Person, Polis, Planet

Person, Polis, Planet

Essays in Applied Philosophy

DAVID SCHMIDTZ

Oxford University Press, Inc., publishes works that further
Oxford University's objective of excellence
in research, scholarship, and education.

Oxford New York
Auckland Cape Town Dar es Salaam Hong Kong Karachi
Kuala Lumpur Madrid Melbourne Mexico City Nairobi
New Delhi Shanghai Taipei Toronto

With offices in
Argentina Austria Brazil Chile Czech Republic France Greece
Guatemala Hungary Italy Japan Poland Portugal Singapore
South Korea Switzerland Thailand Turkey Ukraine Vietnam

Copyright © 2008 by Oxford University Press, Inc.

Published by Oxford University Press, Inc.
198 Madison Avenue, New York, New York 10016
www.oup.com

First issued as an Oxford University Press paperback, 2011

Oxford is a registered trademark of Oxford University Press.

All rights reserved. No part of this publication may be reproduced,
stored in a retrieval system, or transmitted, in any form or by any means,
electronic, mechanical, photocopying, recording, or otherwise,
without the prior permission of Oxford University Press.

Library of Congress Cataloging-in-Publication Data
Schmidtz, David.
Person, polis, planet : essays in applied philosophy / David Schmidtz.
p. cm.
Includes bibliographical references.
ISBN 978-0-19-536583-2 (hardcover); 978-0-19-986170-5 (paperback)
1. Ethics. 2. Applied philosophy. I. Title.
BJ1012.S345 2008
170—dc22   2007043147

Printed in the United States of America
on acid-free paper

ACKNOWLEDGMENTS

I thank Randy Kendrick for all she did in 2003 to help me when I had a nearly inoperable brain tumor, and for all that she has helped me do in my life and career since then. It is in her honor that my current position is named the Kendrick Chair of Philosophy.

I have hundreds of friends and colleagues to thank for their help and support over the years, both in general and with respect to the particular articles reprinted here. If I tried to name them all here, I might exceed Oxford's word limit before the end of this note. I thanked them by name in the original articles, though, and I will not forget all that I owe them.

Special thanks to Cathleen Johnson: for her expertise as an economist and for her high-octane editorial common sense, when that was what I needed, and for bird-watching, hiking, teaching me to salsa dance, exploring new recipes with me, and marrying me, when that was what I needed.

CONTENTS

1. Introduction   3

Person
2. Choosing Strategies   15
3. Choosing Ends   37
4. Reasons for Altruism   62
5. What Nozick Did for Decision Theory (*with* Sarah Wright)   78

Polis
6. How to Deserve   93
7. Moral Dualism   117
8. Separateness, Suffering, and Moral Theory   145
9. Diminishing Marginal Utility   165
10. Guarantees   174

Planet
11. The Institution of Property   193
12. Reinventing the Commons: An African Case Study
    (*with* Elizabeth Willott)   211
13. Natural Enemies: An Anatomy of Environmental Conflict   228
14. Are All Species Equal?   239

Works Cited   249
Index   257

Person, Polis, Planet

1

Introduction

What counts as a life well lived? The question, as I see it, is a three-pronged challenge: how to live in nature, how to live in society, and how to live with ourselves. I work on the "why be moral" question, on connections between being moral and being rational. I work on a more political question of what counts as a life well lived given that we want to live together. I also work on a more ecological question of what counts as a life well lived given that we want to live well in the natural world.

What unifies these explorations? Roughly this: I treat "why be moral" as a question of what morality would have to be like for being moral to be both individually and collectively rational—advantageous to people around us without encouraging people around us to be free riders. Morality is about being a reciprocator, neither a free rider nor someone who enables others to free ride. My answer to the "why be moral" question now considers how respecting nature bears on moral duty, plus how loving nature bears on moral aspiration.

I group these essays in three categories. Several could just as well be in one category as another. For example, "Reasons for Altruism" argues that it would be a failure of self-interest to care only about ourselves. We must care about something beyond ourselves. Otherwise, we won't have enough to care about, and will as a result be unhealthy. "Moral Dualism" unites a theory of personal aspiration with a theory of social obligation. "The Institution of Property" describes social and ecological functions of property institutions. "Are All Species Equal?" offers reasons grounded in personal morality for valuing and respecting our nonhuman neighbors—reasons grounded in human nature rather than animal nature, thus not depending on extravagant claims about all living things being equal. "How to Deserve" conceives justice as a matter of personal redemption, not only interpersonal obligation. "Natural Enemies" argues that in the context of environmental conflict resolution, economics and ecology need to be done together.

Among the overall themes of this collection: (1) Properly caring for ourselves requires that we take an interest in and develop a healthy respect for the world around us. (2) Properly caring for other people requires (a) that we take care of ourselves, and (b) that we take care of the natural world in which we and others must live.

(3) Properly caring for nature—loving it as well as respecting it—requires that we treat humans (both city dwellers and people who live close to the land) as having a proper place in it; misanthropy is bad for the environment.

Another theme: nature does not belong to us. We must treat nature with respect lest our lives be so unexamined as hardly to be worth living. More obviously, *other people* do not belong to us. We must treat other people with respect lest our lives be so unexamined as hardly to be worth living. The *choices* we make, though, *do* belong to us. We are responsible for what we choose to respect. One is responsible for what one chooses, mindfully or otherwise, as the organizing aims of one's life. (An examined life, though, need not treat self-examination as the most important thing in life.)

There is a time-honored approach in epistemology (foundationalism) that involves looking inside one's head for evidence guaranteeing the truth of one's beliefs about the external world. An alternative approach (reliabilism) is to study ourselves from the outside, observe how we come to believe one thing rather than another, and study by experimental methods how reliable our belief-forming processes are. Perhaps our choice in ethics is somewhat analogous. I could start with a belief I regard as absolutely certain (such as that I ought to save a baby drowning in the pool beside me when I can do so at no cost), then treat that previously accepted hypothesis as a reason to reject any new hypothesis that contradicts it. An alternative is to do ethics from outside in, asking which beliefs, principles, actions, customs, habits, and laws actually help us (so far as we can tell) to live environmentally friendly, socially constructive, personally gratifying lives. Perhaps our beliefs about what we owe to babies in backyard pools are not easily reconciled with our beliefs about what we owe to babies in underdeveloped economies, but the empirical question for ethics is whether that combination of beliefs helps us live better lives together. Perhaps we live better lives when we acknowledge that even our best moral theory cannot be the answer to all questions.

The individual articles included here are more or less heavily edited versions of the originals. Several have been reprinted before. Over the years, editors of various anthologies have asked for revisions, many of which are improvements, not just shortenings, so I include the more recent versions here.

Person

Part I consists of essays that develop core themes of my theory of humanly rational choice. How do we make decisions when we have no reliable recipe for making decisions? The challenge is not only that we have limited ability to process information, limited attention spans, limited will power, and that we are encumbered by emotional baggage. It is not only that we have modular brains, the parts of which evolved under different pressures and serve different and not always compatible purposes. Humans are indeed limited, but decision theory itself is limited, and essentially so. Finally, human beings are not only less than but also in some ways more than the mathematically tractable abstractions we use to build the theorems of formal decision theory. We can give our word, and we can make our word mean something.

We can have a range of concerns extending beyond the tangible payoffs we face in everyday concrete cases. We can and we do care about what we are, not only about what we get.

These "Person" essays also bear directly on the task of defining the personal strand (and indirectly on defining the interpersonal strand) of the moral theory discussed in part II.

"Choosing Strategies" (1992)

The original title of this essay was "Rationality within Reason." I now call it "Choosing Strategies" to flag how it complements my more recent essay on choosing ends.

Although I admire David Hume and Adam Smith, I am not a consequentialist in the way the word is now used. I do not think being moral is closely connected to being a maximizer, as maximizing came to be construed in the twentieth century.

I also think being *prudent* has little to do with being a maximizer. To identify genuine, substantive connections between being rational and being moral, I now believe, we will have to work with *humanly* rational choice and humanly moral agency as they really are, not with mathematically tractable idealizations of them.

"Choosing Ends" (1994)

This essay began with my unwillingness to accept the instrumentalist idea that the scope of rational choice is the selection of means to given ends, leaving us with nothing substantive to say about the rationality of ends themselves. To me, some ends obviously are better—they make for better lives—than others.

I had no interest in merely insisting on the obviousness of that point, though. Is there a non-question-begging proof that ends could be rationally chosen? Could instrumental rationality *all by itself* (conjoined to descriptive truisms about human psychology) underwrite the choice of some ends rather than others, or some ends rather than none? I did not argue that ends as such were rational, because that was never the question. The question is about ends we *choose*. So the real question is not whether final ends can be rational so much as whether final ends can be rationally *chosen*.

"Reasons for Altruism" (1993)

Over the years, the Social Philosophy and Policy Center at Bowling Green State University put me in a position to do some of my best essays. This one was the first, written for a conference and then an issue of the journal *Social Philosophy and Policy* on the topic of altruism. (That issue also contained Jean Hampton's "Selflessness and the Loss of Self," about which Jean and I had many fruitful discussions. She taught me something about the philosophical rewards of paying attention to life as actually lived all around us.) My aim was more or less genealogical—to show how self-interested rationality all by itself has the potential (conjoined to descriptive truisms about human psychology) to underwrite concern and respect for others.

"What Nozick Did for Decision Theory" (2004)

In 1999, Terry Moore told me about a series he envisioned on major contemporary philosophers. He asked me to edit a volume on Robert Nozick. As I was assembling a slate of authors, I thought I might include an essay of my own on decision theory.

Nozick was, to be sure, more a fox than a hedgehog, intellectually, but one topic that consumed him for his whole career was the meaning of life. After the first authors I invited to write on that topic declined to do so, I decided to write that essay myself, shelving my paper on decision theory.[1]

When Peter French invited me to write on Nozick for an issue of *Midwest Studies In Philosophy* on American philosophers, I told Peter I was not interested in writing another article on political philosophy, but I still wanted to finish that essay on Newcomb's problem some day, the gist of which I had been teaching in courses on decision theory since 1998. Peter welcomed the proposal.

I had concluded that Nozick's most profound insight had gotten lost in the ensuing debate about the rationality of being a one-boxer versus a two-boxer. Nozick's profound (even if largely implicit) insight was that decision theory inherently lacks the resources to answer seemingly paradigmatic decision-theoretic questions. In particular, we must choose among decision theories, and this prior choice cannot itself be decision-theoretic. As Peter French and I were negotiating, Sarah Wright (currently at the University of Georgia) was just completing an interdisciplinary seminar on decision theory, and was organizing a workshop on decision theory. She was a natural as a coauthor, and contributed to virtually every sentence of the final product.

Polis

"How to Deserve" is continuous with "Reasons for Altruism" and "Choosing Ends," insofar as it takes as a central issue the problem of having a self worth caring about, of becoming and remaining a self worth living for. "Moral Dualism" is a step toward converting these considerations into a comprehensive moral theory, with personal and interpersonal strands. The remaining essays in Part II, namely "Separateness, Suffering, and Moral Theory," "Diminishing Marginal Utility," and "Guarantees," express concerns about different ways of thinking about justice and prosperity. Though I did not write them with this in mind, we could see these essays as ways of fleshing out moral dualism's interpersonal strand.

---

1. I was invited to give a general-audience talk at Boston University in December 1999. Wondering what I could say that might be worthy of an end-of-millennium general audience, I decided to present "The Meanings of Life." (I later gave the talk in Cape Town. It was advertised by radio and newspaper, and remains the only talk I've ever given for which tickets were sold.) A few weeks before the Boston event, Nozick emailed me to invite me to dinner after the talk. I said I would be with my wife, adding that Elizabeth had read some of his work and would love to meet him. Nozick said that by all means she was invited, too. When we arrived, not only had Nozick read several pieces of mine, he had looked up Elizabeth too, tracked down a couple of her articles on insect biochemistry, and asked her some sophisticated questions. He wasn't showing off. He was honestly fascinated. That was the only time I ever met Nozick, yet still, I miss him. He made the world more colorful.

"How to Deserve" (2002)

It is at very least a prominent view among political philosophers that common sense is mistaken in its optimism about the possibility of our being deserving. One reason is ideological: many high-profile academic conceptions of distributive justice are incompatible with common-sense thinking about what we deserve. Another reason is that it is, after all, startlingly difficult to come up with a philosophical framework that grounds significant claims about what individuals deserve. We are born, we are raised, we are given opportunities, and we are made into beings who can to some extent take advantage of opportunities. It is hard to see any room in that mechanistic picture for being deserving.

I was raised Catholic, and taught along the way that pride is a sin and that thinking there are things we can do to be deserving is a paradigm case of this sin. Then I found a remarkably similar view infusing secular political philosophy. Oddly, on the topic of desert, philosophy seems more in the grip of Augustine; by comparison, common sense is Aristotelian.

"Moral Dualism" (1998)

As a contribution to the traditional philosophical enterprise, developing the theory I call moral dualism is among the more important things I've done. I prepared this paper for a conference organized by Peter Danielson entitled "Modeling Morality, Rationality, and Evolution," which became an anthology by the same name. I also presented it to a workshop at Torcuato di Tella Law School in Buenos Aires. It sparks enthusiastic discussion wherever I present it, but the printed version never did, so far as I know. I set out the same theory, in more detail, over four chapters of *Rational Choice and Moral Agency*. If there were anything I've written that I wish had gotten more attention, this would be it.

From my perspective, the overwhelming problem with twentieth- century utilitarianism is that it collapses into what we today call act-utilitarianism. It depicts morality as a decision procedure leaving no room to live a humanly normal life. By contrast, I see being moral as the sort of thing that you would want for your children, for their sake. As per the more recent essay on "Separateness, Suffering, and Moral Theory," moral theorizing is not a game we win by devising the most demanding theory. Neither was I attracted to nonconsequentialist views depicting morality as the correcting antithesis of normal self-interest. I aimed to develop a conception of morality as leaving us room to breathe, acknowledging that our most important choices tend to fall into the category of permissible but not required. I also wanted to avoid representing this room to breathe as a compromise between ideal morality and the corruptness of human nature. I wanted instead to represent the ideal of being true to oneself—being the kind of person we aspire to be, within the constraints of the interpersonal strand—as our highest moral calling. Moral dualism's personal strand sets out a theory of the good life for an individual person.

The interpersonal strand sets out a theory of what we owe each other, the core idea of which is that we ought to pursue our individually rational goals within collectively rational constraints. As ordinary moral agents, we need something unlike the sort of rule-utilitarianism that collapses back into act-utilitarianism. The versions of rule-utilitarianism that collapse are those that continue to try to define a procedure for picking acts. (The traditional version, for example, says act in accordance with the set of rules that will have better consequences than any alternative set if everyone follows it.) Act-utilitarianism is a theory that aims at the wrong thing. The kind of utilitarianism that would have actual utility would aim at something else.

My theory (the interpersonal strand of it) is that agents should respect those actually existing institutions that have a history of making people better off. In asking us to respect and abide by institutions that have a history of putting us in a position to live better lives together, the theory asks a lot (and in particular it asks us to deal with the world of partial compliance as it is), but it does not ask us to sacrifice our lives.[2] Moreover, it has nothing to do with which institutional rule would be optimal *if* people obeyed it. What it asks is that we identify, and live up to, the highest standards implicit in our fellow citizens' normal behavior. Or at least, that is what we owe to others. We owe more than that to ourselves.

We may (from the outside) judge persons by their intentions. There is a point in doing that. There is no analogous point in evaluating *policies* and *institutions* by asking whether they are well intentioned. *People* may need to be forgiven. *Institutions* do not. When tools malfunction, they need to be repaired or replaced, not forgiven. And if our replacement tools function even worse than the "broken" ones, it does not matter that our intentions in replacing them were good. By the same token, if we only *thought* the old tools were broken when they were functioning as well as any tool could under the circumstances, then again (so far as evaluating the tools goes) it does not matter that we meant well.

Personal and institutional moralities are related but distinct topics. Still, moral dualism aims to cover both topics in integrated fashion.

"Separateness, Suffering, and Moral Theory" (2008)

I wrote this essay in response to an invitation from Jeff Schaler to contribute to a volume called *Singer under Fire*. When Jeff invited me, I told him I had been harshly critical of Singer in previous work. So, I told Jeff, I would not blame Singer if he were disappointed to find me included in a volume celebrating his work. Schaler replied that on the contrary I was among a small handful of people Jeff was inviting at the specific request of Singer himself.

I had a second reason for writing this article. I once had a long conversation about Singer with Michael Smith, over several beers. Michael and I had no quarrel

---

2. In the real world, the degree of compliance is an endogenous variable, which means the degree of compliance depends on what people are being asked to comply with. It is not respectable to construct an "ideal" theory while setting aside the problem of compliance, as if compliance issues become relevant only at a later stage of practical implementation. In fact, when we choose a principle of justice, we choose the particular compliance problem that goes with it. If it would take a KGB to achieve compliance, the principle is a bad principle, period.

over Singer's importance or influence, and no great quarrel over the merits of Singer's conclusions, but we had some considerable disagreement over the philosophical quality of Singer's arguments. It was a great conversation, in part because any conversation with Michael Smith is great, but also in part because we both knew Singer's arguments in considerable detail, and some of the details Michael grasped had escaped me. So I wrote this essay partly to honor Singer, and partly to honor a true friend in Michael Smith, hoping to prove to Michael that I was not as dense about Singer's virtues as some of those beers may have made me sound. I include the article here because it presents my initial thoughts on a current project—studying the point of moral theorizing—and locates them in a practical context. Singer's conclusions are not like mine. To me, though, the more philosophically interesting differences are methodological. Singer's conception of the aim of moral theorizing is altogether unlike mine.[3]

"Diminishing Marginal Utility" (2000)

This short essay argues that the idea of diminishing marginal utility does not in the usually assumed way ground a utilitarian argument for egalitarian redistribution. Even when the marginal utility of consumption decreases, and indeed partly *because* the marginal utility of consumption decreases, people at some point invest marginal units in production, not consumption. Everyone's long-run welfare depends on at least some people being so rich that they have nothing better to do with their excess wealth than invest it.

The essay attacks one specific idea routinely mentioned in theoretical support of egalitarian redistribution. It is not a broadside against redistribution per se. Even so, the essay is disturbing enough to have a history of provoking the "That can't be right, but if it is, then I already knew it" kind of reaction.

"Guarantees" (1997)

This essay was an overture to *Social Welfare and Individual Responsibility*, which I had the honor of coauthoring with Robert Goodin. We have been trained to think of distributive justice as fundamentally a question of how to distribute things. The very name (backed by the custom of the profession) seduces us into thinking this way, but thinking this way often is a mistake. In the real world, as Nozick observed, goods do not appear on the table, waiting for contractarians to agree on how to divide them. Instead, goods exist as a result of generations of people pouring the best within them into positive-sum games. When philosophers treat distributive justice as above all a question of how to distribute goods, they are implicitly seeing people as, above all, consumers. To me, though, the overwhelmingly important question of distributive justice is the question of how to respect producers.

---

3. I include this article rather than the related "When Justice Matters" because I prefer how the essay on Singer, despite its officially critical mission, sticks to the positive task of reflecting on how to construct a moral theory.

Planet

Several of my essays speak to the just-mentioned question of justice for producers, perhaps none more so than "The Institution of Property." However, I place this essay in Part III because it was the beginning of my thinking about questions of sustainability.

I first met Don Scherer in 1991. He had just read a draft of what became "Choosing Strategies." He said he saw the essay as altogether in the tradition of ecological thinking. In 1994, I came to Bowling Green State University, one of the main attractions of which was the opportunity to team-teach environmental ethics with Don.[4]

What I liked about environmental ethics was that, in my mind, it represented what ethics in general could be if it took seriously the imperative to reflect on what our theorizing would have to be like to bear directly on questions of how we ought to live, here and now. Questions about the nature of value, about intrinsic value, and so on, were questions with tangible implications for the morality of specific practices: for right and wrong ways of treating trees, and so on. Environmental ethicists were taking up such questions most energetically, but the relevance of such questions extends far beyond that small academic pond.

"The Institution of Property" (1994)

After writing my initial contribution to the literature on property rights ("When Is Original Appropriation *Required*?") I sat in on two courses on property at Yale Law School, taught by Robert Ellickson and Carol Rose, respectively. Their courses transformed my thinking. Anyone who reads "The Institution of Property" will see their influence. I began to see how wonderfully complicated are the real-world problems to which property law evolved as a solution.

Kate Johnson and I visited Jamestown, Virginia, in 2007, on our honeymoon. (Kate was delighted to show me around. She grew up 15 miles from the original site, fascinated by Jamestown lore and well versed in its history.) Ongoing excavations of the fort, rediscovered in 1996, are yielding a steady stream of surprises. This revision incorporates some of what I learned on that visit.

---

4. I moved back to Arizona in 1995, and created Arizona's first course in environmental ethics. In 1997, a bright, front-row student asked, in response to a conversation about externalities that left him exasperated, "Why don't we make some federal regulatory agency responsible for determining what level of fossil fuels it would be optimal to consume, then setting prices so as to engineer that level of consumption?" He paused, stunned by his own insight, then added, "It's so simple. Why hasn't anyone thought of this before?" Someone at the back who had not spoken all semester replied, "Have you heard of the Berlin Wall?" I have no idea why he said "Berlin Wall" rather than "Soviet Union" or "central planning." In any case, the first student shyly responded that while he had heard the phrase, he didn't know what it referred to. Now I was the one who was stunned. A person's memory may be short, but the revelation was that a *society's* memory is *shorter*, not longer, than the memory of individual citizens. Every year, a crop of seventeen-year-olds turns eighteen and becomes a new set of decision-makers on which society's future will depend. Those young citizens have no clue what the world was like just a few years ago. (My student in 1997 was ten when the Berlin Wall fell a mere eight years earlier.) They know the Nazis were bad, but do not know what a Nazi is. They know even less about communism.

People talk about how valuable land is, as if land itself rather than human effort and ingenuity were the ultimate producer of the explosion of wealth we see occurring all around us. But consider: nowadays, no one stays home in the hope of inheriting the family farm. The farm isn't worth waiting for (unless would-be heirs hope to get rich off subsidies, that is, the productivity of other taxpayers, rather than off the productivity of the land per se). The fortunes of people today are made up mainly of their job skills, so long as they are free to move to where their job skills are in demand.

By contrast, land *within* cities is increasingly expensive. Why? Why is housing in Silicon Valley so expensive? Why have housing prices in Seattle risen so explosively? Answer: Because many, many people are quite rationally willing to pay a huge premium to live in close proximity to increasingly productive concentrations of job skills.

"Reinventing the Commons" (2003)

This essay is a sequel to "Institution of Property," which takes a comparative institutions approach to evaluating private and public property regimes. It also describes processes by which publicly held property tends to evolve into privately held property. "Reinventing the Commons" is a case study in the reverse phenomenon: a system of private property whose owners voluntarily (and profitably) converted their holdings into communally held property.

In 2001, Elizabeth Willott (currently at the University of Arizona) and I toured several private game preserves bordering Kruger National Park in South Africa. We deliberately went with no particular hypothesis, knowing we'd find something interesting to write about, so our aim was simply to be open to inspiration. It hit me after a week of touring and casual interviewing that we were looking at an accidental rediscovery of the kind of communal property regime Elinor Ostrom had described as arising in medieval Europe. We talked about how to do the analysis, what to treat as the analog of medieval sheep. Obviously, the wildlife were a cash crop, roughly as sheep were in the medieval commons. The parallels were shocking, though, when we treated the *tourists* rather than the wildlife as the cash crop.

"Natural Enemies" (2000)

In 1993, *New York Times* reporter Raymond Bonner, a person of impeccable left-wing credentials, published *At the Hand of Man*, which chronicles what befalls both people and wildlife in Africa when the interests of people on the ground are ignored. Bonner's book inspired my first article on the subject, "When Preservationism Doesn't Preserve."

When Elissa Morris and Robert Martin at Oxford University Press asked me to consider doing a textbook in environmental ethics, then when shortly thereafter Michael Pendlebury asked me to consider a visiting position at Witwatersrand University in Johannesburg, and David Benatar followed up with an invitation to a conference in Cape Town, I decided to coedit the textbook with Elizabeth and to investigate firsthand the community-based wildlife management programs I had researched for the original article.

"Natural Enemies" is a sequel to "When Preservationism Doesn't Preserve." I was teaching decision theory. The course, as I teach it, includes a module on conflict resolution. One of the points of the essay is that sometimes the point of conflict resolution is to arrive at *habitable* solutions rather than *just* ones.

"Are All Species Equal?" (1998)

I first came across Paul Taylor's work, arguing for the equal worth of all living things, while team-teaching with Don Scherer. Don asked me to take responsibility for teaching the part of the course that covered Taylor. I admired Taylor's reverence for all living things, combined with his common-sense acknowledgment that to care about life is to care about life surviving, and living things can't survive just by revering each other; they have to eat. At the same time, I saw no plausible segue from revering living things to ranking them as equals. This essay sorts out my differences with Taylor while trying to show Taylor some of the reverence he so generously accords to the world around him.

In closing, the question on which I have spent most of my career is this: What counts as a life well lived, a life worthy of aspiration, given that we live in a social and a natural world? I work on many subjects, but the essays collected here are steps toward forming an overall view about what it takes to live well in a world like ours.

I especially thank Paul Bloomfield, Jason Brennan, Cathleen Johnson, Cara Nine, Peter Ohlin, Kevin Vallier, and Matt Zwolinski for comments on drafts of this introduction, and copy editor Martha Ramsey and hundreds of readers over the years for helpful comments on earlier versions of all the essays herein.

PERSON

2

Choosing Strategies

Suppose I need to decide whether to go off to fight for a cause in which I deeply believe, or stay home with a family that needs me and that I deeply love. What should I do? My friends say I should determine the possible outcomes of the two proposed courses of action, assign probabilities and numerical utilities to each possibility, multiply through, and then choose whichever alternative has the highest number.

My friends are wrong. Their proposal would be plausible in games of chance where information on probabilities and monetarily denominated utilities is readily available. In this case, however, I can only guess at the possible outcomes of either course of action. Nor do I know their probabilities. Nor do I know how to gauge their utilities. The strategy of maximizing expected utility is out of the question, for employing it requires information that I do not have.

Nevertheless, my friends have not given up trying to help, and so they point out that I could simulate the process of maximizing expected utility by assuming a set of possible outcomes, estimating their probabilities, and then making educated guesses about how much utility they would have. I could indeed do this, but I decide not to, for it occurs to me that I have no reason to trust the formula for maximizing expected utility when I have nothing but question marks to plug into it. Better strategies are available.

1. Two Kinds of Strategies

This section distinguishes between optimizing and satisficing strategies, and between moderate and immoderate preferences. The following three sections discuss, in turn, when satisficing strategies are rational, when they are not, and when cultivating moderate preferences is rational. Later sections offer a way of characterizing rational choice in situations where the agent's alternatives are incommensurable.

In the simplest context, one has a set of alternatives clearly ranked in terms of their utility as means to one's ends. If one is an *optimizer*, one chooses an alternative that ranks at least as high as any other. In contrast, if one is a *satisficer*, one settles for any alternative one considers satisfactory. In this static context, though, it is hard to see the point of choosing a suboptimal alternative, even if it is satisfactory.

In a more dynamic and more typical context, we are not presented with a set of nicely ranked alternatives. Instead, we have to look for them, judging their utility as we go. In this context, optimizing involves terminating one's search for alternatives upon concluding that one has found the best available alternative. However, although optimizing involves selecting what one judges is best, it need not involve judging what is best "all things considered," because sophisticated optimizers recognize that considering all things is not always worth the cost. There may be constraints (temporal, financial, and so on) on how much searching one can afford to do. A person who stops the search upon concluding that prolonging the search is not worth the cost is also employing an optimizing strategy, albeit one of a more subtle variety.[1]

Satisficing, in contrast, involves terminating the search for alternatives upon concluding that one has identified a satisfactory alternative. What distinguishes satisficing from optimizing in the dynamic context is that the two strategies employ different *stopping rules*.[2] Thus, if options emerge serially, a subtle optimizer might choose a known option in preference to the alternative, namely, searching for something better with no guarantee of ever finding it. The difference between satisficing and this more subtle kind of optimizing has to do with what the two strategies take into account in reaching a stopping point. At any point in the search, we may let the expected utility of stopping the search equal U, the utility of the best option we have turned up so far. The expected utility of continued search equals the probability of finding a better option, $P(fbo)$, multiplied by the utility of finding a better option, $U(fbo)$, minus the cost of further search, $C(fs)$. At some point, the satisficer stops because he believes U is good enough. In contrast, the subtle optimizer stops because she believes that $P(fbo)U(fbo) - C(fs)$ is less than zero. Even if the two stopping rules happen to converge on the same stopping point, they do so for different reasons and require different information.[3]

Unlike the optimizer, who stops searching when she either has considered all her options or has run up against things like time constraints, the satisficer stops the

---

1. Stocker (1990, 311–316) argues that optimizing, even in this subtle sense, is morally and rationally problematic.

2. Herbert Simon's (1955) idea is that, given our limited capacity to acquire and process information, we economize on our limited capacity by setting a concrete goal and then reasoning back to conclusions about what course of action would achieve that goal. This is what Simon means by satisficing. The notion of satisficing as a stopping rule is implied, and later becomes explicit (in Simon 1979, 3). Simon treats satisficing as a surrogate for optimizing under particular information constraints and, so far as I know, treats our limited information as an external constraint. I think such constraints are often more accurately viewed as being partly self-imposed. Within the context of constraints that are in part self-imposed, the distinction between satisficing and optimizing becomes more interesting, as explained in section 2.

3. When pressed to justify stopping a search upon finding a satisfactory alternative, people may say further search would not have been worth the cost. Does that mean they were optimizing after all? Only if the cost of further search was what in fact made them stop. If the circumstance that actually stops a search is the finding of a satisfactory alternative, then it is a case of satisficing, no matter what people say after the fact in defense of the choice. One can defend two acts in the same way without implying that the two acts are the same kind of act. For more on how the two stopping rules differ and on how they might usefully be combined, see the appendix to this chapter.

search upon identifying an alternative as good enough.[4] For example, suppose you enter a cafeteria seeking a nutritionally balanced and reasonably tasty meal. You then proceed down the cafeteria line surveying the alternatives. If you are satisficing, you take the first meal that you deem nutritionally and aesthetically adequate. If you are optimizing, you continue down the line surveying alternatives until you reach the end of the line or run out of time. You then take the meal you consider optimal, either in comparison to the other known options or in comparison to the alternative of further search. A satisfactory meal may or may not be optimal. Likewise, as cafeteria patrons know only too well, the best available meal may or may not be satisfactory. Of course, if you switch from one stopping rule to the other, you might end up choosing the same meal, but you will be choosing it for a different reason. Therefore, neither rule is reducible to the other.

Neither can satisficing be equated with the more subtle kind of optimizing that takes the cost of searching for more-than-satisfactory alternatives into account. Satisficers select the satisfactory alternative because they find it satisfactory, not because they find that stopping the search at that point would maximize utility.

With this characterization of satisficing in mind, we can now clarify the difference between satisficing and *moderation*. Satisficing contrasts with optimizing. Being moderate, however, contrasts not with optimizing but with being immoderate. Being an optimizer does not entail being immoderate, and being a satisficer does not entail that one would be satisfied with a moderate bundle of goods. A person could be both a moderate and an optimizer, for the maximally satisfying bundle of goods for a given person may well be of moderate size. Likewise, a person could be both a satisficer and an immoderate, for a given satisficer may have wildly immoderate ideas about what counts as satisfactory. Consider a person whose goal in life is to be a millionaire—not a billionaire, mind you, just a millionaire—by the age of thirty.

2. When Satisficing Is Rational

There is an apparent incongruence between the theory and practice of rational choice. Theory models rational choice as optimizing choice, yet in practice, satisficing is ubiquitous. We could explain the incongruence away by saying that when people think, they seek something satisfactory, what they really seek is something optimal. But satisficing can be reconstructed as a subtle kind of optimizing strategy only on pain of attributing to people calculations they often do not perform (and do not have the information to perform) and intentions they often do not have. This section tries to explain satisficing in terms of thought processes we can recognize in ourselves.

---

4. There may be no precise way to characterize "good enough". But what people consider good enough seems relative to expectations. As expectations rise, the standards by which an option is judged good enough also tend to rise. This fact can be tragic. It can rob people of the ability to appreciate how well their lives are going, all things considered. Of course, it is rational to set *goals* with an eye to what is attainable, raising one's sights as higher goals become attainable. But raising the standard by which we deem our situation satisfactory is harder to fathom. Perhaps people are psychologically incapable of aiming at higher goals without simultaneously reformulating their notions of what is satisfactory. I do not know.

Satisficing will emerge as a real alternative to optimizing, and thus as a strategy that can be evaluated, criticized, and sometimes redeemed as rational.

We begin with the observation that people have a multiplicity of goals. For example, a person can desire to be healthy, to have a successful career, to be a good parent, and so forth. Some goals are broad and others narrow, relatively speaking. Further, a given goal might be encompassed by another, in the sense that the narrower goal's point—the reason for it being a goal—is that it is part of what one does in pursuit of a larger goal. For example, Kate might want to upgrade her wardrobe because she cares about her appearance because she wants a promotion because she cares about her career. Suppose she believes that achieving her various goals is instrumental to or constitutive of achieving a broader goal of making her life as a whole go well. To mark the difference in breadth between Kate's concern for her life as a whole and her concern for particular aspects of her life (such as her health or her career), let us say Kate seeks a *local* optimum when she seeks to make a certain aspect of her life go as well as possible. Kate seeks a *global* optimum when she seeks to make her life as a whole go as well as possible.[5]

Optima can be defined as such only within the context of the constraints under which goals are pursued. (Thus, when economists speak of maximizing utility, it goes without saying that they are talking about maximizing utility subject to a budget constraint.) We pursue goals subject to the limits of our knowledge, time, energy, ability, income, and so on. More intriguing, however, is that we typically operate under additional constraints that we have deliberately imposed upon ourselves, as if the constraints imposed on us by external circumstances were too loose. For example, if Tom spends an evening at a casino, he is externally constrained (by his savings and his borrowing power) to spend no more than, say, $50,000. What actually defines his set of options over the course of the evening, though, is the $100 budget constraint that he has *chosen* to impose on himself.[6]

To give another example, in fleshing out the task of buying a house, we need to make some prior decisions. We decide how long to look, how much money to spend, what neighborhoods to consider. We knock only on doors of houses displaying "for sale" signs rather than on every door in the neighborhood. To some extent, these constraints are imposed on us by mundane external factors, but they also have a striking normative aspect, for they are in part rules of conduct we impose on ourselves; we take it upon ourselves to make our constraints more precise and more limiting so as to make our choice set more definite. Local optimizing would often be neurotic and even stupid if local goals were not pursued within compartments partly defined by

---

5. I borrowed the terms "local" and "global" from Elster (1984, 9), although a rereading of his text reveals that the way he uses the terms bears little resemblance to the way they are used here. (Elster says the definitive difference between locally and globally maximizing machines is that the latter, unlike the former, are capable of *waiting* and *indirect* strategies.)

6. For someone wanting to construct a tractable mathematical model, it may be easier to ignore the felt experience of pursuing local goals under self-imposed constraints and concentrate instead on the global perspective, from which self-imposed constraints appear, more or less, as preferences about how to operate within external constraints. I want to explain satisficing in terms of thought processes we can recognize within ourselves, though. So for my purposes, the fact that we have both broader and narrower perspectives cannot be ignored.

self-imposed constraints. The constraints we impose on our narrower pursuits can keep narrower pursuits from ruining the larger plans of which they are part.[7]

If we look at life as a whole, we see that life as a whole will go better if we spend most of it pursuing goals that are narrower than the goal of making life as a whole go better. That is why it is rational to formulate and pursue local goals. But it also is rational to prevent narrower pursuits from consuming more resources than is warranted by the importance (from the global perspective) of achieving those narrower goals. Accordingly, when we pursue narrower goals, we pursue them under self-imposed constraints.

Although the constraints we impose on ourselves are imposed from a more encompassing perspective, it is only within the narrower perspective that we become subject to self-imposed constraints. (Of course, we are subject to external constraints, limited incomes and such, from any perspective.) Self-imposed constraints can be applied only *to* narrower pursuits and can be applied only *from* the perspective of a more encompassing pursuit. In more familiar terms, the point is that, because we have broader objectives, there are limits to what we will do for the sake of our wardrobe, or for the sake of a promotion, or for the sake of a career.

Having distinguished between local and global optimization, we can now explain when satisficing is rational. Michael Slote believes the optimizing tendency can be self-defeating. He says, "A person bent on eking out the most good he can in any given situation will take pains and suffer anxieties that a more casual individual will avoid." And he asks us to consider "how much more planful and self-conscious the continual optimizer must be in comparison with the satisficer who does not always aim for the best and who sometimes rejects the best or better for the good enough."[8] In short, that one has an opportunity to pursue the good is not by itself a compelling reason to pursue the good. Surely, Slote has an important point. Just as surely, however, his point applies to local optimizing rather than to optimizing as such. From the global perspective, seeking local optima can be a waste of time. Global optimizers seek local optima only when doing so serves their purposes. For that reason, satisficing is a big part of a global optimizer's daily routine. A compulsive seeking of local optima may go with being immoderate, but not with being a global optimizer. Effort can have diminishing returns, so a global optimizer will be careful not to try too hard. Local optimizing often gives way to satisficing for the sake of global optimality.

From the global optimizer's point of view, the process of buying a house provides a good example of how satisficing can be rational. When we choose a house, we might proceed by seeking the best available house within constraints—within a one-month time limit, for example. We impose such a limit because we have goals other than living in a nice house, and finding a house competes with them for our time and energy. Or we might look for a satisfactory house and cease looking when

---

7. As Jules Coleman has pointed out to me, what Gauthier (1986, 170) calls constrained maximization is a particularly interesting kind of local optimizing under self-imposed constraints. Constrained maximizers seek maximum payoffs in prisoner's dilemmas, subject to this constraint: they will cooperate (and thus pass up the opportunity to unilaterally defect) if the expected payoff of cooperating is higher than the known payoff of *mutual* defection, which it will be if and only if they expect their partners to cooperate.

8. Slote (1989) 40.

we find one. Like local optimizing, satisficing can serve our larger plans by setting limits on how much effort we put into seeking a house at the expense of other goals that become more important at some point, given the diminishing returns of remaining on the housing market. An optimizing strategy limits how much we are willing to invest in seeking alternatives. A satisficing strategy limits how much we insist on finding before we quit that search and turn our attention to other matters.[9]

The two strategies need not be inflexible. People sometimes have reason to switch or revise strategies as new information comes in. If we seek a satisfactory house in an unfamiliar neighborhood and are shocked to find one within five minutes, we may stop the search, acknowledging the stopping rule we previously imposed on that activity. Or, we may conclude that, having formulated our aspiration level under unrealistically pessimistic assumptions, we should resume our search with a satisficing strategy revised to reflect a higher aspiration level. Or we may switch to a local optimizing strategy, spending another day or two looking at houses, then taking the best we have found so far. Or we may do both, looking until we either reach our new aspiration level or reach our time limit. In this way, the two strategies often are interactive.

Likewise, suppose we started out planning to seek the best house we could find within a one-month time limit but have so far been terribly disappointed with our options. In this case, when after two weeks we finally find a house that meets our plummeting aspiration level, we may find ourselves embracing a sadder but wiser aspiration level as a stopping rule, abandoning our original plan to seek a local optimum relative to a one-month time constraint.

Typically, the more concrete our local goals are, the more reason there is to satisfice. If we do not know exactly what we are looking for, then we usually are better off setting a time limit and then taking what we like best within that limit. But if we know exactly what we are looking for, then it is rational to stop searching as soon as we find it.[10] So, having detailed information about our *goals* weighs in favor of using that information in formulating aspiration levels as stopping rules. Conversely, the more we know about our *set of alternatives*, the easier it is to identify which alternative has the highest utility, which weighs in favor of seeking local optima.

The stakes involved are also pertinent—indeed crucial. The less we care about the gap between satisfactory and optimal toothpaste, for example, the more reason we have to satisfice—to look for a satisfactory brand and stop searching when we find it. Note the alternative: instead of satisficing, we could optimize by searching among different brands of toothpaste until we find the precise point at which further search is not worth its cost.

But notice: an optimal stopping point is itself something for which we would have to search, and locating it might require information (about the probability of finding a better brand of toothpaste, for example) that is not worth gathering, given the stakes involved in the original search for toothpaste.

---

9. The appendix to this chapter uses graphical analysis to contrast the two kinds of self-imposed limit.

10. Jay Rosenberg tells me that before he began looking for a house, he made a list of desirable features, telling himself he would take the first house having 85 percent or more of those features. As it happens, the first house he looked at scored 85 percent. He stopped looking, bought the house, and has lived there ever since.

Against this, one might object to my assumption that we need precision in the search for an optimal stopping point. Why not seek to learn *roughly* when looking for better toothpaste is not worth the cost? In the search for a stopping point that we might graft onto the original search for toothpaste, it can be more rational to seek to be tolerably close to an optimum than to seek to be at an optimum.

But that is my point: there are cases where we do not care enough about the gap between the satisfactory and the optimal to make it rational to search for the optimal. Searching for optimal toothpaste can be a waste of time, but so can searching for the optimal moment to quit looking for toothpaste.

One way or another, satisficing enters the picture. There will be times when even the most sophisticated optimizing strategies will be inappropriate, for they require information that we may not have and that may not be worth acquiring. And a less sophisticated "all things considered" strategy will nearly always be inappropriate. Rational choice involves considering only those things that seem worthy of consideration, which is to say rational choice involves satisficing, i.e., having a stopping rule that limits how comprehensive a body of information we insist on gathering before stopping the search and turning our attention to other matters.

There is also something to be said for having a moderate disposition—a disposition that allows one to be content with merely satisfactory states of affairs. Part of the reason why is that starting a search too soon can be every bit as wasteful as stopping a search too late. Searching for a house is costly. It is costly partly because people have other goals; the time and energy you spend searching for a house could have been spent on other things. Even if you find a better house than you already have, the process of moving will also be costly. Moreover, it takes time living in and enjoying a house in order to recoup these costs. If you move every month, you will always be paying the costs and never enjoying the benefits of better housing. Moving into a house is part and parcel of a decision to stay a while, for it is only in staying that you collect on the investment of time and energy you made in moving. The general lesson is that costly transitions to preferred states of affairs require intervening periods of stability so that transition costs can be recovered and thus rationally justified. The stability of the intervening periods requires a disposition to be content for a while with what one has—to find something one likes and then stop searching.

Further, even if transition costs are relatively minor, there still can come a point when we should abandon the search for, say, a better job or a better spouse, not because such goals are unattainable or even because the transition costs are too high, but rather because such goals eventually can become inappropriate. At some point, we have to start collecting the rewards that come only when we make a genuine commitment—when we stop looking for something or someone better. We need to be able to satisfice within various local compartments (those defining our searches for spouses, jobs, and so on) in order to make our lives as a whole go well.

3. When Satisficing Is Not Rational

Slote says "choosing what is best for oneself may well be neither a necessary nor a sufficient condition of acting rationally, even in situations where only the agent's good is at stake." For example, a person who is moving and must sell his house might seek "not to maximize his profit on the house, not to get the best price for it he is likely to receive within some appropriate time period, but simply to obtain what he takes to be a good or satisfactory price." When he receives a suitable offer, he may rationally accept it immediately, even though there would be no cost or risk in waiting a few days to see if a higher offer materializes. "His early agreement may not be due to undue anxiety about the firmness of the buyer's offer, or to a feeling that monetary transactions are unpleasant and to be got over as quickly as possible. He may simply be satisficing in the strong sense of the term. He may be moderate or modest in what he wants or needs."[11]

Slote does not offer an analysis of rationality. Nor do I want my argument to rest on any particular analysis of rationality. I do, however, offer this as a necessary condition of rationality: one's choice is rational only if one does not recognize clearly better reasons for choosing any of one's forgone alternatives. This necessary condition begs none of the questions that concern us here. It does not entail that rational choice is optimizing choice. Rather, it allows that one could rationally choose an alternative because it is satisfactory, terminating the search of one's choice set at that point.[12] Moreover, it also allows that if one has two satisfactory alternatives, one could choose the more moderate of the two on the grounds that it satisfies a preference one happens to have for moderation.

On the other hand, although a suboptimal option may be good enough to be worthy of choice in a given case, that does not mean it is worthy of being chosen in preference to something that is clearly better. If one has two choices and one alternative is satisfactory but the other is not, then the satisfactory choice is rational because it is *better*. But suppose one has two choices and both are satisfactory. (E.g., suppose your house is for sale, and you simultaneously get two satisfactory offers, one for $200,000 and another for $210,000, and you prefer the larger offer.) In this case, one does not give a rationale for choosing the inferior alternative merely by pointing out that the inferior alternative is satisfactory. The inferior option is satisfactory, but since this is not a difference, it cannot make a difference either. By hypothesis, the superior option is also satisfactory.

Why, then, should we choose the superior option? Presumably because it is better. Whatever it is in virtue of which we deem that option superior is also a reason

---

11. Slote (1989) 1, 9, 18.

12. That is, an optimizer might choose a satisfactory option in preference to searching for better options that may never materialize. Slote, however, says we intuitively recognize the rationality of taking the first satisfactory offer even apart from real-world risks and anxieties of selling one's house (1989, 18). However, if we are going to talk about common sense allowing a seller to immediately accept a firm offer even when the seller has the option of waiting a few days in hope of a higher offer, then we have to stick to conditions under which common sense holds sway. We do indeed have intuitions about what to do in risky situations, but we cannot, as Slote wants to do, simply *stipulate* that our intuitions regarding risky situations have nothing to do with the fact that they are risky. In the real-world housing market, to turn down an entirely satisfactory offer in quest of something better is to tempt fate. This is one reason why it is common sense, and rationally explicable common sense, for a global optimizer to be hesitant about turning down a satisfactory offer. Even from a local perspective, the expected gain from further search may not be worth risking the potential loss.

for us to choose it.¹³ Oddly, Slote denies this. It can be rational to choose the inferior option, Slote insists. Nor do we need a reason to choose the inferior option, Slote argues, because rationality does not always require people to have a reason for choosing one alternative rather than another.¹⁴ For example, Kate might rationally grab a blouse out of her closet in the morning without being able to explain why she chose that one over the similar blouses hanging beside it. To call her irrational simply because she cannot explain her choice would be a mistake.

This seems right, as far as it goes; not all choices have to be or can be explained. To deem a choice rational, however, is to imply there is an explanation of a certain kind. A person can be rational without being aware of reasons for everything she does, but the things she does for no reason are not rational, and we do not show them to be rational merely by pointing out that they were done by a rational *person*. The person who simply grabs a blouse may be choosing, perhaps rationally, to forgo the opportunity to rationally choose which of her several blouses she ends up wearing. If Kate is running late for the train, then anything that counts as a blouse will be good enough for Kate under the circumstances, so she leaves to impulse the selection from her set of blouses. (In this case, the process of searching among alternative blouses virtually vanishes—there is hardly any choice at all. If she instead gives herself a few seconds to make sure she avoids the blouses with valentine or hammer-and-sickle patterns on them, then she will be choosing within a tiny but still real local compartment.)

There may be a blouse in her closet that, given time, would emerge as best. Kate judges, however, that it is not worth her time to wait for this to happen. She is not literally compelled to simply pick something, but it serves her broader ends to forget about seeking the optimal blouse and instead just grab something out of the closet. If Kate is running late for the train, she has reason simply to grab a blouse in preference to the clearly inferior alternative of wasting precious time seeking the optimal blouse. Initially adopting an end and creating a compartment within which to pursue it is itself a goal-directed activity and, from the standpoint of the global optimizer, not one to be engaged in frivolously. Therefore, we can endorse her *method* of selecting a blouse even though we anticipate having no particular reason to endorse her actual selection.

On the other hand, *deliberately* choosing the worse over the better would be irrational, and we do not give ourselves reason to soften this verdict merely by reminding ourselves that rational people sometimes leave their choices to impulse. Rational choice theory can tell us a story about why Kate finds herself going to work in a green blouse with orange polka dots, but the story will require an implicit or explicit distinction between more and less encompassing perspectives. Without the distinction, an optimization story would be blatantly false, for she does not in fact choose the optimal blouse, and a satisficing story would have neither explanatory nor justificatory power, for the point of choosing a merely satisfactory blouse when better ones were available would remain a mystery. To see the point of what she does at the local level, we have to step back and look at her actions from a broader perspective. From a broader perspective, Kate may have good reason to simply grab a blouse out

---

13. Pettit (1984, 172) makes the same point.
14. Slote (1989) 21.

of the closet, knowing it will be satisfactory even if it is not her favorite. However, it cannot be rational to choose something because it is satisfactory while at the same time having a clearly better option in hand.

4. When Moderation Is Rational

When we need to decide between two satisfactory alternatives, it does not help to point out that one of them is satisfactory. We could, however, choose on the grounds that one of them is more moderate. For example, Slote says it "makes sense" for someone to desire

> to be a really fine lawyer like her mother, but not desire to be as good a lawyer as she can possibly be. This limitation of ambition or aspiration may not stem from a belief that too much devotion to the law would damage other, more important parts of one's life. In certain moderate individuals, there are limits to aspiration and desire that cannot be explained in optimizing terms.[15]

I agree that common sense can recognize moderate aspirations as rational, but to note this fact in an off-the-cuff way is hardly to provide an explanation of moderate aspirations. Our common-sense recognition is precisely what has to be explained. If all we have is an intuition that an act makes sense, but cannot say what the act makes sense *in terms of*, then we are jumping to conclusions if we say we were approving of the act as rational. In contrast, if we explain a show of moderation in terms of its conduciveness to overall satisfaction, then we have explained it as rational. We have not merely claimed it makes sense; rather, we have actually made sense of it. We have shown that we had reason to choose as we did, while not having better reasons to choose differently.

How, then, might we explain having moderate career goals? First, as Slote mentions, there is the issue of trade-offs. One might cultivate an ability to be content with moderate career goals not because one prefers moderate success to great success but because one cares about things other than success. Thus, one point of cultivating modest desires with respect to wealth is that it might improve a person's ability to adhere to a satisficing strategy with respect to income, thus freeing herself to devote time to her children, her health, and so on.

There are also ways moderation can have instrumental value that do not depend on the need to make trade-offs. There can be reasons for striving to be as good a lawyer as one's mother even if one wants to be as good a lawyer as possible. For example, a person might aim at being as good as her mother as a stepping-stone to becoming the best lawyer she can be. The modesty that enables a person to concentrate on successfully making smaller steps may eventually put her within reach of loftier goals. There is also value in concreteness. A person may have no idea how to go about becoming the best possible lawyer but may have a much clearer idea about how to become as good as her mother, because the more modest goal is more

---

15. Slote (1989) 2.

concrete. Further, even given two equally concrete goals, an optimizer might very well choose the lesser on the grounds that only the lesser goal is realistic. Thus, one might become a better lawyer by emulating one's highly competent mother than by wasting one's time in a fruitless attempt to emulate her superstar partner.

Finally, we can imagine moderation being a preference in itself—not just a quality of a desire but itself the thing desired.[16] One might explain the cultivation of such a preference on the grounds that moderation is less distracting than extravagance, with the consequence that the moderate life is the more satisfyingly thoughtful and introspective life. In various ways, then, moderation can have instrumental or even constitutive value from the global perspective. Insofar as moderate preferences can be deliberately cultivated, their cultivation is subject to rational critique, and can thus be defended as rational.

5. When Seeking Optima Is Not Rational

To seek optima strikes us as generally a reasonable strategy, but it is not necessarily so. Section 2 noted that local optimizing can be a waste of time from a global perspective, but this is not the only circumstance that can make it inappropriate to seek optima. For one thing, a set of alternatives need not contain a well-defined optimal choice at all, let alone one that can be easily identified. To borrow a fanciful example from John Pollock, suppose you are immortal, and are also fortunate to have in your possession a bottle of EverBetter wine. This wine improves with age. In fact, it improves so steadily and so rapidly that no matter how long you wait before drinking it, you would be better off, all things considered, waiting one more day. The question is, when should you drink the wine?[17]

A rational *person* presumably would simply drink the wine at some point (perhaps after artificially constraining himself to drink the wine by year's end, and then picking New Year's Eve as the obvious choice within that time frame), but the person would not be able to defend any particular day as an optimal choice. Indeed, it is part of the story that no matter what day the immortal chooses, waiting one more day would have been better. There are no constraints with respect to which he can regard any particular day as the optimal choice, unless he imposes those constraints on himself.

There is something rational about choosing New Year's Eve, but the rationality lies in something other than how that day compares to the alternatives. Although the immortal could not defend choosing New Year's Eve in preference to waiting one more day, the choice is defensible in the sense that he did not have a better alternative to picking *something or other*. Indeed, picking something or other was optimal, because it was better than the only alternative, namely, sitting on the fence forever. The distinction between local and global optimizing thus allows us to explain without paradox the sense in which choosing New Year's Eve was rational. Picking something or other—and thus closing the compartment within which he seeks to set

16. I thank Mark Ravizza for this point.
17. Pollock (1984) 417.

a date for drinking the wine—was rational from the global perspective despite the fact that from within that compartment, it was not possible to have a rationale for the choice of any particular day.[18]

The EverBetter wine story is fantasy, of course, but it shows that we can imagine a set of alternatives with features making it inappropriate to seek the set's optimal member. Therefore, seeking optima may serve our ends, but if this is so, it is not a necessary truth but rather a contingent truth about the world and the kind of choice sets we find within it. In the EverBetter Wine case, the set of alternatives has no optimal member. Consider a more realistic story with a somewhat similar structure. Suppose a house comes up for sale in January. Out of curiosity, you take a look and find that you prefer it to the house you now own. When you look into the cost of selling your house and buying the new one, you find that the only cost you care about in the end is the cost and inconvenience of actually moving your belongings and settling into the new house. Suppose this cost, all things considered, amounts to $1,000. Moreover, it is clear to you that such moving costs will be amply repaid over time. You can see that the stream of revenue or utility from the new house will be worth $100 per month more than what you will receive if you stay where you are. Thus, the cost of the move will be repaid in ten months. This is hardly a wild fantasy, and so far, buying the house is intuitively reasonable. We see the point.

Now, to make the story more improbable, suppose you change houses in January and, four months later, it happens again. You find another house for sale. The move will cost another $1,000 but the new house will be worth $100 per month more than the one you now own. However, if you choose to move in May, that choice will make your January move retroactively suboptimal, a net loss of around $600. Should you move?

Perhaps opportunities to move to ever better houses will surface again and again. You do not know.[19] But you do know this: for any move to be optimal, something must subsequently make you stay put long enough to recover the cost of that particular move. If you keep waiting for and expecting the day when the world stops presenting you with such opportunities, and if that day never comes, then sooner or later you will have to begin turning your back on them. As in the EverBetter wine story, there is no particular point at which it is especially rational to stop moving. Indeed, whenever you finally reject an opportunity to move, it will be true that if you moved one more time, you eventually would be better off. Nevertheless, you have reason to commit yourself to being satisfied for a time with the house you have. Recall that optima are defined with respect to constraints. If you resolve in May that, once you choose, you will not look at another house for at least ten months, then choosing to move is optimal with respect to the choice set defined in part by that self-imposed constraint. Your January move will then have been a waste, but

---

18. Ullmann-Margalit and Morgenbesser (1977, 758–759) say one *picks* between A and B when one is indifferent between them and prefers the selection of either A or B to the selection of neither. What I call "picking" presumes the latter but not the former condition, for one could be in a picking situation even if one was not indifferent between one's alternatives. In the EverBetter wine case, one cannot find even a pair of alternatives over which one is indifferent. Even so, one still is forced to simply pick.

19. If you knew that ever better opportunities will keep coming in a steady stream, the optimal long-run strategy would be to make a big move up every ten months, skipping intervening steps.

your move in May will be worthwhile, provided that your self-imposed constraint remains firm.

Satisficing strategies strike us as reasonable in part because of contingent facts about ourselves and our world. For creatures as limited as ourselves, satisficing often makes a lot of sense. Perhaps less obvious is that the intuitive reasonableness of optimizing is no less contingent. Seizing on opportunities to make optimal moves serves a purpose partly because the real world is such that we can take for granted that there will time between moves to enjoy our improved situation. In the real world, opportunities to improve our situation do not come along so rapidly that we find ourselves stepping higher and higher without having time to enjoy the steps along the way. The real world limits our access to opportunities to improve our situation, and if such limits did not exist, we would have to invent them. We would have to give ourselves time to enjoy our situation even if that meant rejecting opportunities to improve it.

This section explained why seeking optima is only contingently rational. The argument went beyond the idea that different local goals can come into conflict. To be sure, there can be conflicts between the pursuit of local optima and the attainment of global optima, and such occasions give us reason not to pursue local optima. This section, though, articulated a different kind of reason not to pursue local optima, because the conflict discussed in this section could occur even if one had no goals beyond, for example, living in the best possible house. The nature of the conflict is that, ironically, *seeking* the best possible house could leave us with no time to actually live in the best possible house.

6. Trade-offs among Incommensurable Values

As explained in previous sections, moderate preferences and satisficing strategies can be of instrumental value from the global perspective. Section 4 closed with the speculation that moderate preferences might even be considered essential constituents of the good life and thus have more than merely instrumental value. Satisficing strategies, however, are of instrumental value only. This is because to satisfice is to give up the possibility of attaining a preferable outcome, and giving this up has to be explained in terms of the strategic reasons one has for giving it up. Local optimizing must likewise be explained, for it, too, consists of giving something up, namely the opportunity to invest one's efforts in some other compartment.

Global optimizing, however, is not open to question and subject to trade-offs in the ways local optimizing and satisficing are. Local goals can compete with each other, but there are no goals that compete with optimizing at the global level, at least not in the arena of rationality. A global optimum is not one among several competing goals; rather, in encompassing our lives as a whole, it also encompasses our competing goals. It represents the best way to resolve the competition from the standpoint of life as a whole. Local optimizing can be a waste from the global perspective. Global optimizing cannot be.

What, then, is the nature of the global perspective? Do we ever actually assume the global viewpoint or is this merely a theoretical postulate? The answer is that we can and do assume the global viewpoint every time we do what we call "stepping back to look at the big picture." We do sometimes ask ourselves if the things we do to advance our careers, for example, are really worth doing. We do not spend all our waking hours looking at the big picture, of course. Nor should we, for when we look at the big picture, one thing we see is that it is possible to spend too much time looking at the big picture. Reflection is a crucial part of the good life, but it is only a part. Part of attaining a global optimum involves being able to lose ourselves for a time in our local pursuits.

Previously, we saw that, at least in imaginary cases, there can be rational choice regarding a set of alternatives even when the set has no optimal members. The lesson applies to more realistic situations as well. In particular, as Isaac Levi notes, a person torn between ideals of pacifism and patriotism need not feel that his eventual choice is best, all things considered. Rather, he may feel that his eventual choice is best according to one of his ideals and worst according to another. What we have in such a case is what Levi calls "decisionmaking under unresolved conflict of values."[20] If you have several goals, none of which are subordinate to any other, and you find yourself in a situation where these goals are in conflict, the globally optimal trade-off may not exist. And such situations (involving concerns for one's loved ones and for one's ideals, for example) may be common.

Yet even in situations where there is no such thing as a global optimum, we can still take a global perspective. We can still look at our lives as a whole, even if nothing presents itself as optimal from that perspective. Indeed, conflict of values is precisely that from which broader perspectives emerge. We confront the big picture precisely when we stop to consider that there is more to life than pursuing a career or buying a house or raising children. It is from broader perspectives that we attempt to resolve conflicts of values, with or without an algorithm for resolving them in an optimal fashion.[21]

One might think unresolved conflict is a sign of poorly chosen values. Why should global optimizers risk adopting goals that could leave them having to make decisions under unresolved conflict? One reason is that some of our goals realize their full value in our lives only when they develop a certain autonomy, when we pursue them not as means of making our lives go well but as ends in themselves. We begin to tap the capacity of our ideals, our spouses, and our children to enrich our lives only when we acknowledge them as having value far beyond their capacity to enrich our lives. (Cherishing them becomes more than an instrumental means of making life go well; it becomes constitutive of life going well.) And goals we come to cherish as ends in themselves tend to become incommensurable.[22] We may, for instance, find ourselves in a position where we cannot fight for a cause in which we deeply believe without compromising the care that our loved ones need from us and that we wholeheartedly want them to have. Nevertheless, this is the

---

20. Levi (1986) 13.

21. As Gibbard (1990, 321) says, we have ways of coping other than by resolving everything.

22. Seung and Bonevac (1992) distinguish *incommensurate* rankings (no alternative is best) from *indeterminate* rankings (several alternatives are tied for best). Most of what follows concerns incommensurate rankings. In contrast, most of the cases discussed in Ullmann-Margalit and Morgenbesser (1977), like the case where a shopper chooses among identical cans of tomato soup, concern indeterminate rankings.

price of the richness and complexity of a life well lived. To have both ideals and loved ones is to run the risk of having to make decisions under unresolved conflicts of value.

Because some of our values are incommensurable, we sometimes have no method by which to identify optimal trade-offs among conflicting local goals. In such cases, the goal of making life as a whole go as well as possible remains meaningful, although there may not be any course of action that unequivocally counts as pursuing it. Even if would-be global optimizers cannot identify optimal options, they can still reject alternatives that fail to further any of their goals. In particular, if no better way of resolving the conflict emerges, simply picking something or other will emerge as optimal compared to the alternative of remaining on the fence, for we eventually reject fence-sitting on the grounds that it fails to further any of our goals.

This may seem a grim picture of rational choice at the global level, but there are two points to keep in mind. First, when faced with a situation in which we must simply pick something, we are likely to have regrets about paths not taken, but we naturally adapt to the paths we take, and regret can fade as we grow into our choice. Thus, an alternative somewhat arbitrarily picked from a set within which no optimum exists can eventually come to be viewed as optimal from the perspectives of people we are yet to become, even if it could not have been considered optimal at the moment of choice. Second, this discussion of underdetermined rational choice concerns a worst-case scenario. Global optimizers carry out the highest-ranked life plan when they have one. Often, however, there is no highest-ranked plan for life as a whole and thus no well-defined global optimum; there is only a need to cope with competing and sometimes incommensurable local goals. In the worst case, no course of action unambiguously qualifies as making life as a whole go as well as possible, except insofar as it is unambiguously better to move in some direction rather than none. But this gives us enough to avoid paralysis even in the worst case. By hypothesis, simply picking something emerges as the best the agent can do, and thus to pick something is to optimize with respect to the choice of whether to spend more time sitting on the fence.

It would be natural to say rational choice is choice "all things considered." The trouble is that we often find ourselves not knowing what to consider, and it would be bad advice to tell us to consider all things. We can consider all things within a limited range, perhaps, but the limits of that range will themselves tend to be matters of choice in large part. We start out knowing that in some sense we want each aspect of our lives to go as well as possible, yet we realize that our resources are limited and that our various pursuits must make room for each other. When looking at our lives as a whole, what is most clear is that rationally managing a whole life involves managing trade-offs among life's various activities. If the benefits that will accrue from our various pursuits are known and commensurable, then managing the trade-offs is easy, at least theoretically; we simply maximize the sum of benefits. However, in many everyday cases, the benefits are neither known with any precision nor straightforwardly commensurable with other benefits. Even so, we can effectively manage trade-offs among particular pursuits by setting limits on how much of our lives we spend on particular pursuits. We can also set limits on how much benefit we insist on getting from particular pursuits. To impose the latter kind of stopping rule on a particular pursuit is to embrace what I have called a satisficing strategy.

Both kinds of constraint play a role in rational choice. Why? Because if we recognized only temporal limits, say, then we would automatically spend our full allotment of time in a given compartment even when we already had an acceptable option in hand. But if we also have strategically limited aspiration within that compartment, then finding an acceptable option will trigger a second kind of stopping rule. The second stopping rule closes the compartment and diverts the unused portion of the compartment's time allotment to other compartments where our need to find an acceptable option has not yet been met. Cultivating moderate preferences may also be advantageous in a supplementary way, insofar as moderate preferences may help us adhere to the kind of limit we impose on a pursuit when we embrace a satisficing strategy.

Against the idea that our most important goals tend to become incommensurable with each other, one might suppose our global end is simply to flourish or to be happy—and that our local goals therefore *must* be commensurable in such terms. This would be a tidy climax to an otherwise rather untidy story about rational choice under unresolved conflict of values, but the tidiness would be superficial. One hardly gives people an algorithm for resolving conflicts when one advises them to be happy. What makes such advice vacuous is that flourishing and being happy cannot be concrete goals at the global level in the way that finding a house can be at the local level. Of course we *want* to flourish, but we *aim* to flourish only in an especially metaphorical sense. The fact is that we flourish not by aiming at flourishing but by successfully pursuing other things, things worth pursuing for their own sake.

Likewise, happiness can be a standard by which a life as a whole is judged, perhaps, but it cannot be a goal at which a life as a whole is aimed. We do not become happy by pursuing things there would otherwise be no point in pursuing. Rather, there must be a point in striving for a certain goal before striving for it can come to have any potential to make us happy. To aim at happiness is to aim at a state that emerges only in the course of aiming at something else.[23] So, the point about happiness and flourishing leaves us where we started, having to choose among things we value for their own sake, hoping we will be happy with our choice.

We might add that happiness derives from a variety of local sources, and the different elements of a person's happiness are not interchangeable. Our various local pleasures are not fungible; different dollar bills are all the same, functionally speaking, but different pleasures are not all the same, and are not experienced as interchangeable units of the same kind of stuff. We can find happiness in our careers and in our marriages, but the vacuum left by a shattered career cannot be filled by domestic bliss.[24]

---

23. As Williams (Smart and Williams, 1973, 113) puts it, one has to want other things for there to be anywhere that happiness can come from. See also the eleventh of Butler's *Fifteen Sermons* (1874, 139).

24. I thank Nick Sturgeon for a discussion from which this point emerged. See also Stocker (1990, chap. 6) and, of course, chap. 2 of Mill's *Utilitarianism*.

7. An Infinite Regress of Perspectives?

The global perspective is the perspective encompassing our lives as a whole. Decision-making at this level disciplines the amount of time we devote to particular local compartments. It seems that we are capable of taking a perspective this broad even in worst-case scenarios where there is no well-defined global optimum. But even if we suppose we can take a perspective encompassing our whole lives, why should we suppose this is the broadest perspective we can take?

Perhaps there can be broader perspectives than what I call the global perspective. Indeed, I argue elsewhere (see chapters 3 and 4) that we do have access to a larger perspective, that there are aspects of morality that we cannot appreciate except from a larger perspective, and that it can be rational to try to achieve this perspective. Yet, it would be unrealistic to suppose there is an infinite regress of levels. We need not prove that an infinite regress is impossible, but insofar as an infinite regress is unrealistic, it is important to show that my theory does not *presuppose* an infinite regress.

The threat of infinite regress arises in the following way. I said we cannot spend all our time looking at life as a whole; we must be able to lose ourselves (or perhaps I should say, find ourselves) in our local pursuits. How much time, then, should we spend pondering conflicting values? How much time should we spend looking at life as a whole? From what perspective do we choose to limit the amount of time we spend looking at our lives from the global perspective? Perhaps we need a "superglobal" perspective in order to answer these questions. After all, how could we decide how much time to spend at a given level unless we did so from a still more encompassing perspective?[25]

It seems my theory can explain the time we allot to a given perspective only by supposing that we retreat to a broader one, ad infinitum. Not so. The theory presumes no such retreat. There are simpler, more realistic ways to explain the amount of time we spend looking at life as a whole.[26] Here are two.

1. There are things, like sleeping, that we do as the need arises. Since we do not *decide* how much time to spend sleeping, we do not decide from a broader perspective, either. Indeed, we might be better off sleeping as we feel the need rather than trying to set aside a calculated amount of time for sleep. Perhaps the same holds true of the activity of looking at life as a whole. Insofar as our purpose in looking at life as a whole is to resolve conflicts arising between various aspects of our lives, so that life as a whole may go well, there will come a time when taking a global perspective has served its purpose. At that time, the compartment in our lives reserved for the activity of resolving local conflicts naturally closes until subsequent conflict forces it open again. There is no residual conflict awaiting resolution at a higher level.

25. Holly Smith (1991) worries about the same sort of problem.

26. The simplest way to explain time spent at the global level would be to say we take whatever time we need to consider *everything*. The trouble is that we do not have time to consider everything that may be relevant to life as a whole, any more than we have time to consider everything that may be relevant to purchasing a house. The explanation will have to be more complicated than this; hence the line of thought pursued in the following text.

Thus, the question of how much time to spend in contemplation need not itself require contemplation. Rather, we take whatever time it takes to genuinely resolve a conflict, or else we reach a point where we must simply pick something. More generally, we stop contemplating when we judge that pursuing our local goals has come into conflict with—and has become more important than—the activity of thinking about how to juggle them. (For example, we would not dwell on the big picture if we were starving. Conflicts are rarely so important that contemplating them could preempt securing our immediate survival.) In this scenario, we are driven *to* the global level by local conflict and eventually are driven *from* that level by a need to get on with our lives.[27] The question of how much time to spend looking at life as a whole resolves itself.

2. We also can imagine a scenario in which the question does not resolve itself but is instead answered by deliberate calculation, in the same way we could imagine deliberately calculating how much time to spend sleeping. Could we make a conscious decision of this kind without taking a superglobal perspective? Yes, we could. Consider that contemplation is an activity that must find its place in our lives along with other activities. For example, I might spend the month of July in a rented cabin, not doing anything to pursue my career, but just thinking about why I ever wanted to be a philosopher and about whether my original reasons still hold. This compartment in my life is reserved for contemplating my career. It is separate from the compartment or compartments within which I actually pursue my career. I also have a compartment, similar in many respects, within which I contemplate life as a whole. But although the subject I contemplate is the whole of my life, the contemplation itself is not. The contemplation is only one of many activities about which I care.

Now, if I need to decide how much time to reserve for contemplating life as a whole, I take a global perspective, trying to gauge how important such contemplation is to my life as a whole. Notice, then, what is unique about the compartment I reserve for the activity of contemplating my life as a whole. The compartment is unique because its boundaries are set by the activity that takes place within it. In the course of contemplating life from the global perspective, I decide how much time to reserve for any given activity, including contemplation in general and contemplating life as a whole in particular. In this second scenario, as in the first, there is no residue. Once we finish making the kinds of decisions we make at the global level, we are done. No boundary-setting issue is left to await resolution at a higher level.

I have outlined two possibilities. In the first case, we use whatever time we need for resolving conflicts, subject to preemption by activities that in the short run are more important than conflict resolution. In this case, no decision is required.

---

27. We also can be driven to a global perspective by the resolution of conflicts. Thus, when we finish a major project that has forced other pursuits to take a back seat, we often take time to evaluate self-imposed constraints and decide how to divide our extra time among previously neglected projects. And what drives us from the global perspective is the eventual resolution of a local conflict between savoring the big picture (a satisfying activity indeed when just finishing a major project) and the need, say, to start making dinner.

The discipline is automatic. In the second case, we discipline the compartment from within, as our contemplation of trade-offs leads us to conclude that we should reserve time for contemplation along with our other local activities. Therefore, we do not need a superglobal perspective to decide how much time to reserve for the activity of taking a global perspective. Such decisions are precisely the kind we make from the global perspective itself, when we need to make them at all.

8. Conclusion

This essay sets out part of a normative ideal of rational choice suitable for the kind of beings we happen to be, beings who would only hurt themselves if they tried to maximize their overall utility in every waking activity. This essay defines satisficing and local optimizing as strategies for pursuing goals within constraints that are in part self-imposed. Satisficing emerges not as an alternative to optimizing as *a model* of rationality, but rather as an alternative to local optimizing as *a strategy* for pursuing global optima.

Under normal conditions, we employ a combination of heuristics, such as (1) compartmentalizing our pursuits so as to narrow the scope of any particular optimization problem to the point where our limited knowledge becomes sufficient to identify an optimal solution; (2) accepting self-imposed constraints for the same reason as well as to keep particular pursuits from preempting more important ones; and (3) satisficing, which has the effect of closing compartments as soon as they serve the purpose for which they were created. Under normal conditions, where we lack the information we need to assign probabilities and utilities, this combination of strategies is more effective at making our lives as a whole go well than the alternative of plugging guesswork into a formula for maximizing expected utility. Thus, it is no wonder we so rarely find ourselves trying to calculate expected utilities, for the truth is that we usually have better things to do.

When goals are in conflict, there may not be any well-defined sense in which one way of resolving the conflict is, from the viewpoint of one's life as a whole, better than the alternatives. Of course, we do well to cultivate moderate preferences, so as to reduce the frequency and severity of conflicts of value. But at the same time, there are limits to what one should do to avoid situations of underdetermined choice, for the risk of finding oneself in such situations is a risk one assumes in the process of becoming rationally committed to particular ends as ends in themselves. A life with no regrets (about decisions made under unresolved conflict) is preferable, all other things equal, but if the lack of regret is purchased at a cost of not having goals that can come into irresolvable conflict, the price is too high. A person who adopts a number of goals as ends in themselves risks finding himself in situations where global optima do not exist, but there are reasons why a global optimizer would take that risk.

Admittedly, these conclusions about rational strategy are not neat and tidy, certainly not in comparison to the simple maximization model. But tidying up the conclusions at the expense of realism would be a mistake, for the conclusions are meant to be about us, not about mathematically tractable caricatures of us. Rational choice theory developed along the lines indicated here has more power than simple maximization models to explain why we live as we do, but it does not thereby become merely a self-congratulating description of how we live. Rather, it sets out a normative ideal of rational choice that it would be natural and healthy for us to try to live up to.

Appendix: The Difference between Satisficing and Local Optimizing

I distinguished between satisficing and local optimizing as stopping rules. Some readers may find it helpful to consider a graphical representation of that distinction. We might represent a choice among alternatives in two-dimensional Cartesian space with Utility on the y-axis and our set of alternatives arrayed along the x-axis. If we know the shape of the utility curve, we simply pick the highest point. No controversy arises. (See fig. 2.1.) This essay concerns what to do when we are looking at a blank; that is, we may suppose there is some curve or other, but often we do not know what it looks like. (See fig. 2.2.)

Further, suppose we look at our lives from a global perspective, wanting life as a whole to go well. What do we see? We don't see one big graph, blank or otherwise. Rather, we see a bunch of little graphs, some of which are more or less blank. The question then arises: within a particular compartment, how do we make decisions when we do not know the utility function's shape? The answer is that we search the set of alternatives. We see how much utility a_1 has. We see how much a_2 has, and so on. And since other decisions (searches) are also calling for our limited resources, we pick something at some point.

At what point do we rationally stop searching and pick something? The answer is, we impose two kinds of constraints on our search of the particular local utility space. We impose vertical constraints on how many alternatives we will consider (or if we defined the x-axis differently, on how much time or money or other resources we invest in the search). In other words, we operate with limited *inputs*. Or we impose horizontal constraints on how much utility we insist on getting before we stop searching. In other words, we operate with limited aspirations, limits on aimed-at *output*. Or we do both. Then, when we run up against either kind of limit, we stop searching in that local utility space, pick something, and turn our attention to some other local utility space. (See fig. 2.3.)

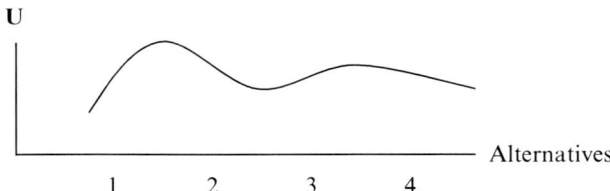

FIGURE 2.1. Searching among alternatives with known utilities.

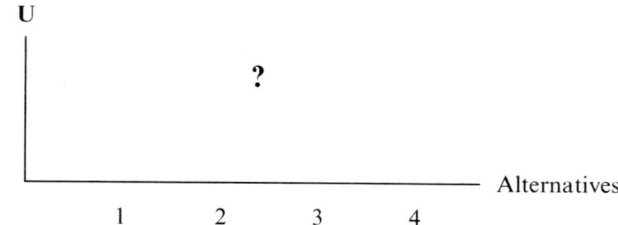

FIGURE 2.2. Searching among alternatives with unknown utilities.

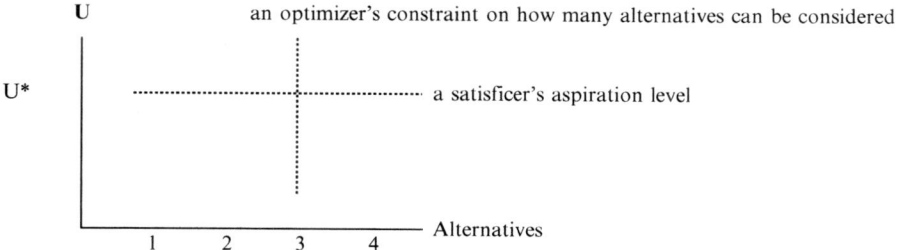

FIGURE 2.3. Two stopping rules contrasted.

In figure 2.3, the horizontal line represents the point at which $U = U^*$, where U^* is the level of U with which the agent will be satisfied. As mentioned earlier, we can let the expected utility of continued search equal the probability of finding a better option, $P(fbo)$, multiplied by the utility of finding a better option, $U(fbo)$, minus the cost of further search, $C(fs)$. In that case, the vertical line in figure 2.3 represents the point along the x-axis at which, the agent judges, it becomes true that $P(fbo)U(fbo) - C(fs) \leq 0$, where $P(fbo)U(fbo)$ is the expected utility of further search and $C(fs)$ is the cost of further search.

In figure 2.3, vertical constraints are constraints on inputs, and define the search as local optimizing, taking the best alternative we discover prior to hitting that constraint. Horizontal constraints are constraints on aimed-at output, and define the search as satisficing, taking the first alternative we find with that high a utility. The two strategies can be employed simultaneously, of course. I argued that this is how we actually live and that a global optimizer would have no reason for wanting to do things differently.

The vertical constraints partition our various activities in terms of how much of our total resources are allotted to those activities. Note that we do not need to be able to prioritize our activities in order to ration our resources among them. If necessary, we can arbitrarily set vertical constraints on how much (time, money, and so on) we are willing to spend within a particular compartment. As illustrated by the story about imposing time constraints on our search for optimal toothpaste, we tend to be satisficers when gathering information about *where to set vertical constraints*. The less we know about what our different endeavors mean to us, relatively speaking, the more arbitrariness there will be when we set the vertical constraints that delimit the different compartments. By the same token, the more comparability we have in terms of the relative importance of our different activities, the less arbitrary will be the boundaries we draw between them.

This chapter revises "Rationality within Reason," *Journal of Philosophy* 89 (1992): 445–66. Reprinted by permission of the Journal.

3

Choosing Ends

> "Reason" has a perfectly clear and precise meaning. It signifies the choice of the right means to an end that you wish to achieve. It has nothing whatever to do with the choice of ends.
>
> Bertrand Russell, *Human Society in Ethics and Politics* (1954)

Rational choice, on a means-end conception, involves seeking effective means to one's ends. From this basic idea, the social sciences have developed an instrumental model of rationality. The instrumental model goes beyond a means-end conception by inferring from it not only that rational choice involves seeking effective means to one's ends but also that rational choice involves nothing beyond this. Ends must be taken as given, as outside the purview of rational choice. All chains of justification eventually terminate in something unjustified.

Or so the story goes. This essay, though, shows how we can have a chain of means and ends whose final link is rationally justified. One might assume that justifying final ends requires a conception of justification foreign to rational choice theory. Not so. Admittedly, defenders and critics alike agree that "the theory of rational choice disclaims all concern with the ends of action."[1] But such quietism about ends is not necessary. A means-end conception of rationality can be made consistent with our intuition that we can be rational in a more reflective sense, questioning ends we happen to have, revising them when they seem unfit.

One could define ends as items we *ought* to pursue, but I define ends descriptively, as items we do pursue. Human beings are capable of having ends in this descriptive sense. Are we also capable of having ends that we were rational to adopt as items to pursue? This essay tries to craft a philosophically and psychologically

---

1. Gauthier (1986) 26. Resnik puts it dramatically: "Individual decision theory recognizes no distinction—either moral or rational—between the goals of killing oneself, being a sadist, making a million dollars, or being a missionary" (1987, 5).

plausible account of how the answer could be yes, thus looking beyond a purely instrumental model to something more reflective, a model in which agents choose and criticize ends as well as means.

There is, of course, a problem. The instrumentalist model is standard equipment in the social sciences, in part because it is useful, but also because it is hard to imagine an alternative. Evaluating a proposed means to a given end seems straightforward. We ask whether it serves the given end. But when we talk about being reflectively rational, we are talking about evaluating ends as such. Now, we evidently can and do judge some ends as not worth pursuing—but how?

1. Three Kinds of Ends

My answer draws on distinctions between four kinds of ends, three of which are well known among philosophers. Suppose I wake one morning wanting to go for a 2-mile run.

1. Perhaps I have this goal as an end in itself; I want to run 2 miles just for the sake of being out there running. In this case, the goal of running 2 miles is a *final* end.
2. Or perhaps I want to run for the sake of some other goal. I run because I want to be healthy. In this case, running 2 miles is an *instrumental* end, instrumental to the further end of being healthy.
3. Or suppose I want to run 2 miles because I want some aerobic exercise. In this case, running 2 miles is not exactly a mere means to the further end of getting some exercise. Rather, running 2 miles constitutes getting some exercise. So, in this third case we can speak of going for a run as a *constitutive* end.[2]

A variety of subsidiary criteria often help us to assess the relative merits of alternative constitutive ends. For instance, if my further goal is to get some aerobic exercise, and it occurs to me that I could ride my stationary bicycle rather than run 2 miles, I could ask myself which is easier on my knees, which will use less time, whether the bicycle's noise will bother the neighbors at this hour, and so on. If subsidiary criteria do not tell the difference between alternative constitutive ends, then the best I can do is to pick a form of exercise and get on with it.

The three categories are not mutually exclusive. An end like running 2 miles could be both final and instrumental, pursued for its own sake and for the sake of further ends. Nevertheless, distinguishing among these three ends is useful. For one thing, the distinction makes it easy to see how we can rationally choose some of our ends. In particular, we can choose instrumental and constitutive ends as means to further ends, and so such ends can be rational in the sense that choosing to pursue

---

2. The distinction between instrumental and constitutive ends is formalized by Ackrill (1980, 19). I am also borrowing from MacDonald (1991).

them can serve further ends. By the same token, we criticize such choices by asking whether pursuing the chosen end really helps to secure the further end, or whether pursuing it truly constitutes pursuing the further end.

The final end that terminates a chain of justification, though, cannot be justified in the same way we justify the links leading up to it. Final ends as such are neither constituents of nor instrumental to further ends. They are pursued for their own sake. Thus, the justification of final ends will be a different kind of story, a story that cannot be told within the confines of an instrumentalist model.

2. A Fourth Kind of End

What sort of story? To give an example: suppose that, for Kate, becoming a surgeon is an end. Perhaps it is an end because Kate thinks becoming a surgeon will be prestigious, in which case becoming a surgeon is an instrumental end. Kate becomes a surgeon in order to do something else, namely, to secure prestige. But maybe, for Kate, becoming a surgeon is an end in itself. How could a career in medicine come to be a final end?

Maybe it happened like this. When Kate was a teenager, she had no idea what she wanted to do with her life, but she knew she wanted to do something. She wanted goals to pursue. In particular, she wanted to settle on a career and thus on the goal or set of goals that a career represents. At some point, she concluded that going to medical school and becoming a surgeon would give her the career she wanted. So she went to school to pursue a career in medicine. She has various reasons to pursue this goal, of course, but she also pursues it as an end in itself, much as I might run just for the sake of being out running.

The interesting point is that Kate's story introduces a fourth kind of end, an end of acquiring settled ends, an end of choosing a career in particular. The goal of choosing a career is what I shall call a *maieutic* end—an end achieved through a process of coming to have other ends. People sometimes describe Socrates as having taught by the maieutic method or method of midwifery. The idea: students already have great stores of inchoate knowledge, so a teacher's job is to help students give birth to this latent knowledge. I use the term "maieutic" to suggest that we give birth to our final ends in the process of achieving maieutic ends. In this case, Kate achieves a maieutic end by coming to have particular career goals. As I said, she settles on a career by deciding to pursue a career in medicine. Thus, just as final ends are further ends for the sake of which we pursue instrumental and constitutive ends, maieutic ends are further ends for the sake of which we choose final ends.

The immediate worry here is that there may appear to be an inconsistency in the way the terms are defined. I said we could choose a final end as a way of achieving a maieutic end. On the contrary, one might respond, if Kate chooses a career in medicine as a way of achieving a maieutic end, she must be pursuing that career not as a final end but rather as an instrumental end. This is a natural response. It may even seem indisputable.

But the natural response is a mistake. It overlooks the distinction between *pursuing* a final end (which by definition we do for its own sake) and *choosing* a final end (which we might do for various reasons). By definition, final ends are pursued for their own sake, not for the sake of maieutic ends. Yet, even if Kate pursues an end purely for its own sake, it can still be true that there was, in Kate's past, a process by which she acquired that end. It can also be true that going through the process (of acquiring the new goal) served ends she had at the time. The supposition that the choice process is a means to an existing end leaves open whether the outcome of the process, the chosen end, will be pursued as a means to the same end. The new end may well be something Kate subsequently pursues for its own sake. The distinction between reasons for choosing and reasons for pursuing an end thus lets us speak coherently of choosing a final end for the sake of further ends.

Against the distinction, however, one might object that when we choose an instrumental or a constitutive end, we *necessarily* pursue it for the same reason we originally chose it, namely, the further end to which we chose it as a means. Analogously, the objection continues, when we choose a final end we thereby take it to be good in itself. Consequently, our grounds for choosing X specifically as a final end must necessarily be the same as our grounds for pursuing X specifically as a final end—its being good in itself.[3]

This objection is more complicated than it looks. The alleged relation of identity between reasons for choosing and reasons for pursuing an end is by no means analytic. Even if it is true by definition that an instrumental end is both chosen and pursued as a means to a further end, it does not follow that the further end for which we chose it is identical to the further end for which we pursue it. Even if it were safe to assume that they will be identical, it is nevertheless an assumption, resting on further assumptions about human psychology. It is an empirical issue whether people tend to pursue ends for the same reasons they originally chose those ends as ends.

Similarly, even though it is true by definition that final ends are pursued for their own sake, it remains an open question whether further purposes were served by the process of coming to have final ends. For example, I may write in part because I love to write, but that supposition leaves open a possibility that other purposes were served by the process of becoming so devoted to writing. Developing that kind of devotion may have been what made it possible for me to get a job at a research-oriented university in the first place. I may even have been aware that good things happen to people who love to write when I began doing the things that led me to develop my taste for writing. My point is that these are empirical matters. Some might insist that my reasons for choosing to pursue an end simply cannot—cannot *possibly*, cannot *conceivably*—differ from my subsequent reasons for pursuing that end. However, we just conceived of a difference between what drives me to write and what drove me to nurture my drive to write. Therefore, it is demonstrably false that we cannot conceive of them as distinct. If there is any truth in the idea that the two reasons cannot be distinct, it will be a truth grounded in human psychology rather

---

3. I thank Scott MacDonald for suggesting this objection.

than in analysis of terms. It will be a psychological truth that if ever I nurtured my desire to write because I thought it would further my career, then my ultimate reason to write must forever remain that I think it will further my career. (Think about it. Is it plausible that there is *no chance* of my still desiring to write after I retire?)

My own understanding is that an act of adopting something as an end often changes our attitude toward it. If so, then it is a mistake to assume that our future grounds for pursuing X will be like (and a bigger mistake to assume our future grounds *must* be like) our present grounds for adopting X as an end. My student may feel ambivalent about each of the subjects she might major in, but if she anticipates coming to view the study of philosophy as good in itself, then her anticipation of this new attitude can be grounds for choosing to study philosophy in the first place. Similarly, sometimes one of our core reasons to choose a career is that we want—*and do not yet have*—the attitude that goes with pursuing a given career in a wholehearted way. We might have reasons to choose an end in part because of reasons we expect to develop for pursuing that end.

Observe, then, how the relation between maieutic and final ends differs from the relation between final and constitutive ends. The end of getting some aerobic exercise is schematic; we cannot do what it tells us to do until we choose a specific way of getting exercise, such as a 2-mile run.[4] Choosing specifics is a necessary preface to achieving the end. This is not how it works, though, when the further end is a maieutic end. Choosing specifics is not merely a preface to achieving a maieutic end. On the contrary, a maieutic end just is a goal of settling on a specific end. In settling on a specific goal and thereby meeting the maieutic end's demand, one is achieving the maieutic end, not merely choosing a specific way of pursuing it.

For example, my attempt to jog 2 miles constitutes my attempt to get some exercise, but Kate's attempt to become a surgeon does not constitute her attempt to choose a career goal. On the contrary, when Kate goes to medical school in an attempt to become a surgeon, she is not just attempting to choose a career goal. At that point, she has chosen a career goal, namely, to be a surgeon. In the jogging case, I pursue goal A as a way of *pursuing* goal B. In the second case, Kate chooses goal A as a way of *achieving* goal B. Note that in the jogging case, A is the constitutive end, while in the other case, B is the maieutic end. Therefore, even if the relation between A and B were the same in both cases (which it isn't), constitutive ends and maieutic ends would still be different, for the two kinds of ends are found at opposite ends of the relation.

We also can see how the relation between maieutic and final ends differs from the relation between final and instrumental ends. When one end is pursued purely for the sake of another end, then the rationale for its pursuit depends on its ongoing relation as a means to the further end. For example, if pursuing a career in medicine is merely a means of securing prestige, and Kate one day loses her desire for prestige, then she also loses her grounds for becoming a surgeon. The rationale for her career depends on the persistence of the further end of securing prestige. In the other

---

4. Constitutive ends can be either specific ways of pursuing a more formal further end (putting on a suit can be constitutive of being well-dressed) or constituent parts of the further end (putting on a tie can be a constituent of putting on a suit).

scenario, though, the rationale for her career does not depend on the persistence of the teenage end of settling on a career. On the contrary, her evolving career goal *replaces* the teenage end with something quite different. As long as Kate is settled in her career as a surgeon, she has attained the goal (of settling on a career) that she had as a teenager, thus eliminating the earlier goal as an item to pursue. For Kate, the maieutic end of settling on a career reemerges (as an item to pursue) only if Kate at some point rejects her career as a surgeon and longs for something new.

Some readers might worry that a maieutic end is never really eliminated and that the new end it spawns is subsequently pursued, implicitly if not explicitly, as a means to the maieutic end. When Kate settles on a career, her subsequent pursuits might be motivated by the same concerns that drove her as a teenager to settle on a career. My response is, of course this will be true in some cases; some people, after settling on a career, subsequently pursue their careers instrumentally (instrumental to the further end of making money) or constitutively (constitutive of the further end of keeping busy). In other words, maieutic ends can give birth not only to final ends but to other kinds of ends as well.[5] But such cases are beside the point. If our task were to explain how instrumental or constitutive ends could be rationally chosen, such cases would be relevant. Our actual objective, though, is to explain how final ends can be rationally chosen, which means we need to focus on cases where the chosen ends are subsequently pursued as ends in themselves. Only in those cases are maieutic ends relevant to the puzzle of how final ends can be rationally chosen.

But, a critic might persist, how can we be sure that maieutic ends *ever* give birth to final ends? One could argue that, if the desire to have a career is what leads Kate to choose a career, then the same desire will be the further end for the sake of which she pursues her career. If she chooses a career as a mere means to the further end, then she will pursue the career for the same reason. In response, we need not deny that there can be a value Kate attaches to having a career that persists through her choice and pursuit of a particular career. To say Kate eliminates "settling on a career" as an end, that is, as an item to pursue, is not to say she ceases to value having a career. We need to distinguish between something being valuable and something being an item to pursue.

For example, my car is valuable to me. And if I leave it parked on a hill and the parking brake fails, then it also becomes an item to pursue. The car is valuable to me both before and after I secure it, but it ceases to be an item to pursue after I secure it. Similarly, if Kate already has a career, then having a career may be valuable to her, but it isn't an item to pursue; it is an item she already has. Of course, Kate continues to value having a career even as she pursues one. (That is, she pursues the particular goals making up her particular career. Once she has a particular career, though, she does not pursue the generic goal of having a career.) But this is no reason to doubt that she now has goals, acquired in the course of settling on her particular career, that she pursues for their own sake.

Maieutic ends are not the only kind of end that can be eliminated as items to pursue, but their elimination has a unique upshot. In the means-end relation between instrumental and final end, eliminating the further end renders the means pointless, robbing them of normative significance. In contrast, in the means-end relation

5. The issue came up in discussions with Lainie Ross.

between final and maieutic end, eliminating the further end is an essential part of the process by which final ends acquire their characteristic normative significance.

Maieutic ends are not merely a theoretical postulate. They are real. The drive to find a career or a spouse can be powerful, even painful, and such drives are drives to settle on a particular career or particular person. Recall what it was like to choose a major in college or to choose a career. One way or another, we had to choose something, and, for some of us, not having done so yet was an occasion for considerable anxiety. Some of us had hardly a clue of what we really wanted, but it felt better to settle on some end or other than to let that part of our lives remain a vacuum. Of course, there were institutional and parental pressures as well, and some of us felt only those, but many of us also felt pressure from within.

None of this denies that some people are simply gripped by particular final ends.[6] Perhaps such ends are not acquired by choice. If not, then questions about how they could be rationally chosen are moot. But that does not mean all questions are moot, for we can still ask whether further ends are served by the process of coming to have a final end. Regardless of whether ends are deliberately selected from a set of alternatives, my model has something to say. It addresses the question of whether an end's acquisition serves further ends.

That, then, is my theory about how an end, pursued as a genuinely final end, could have been rationally chosen. There are ends—maieutic ends—to which a final end could be chosen as a means. In passing, although the four categories of ends are conceptually distinct, they are not mutually exclusive. An end could be final, pursued for its own sake, and at the same time instrumental, pursued as a means to some further end. Moreover, section 4 presents three formal models of reflective rationality, the first of which models a maieutic end as a final end and the third of which models a maieutic end as an instrumental end. That an end falls into one category does not preclude it from falling into others.

Section 3 explains how unchosen ends might serve as parts of a framework for judging a choice of ends. Section 4 then considers whether explaining the rational choice of one final end presupposes further ends. That is, we have seen how final ends could be rationally chosen, but are "loose ends" inevitable?

3. The Role of Unchosen Ends

Although some of our ends are chosen, some are not. For most of us, the goal of survival is a goal we simply find ourselves with. Likewise, we want to be good at what we do, and this goal also seems unchosen, something we simply have. We want to be competent.[7] We do not need reasons to choose our unchosen ends, since we do not

---

6. The issue came up in discussions with Ruth Marcus and Michael Della Rocca.

7. It is not a conceptual truth that human beings desire to be competent, but nor is that desire merely a local phenomenon. Probably it is conspicuously present in all societies. White (1971) says exploratory and playful behavior in children and even young animals serves to develop competence in dealing with the environment and that a sense of competence is a vital aspect of self-esteem. Broadie says the joy human beings take in doing things well "is so natural that people set up all sorts of trivial ends in order to have the satisfaction of achieving them correctly" (1991, 92).

choose them. We simply have them. Even unchosen ends can be rejected, of course, but to rationally reject them, one needs a reason to reject them. Unchosen final ends, therefore, have a certain normative inertia, which means they can form a relatively stable frame of reference in terms of which we evaluate ends we might acquire by choice. Not every pursuit, for instance, is conducive to survival.

Harry Frankfurt goes a bit farther, holding that fixed ends are a *necessary* part of a normative frame of reference. The problem of choosing ends presupposes a frame of reference against which one assesses one's options, and not all of this framework can be an endogenous product of choice. As Frankfurt puts it,

> it is only if his volitional nature is in certain respects already fixed that a person can effectively consider what his final ends should be—what is to be important to him, or what to care about. He will not be in a position to inquire into the question of how he should live unless it is already the case that there are some things about which he cares.[8]

Frankfurt has a point. We need a fairly stable frame of reference to get started in assessing prospective ends.

At the same time, the stable foundation need not, as Frankfurt himself notes, "be fixed unalterably."[9] Thus, although I accept a version of Frankfurt's point, three related complications bear mentioning. First, the stable foundation need not be permanently fixed. Indeed, it may be something needing to be left behind. Childhood is the foundation for adulthood, but childhood is something we outgrow. Second, in the long run the foundation might not be fixed independently of choice. Rather, some parts of the foundation (character traits, in particular) may arise and change through a process of habituation driven by ongoing patterns of choice. Third, even when an end is acquired by choice, the process of settling on that end often is not a simple act of will. On the contrary, often we settle on an end partly by habituating ourselves toward aiming at it. For instance, we want to have someone to love. This is a maieutic end that we achieve when we come to love particular people and accept spending time with them and making them happy as ends worth pursuing for their own sake. But coming to love and be devoted to a person obviously is not an act of will so much as growing into a commitment, step by step.

So, some items come to be pursued as final ends through a process of habituation. And although Kate's character is stable with respect to particular decisions, it is also a part of her that, over the long run, she shapes in incremental ways through her choices. If all goes well, she will grow into the career (and the husband) she has chosen, and the person she becomes will some day find that career (and that husband) intrinsically worthy of her ongoing commitment.

Of course, circumstances help determine whether a prospective end is appropriate. Indeed, circumstances determine whether a particular option even exists. A given activity counts as a prospective career, for example, only if there is a market for that kind of activity. (Does becoming a chess player count as settling on a career?) The

---

8. Frankfurt (1992) 17.
9. Frankfurt (1992) 18.

nature of maieutic ends also depends on circumstances. For example, settling on a spouse can be a maieutic end only if a certain kind of social structure exists to render that end intelligible. To a large extent, culture dictates both the range of maieutic ends one could have and also the range of final ends whose choice would achieve a given maieutic end.

Another part of a framework for assessing prospective ends is supplied by an aspect of maieutic ends that I have yet to discuss. A maieutic end is an end of bringing ends into existence, of giving oneself ends to pursue. To have ends to pursue is to have something to live for. If we have a single overarching and possibly unchosen maieutic end, I would say it is the end of finding things to live for.[10] The various maieutic ends (settling on a major in college and then a career, defining ideals, choosing a spouse, finding ways of contributing to the community, and so on) are all species of a generic and overarching maieutic end of finding things to live for, ends to which one can devote oneself. In different words, the end of finding something to live for is the end of acquiring ends in general, the end of having one's life be spent on something rather than nothing.

That does not mean we are always looking for things to live for. Sometimes our existing corpus of ends gives us plenty to do, leaving us with neither need nor opportunity to look for more. Sometimes feeding ourselves or our children is a challenge, keeping our hands so full that taking time to ask what we are living for is out of the question. To have no time for ends beyond survival is to have no need for ends beyond survival. But when daily survival becomes too easy to keep us busy, that is when we need something else to aim at, lest we find ourselves with too much time to ponder the fact that there is nothing for the sake of which we are surviving.

In effect, insofar as bare survival originally presents itself as a final end, we need to convert it into something else, a form of survival that has instrumental value as well. When we do this, we change survival from something we happen to seek as a matter of descriptive biological fact into something with normative weight—a goal we have reason to seek. In this way, we redeem survival as a goal. But to do this, we need to settle on further ends to which survival can serve as means.[11] The next section incorporates these ideas into a model of reflective rationality. After we have the model in front of us, I will consider how we compare prospective final ends.

4. A Model of Rational Choice with No Loose Ends

Means-end conceptions of rationality posit instrumental ends. Sophisticated versions also posit constitutive ends. A means-end conception also posits final ends, which rationally justify instrumental and constitutive ends. Instrumental or static rationality involves seeking effective means to given ends. The essence of reflective rationality

---

10. I speak interchangeably of having, finding, getting, or coming to have something to live for.
11. It seems that some people would rather die than live without goals they consider worth living for. Suicide often might be understood not as a repudiation of the unchosen end of survival but rather as the ultimate confirmation of the intolerability of failing to achieve the maieutic end of finding something to live for.

46 PERSON

is that, although it involves means-end reasoning, it goes beyond instrumental rationality because it does not take ends as given. Reflectively rational choosers realize that their preference functions change over time and that some changes will serve their current ends better than others. To be reflectively rational is to manage one's changing preference function, to do what one can to become the sort of person one wants to become.

In figure 3.1, F, *c*, and *i* stand for final, constitutive, and instrumental ends. An arrow from *c* to F signifies that pursuing *c* is a means to F.

There will be as many chains of justification as there are final ends, and instrumental or constitutive ends pass as rational only if they are links within one or more chains, which is to say they serve as means to one or more final ends. The final ends that top the chains, though, are not justified within the instrumentalist model.

A model of reflective rationality adds the following elements to the means-end conception of rational choice. Keep in mind that the point is to complete the means-end conception rather than to supplant it, in the process showing how, without adding any new normative machinery to the standard instrumentalist model, we can construct a model where even final ends can be rationally chosen. First, the model posits particular maieutic ends. Insofar as settling on final ends is our way of achieving maieutic ends, the choice is rational if it serves the purpose. Second, we pursue particular maieutic ends (like choosing a career) as constitutive ends relative to the overarching maieutic end of finding something to live for. Getting a career is a way of getting something to live for (see fig. 3.2).

In figure 3.2, an arrow from *i* to F signifies that pursuing *i* is a means to F. An arrow from F to *m* signifies that choosing F is a means to a particular maieutic end *m*. An arrow from *m* to M signifies that pursuing *m* is a means to the overarching maieutic end M.

The model that emerges from this has several variations; we will look at three of them. In the first version, this is where we stop. We take the overarching maieutic end as a final end that is simply given. This first model is noteworthy in two ways. First, it explains how an end, pursued for its own sake, could nevertheless be rationally chosen. Second, this model identifies and characterizes further ends to which the choice of final ends could be a means. The model takes at least one final end as given, though, so from a theoretical standpoint is not entirely satisfying. It goes beyond the instrumentalist model by showing how even final ends (most of them) could be rationally chosen, but shares with instrumentalist models the property of necessarily leaving us with loose ends—terminal ends not justifiable within the model.

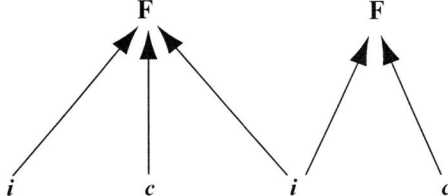

FIGURE 3.1. The means-end conception.

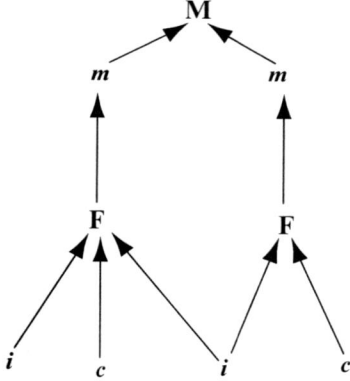

FIGURE 3.2. The reflective model, taking the overarching end as given.

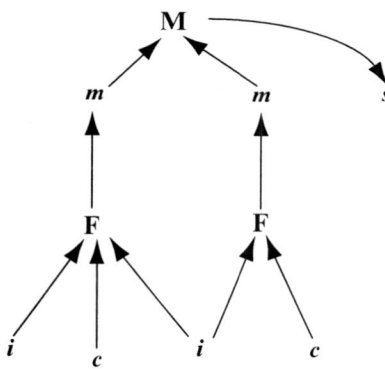

FIGURE 3.3. The reflective model, taking survival as given.

Judging from the first model, then, it still seems reasonable to suppose that, as Bernard Williams writes, "there will have to be at least one reason for which no further reason is given and which holds itself up."[12] The second model, however, goes further. Instead of taking the overarching maieutic end as given, we note that finding reasons to live improves our survival prospects. To whatever extent we care about survival, and to whatever extent finding things to live for strengthens our will to survive and thereby improves our survival prospects, we have a rationale for the overarching end. Finding things to live for is instrumental to the further end of survival. In the second model, we stop here. We take survival as a given final end. (See fig. 3.3.)

In figure 3.3, an arrow from M to s signifies that pursuing the overarching end M (finding things to live for) is a means to the end of survival.

---

12. Williams (1985) 113. Williams expresses skepticism about the "linear model" of reason-giving at issue in the cited passage, yet his belief that it is impossible for rationales to go "all the way down" is unwavering.

Should we take the end of survival as given? Since we are given the end of survival as a matter of biological fact, why not? One problem is that we would still be left with a theoretical loose end, an end accounted for in descriptive biological terms but not in normative terms. There is also a practical reason why we cannot take survival as given. We cannot take it as given because, as a matter of fact, our commitment to the biologically given end of survival is not an all-or-nothing matter. Our commitment is a matter of degree, variable even within the stages of a particular life. The point is not that some people lack the end of survival. (Even if some people lack the end of survival, this need not affect its normative force for the rest of us.) The more crucial fact is that, even for those of us who have the end of survival, the strength of our will to survive can change. Further, the strength of our will to survive is in part a consequence of our choices.

Accordingly, the third and final model of reflective rationality goes one more step. Survival is a final end with which we begin as a matter of biological fact, but it will be subverted as an end unless we find something that survival is *for*, that is, unless we find reasons to live. With some ends, of course, a threat of subversion would not matter. Thus, if Ulysses expects the Sirens to subvert his desire for broccoli, he shrugs his shoulders and plans to eat something else. By contrast, if Ulysses expects the Sirens to subvert his desire to survive, he binds himself to the mast. He wants to survive his encounter with the Sirens no matter how he will feel about survival when the time comes.

Therefore, broccoli and survival are different. Unlike a desire for broccoli, the biologically given desire for survival has a certain intransigence. It resists its own extinction. It drives us to find things to live for, as proof against its own subversion.

As we find things to live for, the goal of survival with which we begin as a biological instinct becomes something more than that. It becomes a means to final ends acquired in the process of achieving maieutic ends. And as those new goals insert themselves into our corpus of ends, the goal of bare survival evolves into something else. There comes a time when bare survival is no longer what we are after. By acquiring the final ends that make life instrumentally valuable, we convert bare survival from something we happen to pursue into something we have reason to pursue as part of an increasingly complex hierarchy of ends.[13]

This suggests a circular chain of reasoning (a nonvicious circle, since the links have empirical content). Constitutive and instrumental ends are justified as means to final ends. We pursue final ends for their own sake, while the *choice* of final ends is justified as a means of achieving particular maieutic ends. Particular maieutic ends are then justified as constitutive means to the overarching maieutic

---

13. For those with no desire to live in the first place, this argument does not get off the ground unless they have some other desire that can play a similar role in the model. But we are not concerned here with the likelihood that some people's ends cannot be rationally justified in this way. Perhaps some ends cannot be rationally justified at all. Be that as it may, the objective is to show how a final end could be rationally chosen. We need not argue that *all* ends are rationally chosen.

end of finding something to live for. Finding something to live for is instrumentally justified to the extent that, given our psychology, achieving the overarching maieutic end (thus producing reasons to live) helps us survive. And closing the circle, survival and the consequent preservation of our ability to pursue goals has come to be instrumentally justified as a means to the pursuit of final ends. (See fig. 3.4.)

In this model, survival is a means in the sense of being needed for the sake of other goals. To be an instrumental end, and thus an item to pursue, there must also be something one needs to do to secure it. So, as I use the terms, being an instrumental end entails being a means, but not vice versa. Survival is not unique in this respect. For example, suppose Bob needs a car in order to attend a concert. If Bob already has a car, though, then having a car is not an item to pursue and thus not an end and thus not an instrumental end, even though it is a means of attending the concert.

We might think there is an easier way to close the circle. That is, we could eliminate maieutic ends from the picture and suppose more simply that survival is justified as a means to our final ends, while our final ends are justified by the fact that acquiring those ends gives us reason to live and thereby improves our survival prospects. But how could acquiring final ends improve our survival prospects? Acquiring final ends could improve our survival prospects by giving us reasons to live, but that way of closing the circle presupposes maieutic ends. Maieutic ends enter the picture even if the name I gave them does not.

Another way of closing the circle involves standard instrumental reasons for wanting some of our ends to be final ends. For example, one might be healthier eating broccoli as an end in itself—just for the taste—rather than for the sake of one's health.[14] In this way, we can rationalize intermediate links in a chain of ends, and thus can rationalize ends that have final as well as instrumental aspects. We cannot

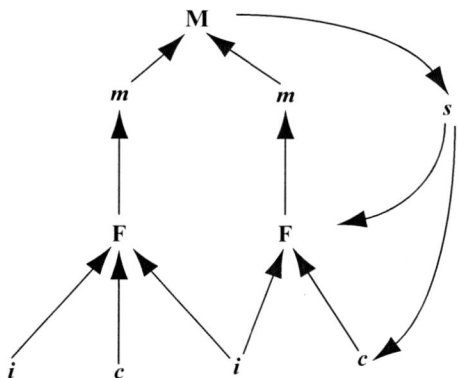

FIGURE 3.4. The reflective model, with no loose ends.

14. I thank Sara Worley for this point.

explain terminal links in this way, though. The rationale for the end of eating broccoli presupposes a *persisting* further end of being healthy. By contrast, maieutic ends are achieved, not merely furthered, by a process of acquiring final ends. Their persistence is not presupposed. Maieutic ends can drop away while leaving intact the chosen end's rationale, which is what we need if we are to explain how even a link that terminates a chain of ends could have been rationally chosen.

Does this mechanism drive the emergence of everyone's corpus of ends? It is hard to say. In any event, the models are not meant to be depict an invariant feature of human nature. They are meant to depict a possibility, how a human being could be what (at least some) human beings seem to be; that is, they show how someone, starting from something as mundane as the survival instinct, could have reason to develop the complicated set of ends that beings like us actually have. The models also show how each element of an emerging corpus of ends can come to have its own normative force without any end's normative force being simply taken as given. Survival enters the second model as a biological given, but the third model depicts a process by which this biological given eventually becomes something more than that. The third model thus exhibits a striking completeness, since within it there are no loose ends.

One might be tempted to ask for a justification of the chain as a whole, but to justify every link is to justify the whole chain. The chain metaphorically represents a series of choices wanting justification in rational choice terms, together with interrelationships that help them justify each other. When we forge a chain in such a way that no link is without justification (that is, no choice is without justification, including basic existentialist choices such as to seek survival or to cultivate ends beyond survival), then no issue of rational choice remains to be represented by the metaphorical chain as a whole.

Even as astute a critic of foundationalism as Bernard Williams joins foundationalists in embracing the least plausible implication of the foundationalist metaphor, namely the idea that starting points are what subsequently erected edifices must rest upon.[15] We should not be fooled by the metaphor. We should realize that our starting points can be—and in fact are—more like launching pads than like architectural foundations. A launching pad serves its purpose by being left behind. Even if we inevitably start by taking some end as given, it remains open whether a corpus of ends will always include ends taken as given.

Further, survival is not the only descriptively given end capable of launching the normative rocket. If the primeval desire for survival does not drive a person to develop a corpus of ends, something else might. A desire for happiness also can drive us to find things to live for, because we secure happiness by pursuing ends we care about for their own sake. (If we did not independently care about achieving those ends, then there would be nothing in the achievement to be happy about.) A primeval desire to avoid boredom might have similar consequences.[16] To launch the normative rocket, all we need is some sort of given desire that gives us reasons to find things to live for. I used survival as an example of such a primeval desire,

---

15. Williams (1985) 113–17.
16. I thank Harry Frankfurt for this suggestion. See also Frankfurt (1992) 12.

partly because it is in fact biologically given, partly because we can see how bare survival could start out as a biologically given final end only to drive the process by which survival evolves into a complex instrumental end, thereby leaving us with no loose (i.e., simply given) ends.

Perhaps it is curious that organisms would have a survival instinct in the first place. The reason they have it, presumably, is this. Organisms having no instincts other than an instinct to replicate would not be good at replicating and thus would have declining representation in successive generations. The goal of replicating, the ultimate biological given, is better served in organisms that combine or replace that goal with other goals: to survive, to have sex, to eat, and so on. Organisms are not guaranteed to have more offspring in virtue of having a complex corpus of ends, but whether the rule has exceptions is not the issue. The issue is whether the probability of replication goes up or down as a corpus of ends becomes complex.

Sociobiological speculation aside, it remains the case that, having posited an initial goal of bare survival, we can see why this goal would fall away as a driving force in just the way launching pads are supposed to fall away, to be replaced by a set of ends that add up to a commitment to survive in a particular way, as a being with a particular hierarchy of ends. In circumstances like ours, to have the thinner goal is to have reason to try to replace it with its thicker analog. (The reason is that the end of bare survival is too thin to sustain itself as a corpus of ends. Unless survival acquires instrumental value, our commitment to it will decay.) It would have been simpler to posit a thicker goal (of surviving in a humanly dignified way, for example, or of having a life filled with happiness) as a biologically given final end, but that would have made the model much less interesting and its premises much more controversial.

One might find it odd to model final ends as ends we acquire by conscious choice. But these models do not presume we acquire final ends only by conscious choice. We sometimes make choices unintentionally, habituating ourselves toward aiming at an end without realizing it. Some of our ends simply captivate us. Nor is anything necessarily wrong with acquiring ends unintentionally. When we find ourselves simply gripped by an end, we have no practical need to formulate a rationale for our ends. (There is a saying: "If it ain't broke, don't fix it.") Nevertheless, there might be a rationale for one's final ends regardless of whether one has reason to identify it. Final ends can give us something to live for regardless of whether we view them as serving that purpose.

Thus, the three models have a normative force pertaining not only to ends we acquire by deliberate choice but also to ends by which we are simply gripped. They explain not just how we could come to have final ends but how we could come to have *rationally chosen* final ends, and such an explanation can have justificatory force even when not descriptively accurate.[17] For example, if Kate is simply gripped by the end of learning to play jazz guitar, and did not choose it at all, then she did not rationally choose it either. Nevertheless, we can say her end is in some sense rational if the process of adopting it served an end she had at the time, and in particular if

---

17. Nelson (1986) discusses the relation between explanation and justification.

adopting the end gave her something to live for. And we can say this even when she neither chooses nor pursues the end with that further purpose in mind.

We have seen how final ends could be rationally chosen. In addition, the third model shows that a chain of ends need not terminate in an end that is simply given rather than rationally chosen. Note that these models rely only on the ordinary means-end conception of rational choice. The choice of instrumental, constitutive, final, and maieutic ends are all explained as means to further ends. (By definition, the *pursuit* of final ends cannot be so explained, but even so, the *choice* of final ends can be.) This shows that the means-end conception of rational choice has resources to go beyond the instrumentalist model. I do not assume means-end reasoning is the only kind of rationality there is. Rather, the point of the exercise is to show how even this narrowest of conceptions of rational choice has resources to explain the rational choice of ends, and further, to do so without leaving loose ends.

Aristotle said we deliberate not about ends but about ways and means.[18] But I believe we have maieutic ends. And if we deliberate about means to maieutic ends, then we deliberate about ends. It is through means-end deliberation with respect to maieutic ends that final ends are brought within the purview of rational choice. To belabor the obvious, though, only choices can fall within the purview of rational choice. Therefore, my aim here has been to show how final ends can be rational as choices, not as ends per se. Even when there is nothing to say about the rationality of ends per se, we saw, one can rationally choose final ends in the sense that choosing them can serve further ends.

This completes the formal description of my model, leaving us with practical questions about how to compare ends. The remaining sections (1) look at what can make one end better than another; (2) discuss the process by which we become devoted to our chosen ends—how they acquire independent normative force in our lives; and finally (3) consider whether it can be rational to organize our lives around purely self-regarding ends.

5. Comparing Ends

Having chosen to become a surgeon, Kate now has ends she can pursue. Still, she had alternatives. She could have tried for a career as an astronaut or a jazz guitarist, which raises a question. Did she make the right choice?

The funny thing is, few people are totally satisfied with their ends. Within an instrumentalist framework, that would be inexplicable, but it is true. People often are dissatisfied not only with the effectiveness of the means at their disposal; they have reservations about their ends as well. Maieutic ends (like choosing a career)

---

18. *Nicomachean Ethics* 1112b11–12. Aristotle believed we deliberate about constitutive as well as instrumental means, and some commentators (e.g., Irwin in the notes to *Nicomachean Ethics* [Aristotle 1999, 318]) suggest that if we deliberate about a constitutive means to a final end, we thereby deliberate about the final end. On the contrary, we may deliberate about whether to run 2 miles without deliberating about whether to get some exercise. We may deliberate about whether to wear a maroon tie without deliberating about whether to wear a suit. And so on. We do not get to a perspective from which to assess final ends merely by deliberating about constitutive means.

can be achieved in various ways (e.g., by various career paths) and many people easily can imagine how the process of choosing ends could have gone better. There is a purpose served by the choice of final ends. Some choices serve this purpose better than others.

Unfortunately, as the phenomenon of dissatisfaction suggests, there is no sure way to anticipate how well a given choice will serve its purpose. Even if there were a fail-safe recipe for choosing ends, that is not what we are looking for here. What we seek is not a recipe for choosing ends so much as a characterization of well-chosen ends. Asking what makes some ends better than others is like asking what makes some cakes better than others. It is not like asking for a cake recipe. I have ideas about what to look for when assessing ends, and those ideas can guide action, but the guidance is by heuristic rather than by recipe.

It may be an oversimplification, though, to think of recipes as analogous to algorithms. When a recipe tells us to bake something until it is golden brown, it is not giving us an algorithm.[19] We need to interpret the instruction in light of previous experience, and may need to repeat the procedure a few times before we fully grasp what the recipe is telling us to do. Conditions supporting rational endorsement can be like recipes so construed, telling us what to look for without being necessary or sufficient conditions.[20] And just as there can be more than one way to bake a cake, there can sometimes be other grounds for endorsement.

Consider another analogy.[21] When a stockbroker tells us to buy low and sell high, she has not given us an algorithm for portfolio management. Nevertheless, she still has stated a criterion of successful portfolio management. This section seeks to identify analogs of the dictum "Buy low, sell high." Such things can guide action, insofar as they give a person a rough idea of what to look for, but do not add up to a decision procedure.

When comparing prospective career paths, settling on any one of them might fully satisfy one's maieutic end of settling on a career. So this in itself is no reason to choose one career path over another. Still, there is the overarching end of finding something to live for, and this end is achievable in degrees. Accordingly, we might assess prospective ends in terms of *how much* they would give us to live for. This is a central question when assessing ends. We answer it (if we can answer it at all) in terms that are unavoidably subjective. An end gives us something to live for to the extent that pursuing it makes us feel we are doing something important.

The importance of our pursuits is partly a matter of opinion, of course. But so long as our goals grip us, making us feel our pursuits are worthy, it won't be merely a matter of opinion that our goals give us something to live for; it will be a matter of fact. Although the conviction that our pursuits are important is subjective, it remains a fact that when we have such a conviction, we have something to live for. The sense of importance, or the possibility of developing it, is one thing to look for when assessing prospective ends.

19. The example comes from Irwin (1993) 327.
20. See chapter 8 for discussion of *supporting* conditions as alternatives to necessary and sufficient conditions as the goals of philosophical analysis.
21. This one is borrowed from Pettit (1991) 166.

The sense of having something to live for is not a simple function of the importance of the goals being pursued. For example, we might believe ending world hunger is more important than coaching Little League football. Yet, we might feel a sense of responsibility and achievement (adding up to a sense of having something to live for) when teaching Little Leaguers to punt, while feeling overwhelmed and frustrated when trying to end world hunger. Coaching Little Leaguers, therefore, might give us more to live for. I do not think one should try to literally maximize the importance of one's pursuits. When one's pursuits become overwhelmingly important, they swallow one's life rather than give it meaning. The sense of importance that best sustains our sense of having reason to live need not be the same as a sense of maximum importance.[22] Nor is the sense of having something to live for a straightforwardly quantitative notion. Sheer multiplication of ends gives us more to live for if we have time for them. But when we take on so many projects that they begin to detract from each other, forcing us to race from one halfhearted pursuit to another, we end up with less to live for rather than more. How much we have to live for has more to do with the wholehearted intensity we bring to our pursuits than with their number.

On the heels of that, we must acknowledge that the sense of importance can be misleading. A grand master may feel chess is important, while others see that his devotion to chess is stunting his capacity to find things important. He finds chess supremely important partly because his capacity to find anything else important is withering away. His choices shape him in such a way that he becomes someone who is maximally satisfied by the choices he has made. Even so, had he chosen differently, his capacity for satisfaction might have been greater. Therefore, we can question the choices of even a maximally satisfied chess champion if we have reason to think he has less to live for than he could have had.[23] He still has something to live for so long as he believes his pursuits are important, but he may have less than he could have had. Perhaps even worse is the thought that if he ever gets tired of chess, he will then have nothing.

We should, no doubt, be cautious about judging the goals of a chess grand master, for the risks associated with single-mindedness need not materialize.[24] Nor can we assume he would become capable of a more profound satisfaction if we forced him to give up chess. We should not expect people to be shaped in so intimate a way by other people's choices as by their own. We do not have the same psychological push to grow into choices others make for us as we have to grow into choices we make for ourselves. Force of habit and the drive to resolve cognitive dissonance do not attach in the same way to choices others make for us. So, some cases are hard to judge, and even well-grounded judgments generally do not weigh in favor of using force.

22. I owe this point to Harry Frankfurt. In his words, "A human life may be full of meaning for the person who lives it, even though it has no significant impact upon history or upon the world, and is therefore in that sense quite unimportant" (1992, 7).

23. Chapter 4 levels the same criticism against those, like Thrasymachus, who profess no reason to be moral. Being someone who has no reason to be moral can be a great misfortune.

24. Paul Hoffman wrote of a mathematician named Paul Erdös having "no wife or children, no job, no hobbies, not even a home, to tie him down. He lives out of a shabby suitcase and a drab orange plastic bag" (1987, 60). But Erdös lived to be eighty-three, and published around fifteen hundred papers. I owe this example to Walter Glannon.

Nevertheless, we do have grounds for judging alternatives, and some cases are easy. Suppose Bob wants to be high on drugs, and views being high as a good in itself. Even so, Bob might reject intoxication as an item to pursue. For one thing, it would compromise his capacities for pursuing goals in general. Bob would have less to live for in part because he would have less to live with. Not only would Bob be less capable of pursuing goals; he predictably would be less committed to pursuing goals. So, this is a clear case of a prospective end the pursuit of which would undermine Bob's sense of importance, thereby giving him less to live for.[25] Another point is that we feel our pursuits are important when we believe something or someone depends on us. When others depend on us, we are important to them. That, perhaps more than anything else, confirms that what we do is worth doing (especially when people appreciate our efforts). So, when Bob's drug habit makes it impossible for others to depend on him, it poisons a primary source of his sense of importance.

Thus, our chosen pursuits predictably affect our capacities, both for pursuing goals and, more fundamentally, for caring about goals. Further, an end may be incompatible (under actual or expected circumstances) with our other ends, and specifically with our unchosen end of being good at what we do. Playing jazz guitar is something Kate does for its own sake. However, since her friends all describe her playing as intolerable, she realizes the activity will never draw on her talents in a satisfying way. It will never give her a sense of competence, and so it cannot give her the unequivocal sense of importance she can get from practicing medicine. As a surgeon, Kate finds it important not only that her ends be pursued but that she in particular is pursuing them. Her particular talents make her well suited for a career in medicine, and so she finds it fitting to have the ends she has.

Combined with the question of how a prospective end would mesh with one's desire to be competent is a question about whether a pursuit will be sufficiently demanding. Kate wants ends she will not be able to meet too easily, for if she meets them too easily, maximal satisfaction will not really be satisfactory. She will not have lived for her goals in a sufficiently intense way. Consider builders of model ships. The end products are things of beauty to the builders. Otherwise, the activity would not be rewarding. Yet, the beauty of the end product is only part of what is rewarding in the activity, for the builders also want the activity to be a delicate and intricate challenge. If such ships took only a moment to assemble, then the point of building them would be lost. The nature of the activity is part of the point of aiming to create the final product.[26] Metaphorically, we want a cup that will not run over too easily, something it takes work to fill. On the other hand, we do not want a cup so big that we find it overwhelming. Challenges can be too small or too big. They have an optimal size (which by a different route brings us to the conclusion of chapter 2 that we can have reason to cultivate moderate desires). When an end is a real challenge, but one we are competent to meet, the end has key ingredients of a recipe for giving us a sense of having reason to live.

25. Particular pursuits also can *re*generate one's capacity to find things to live for. Undertaking an exercise program, for example, often reinforces or restores a sense of overall purpose.

26. Suppose a person could do much good merely by pressing a button. Frankfurt observes: "A life devoted to bringing about that benefit, in which the only meaningful activity was pressing the button, would be less meaningful than one devoted to a final end that was of smaller value but that could be pursued only by complex and varied activity" (1992, 9n).

If none of Kate's alternatives leaps out as the final end whose adoption would give her something to live for, then she must proceed in a more deliberate fashion, asking herself which alternatives are truly feasible, which of them draw well on her particular talents and positional advantages, and so on. If we have a procedure for saying which prospective end will give us the healthiest, most intense, or most enduring sense of having reason to live—so much the better. Suppose, though, that there is no algorithm, and that none of Kate's alternatives grips her. This is not to say the choice does not matter. On the contrary, it may matter a great deal. Kate might be acutely conscious of how different her life will be if she chooses one alternative rather than the other, but the differences between the alternatives may not help her to rank them. Suppose she looks for a decisive reason to choose one end in preference to alternatives, and fails. Even in that case, something eventually emerges as the best she can do. If she cannot afford to wait, or if waiting does not resolve her ambivalence, then at some point the best she can do is pick something and get on with her life, hoping she will grow into that pursuit and become a person on whom that end acquires a grip. Therefore, it can be rational for Kate to choose an end even when she lacks decisive reasons for choosing that end in preference to alternatives.

This may seem to leave the choice of ends peculiarly underdetermined, but in fact, the same thing happens when we choose mere means to given ends. Suppose Bob wants to buy a car, but none of his prospective purchases emerges as the best means to his ends. Still, he sees that it is rational to pick an alternative and get on with it, because even if none of his prospective purchases is clearly best, he eventually reaches a stage when choosing an alternative becomes clearly better than not choosing one. Eventually, it becomes clear that staying on the fence is costing too much, at which point choosing something or other becomes unequivocally rational. There is no general algorithm for rationally choosing final ends. But there is no general algorithm for choosing means to given ends, either, at least not for beings like us. We have no recipe for rational choice.[27]

People sometimes pursue maieutic ends as if they expect to find uniquely suitable means to those ends. People once spoke, for example, of "looking for Mr. Right." What often is called for, though, is underdetermined choice. When given ends like survival first begin pressing us to find something to live for, that new end is too vague to guide us in ranking alternatives. When we realize this, we begin to understand one of the roles that underdetermined choice plays in a thoroughly rational life plan. Underdetermined choice launches the process of coming to have a thoroughly rational life plan.

It is in the process of choosing ends that our lives and thus our corpus of ends becomes a particular framework for ranking alternatives in a nonarbitrary way. As one develops increasingly well-defined images of oneself and one's goals, one develops increasingly concrete criteria for judging whether a prospective end is really something for oneself in particular to live for. But we do not start our lives with such criteria. Nor are they revealed by reflection. We know only so much about ourselves. And in the beginning, there is only so much to know. As we become too reflective to be sustained by a goal of bare survival, we become reflective enough to choose goals

---

27. In chapter 2, I offered an analogous argument for the rationality of underdetermined choices of means to given ends.

that go beyond bare survival. In time, our corpus of ends conceivably may come to be thoroughly justified, but it cannot start out that way. The process by which a circle of ends completes itself is a process that takes time.

That is one reason why, in abstraction from the context provided by a particular agent's corpus of ends, it is so difficult to say anything concrete about which ends the agent should choose. Still, this section discussed several ways in which we compare prospective ends. It explained why we would be wrong to interpret the question of how to compare prospective ends as a question that can be answered only by giving a recipe for rational choice. I considered examples of the elements of reasoned judgment about prospective ends. I also showed how rational agents might proceed when reasoned judgment is inconclusive, as I think it often is.

6. The Possibility of Devotion

I explained how, when we achieve a maieutic end by choosing a final end as an item to pursue, the maieutic end does not persist. Having been achieved, it no longer exists as an item to pursue. If this is right, then one cannot be pursuing a chosen end as a means to the maieutic end, for one no longer has the maieutic end. Final ends are chosen as, but not pursued as, means to maieutic ends. They really do take on a life of their own.

Here is the problem. Although particular maieutic ends do not persist, the overarching maieutic end could.[28] For example, Kate does not keep trying to settle on a career when she has already settled on one, but she may well continue to seek things to live for even though she already has things to live for. The overarching end of finding things to live for cannot be satiated in the way particular maieutic ends can be.

This seems to cut against my argument that so-called final ends cannot have an ongoing means-end relation to maieutic ends. Final ends replace particular maieutic ends as items to pursue, but they do not replace the overarching maieutic end. And if the overarching maieutic end persists, then we could be pursuing our allegedly final ends not so much for their own sake as for the sake of the one maieutic end that endures. Accordingly, there is some doubt here about whether my model's positing of an overarching maieutic end, intended to explain the choice of final ends, leaves room for final ends at all.[29]

In response, we can admit that the overarching end persists, but it persists only in the sense that, unlike more particular maieutic ends, its satisfaction is a matter of degree. And if this is the sense in which the overarching maieutic end endures, there are two things to say. First, even an overarching maieutic end conceivably could be attained and thus not persist as a further end to which purported final ends could serve as mere means. We can envision reaching a point where we already have so much to live for that, if we had an opportunity to take on a new project that would give us

---

28. I thank David Kelley for noticing this.

29. One might suppose this argument does not get off the ground because Kate's career, say, cannot plausibly be construed as a means to the further end of finding more to live for. She lives for her career, but it is not part of her search for things to live for beyond her career. I am not so sure. The day-to-day activities that make up her career might well be part of a search for things to live for—a search for patients to help, for puzzles to solve in her research, and so on.

a great deal to live for, we should regretfully decline, for our hands are already full. (Unfortunately, it is possible to go beyond this point without knowing it. Fear of not being sufficiently busy drives some people to overload themselves with projects, and the consequent dilution of time and energy leaves them unable to do anything in a wholehearted way. In the end, they have less to live for rather than more.)

I do not want to lean too heavily on this point, however, for although such satiation may actually occur, I want to say that even when satiation does not occur, and thus even when the overarching maieutic end persists, an end initially chosen as a means to a maieutic end can still become a final end. Accordingly, the second thing we should say is that even when the overarching end remains unsatiated and thus persists in degrees, an end whose choice gives us something to live for can still take on a life of its own. Consider how people become devoted to their chosen ends. When Kate settles on a particular spouse, she can become devoted to him for his sake—devoted to him as a particular person, not just as a convenient occasion for goal-directed activity on her part. If Kate's devotion persisted merely as a means of having something or someone to live for, then her devotion should cease as soon as it no longer serves the purpose of giving her something to live for.

So when Kate loses her spouse in a car accident, her devotion to him no longer serves its alleged purpose, which suggests she should erase her devotion and go back to where she started, with a clean slate and a once-familiar maieutic end of settling on a spouse—on someone to whom she can devote herself. But Kate does not do this. She can't. Devotion does not work that way. Kate may remember a time when she liked to say there are "lots of fish in the sea," but having lost her spouse, the breadth of choice she once perceived will never again present itself in the same way. That part of her life is now empty, but it is not the same emptiness that once could have been filled by a process of choosing someone or other as a spouse.

The point of the story is that we can reach a stage when we are heavily invested in the particular ends we have chosen, so heavily invested that the corresponding maieutic ends cannot easily be resurrected as items to pursue. If we cannot live for the sake of the particular ends we have already chosen, we may not be able to live for the sake of substitutes, either. We cannot always wipe the slate clean and seek to choose a final end as if we had not already chosen one. This is part of what underlies the thought that our attitude toward a prospective end typically changes after we adopt it as an end, and thus our grounds for choosing it will not be the same as our subsequent grounds for pursuing it.

Metaphorically speaking, particular compartments in our lives initially are given shape by maieutic ends. These compartments wait to be filled by a choice of final ends. As we choose, the compartments are reshaped by what fills them—by the process of growing into our choices. In time, a once-amorphous shape conforms to a particular chosen end, so that alternative ends that once could have fit into that compartment no longer can. Thus, if the chosen end that once filled a compartment is somehow lost, one might simply be stuck with an empty compartment.[30]

---

30. Extending the metaphor, we might say compartments have a certain elasticity. A compartment contoured to a particular lost end can return to an approximation of its more loosely defined original shape. Kate can recover the motivation she once had to pursue the maieutic end of settling on a spouse. But it takes time.

At that stage, it rings false to say one's ongoing devotion to the particular end was a mere means of having or getting something to live for. The truth is that one came to live for the particular end, period. The end acquired a genuinely terminal status, and its status as a final end is not affected by the fact that, in other compartments of one's life, one is still trying to settle on goals to pursue so that one will have more to live for.

We might wonder why would Kate let herself grow into a commitment so deep that it becomes independent of the end she originally achieved by choosing the particular object of devotion? Why risk becoming so devoted to an end that it takes on a life of its own and becomes a final end? Presumably because that kind of devotion gives Kate more to live for. Kate's career and her spouse give her so very much to live for partly because the depth of her commitment to them has gone beyond considerations of how much they give her to live for.[31]

We also might wonder whether the overarching maieutic end itself is a final end. It could be; the categories are not mutually exclusive. Even so, it is importantly unlike other final ends. Kate's other final ends guide her choice of means. Although her need to find things to live for pushes her to make choices, that need does not guide her choices in the way her decision to pursue a career as a surgeon guides her subsequent choices. Nor does her end of finding things to live for make her feel she has things to live for in the way her final ends do.

For a similar reason, there is a problem with thinking of happiness as an end. If my student says she wants to be a professional philosopher, it sounds like she has something to live for. But if she says all she wants is to be happy, it sounds like finding something to live for is exactly what she needs. Happiness is something she hopes for, but not something to live for. She values happiness, yet the fact remains that she will become happy not by adopting happiness as an end, an item to pursue, but only by adopting, pursuing, and achieving other ends, items worth pursuing for their own sake.[32]

For the sake of argument, though, suppose we say the overarching maieutic end is itself a final end, an unchosen final end. Would that threaten my theory? No. The real threat—the threat discussed in this section—consists of the argument that my model leaves no room at all for final ends, and thus cannot begin to explain how final ends could be rationally chosen. I responded to this threat by showing that the model allows for, and even gives reasons for, the process of coming to view ends as worth pursuing for their own sake.

7. The Inhuman Rationality of *Homo Economicus*

I argued that although final ends are pursued for their own sake, their choice can be a means to what I call maieutic ends. Moreover, a corpus of ends need not have loose ends, ends we must take as given. On the contrary, a corpus of ends can evolve into something of which every member has a rationale. Later sections asked two

---

31. On the instrumental value of noninstrumental emotional commitment, see Frank (1988).
32. I thank Carol Rovane for suggesting both the example and the point it exemplifies.

further questions. First, is there a procedure for choosing among prospective ends? Probably not, but even if there is no such procedure, people still have various common-sense criteria by which they often (if not always) manage to sort out which of their options will give them something to live for—which of their options will grip them with a sense of life's instrumental value. Second, when an agent cannot sort out which prospective end best meets common-sense criteria for choosing among ends, is it nevertheless possible for the agent to make a recognizably rational choice? Yes, because even then, agents can see that their corpus of ends is better served by picking something than by picking nothing. When the best one can do is pick something, hoping to grow into the choice, then choosing to pick something and get on with one's life is eminently rational.

Finally, a comment on how this model of rationality bears on the task of developing a conception of characteristically human self-regard, a conception that can help us make sense of our lives as moral agents. The conventional instrumentalist conception of rational choice sometimes is combined with a substantive assumption of mutual unconcern (i.e., that rational agents are immediately concerned with no one's welfare but their own). This combination produces a model of rational agency that has become notorious in the social sciences: *Homo economicus*. By hypothesis, *Homo economicus* is purely self-regarding.[33]

It is commonplace to note that the *Homo economicus* model, so defined, does not accurately describe human agents. Like *Homo economicus*, we have preferences. Unlike *Homo economicus*, we have preferences directly relating to the welfare of others. Some may regard this as controversial. Psychological egoism is the thesis that all human behavior is purely self-regarding. Responding to obvious counter-examples, defenders of psychological egoism sometimes say we act in apparently other-regarding ways only because we reap "psychic" rewards from helping others. As philosophers well know, psychological egoism thus embellished becomes airtight at a cost of becoming literally inconsequential. It does not tell us that soldiers will never give their lives for their countries or that people will never make anonymous donations to charity. It does not predict that Ebenezer Scrooge will never buy Bob Cratchit a Christmas turkey. It offers no testable predictions. Instead, it avoids having false implications by having no implications whatsoever. It merely expresses a determination to stretch the concept of self-regard as far as necessary to fit all behavior, no matter how diverse observed behavior actually turns out to be.[34]

Insofar as there is any real content to the claim that we get psychic rewards from helping others, we can admit that, of course, we tend to feel good about helping others. But this fact does not begin to suggest that our real objective is psychic benefit rather than other people's welfare. On the contrary, there can be no psychic reward

---

33. This is the *Homo economicus* model as it enters into the fundamental theorems of welfare economics. Models incorporating (or claiming to incorporate) other-regarding preferences also are referred to sometimes as *Homo economicus*, but the term is used here in its narrower sense.

34. Most of the professional economists I know do not make this mistake. They construe psychological egoism not as true but rather as a useful working hypothesis. Not all human action is driven by self-interest; nevertheless, we often arrive at a better understanding of observed behavior by looking for motives of self-interest.

for helping others unless we care about others. Imagine Bob helping someone across the street and then saying to her, "Other things equal, I would rather you had been hit by a bus. Unfortunately, helping you is the price I have to pay in order to reap psychic rewards." The fact that we get psychic rewards from helping others *proves* we are directly concerned with the welfare of others. The mark of a purely self-regarding person is not that he really wants to help others but rather that he really doesn't.[35] That is the obvious and much celebrated difference between *Homo economicus* and us.

The less obvious and more interesting difference is this: *Homo economicus does not have maieutic ends. Homo economicus* wants to maximize profit; the question of how *Homo economicus* developed or settled on such an end does not arise. (The end did not develop; it was stipulated.) But whereas *Homo economicus* deliberates only about alternative means of achieving stipulated ends, we deliberate about ends themselves. We sometimes stop to wonder whether an end like maximizing profit is worth having. We have self-regarding ends, to be sure, but they are not given to us in the same way they are given to *Homo economicus*. On the contrary, we shape ourselves and our ends as we go. We are the outcomes as well as the makers of our choices.

Admittedly, *Homo economicus* is a useful model in the social sciences. But we are not *Homo economicus*, and what is good for us is not the same as what would be good for *Homo economicus*. Thus, *Homo economicus* is a poor model of rational choice even when self-interest is all that matters, for even then there is a crucial difference between *Homo economicus* and beings like us. The difference is this: we need to worry about our goals in a way *Homo economicus* does not. *Homo economicus* does not have to work at maintaining an attitude that his goals are worth living for, but we do.

This essay revises "Choosing Ends," *Ethics* 104 (1994): 226–51. Reprinted by permission of the University of Chicago Press.

---

35. For a classic critique of psychological egoism/hedonism, see Feinberg (1981).

4

Reasons for Altruism

> We like to flatter ourselves with the false claim to a more noble motive... but if we look more closely at our planning and striving, we everywhere come upon the dear self.
>
> Immanuel Kant, *Grounding for the Metaphysics of Morals* (1785)

According to a well-known version of the instrumental model, rational choice consists of maximizing one's utility, or more precisely, maximizing one's utility subject to a budget constraint. We seek the point of highest utility lying within our limited means. The term "utility" could mean a lot of different things, but in recent times theorists have often taken it to mean something related to or even identical to preference satisfaction (and thus utility functions are sometimes called preference functions). To have a preference is to *care*, to want one alternative more than another.

People are self-regarding insofar as they care about their own welfare.[1] People are *purely* self-regarding if they care about no one's welfare other than their own and recognize no constraints on how they treat others beyond those constraints imposed by circumstances: their limited time and income, legal restrictions, and so on. The question is, is it rational—is it *uniquely* rational—to be purely self-regarding? The instrumentalist model does not say. For that matter, neither does the instrumentalist model assume people care about welfare (their own or others'). The instrumentalist model allows that Hume could "prefer the destruction of the whole world to the scratching of my finger."[2]

---

1. Insofar as we can distinguish between interests and preferences, welfare is a matter of serving interests rather than satisfying preferences. There is a perfectly natural sense in which many people have preferences the satisfaction of which is not in their interest.

2. Hume (1978) Part 3, sec. 3.

1. An Analysis of Other-Regard

The departures from pure self-regard that concern us here come in two varieties. First, we might care about other people, which is to say their welfare enters the picture through our preference functions. Indeed, a desire to help other people often is among our strongest desires. Second, the welfare of others can enter the picture in the form of self-imposed constraints we acknowledge when pursuing our goals. In different words, an otherwise optional course of action may be seen as either forbidden or required, depending on how it would affect others. There may be limits to what we are willing to do to others in the course of pursuing our goals.[3]

Insofar as one's other-regard takes the form of caring about other people's welfare, one exhibits *concern*. Insofar as it takes the form of adherence to constraints on what one may do to others, one exhibits *respect*. As I use the terms, we have concern for people when we care about how life is treating them (so to speak), whereas we respect people when we care about how *we* are treating them, and constrain ourselves accordingly. Note that what motivates one kind of other-regard need not motivate the other. Joe may find it out of the question to violate other people's rights but at the same time be unconcerned about other people's welfare.[4] Jane may care about feeding the poor and have no qualms about taking other people's money to buy the food. In short, unconcerned people can be principled, and concerned people can be ruthless.

I use the term *altruism* to characterize a kind of action. In particular, an action is altruistic only if it is motivated by regard for others. Expressing concern or respect as a mere means to some other end is not altruistic. The expression is altruistic only if concern or respect for others is what motivates it. (People can act from mixed motives. Robin Hood may undertake a course of action in order to help the poor, make himself look good, and hurt the rich. His action is at once altruistic, self-serving, and vicious.) Whether altruistic action is coextensive with other-regarding action is a terminological matter. Some classify respect for others as altruistic; others would say that to respect others is merely to give them their due, to do what justice requires, and thus cannot count as altruistic.

This definition of altruism leaves open questions about how altruism relates to justice and other essentially moral concepts. There is good reason not to try to settle

---

3. People have tried to distinguish between self-regarding and other-regarding actions, separating actions affecting only the agent from actions affecting others as well. (See Mill's *On Liberty*, for example.) The distinction is supposed to define a sphere of self-regarding activity with which society may not interfere, but the line has proven notoriously difficult to draw, because a person seeking to justify interference with activities she dislikes can always claim she is being *affected* in some way, and thus that the activity is not purely self-regarding. By contrast, the distinction between self-regarding and other-regarding concerns is unproblematic. However hard it is to find important examples of actions that affect only oneself, the distinction between caring about others and caring only about oneself remains sharp.

4. The distinction between respect and concern does not correspond to a distinction between duties of noninterference and duties to provide positive aid. Expressions of concern typically will involve lending aid; yet, out of concern, one might resist one's urge to help a child, knowing that children need to learn to take care of themselves. And expressions of respect typically will involve noninterference; yet, out of respect, one might lend aid to a war veteran.

these questions with definitions. For example, if we elect to stipulate that an act cannot be altruistic unless it goes beyond requirements of justice, then we cannot count ourselves as observing instances of altruism until we settle what justice requires. Someone might wish to define altruism as other-regarding action that goes beyond requirements of justice, but identifying acts as altruistic would then be fraught with difficulties, and pointlessly so. The difficulties would be mere artifacts of a bad definition.

Terminological issues aside, the issue of substance is twofold. We have both concern and respect for others, which raises a question about whether these departures from pure self-regard are rational. This chapter explores reasons for both departures, while acknowledging that some people consider one or the other to be the canonical form of altruism.[5]

Of course, one account of our reasons for altruism is built into altruism's definition. As it happens, we are not purely self-regarding. We have other-regarding preferences that can weigh against our self-regarding preferences. If we prefer on balance to act on our concern for others, then by that very fact we have reasons for altruism. The reasons are not purely self-regarding reasons, to be sure, but they are still reasons, and reasons from our points of view. Therefore, given that we are as we are, altruism sometimes is rational.

It hardly needs to be said, though, that no one would be satisfied with an argument that stopped here. A satisfying account of our reasons for altruism will not take our other-regarding preferences as given. Neither is it enough to offer a purely descriptive account of concern and respect—a biological or psychological or sociological account of what causes us to develop concern and respect for others. Biology and psychology are relevant, but they are not enough. We want an account according to which it is rational for us to have other-regarding preferences in the first place.

The interesting question, then, is this: if we were to abstract from our other-regarding interests and consider the matter from a purely self-regarding perspective, would we have reason from that perspective to affirm our other-regarding interests? This section has characterized altruism as action motivated either by respect or concern for others. The task now is to explain how self-regarding concerns could give people reasons to cultivate concern and respect for others.[6]

Since this essay aims to rationally ground respect and concern for others, readers may expect me to take for granted that self-regard is the fixed point around which all else must revolve if altruism is to have a place in rational choice theory's normative universe. That is not the plan. To be sure, self-regard enters the argument as an explanatory tool rather than as the thing to be explained, but that does not mean we can take it for granted. On the contrary, my conclusion is this: human self-regard is a fragile thing. *Self-regard's fragility is one source of its explanatory power.* Although

---

5. The people I have polled usually agree that one of the two is the canonical form, but it turns out that they are evenly split on which one it is.

6. It may seem that if the original motivation is self-regarding, then we cannot be talking about genuine altruism. Not so. The point of the discussion is to consider whether we can be motivated by reason A to endorse a disposition to be motivated by reason B. (Can one be led by concern for one's health to try to cultivate a liking for vegetables?) Whether the acts motivated by reason B are altruistic depends on the nature of reason B, not reason A. If reason B consists of respect or concern for others, then acts motivated by it are altruistic. It makes no difference whether reason A consists of something else.

we have a certain amount of respect and concern for ourselves, this amount is not unlimited and is not fixed. It varies. It is influenced by our choices, and this fact has a direct bearing on how regard for others fits into the lives of self-regarding human agents. The following sections elaborate.

2. *Homo Economicus*

As already mentioned, to be instrumentally rational is to be committed to serving preferences *of* oneself, but one may or may not be committed to serving preferences *regarding* oneself. When we combine the instrumental model of rationality with a stipulation that rational agents are purely self-regarding, the result is the *Homo economicus* model of rational agency. I want to stress that the reasons given here to nurture other-regard are reasons for beings like us, not for beings like *Homo economicus*. The *Homo economicus* model leaves no room for altruism. The fact that the *Homo economicus* model assumes pure self-regard, however, is only part of the reason why it leaves no room for altruism. The real problem lies in how the assumption of pure self-regard works when combined with the underlying instrumental model of rationality.

The instrumental model of rationality is static, in the sense that it does not provide for rational choice among ends. The instrumental model can (and for my purposes should) be enriched by allowing for the possibility of endogenous preferences (that is, preferences that change in response to choices). This enriched model might explain how we develop our preferences. Even so, something is missing, because a person could have endogenous preferences and still think preference satisfaction is all that matters. For *Homo economicus*, there remains only one question: how much can I get? We go beyond *Homo economicus* and develop a truly reflective rationality as we come to see that the quality of our lives is a function not only of what we get but also of what we are.[7] And what we are, no less than what we get, depends on what we choose.

This section's main point is that whether or not we intend to do so, we develop new preferences as we go, which creates the possibility that beings like ourselves might come to be other-regarding. The next section argues that the same fluidity and capacity for reflecting on our ends that makes possible the cultivation of other-regarding concern also makes it important. There are reasons to embrace and nurture our concern for others, reasons that have to do with what is conducive to our own health, survival, and growth.

3. Reasons for Concern

As Nagel sees it, "altruistic reasons are parasitic upon self-interested ones; the circumstances in the lives of others which altruism requires us to consider are circumstances which those others already have reason to consider from a self-interested

---

7. I thank Jean Hampton for suggesting this way of describing the contrast.

point of view."[8] Altruistic reasons could be parasitic on self-regarding reasons in a second way, insofar as reflective self-regard is the seed from which our regard for others must grow. Or perhaps the last claim is too strong. Respect and concern for others might, for all we know, be the phenotypic expression of a recessive gene. Even so, it remains the case that we do not really give a rationale for other-regarding concerns until we explain how people could abstract from their other-regarding concerns and still find reason from a purely self-regarding perspective to embrace concern for others. Thus, for those who seek to explain how other-regard could be rational, it seems obvious that our other concerns, that is, our self-regarding concerns, must inevitably have explanatory primacy. If we take this approach, it seems we are committed to viewing other-regard as parasitic on self-regard for its rational reconstruction even if not for its literal origin.

However, this is only half of the picture. On closer inspection, the apparently parasitic relationship between other-regard and self-regard turns out to be symbiotic. Insofar as other-regard has to be nurtured, we need self-regarding reasons to initiate the nurturing process. But self-regard is not automatic either. (It may be standard equipment, so to speak, but even standard equipment requires maintenance.) Our interests are not static. They wax and wane and change shape over time, and self-regarding interests are not exempt. An enduring self-regard requires maintenance.

How, then, do we maintain self-regard? Consider that our preference functions are, in effect, a representation of what we have to live for. To enrich the function by cultivating new concerns is to have more to live for. As we increase our potential for happiness, it may become harder to attain our maximum possible happiness, but that is no reason not to expand our potential. New concerns leave us open to the possibility of new frustrations and disappointments, but also to the possibility of deeper and broader satisfaction. And one crucial way to nurture self-regard is to nurture concerns that give us more to live for than we have if we care only about ourselves.

It is rational for beings like us to be peaceful and productive, to try to earn a sense of genuinely belonging in our community. Not many things are more important to us than being able to honestly consider ourselves important parts of a community. When evaluating our goals, we have to ask whether pursuing them is an appropriate way to use our talents, given our circumstances and tastes. We also have to ask how valuable our services would be to others in the various ways we could employ our talents.

The latter consideration is not decisive, of course, for if you are bored by computers and feel alive only when philosophizing about morality, then devoting yourself to computer programming might be irrational, even though your programming services are in greater demand. (What might make it irrational is that you would be responding to others at the cost of becoming unresponsive to yourself.) Nevertheless, to create a place for ourselves in society as peaceful and productive members, we must have regard for the interests of others, for serving the interests of others develops and gives value to our own latent productivity. For many of us, being honest

---

8. Nagel (1970) 16.

and productive members of a community we respect is an end in itself. Even when it is not, it remains that much of what we want from life (and from our communities) comes to us in virtue of our importance to others.[9]

This is not to deny that when personal survival is an urgent concern, it can be quite sufficient to capture our attention. In such cases, we may have no need for other-regarding concerns. Indeed, we may view ourselves as not being able to afford other-regarding concerns. To cultivate additional preferences when our hands are already full is to cultivate frustration. But when circumstances leave us with free time, a more reflective kind of rationality will weigh in favor of trying to develop broader interests. We may begin with a goal of survival, but because we are reflective, we need to cultivate concerns other than survival. As per chapter 3, if there were nothing for the sake of which we were surviving, reflection on this fact would tend to undermine our commitment to survival.

Because we are reflective, it is conducive to survival to have a variety of preferences in addition to a preference for survival, preferences whose satisfaction gives significance and value to our survival it otherwise would not have. Paradoxically, it can be healthy to cultivate preferences that can cut against the pursuit of health. Other ends compete with the end of health for our attention, but also reinforce our concern for our health by giving it instrumental value. Developing concerns beyond the interest we take in ourselves is one way (even if not the only way) of making ourselves and our projects important enough to be worth caring about.

I conclude that we have self-regarding reasons to incorporate (so far as we are able to do so) other-regarding preferences into our utility functions, or in other words, to internalize other-regarding concerns. As these new preferences become part of the function, they acquire a certain autonomy, becoming more than mere means to previously given ends. The element of autonomy is crucial. The new preferences must take on lives of their own; we must come to care about them independently of how seeking to satisfy them bears on ends we already had. If they fail to become ends in themselves, then we fail to achieve our purpose in cultivating them, which is to have more to live for. We cultivate a richer set of concerns as a means to a further end, but we cultivate so as to reap new *ends*, not merely new means of serving ends we already have.

That we nurture our emerging ends for the sake of preexisting ends does not stop them from becoming ends we pursue for their own sake. The cultivation *process* is an effective means to existing ends only if the *things being cultivated* are more than that. Our ultimate interest is in having something to live for, being able to devote ourselves to the satisfaction of preferences we judge worthy of satisfaction. Not having other-regarding preferences is costly, for it drastically limits what one has to live for. A person may have no concern for others, but her lack of concern is nothing to envy.[10] Concern for ourselves gives us something to live for. Concern for others as well as ourselves gives us more.

---

9. As Bricker (1980, 401) says, "to be prudent is to effect a reconciliation between oneself and one's world." And, we might add, our world consists in large part of other people.

10. Similarly, Kavka says "an immoralist's gloating that it does not pay him to be moral because the satisfactions of morality are not for him [is] like the pathetic boast of a deaf person that he saves money because it does not pay him to buy opera records" (1984, 307).

This section has argued that, to the extent that we are reflectively rather than instrumentally rational, we cannot afford the poverty of ends that pure self-regard would saddle us with. Under conditions that leave us time for reflection, we need to have a variety of ongoing concerns with respect to which our survival—our selves— can take on value as a means. When these further ends are in place, survival comes to be more than a biological given; an agent who has further ends not only happens to have the goal of survival but can give reasons why survival is important. As a biologically given end, survival can confer value on our pursuits insofar as they take on value as means to the end of survival, but survival can also come to possess its own value insofar as it comes to be a means to our emerging further ends. Survival thus becomes an end we have reasons to pursue, quite apart from the fact that the end of survival is biologically given. The next three sections turn to the topic of other-regarding respect, and the more general phenomenon of commitment and counter-preferential choice. Section 4 discusses how our self-imposed constraints (along with our preferences) change over time, and sections 5 and 6 discuss why we might want them to change.

4. The Mechanism of Commitment

My distinction between concern and respect for others is like Amartya Sen's distinction between sympathy and commitment. Sen says that when a person's sense of well-being is psychologically tied to someone else's welfare in the right sort of way, it is a case of sympathy, whereas commitment involves counterpreferential choice. "If the knowledge of torture of others makes you sick, it is a case of sympathy; if it does not make you feel personally worse off, but if you think it is wrong and you are ready to do something to stop it, it is a case of commitment."[11] Whether or not it is best to follow Sen in describing commitment as counterpreferential choice, at very least we can say that commitment involves a different kind of preference than does sympathy.

What I call concern for others seems essentially identical to what Sen calls sympathy.[12] What Sen calls commitment, however, is broader than what I call respect for others. Commitment involves adherence to principles, whereas respect for others involves adherence to principles of a more specific kind, namely those that specify constraints on what we may do to others in the course of pursuing our goals. This section describes a process by which we can become committed (in Sen's broad sense). Section 5 considers why it can be rational to cultivate commitments (in the broad sense), and section 6 explores reasons why commitment typically seems to involve the more particular kind of commitment that I call respect for others.

Of course, not everyone sees a need to argue that there are processes by which people develop genuine commitments. Indeed, some people believe we become

11. Sen (1990) 31.

12. Sen (1990, 31) considers sympathy to be egoistic, however, on the grounds that sympathetic action is still action done to satisfy one's own preferences. For what it is worth, I disagree. Whether my preferences are egoistic depends on their content, not on the bare fact that I happen to have them.

committed by choosing to be committed and that is all there is to it. Nothing said here is meant to deny that we can simply choose to be committed, but because some people do deny it, this section offers an account of a process by which a person can internalize commitments, thereby making them genuine. This section is addressed mainly to those who are skeptical about whether human commitment is really possible.

Geoffrey Sayre-McCord once proposed a thought experiment in which we imagine we have an opportunity to choose whether we will have a disposition to be moral. "With one hand, say, we might pull a lever that frees us of moral compunction and clears our minds of morality; with the other, we might pull a lever that gives us the will to do what we believe morality demands."[13] Which lever do we have reason to pull, all things considered?

The idea that we could choose a disposition is by no means merely a thought experiment. To borrow Sayre-McCord's metaphor, our actions pull the levers that form our characters. We would not want to pull a lever that would make us act as automatons. Nor can we, for we have no such lever. We would not want to pull a lever that would make us subject to absolute constraints. Nor can we. Again, we have no such lever. But many of us would pull a lever that would strengthen our disposition to be honest, for example, if only we had such a lever.

And in fact, we do. One of the consequences of action is habituation. Because we are creatures of habit, there is a sense in which pulling the lever is possible and a sense in which doing so can be rational. With every action, we have a marginal effect on our own character and on our self-conception. Character is a variable. It is not, however, subject to direct control. Actions that shape character are under our control. Character itself is not. It is neither fixed nor straightforwardly determined by choice. Rather, character is a function of choice. It is shaped by patterns of choice.[14]

Because people are creatures of habit, time eventually leaves a person with the accumulation of dispositions that we think of as a character. We do not face new situations as blank slates. Yet our accumulation of psychological baggage can seem obtrusive at times, leaving us to wonder why we are not blank slates. Why are we creatures of habit to begin with? We evolved as creatures of habit presumably because having routines for coping with repeatedly encountered situations helps us to conserve our cognitive capacities for circumstances that are novel. As Broadie says, "habits of doing what is usually desirable are important, not least because at any level they free the agent to reach for special achievement on a higher level."[15] In any event, if the advantage in developing routine responses is real, we need not regret being creatures of habit. However, the price is that, if we are creatures of habit, shaping our characters as we go, then making sure we can live with the changing shape of our accumulation of dispositions will be an ongoing project.

Habituation, then, is a mechanism of commitment. Of course, this is not to say that habits and commitments are the same thing. Kate can be in the habit of checking her

---

13. Sayre-McCord (1989) 115.

14. Thus, when we interpret Sayre-McCord's thought experiment as a metaphor for habituation, we reproduce a core insight of book 2 of Aristotle's *Nicomachean Ethics*. On the choice of character, see also Long (1992).

15. Broadie (1991) 109.

mailbox twice a day without being committed to doing so. Likewise, Kate can be committed to standing by her husband even if he is arrested for drunk driving, although she has not yet had occasion to make a habit of it. But the fact that habits and commitments are not the same thing does not stop habituation from being one kind of process by which Kate can internalize a general commitment to her husband and thereby make it genuine. (Her general commitment will then be operative in all kinds of circumstances, even the unprecedented circumstance of his being arrested for drunk driving.)

We might wonder why we pay relatively little conscious attention to the ongoing process of habituation by which we internalize commitments. Why are we so often oblivious to the importance of cultivating good habits? Natural selection builds in a bias—a sometimes unhealthy bias—for the concrete. We have a potential for reflective rationality, but its flowering has not been a precondition of genetic fitness. People are built to worry about things that can draw blood, not about the decay of their characters. The cost of damaging our characters is easily overlooked, because it is not reflected in some obvious frustration of our preferences. Rather, it is reflected in something more subtle, in changes to the preferences themselves.[16] And so it turns out that when it comes to sorting out what is in our self-interest, we are relatively inept in situations where what is at stake is our character. Our ineptness notwithstanding, however, it remains possible for us to develop and reinforce our commitments, including commitments that embody respect for others. The next two sections offer reasons why we might want to do so.

5. Reasons for Commitment

Section 3 undertook to show that we have reason to try to enrich our preference functions, for if we develop preferences that go beyond pure self-regard, we will have more to live for. Section 4 explored habituation as a mechanism by which we might internalize self-imposed constraints. This section explains why we might consider some self-imposed constraints worth the price.

There is an important place in our lives for strategic behavior, that is, for seeking effective means to current goals, given how we expect others to act and react. But this important place is not without limits. We want to achieve our goals, to be sure, but we also want to deserve to achieve our goals, and this is not at all like our other goals. (We care about what we are, not only about what we get.) We seek not merely to earn the respect and concern of others; more fundamentally, we seek to earn our own respect and concern. For whatever reason, it is a simple fact that a person of principle inspires more respect than a person driven by mere expedience. Kate may duly note that the object of her attention is herself, but that fact is not enough to guarantee that

---

16. Allan Gibbard (1990, 276) notes that feelings can induce beliefs whose acceptance has the effect of making the feelings seem reasonable. The beliefs induced, we might add, can amplify our original feelings in the course of giving them a rationale. Some of us, when angry at our spouses, are tempted to dredge up a history of slights suffered at the hands of that person so as to justify our present feelings, and our new beliefs about that person's general inhumanity amplify our original anger to the point where our final blow-up is spectacular, and barely intelligible to observers. We need to be careful about our negative feelings, for the beliefs they induce can do lasting damage.

the object will hold her attention. The motivating power of Kate's self-interest is not without limit, and it is not fixed. The more worthy her self is of her interest, the better off she is. Consequently, there is this advantage in having a principled character: we become selves worth struggling for.

Plato took justice to consist of giving each citizen his due, interpreted not as harming enemies and helping friends (Polemarchus's proposal in *Republic*, bk. 1) but rather as possessing what is properly one's own and performing what is properly one's own task (Socrates' proposal in bk. 4). Plato tried to argue that, like unjust cities that degenerate into tyranny and civil war, souls whose parts fail to possess what is properly theirs and do the job that is properly theirs will be at war with themselves. The ultimate point of the argument was to connect justice to rationality (without reducing it to rationality). Few people accept Plato's argument at face value, of course, but even if Plato failed to connect rationality to justice, he did in the course of the argument connect rationality to integrity.

Integrity and justice are analogous, insofar as both are species of the genus "giving each part of the whole its due." To have integrity is to be true to oneself, to give each part of oneself its due. To be just is to give each person, each part of the whole society, its due. Plato's argument went awry when he mistook this analogy for a case of identity, which might be one reason why his conclusion about the rationality of being just rings false.[17] But what rings true is that having integrity is rational.

Having integrity is not merely good strategy, a matter of prudence. On the contrary, it is far more important than that. Being a person of integrity may on occasion be wildly imprudent, but that likelihood is not decisive even on prudential grounds. Indeed, the point here is that people who have no commitment to integrity have less to live for, which in the long run tends to undermine their commitment to prudence as well. Although integrity may be incompatible with prudence in exceptional cases, it also rationally justifies prudence in ordinary cases. Integrity rationally justifies prudence because it involves committing oneself to having a self worth caring about.

A person who does not have commitments has little with which to identify himself. What we are is in large part what we stand for. We think of having to make a stand on behalf of our ideals or on behalf of our loved ones as frightening and painful, and it often is. Yet, to make a stand for what we think is right is one of the most self-defining things we can do.

6. Respect for Others

The reasons offered in section 3 for cultivating other-regarding concern had to do with the value of enriching our set of goals. Our goals are what we have to live for,

---

17. Unlike the analogy between integrity and justice, the often-discussed connection between the soul of the state and the soul of the citizen is much more than a matter of analogy. Lear (1992) argues that Plato believed not only that the souls of citizens and the soul of the state are like each other but also that the reason they are like each other is because they are outgrowths of each other. The state is the milieu within which children grow up, and so the characters of its adult citizens reflect that milieu. At the same time, the state's ongoing evolution or devolution lies in the hands of its adult citizens, and so reflects the characters of its adult citizens.

and enriching our set of goals gives us more to live for. We do not live for our constraints. Nor would enriching our set of constraints give us more to live for in any direct way, but it does help define *who* we are living for. In effect, our constraints help define what we are living with, what means we can employ while still remaining persons worth living for. Defining our constraints is prior to the strategy we formulate and execute within those constraints. It is a prerequisite of prudence.

Why, then, does having a principled character involve respect for others? There is an alternative, namely that we might accept a suitably demanding set of commitments to ourselves. We might, for example, commit ourselves to achieving excellence in particular endeavors. This means that reasons for commitment per se do not automatically translate into reasons for commitments embodying respect for others. What then leads us to develop commitments of an other-regarding nature? Something like this, perhaps: we want more than to be at peace with ourselves. We also want more than to be liked and respected by others. We want to deserve to be liked and respected. Being a liar can hurt one not only by disrupting our purely internal integrity but also by precluding the kind of honest rapport one wants to have with others, precluding one's integration into the larger wholes that would otherwise give one more to live for. As Gerald Postema wisely observes,

> to cut oneself off from others is to cut oneself off from oneself, for it is only in the mirror of the souls of others that one finds one's own self, one's character. The pleasures and satisfactions of conversation and intercourse are essential to human life, because they are essential to a sense of one's continuity through a constantly changing external and internal world.... Thus, a truly successful strategy of deception effectively cuts oneself off from the community in which alone one can find the confirmation essential to one's own sense of self.[18]

The point is that, human psychology being what it is, respect for others turns out to be part and parcel of having integrity, because integrity has external as well as internal components. Being true to ourselves ordinarily involves presenting ourselves truly to others, but integrity involves not only honestly presenting ourselves to the world but also *integrating* ourselves into the world, achieving a certain fit. We give ourselves more to live for by becoming important parts of something bigger than ourselves. A principled character lets one pursue this wider integration without losing one's own identity. People of principled character—those with nothing to hide—can seek integration on their own terms.

We may never quite swallow the conclusion that it is rational to be just, in the sense of giving each person what he or she is due. Yet, it surely is rational to give our own interests their due, and (human psychology being what it is) we have a strong interest in being able to think of ourselves as decent human beings. We identify ourselves largely in terms of what we do, and therefore individual rationality behooves us to do things that can support the kind of self-conception we would like to have. Thus, being a person of integrity rather than an opportunist is rational not only as a prospective policy (i.e., as something that is advantageous in a long-run probabilistic sense);

---

18. Postema (1988) 35.

there is also something to be said for it on a case-by-case basis, even when we see in retrospect that we could have lied or cheated without being caught. We desire integrity not only in an internal sense but also in the sense of being integrated into a social structure—functioning well within structures that make up our environment. We seek real rapport with others, not merely a sham. We want to feel that we belong, and it is our real selves for which we want a sense of belonging, not merely our false facades.

So, how does that give us reasons to fall on grenades for the sake of our comrades? It may not. Considerations weighing in favor of having a principled character in ordinary cases need not do so in extraordinary cases. Nevertheless, ordinary cases are the crucibles within which characters take shape. It is in the ordinary course of events that we create the characters we carry into emergencies. Conversely, in emergencies, we learn something about what we have created. We find out what we are made of, so to speak, and the knowledge can have a lasting effect, for good or ill, as we resume our normal lives. There is a precious dignity in knowing one has a character that does not wither away under pressure.

Insofar as we maintain a critical perspective on our ends, it is conceivable that, in an emergency, we will question the concerns and commitments that call on us to fall on a grenade for the sake of our comrades. Depending on how well we have internalized our concerns and commitments, we may find ourselves able to reject them. If we reject our concerns and commitments, though, we cheapen our past as well as our possible future. We reveal ourselves to have been only superficially concerned and committed. Upon being convicted of corrupting the youth, Socrates willingly went to his death, so the legend goes, because his other alternatives were inconsistent with principles by which he had lived to that point. He was seventy years old, and his life as a whole would not have been improved by running away to spend his remaining years as an escaped convict.

Our reasons for acting as we do in a given situation stem from concerns we bring with us to that situation. Thus the rationality of internalizing a given concern does not turn on the consequences of acting on it in a single case. The relevant consequences are those that follow from a certain concern being part of one's life.[19] This is why the task of providing reasons for altruism is first and foremost the task of providing reasons for altruism of the more mundane variety. It is fine to consider whether it can be rational to die for one's comrades, but in truth, the central cases are cases of simply lending a hand in the ordinary course of events. We stop to give people directions. We push their cars out of snowbanks. We hold doors open for people whose hands

---

19. McClennen (1988) argues that one can be better off as a resolute chooser, i.e., a person who can adopt plans and stick to them. For example, suppose Kate wants to buy a television set, but if she does, she will then need to decide whether to watch game shows. Kate's most-preferred option is to buy the television, resolving never to watch game shows. However, she is not sure she can trust herself never to watch game shows, and would rather not have a television set at all than to end up watching game shows. Subsequently, having bought a television set, how can Kate eschew game shows, if watching them is now her most preferred option? What difference does it make that she resolved last week when she bought her television never to watch game shows? My theory is that genuine resolve is the sort of thing we build over time. Kate is *rational* to build up her capacity for resolve because, as she proves to herself that she can carry out plans calling for resolve, she becomes able to trust herself to make choices that will be optimal if and only if she ignores temptations associated with those choices.

are full. And we walk away from these mundane encounters feeling grateful for the chance to be helpful.[20]

In nurturing concerns that give us more to live for, we develop concerns that can become more important to us than life itself. In the ordinary course of events, this is a splendid result, but in extraordinary situations, concerns worth living for can become concerns worth dying for. One may some day find oneself in a situation where one's other-regarding concerns dictate a course of action that will seriously jeopardize one's purely self-regarding interests. The consequences might lead an observer to avoid developing similar commitments and concerns; the observer has not yet internalized those concerns and commitments, and after witnessing their worst-case results, internalizing them may seem unwise, if not downright impossible. But for us, already having those concerns and commitments (not merely observing them), failing to act on them is what would be irrational. When the emergency comes that calls on one to pay the price of having one's commitments, one no longer has the option of acting as if one's slate of commitments were blank. One got the benefits of integrity by accepting the risks associated with becoming actually committed, and when the emergency comes, one is actually committed.

Gregory Kavka points out that it can be rational to accept a *risk* of death even when it would not be rational to accept *certain* death.[21] And when one develops concerns so deep and genuine that they may some day lead one to willingly give one's life for one's comrades or one's children, one is accepting a risk, not a certainty. Meanwhile, those concerns give one more to live for. One has no intention of actually dying for one's comrades or children, but if one gets unlucky, one may some day find oneself in a situation in which dying for them is one's preferred alternative.

Altruism will involve self-sacrifice in exceptional cases, but not as a matter of routine. Altruism involves costs, of course, as does any action, but that an action is costly is not enough to make it a self-sacrifice. Cost-bearing becomes self-sacrificial only when agents deliberately give up something they prefer more for the sake of something they prefer less. Thus, only purely self-regarding agents will view altruism as necessarily self-sacrificial. For agents who have other-regarding concerns, acting on those concerns will be self-sacrificial if it costs too much, and only if it costs too much.

Needless to say, we may regret sacrificing one goal for the sake of another, even when both goals are of a self-regarding nature, and even when we have no doubt that what we give up is less important than what we gain. I may feel anguish when I give up coaching Little League football in order to pursue my career in a different city, but the regret I feel when I sacrifice one part of my life for the sake of another is neither necessary nor sufficient to indicate that my choice is a self-sacrifice. However painful it feels, I am not sacrificing myself when I sacrifice a less important goal for the sake of a more important goal. On the contrary, in a world that sometimes requires painful

---

20. It would be a mistake to say something cannot be altruistic if you really enjoy doing it. This would put the cart before the horse. If you help other people for their sake, you are altruistic whether or not you like having the concern for others that your action expresses. In the *Grounding of the Metaphysics of Morals*, Kant said getting joy out of an action can rob it of moral worth, which seems wrong, but even if he had been right, enjoying an action can affect its moral worth without changing the fact that the action is altruistic.

21. Kavka (1984) 307–10.

trade-offs, we affirm ourselves and our commitments and our values when we act for the sake of what we consider most important. This is what altruism can amount to for other-regarding agents.[22]

That also reveals the limits of rational altruism. For beings who begin with self-regarding ends, it would be irrational to nurture commitments that lead to self-sacrifice as a matter of course. The point is to have more to live for, and to meet the prerequisites of prudence. We accomplish this by nurturing respect and concern for family, friends, neighbors, the strangers we meet, and so on. There are forms of respect that, under normal conditions, we can easily afford to extend to the whole world, but we have only so much capacity for genuine concern. If we tried to care about everyone, our lives would be impoverished rather than enriched.

This has implications for morality as well as for rationality. Although I think morality requires us to respect everyone, I do not believe it requires us to care about everyone.[23] I have not argued for that conclusion here, but in any event, if morality did require us to care about everyone, then that would be one place where morality and rationality part company.

7. The Fragility of Self-Regard

The model of reflective rational choice is, I have shown, rich enough not only to allow for but even to justify the development of other-regarding concern and respect. In particular, the fragility of self-regard can give us reason to develop concerns and commitments that go beyond self-regard. In the process, one acquires a rationale for one's fragile self-regard and thereby makes it more robust.

The emergence of these new reasons for action is driven by instrumental reasons, but this does not imply that the new reasons are themselves instrumental reasons. The concern and respect for others that is rationally grounded in reflective self-regard may be of an entirely wholehearted and uncalculating kind. Indeed, that is what we are striving for, for those are the most rewarding concerns a person can have.

Does this mean that concern for others is rationally *required*? I would say not. That concern for others is rationally justifiable does not imply that a lack of concern is unjustifiable. To be sure, most of us are rationally required to nurture other-regarding concerns and commitments, but we are rationally required in virtue of social and psychological circumstances that are not quite universal. People whose survival is immediately secure will be driven to cultivate concerns beyond mere survival.[24]

---

22. I thank Lainie Ross for helping me work out the connection between altruism and sacrifice. See also Aristotle's discussion of friendship and sacrifice in *Nicomachean Ethics* (1169a).

23. Galston (1993) distinguishes between progressively more expansive forms of altruism, and draws attention to the moral cost of altruism in its more expansive incarnations. For example, Galston says, the concern expressed by rescuers of Jewish refugees in Nazi-occupied Europe was an expansive, cosmopolitan form of altruism. Commendable though it was on its face, this cosmopolitan form of altruism often went hand in hand with a failure to express concern for family members whom the rescue effort put at risk. The more cosmopolitan form of altruism came at the expense of the more parochial form. More parochial forms of altruism sometimes are not consistent with expressing concern for everyone.

24. See chapter 3.

However, being driven to develop concerns beyond survival is not the same as being driven to develop concern for others. Some people have the option of fashioning more ambitious sets of concerns that would be fulfilling yet would still count as purely self-regarding. Even for such people, caring for others remains reasonable, because caring for others remains a particularly effective way of giving oneself more to live for. But it is not uniquely reasonable. Many kinds of commitments and concerns can be motivated by our need to have something to live for; not all of them are other-regarding, and some of them are evil. People commit acts of vandalism for the sake of having something to do. They go to war for the sake of having something to live for.

Be that as it may, the project of showing that altruism is reasonable does not require us to show that altruism is uniquely reasonable. We do not need to prove that failing to care about others would be unreasonable. For most of us, failing to care about others really would be unreasonable, because for most of us, there are no self-concerns that could give us as much to live for as we have in virtue of caring for others. Section 3 argued that we cannot afford to be purely self-regarding, but that may not be true of everyone. There are reasons for altruism, but there also are people for whom those reasons are not compelling. Is the existence of such people a problem? It surely is a practical problem, insofar as the rest of us need to deal with such people. Some readers might feel that the existence of such people is also a problem for my argument; that is, a person might reply to my reasons for altruism by insisting that not everyone has the kind of reasons discussed here. There are people, sociopaths perhaps, who have no reasons to care about others.

My response is that looking for reasons for everyone is a mistake. If we presume at the outset that our reasons to care about others must be reasons for everyone, the reasons we produce are likely to be reasons for no one. Such reasons likely will be mere philosophical sleight of hand, a distraction from our real-world concerns. Let us face the fact that our reasons for altruism can be real without being reasons for everyone. We must look for the real reasons, and accept that human societies need to deal with the fact that not everyone has real reasons.

In closing, a word on the larger project of identifying connections between rationality and morality. There is a limit to how much other-regard is rational, but whether that opens a gap between rationality and morality is an open question, for there is also a limit to how much other-regard is morally required. This is in part a point about morality leaving room for people to pursue their own projects, but it is also a reminder that the consequences of other-regard are only so good. Whether other-regarding action has better consequences than self-regarding action in a given case is an empirical matter.

Other-regarding action can sometimes seem morally dubious, even apart from its immediate consequences in a given case. *Paternalism*, for example, is a form of altruism, an expression of concern for others (i.e., for their welfare) that overrides one's respect for others (i.e., for their preferences). Altruistic though it might be, paternalism often is objectionable. To give another example, teachers should grade term papers on the basis of what they believe the papers deserve, not what they believe the authors need. Anyone who has ever graded term papers knows how difficult it can be to ignore one's concern for others, but there are cases in which one is morally required to make the effort. From the viewpoints both of the agent and of those persons the agent might affect, neither self-regard nor other-regard is intrinsically exalted. A great deal depends on how a concern plays itself out.

In *The Republic*, Socrates concluded that individuals need justice within themselves for more or less the same reasons and with more or less the same urgency as society needs justice within itself. But this did not answer Glaucon's question. Glaucon did not ask whether the individual needs to give each part of himself its due. He did not ask whether society needs to give each part of itself its due. What he asked was whether the individual needs to give each part of society its due. If Thrasymachus neglects to give other people their due, must he at the same time be neglecting to give a part of himself its due?

He might be.[25] Characters like Thrasymachus have reason to act only when doing so satisfies their purely self-regarding ends. Because almost nothing counts as a reason for Thrasymachus to act (in particular, regard for others does not), his life is impoverished in a certain way. He has fewer reasons to live than the rest of us. (To have *fewer* reasons to live is not necessarily to have less reason to live, but that will be the tendency.) Thrasymachus lacks a kind of respect and concern for others that could have given him reason to pursue a range of goals. I realize that if Thrasymachus were here, he would laugh at me for saying this, for the range of goals I am talking about would mean nothing to him, but the bottom line remains: those goals could have enriched his life.

This essay revises "Reasons for Altruism," *Social Philosophy and Policy* 10 (1993): 52–68. Reprinted by permission of Cambridge University Press.

---

25. Griswold (1994) finds a close connection between justice as an excellence of self and justice as a kind of respect we owe to others, because it is in treating others with concern and respect that we perfect ourselves.

5

WITH SARAH WRIGHT

What Nozick Did for Decision Theory

Robert Nozick's seminal 1969 essay ("Newcomb's Problem and Two Principles of Choice") introduced to philosophers the puzzle known as Newcomb's problem. Nozick returned to the problem in his 1974 essay "Reflections on Newcomb's Problem" and then again in *The Nature of Rationality* (1993). We describe the problem, then explain what it tells us about the nature and limits of decision theory. The problem is as follows.

1. Newcomb's Problem

You are presented with two boxes. A transparent box holds $1,000.[1] A second box is opaque, but you know it contains either nothing or $1 million. You are offered a choice. You may take only the opaque box, or you may take both: that is, you take the opaque box by itself, or the opaque box plus the box that you know to contain $1,000. It seems obvious you should take both boxes, that is, you take the extra $1,000 on top of whatever is in the opaque box.

Here is the catch. There is a predictor who predicted whether you will take one or two boxes. The $1 million is in the box if and only if the predictor predicted you will take only the opaque box. The predictor has a history of being correct 90 percent of the time.[2] What should you do?

---

1. In Nozick's original presentation of Newcomb's problem, both boxes are opaque. We treat the box with the $1,000 as transparent because it makes for easier exposition and does not affect the structure of the original case.

2. In the original presentation, you are said to have "enormous confidence" that the predictor can correctly predict your behavior. We have quantified this expression for use in later calculations.

The literature is full of answers. What we wonder is: what was Nozick's point in asking? Another question: why did the question spark such fierce debate? *Why doesn't decision theory simply settle the matter?*

2. World State Partitions

Suppose we represent Newcomb's problem as a decision matrix. Should the matrix look like this?

	Predictor predicts one box	*Predictor predicts two boxes*
You take one box	M	0
You take two boxes	M + K	K

M = $1 million; K = $1,000

Or should the matrix look like this?

	Predictor is correct	*Predictor is mistaken*
You take one box	M	0
You take two boxes	K	M + K

The second matrix is a different way of representing the same problem. The actions are the same: the top row represents taking one box; the bottom row represents taking two. The columns differ in terms of how they *partition* the states of the world forming the background of your choice (although in either case the world state descriptions are meant to be mutually exclusive and jointly exhaustive; their probabilities sum to one). The first matrix partitions the world into two possible states: the predictor predicts either one box or two. The second matrix partitions the same world along different lines: the predictor is either correct or mistaken.

In Leonard Savage's decision framework, each column in a decision matrix represents a state of the world, and to each column attaches a probability. In the first matrix, the probabilities of columns appear irrelevant to the question of what you should do, because no matter which column you are in (that is, no matter what the world state) you are $1,000 better off taking two boxes. Taking two is a *dominant strategy*.

If you frame the problem the second way, though, you see neither strategy as dominant. So, in weighing your options, you want to know the probability of each column. In the second matrix, there is a 90 percent chance that the first column represents the background state of the world in which you make your decision. Therefore, to people who partition world states the second way, clearly you should take one box; taking one box implies a 90 percent chance of winning a million.

The problem: to those who partition states the first way, clearly you should take both boxes. What would make it better to see the problem in one way rather than the other? Here is a preliminary answer. The first way of partitioning states, implying that you have a dominant strategy, is a mistake when the probability of your being in a given state (that is, a given column) depends on which action you choose. Thus, if choosing one box would make it likely you were in the state represented by the first column, and choosing two would make it likely you were in the state represented by the second column, then choosing one box approximates choosing $1 million in preference to $1,000. Playing your apparent dominant strategy would be a big mistake.

The second way of partitioning world states can likewise be a mistake, but explaining why requires a bit more background.

3. From Savage to Jeffrey

Forget about the Newcomb story for a moment, and just look at Nozick's (1969) example of an uninterpreted matrix of values.

	State 1	State 2
Act 1	10	4
Act 2	8	3

We have not yet assigned numbers to the likelihood of being in state 1 as opposed to state 2. It appears not to matter, because act 1 dominates act 2. But what if your choice of action *affects* the probability of being in state 1? This is the factor that, when present, makes dominance reasoning untrustworthy. To use dominance reasoning, we must start by asking whether we know of a way of partitioning world states such that (1) the probability of being in a given column does not depend on which action you choose, and (2) a dominant strategy exists when the world is partitioned that way.

Since Savage conceived of probabilities as attaching to matrix columns, the only background probability that could be modeled was a kind independent of which row (that is, which action) the agent chooses. Richard Jeffrey revolutionized the framework by developing a theory that lets us consider cases where the likelihood of being in a given state depends on the act chosen. Jeffrey modeled such cases by supplementing his desirability matrix (giving values of each consequence) with a probability matrix (giving a probability of each state given each act).

Desirability Matrix

	Predictor predicts one box	Predictor predicts two boxes
You take one box	M	0
You take two boxes	M+K	K

Probability Matrix

	Predictor predicts one box	Predictor predicts two boxes
You take one box	P(predicted 1 / you take 1) = .9	P(predicted 2 / you take 1) = .1
You take two boxes	P(predicted 1 / you take 2) = .1	P(predicted 2 / you take 2) = .9

This type of matrix lets us represent the Newcomb predictor's accuracy in terms of conditional probabilities. Thus, P (predicted 1 / you take 1) is read as "the probability of predictor having predicted one box given that you took one," which in this case equals 0.9.[3] Jeffrey's probability matrix lets us represent the probabilities of states as depending on the actions chosen, which enables us to develop models of situations where agents can influence the probability of being in a given state. Putting together the two kinds of information—multiplying this conditional probability by the value of taking one box when the predictor has predicted one box, and so on—we can calculate expected utilities and represent Newcomb's problem as follows:

	Predictor predicts one box	Predictor predicts two boxes	Expected utility
You take one box	M x .9	0 x .1	= $900,000
You take two boxes	(M + K) x .1	K x .9	= $101,000

The conditional probabilities are what dominance reasoning ignores, but once we build them into the matrix, Jeffrey's framework appears to give us decisive reason to choose one box. In effect, Jeffrey's apparatus revealed a potential problem with dominance reasoning: sometimes, the appearance of a dominant strategy cannot be taken at face value.

Nozick's contribution, four years later, was to notice a somewhat analogous problem with expected utility reasoning. That is, sometimes the fact of being the option with maximum expected utility cannot be taken at face value either.

4. Probabilistic Connection without Causal Influence

What exactly is it that cannot be taken at face value? To put it somewhat paradoxically, Nozick noticed that the action having maximum expected utility is not necessarily the action that maximizes expected utility.

---

3. This is the standard construal of the relevant conditionals, and we need the standard construal in order to depict the problem in the standard way. Isaac Levi (1975), though, notes that a natural way to represent the idea that the predictor is right 90 percent of the time is with a converse conditional: for example, p(you take 1 / predicted 1) = 0.9, not p(predicted 1 / you take 1) = 0.9. As Levi proves, that p(you take one / predicted 1) = 0.9 does not entail that p(predicted 1 / you take 1) = 0.9. We henceforth assume this caveat goes without saying.

We explained when dominance reasoning leads to error: that is, when it leads us to overlook ways in which probabilities of world states depend on which act we choose. We now can explain when expected utility reasoning leads to a parallel sort of mistake. To get at what is wrong with being a one-boxer, consider a case Nozick proposed that has a causal structure relevantly like Newcomb's: ACADEMIC DISEASE.

Joe knows that Stu or Tom is his father. Stu died of an inheritable disease later in life. Tom did not. Stu's disease also was genetically linked to an academic propensity. Joe now has to choose a career. Other things equal, Joe would rather be an academic, but reasons that if he goes into athletics, he is less likely to be a child of Stu, and thus less likely to get the disease. Nozick says it would be wild to decide on that basis, since there is nothing Joe can do to *make* it less likely that Stu is his father, thus nothing he can do to make it less likely that he will get the disease.[4]

The crucial fact, to Nozick, is not whether a world state is probabilistically linked to your action but whether it is *influenced* by your action.[5] Whether M is in the opaque box seems to depend on whether you choose one box or two. That probabilistic dependence suggests that dominance reasoning is a million-dollar mistake in the Newcomb context. Contra dominance reasoning, you do best when you take one box rather than two.

Why is this not the end of the conversation? The problem is that what normally makes conditional probabilities relevant is missing in the Newcomb situation. If our picking one box would *make* it more likely that the predictor will put $1 million in the opaque box, that would be part of the action's overall utility. Conditional probabilities often indicate a tendency of the action to influence the probability of being in a given state. However, they *need* not, and when they *do* not, they are not relevant. And that kind of conditional probability is the kind we are given in Newcomb's problem. Probably.

5. The Prisoner's Dilemma

Likewise, in a prisoner's dilemma, if one's deciding to cooperate would *cause* one's partner to cooperate, that is one of the effects of one's action, and thus is part of the action's overall utility.[6] Here is the general form of a prisoner's dilemma.[7]

---

4. Another case: John Calvin said the devout go to heaven, but there was ambiguity about why. Do they go to heaven *because* they are devout? If so, expected utility gives the right answer: be devout. Or do they go to heaven because of predetermined grace, a side effect of which is a neurotic urge to be devout? In this second case, assuming it's more fun to be a party animal, then expected utility gives the wrong answer.

5. Nozick (1969) 123.

6. Many have wondered whether the prisoner's dilemma is a Newcomb problem (Lewis 1979, Sobel 1985). We are not making a claim of equivalence here.

7. Here is the classic case from which the dilemma gets its name. You and your coconspirator, a person about whom you care little, and from whom you do not fear retribution, have been arrested and charged with a crime. You are offered the chance to testify against your partner, in which case he gets a long sentence and you go free—unless he testifies against you as well, in which case you each get a medium sentence. If each of you refuses to testify, then each of you gets a short sentence.

Standard Prisoner's Dilemma Partition

	Partner cooperates	Partner defects
You cooperate	M (partner gets M)	0 (partner gets M + K)
You defect	M + K (partner gets 0)	K (partner gets K)

Partitioned in this way, the problem seems to have a dominant strategy solution. No matter what your partner does, you are better off defecting, and likewise for your partner. But there is an issue here that is analogous to Newcomb's problem. The analogous question for dominance reasoning here is, what if your partner is a lot like you? What if you reasonably predict that, if your reasoning is leading you to choose a particular action, then the same reasoning will be leading your partner to the same conclusion?

An Alternative Partition

	Partner plays like you	Partner plays unlike you
You cooperate	M (partner gets M)	0 (partner gets M + K)
You defect	K (partner gets K)	M + K (partner gets 0)

The second matrix is merely a different model of the same situation. In this alternative model, though, there is no dominance. If we consider it likely that "my partner plays like me," then we will calculate that the expected utility of cooperating exceeds that of defecting. Suppose "my partner plays like me" is likely. Your forming an intention to cooperate seemingly makes it more likely that your partner is likewise forming an intention to cooperate. In that case, is cooperation rational? Yes, to judge by the numbers. If we are fairly sure we are working in the first column of the second matrix, then to choose cooperation is, in effect, to choose a payoff of M over a payoff of K. But it depends on causal structure. If cooperation *makes* it more likely (that is, *causes* it to be more likely) that your partner cooperates, then cooperation is in your interest. If not—if you know your partner's choice is independent of your action—then cooperation is not in your interest.

The second matrix is somehow a mistake, although it is not transparently so. It is a mistake insofar as there is in fact a dominant strategy that the matrix fails to reveal. And it is a mistake insofar as the feature that would give the second matrix its point—that it successfully partitions world states in such a way as to reflect *relevant* conditional probabilities—is not actually in place.[8]

---

8. As Nozick later came to express the point, in a prisoner's dilemma, *causal* reasoning recommends the dominant strategy; *evidential* reasoning recommends cooperation when you think the other party is so similar to you that your cooperation can be taken as evidence that the other player will cooperate (1993, 48).

A high conditional probability of your partner cooperating, given that you cooperate, could be a sign that your cooperation tends to induce your partner's cooperation.[9] However, a second possibility is that a high conditional probability may reflect the fact that the same reasoning that leads you to cooperate tends *independently* to lead like-minded partners to cooperate as well. In this second case, expected utility reasoning gives the wrong answer—because it leads you to think of your cooperation as *producing* the preferred outcome, when in fact your action has nothing to do with the process you hope will culminate in your partner deciding to cooperate.

We normally and appropriately treat probabilistic dependence as a sign of causal influence. If we *know* there is no such influence, probabilistic dependence becomes irrelevant.

6. Unknown Causal Structure

So, what if we *suspect* influence? Then we must decide whether and how to take such suspicion into account.

The *Fisher Smoking Hypothesis* begins with the observation that cancer correlates to smoking. We then suppose there are two alternative causal structures that could underlie the correlation. Perhaps smoking causes cancer. In that case, expected utility reasoning gives the right answer: don't smoke. Or, perhaps smoking does not cause cancer, but if not, then why are smokers at a higher statistical risk of getting lung cancer? The Fisher hypothesis is that smoking and cancer are each caused by a defective gene. Thus, there is a statistical correlation not because smoking causes cancer but because smoking and cancer are effects of a common (genetic) cause. In that case, expected utility reasoning gives the wrong answer.

Fisher Hypothesis

	You won't get cancer	*You will get cancer*
You don't smoke	M	0
You smoke	M + K	K

K = the pleasure of smoking; M = utility of not getting cancer

The symbols M and K are awkward here, but the point of using them is to reveal what the Fisher hypothesis is hypothesizing: namely, that smoking is a Newcomb problem, a situation where cancer is probabilistically but not causally linked to smoking. (Compare this matrix to the first matrix in section 2.) If the Fisher hypothesis is correct, you apparently have a dominant strategy. Regardless of whether you are going to get cancer, smoking is fun (we are supposing).

---

9. That could be so in, for example, an iterated prisoner's dilemma, where the game is played over several rounds, and in any given round, your partner can respond to the manner in which you played the previous round. In this case, expected utility gives the right answer: cooperate, so long as your partner is cooperating in return, and so long as your partner likewise would respond to defection by defecting.

Does that mean you should smoke? No! It depends on whether the world state is independent of the action. Although it looks like smoking dominates here, what if Fisher's hypothesis is wrong? What if the reason for the probabilistic link between smoking and cancer is that smoking does indeed *cause* cancer? The next partition models that uncertainty.

Alternative Partition

	Smoking doesn't cause cancer	*Smoking causes cancer*
You don't smoke	M	M
You smoke	M + K	K

Here we have a different partition, where state probabilities clearly are unaffected by the choice of action.[10] That is, my choice of action clearly is not what determines the general truth of the matter regarding whether smoking causes cancer. But in this matrix, smoking does not dominate. Accordingly, this alternative partition suggests the *correct* conclusion that whether you should smoke (assuming smoking is fun) depends on whether smoking causes cancer.[11]

The second matrix is a better way of representing the problem if smoking turns out to cause cancer. What if you do not know? In that case, is it still better to represent the problem in the second way? Yes, because the second matrix makes plain that the question of causal structure is *the* question. The second matrix does not tell us what to do, but it does focus us on the pivotal question.

Maximizing expected utility gets wrong answers in cases like Fisher Smoking Hypothesis. However, the only reason we know it gets the wrong answer is that by stipulation we supposedly know smoking does not cause cancer. If smoking and getting cancer have a common cause but smoking does not per se have direct causal bearing on whether a person gets cancer, then the lowering of expected life span, given that you smoke, is misleading. Therefore, just knowing the numbers (utilities,

---

10. There is a background risk of cancer, of course. In the foregoing matrix, M is the utility of being subject only to this background risk, avoiding the added risk that goes with smoking if smoking causes cancer. Note that the result is the same in both columns of the top row, meaning that so long as you do not smoke, it does not matter whether smoking causes cancer.

11. The literature speaks of deciding under *uncertainty* when the agent cannot be certain of the world state but does know the probabilities. We speak of deciding under *ignorance* when we do not even know the probabilities. If I am ignorant, I can simply assign probabilities of 50 percent to signify that, so far as I know, one state is as likely as the other. Even if that were to get the right answer, though, it is not clear that it would be getting the right answer for the right reason. The procedure simulates the appearance of algorithmic decision theory, but what is really going on is that you are comparing two possibilities: the minor value of K versus a package consisting of K plus an M-sized catastrophe. And you are saying you are not interested in taking such a risk, and would not become interested unless you were sure that the probability of the catastrophe were, let's say, under one in a thousand. So long as you do not know that the risk is under one in a thousand, you cannot exactly know there is a higher expected utility in refusing to take the risk, but that is how a rational gambler would play it.

probabilities) isn't enough. We could know the numbers, and still be in a situation of deciding under ignorance.[12]

Going back to the Newcomb problem, we will rephrase our view. If I *know* my play has no causal bearing on what is in the opaque box, I take both boxes. If I am not sure of the situation's causal structure, and *cannot* rule out the possibility that the prediction is influenced by my choice, I have reason to take only the opaque box.

If all I know for sure is that one-boxers average $900,000 while two-boxers average roughly $100,000, I rationally opt for one box. If the opaque box were to become transparent, though, then average payoffs would no longer be relevant.[13] I would take two boxes. Notice that the only thing that changes when we make the opaque box transparent is that my level of confidence jumps regarding the independence of the state from my action. Yet, given the stakes, that is enough to change a rational contestant from a one-boxer to a two-boxer.

That tells us when expected utility reasoning is apt. Expected utility reasoning is apt for situations where we know we can influence the probability of being in a given world state. Less certainly, we also use, and are not obviously mistaken in using, expected utility reasoning in circumstances where we do not know the situation's causal structure but cannot rule out the *possibility* that our actions influence the probabilities of world states.

A probabilistic link between an act and a state can signify that the act affects the probability of the agent being in the state. Or it could be a sign of influence going the other way, that is, the state influences the likelihood of the agent choosing the act. Or it could be a sign that the state and the act are separate effects of a common cause. If we do not know what correlation has to do with causal influence, we guess. To jump to the conclusion that there is a causal relationship is known in philosophy as *post hoc, ergo propter hoc*. That jump is a fallacy. The premise that B happens after A does not guarantee the conclusion that B happens because of A.

So *post hoc* reasoning is invalid, but is it a mistake? That is a different question.

Food poisoning: I eat mushrooms. I get sick. I jump to the conclusion that the mushrooms made me sick. My inference is invalid, to be sure, but it also leads me to consume less poison than I otherwise would. The *post hoc* fallacy is our heuristic for coping with the kind of ignorance we face every day. We rely on that kind of reasoning. At the same time, interestingly, we do not lightly bet the farm on it. If the alternative to eating mushrooms is to starve, then I do not conclude that mushrooms

---

12. Some theories of causal decision attempt to justify assertions about causal connection entirely in terms of probabilistic dependence (Pollock, 2002). To use probabilistic dependence for this purpose, though, one needs to know various conditional probabilities—the sort of probabilities one would know only in virtue of understanding a situation's causal structure.

13. The parallel point also holds in the Fisher case. Suppose the average person has a gene for cancer, but the phenotypic expression of that gene occurs only in smokers. In that case, smoking causes cancer in the average person. Nevertheless, my real concern is not whether smoking would cause cancer in average smokers but whether it would cause cancer in me. So, if my own genetic "box" is transparent, so that I see I do not have the genetic risk-factor, then the fact that the average smoker gets cancer is not relevant.

make me sick. I draw that conclusion only if the cost of eschewing mushrooms is acceptable. Or perhaps the mechanism is hard-wired. We are wired to dislike foods we ate just before becoming ill. We presumably would not be wired that way except that we evolved under conditions where we had various things to eat, so we could *afford* to be wired to be dislike suspect foods.

We have to know what the causal structure is like before we can be confident we are applying the right decision theory, or applying it in the right way. And if we cannot get that information, and have to go *solely* on information about probabilistic dependence, then what we actually do, and not at all unreasonably, is reason that if something reliably happens after A, it happens because of A. Applying expected utility reasoning, when we only suspect causal influence, is like *post hoc, ergo propter hoc* reasoning. It is fallacious, but not necessarily a bad idea. That is to say, deciding on the basis of expected utility is a heuristic. It may be a good heuristic, but it is in any case a heuristic, not an algorithm. There are times when an expected utility calculation will be a misleading indicator of how much utility there is in an action.

7. Problems of Underdescription

There is a controversy regarding whether to be a one-boxer or a two-boxer. Why? Suppose you have the opaque box under your arm and are walking out the door, not knowing whether the box contains $1 million. Then someone runs up waiving a thousand-dollar bill. Is there any controversy concerning whether you should take the thousand? None at all. Or, if that isn't clear enough, suppose you have already opened the box and know exactly what is inside. Surely now there is no controversy. Take the thousand. At some point, you *know* that nothing can change the amount of money in the opaque box.

In the Newcomb case, what makes some people one-boxers is that it is not merely the *box* that is opaque. The whole *causal structure* is mysterious. Nozick can stipulate that one is in a situation where one's action does not affect what is in the box, but it is hard to believe, after all. And if all we have is Nozick's word, $1 million is a lot to bet on it. So, if there is an opaque box sitting on a stage at the far end of the auditorium, and we can hear someone thumping around underneath the stage, and we know the predictor moonlights as a stage magician, at some point it makes no sense, given the stakes, simply to accept at face value Nozick's assurance that there is nothing we can do to affect the probability of the box containing $1 million.

Lawrence Davis says the choice we face in Newcomb is simple: which is bigger: $1 million or $1,000?[14]

> One box = $1 million (probably)
> Two boxes = $1,000 (plus nothing, probably)

However, those who advocate choosing two boxes also say the choice is simple: do you want the extra $1,000 or not?

14. Davis (1977).

One box = Whatever is in the opaque box + $0
Two boxes = Whatever is in the opaque box + $1,000

Which of these straightforward choices is the real choice? Davis's reasoning seems compelling, until we see that it embodies an assumption contrary to Nozick's stipulation that your action cannot influence the situation's causal structure. Conditional probabilities in the Newcomb case create a curiously (but by no means uniquely) misleading appearance of influence that throws us off, making us less certain of the wisdom of taking both boxes.

Although Nozick himself was a two-boxer, he said the situation is different if it is stipulated that you know the predictor is *never* wrong. In that case, even Nozick finds compelling the case for taking one box. He may be wrong about that, though. To make the case compelling, we would need to know the causal mechanism that explains how it could happen that the predictor is never wrong. Here is one such mechanism. Someone puts the opaque box in your hand, and (as she has done with everyone else) she explains to you the predictor's secret. The secret is that the predictor does not have $1 million, and would not give you $1 million even if he had it to give, and therefore *never* puts $1 million in the box. You can be certain there is no money in the box you have under your arm, and by the way, do you want the $1,000? Like *everyone* before you, each having heard this explanation of why the Predictor is never wrong, you take the $1,000. This is the only scenario we know of, compatible with Nozick's stipulation of genuine causal independence, where we can make sense of the idea that the predictor is never wrong.[15] And in this scenario, contra Nozick, it is two-boxing that is compelling.

We undermine the one-box intuition when we stipulate that the opaque box's payoff is safely in your pocket and you are walking out the door as someone hands you an extra $1,000. Accordingly, a credible case for one-boxing would need to focus on situations where the causal structure is opaque, where there is a real chance (unlike in the scenario just mentioned) that if I choose one box, the predictor will have put $1 million in that one box, and where we reasonably can suspect we somehow influence the predictor. To *nurture* such suspicion in myself, what I would need to do, *prior to the prediction*, is to insist that I be put in a situation where I rationally lack confidence in Nozick's stipulation that I cannot influence the prediction. I will insist that the box be placed on a stage at the far end of the auditorium, on top of the magician's trapdoor! Although I do not know my choice is influencing the predictor, neither can I be sure of the contrary. Meanwhile, if all goes well, the predictor knows I respond to such ambiguity by playing expected utilities. The predictor puts $1 million in the box, and I take away $1 million, although not the extra $1,000.

So, in the Newcomb situation, do you know that Nozick's stipulation (that you cannot now influence the prediction) is true? That is the heart of the controversy.

---

15. What makes it true in our story that the predictor is never wrong would not support a subjunctive counterfactual of the form "But if someone were to choose one box, then the predictor would have predicted one box." In our story, p(predictor chooses 1 / you take 1) would equal zero rather than one, but since you never take one box, it does not affect the claim that the predictor is never wrong.

What does it take, given the stakes, for you to feel absolutely confident that one-boxers are reasoning from a false premise about the problem's causal structure?

8. Absolute Confidence

Nozick's original article launched a vast literature, much of which was a debate between one-boxers and two-boxers. The real payoff of this puzzle, though, is that it stands as something like an incompleteness theorem for decision theory.

In his later book, Nozick concludes: "It would be unreasonable to place absolute confidence in any one particular line of reasoning for such cases or in any one particular principle of decision."[16] If we had absolute confidence in dominance reasoning, we would take two boxes even if there were only a dollar in the transparent box. If we had absolute confidence in expected utility reasoning, we would take only one box even if there were close to a $1 million in the transparent box. Evidently, Nozick is right. We are *not* absolutely confident in any given decision procedure. Indeed, if we were, we would be irrational.

In Newcomb's problem, there is enough vagueness in the problem's description to create doubt regarding the situation's causal structure. If we tighten the description, we resolve the ambiguity about which procedure is called for. That tells us there is work to be done prior to the stage of decision-making addressed by decision theory. *Before* we bring a decision theory to bear on a given decision problem, there are decisions to make.

A decision theory is not the kind of thing we simply follow. A decision theory is something we decide to apply: something whose applicability we must evaluate before deciding to apply it. Our chosen principle is, after all, *chosen*. So, before we embrace dominance reasoning, or expected utility reasoning, what reasoning leads to our choosing that principle? There is a pre-decision-theoretic art to the partitioning with which decision theory begins.

At one level, Nozick's point (to answer the question we began with) is that Jeffrey's conditional probabilities are relevant to decision-making only insofar as conditional probabilities do, or at least may, indicate causal influence. More profoundly, what we seek in a decision theory is an algorithm, and that may not be the right thing to seek.

A decision theory can recommend that we try to partition world states so that the probabilities of the states do not causally depend on the choice of action. Then,

(1) if we have a dominant strategy, given a partition of world states such that the probabilities of the states do not causally depend on the choice of action, we should go with it;
(2) if we have no dominant strategy, given any such partition, we should use conditional probabilities to calculate expected utilities, and go with that.

Recommendation (2) assumes that conditional probabilities indicate causal influence. As Heraclitus once said, though, nature loves to hide. The world does not

---

16. Nozick (1993) 43.

wear its causal structure on its sleeve. Where causal structure is opaque, *post hoc* reasoning is a good heuristic. So, for the same reasons, is using expected utility calculations. But Nozick showed that such calculations are only a heuristic. We do not have an all-purpose decision-theoretic algorithm.

Originally published *in The American Philosophers,* ed. P. French and H. Wettstein, *Midwest Studies in Philosophy* 28 (2004): 282–94. Reprinted with permission of Blackwell Publishing. Sarah Wright is Professor of Philosophy at the University of Georgia.

POLIS

6

How to Deserve

People ought to get what they deserve. And what we deserve can depend on effort, on performance, or on excelling in competition, even when excellence is partly a function of our natural gifts. Or so most people believe. Philosophers sometimes say otherwise. At least since Karl Marx complained about capitalist society extracting surplus value from workers, thereby failing to give workers what they deserve, classical liberal philosophers have worried that to treat justice as a matter of what people deserve is to license interference with liberty.

Rawls likewise rejected patterns imposed by principles of desert, saying that

> no one deserves his place in the distribution of natural endowments, any more than one deserves one's initial starting place in society. The assertion that a man deserves the superior character that enables him to make the effort to cultivate his abilities is equally problematic; for his character depends in large part upon fortunate family and social circumstances for which he can claim no credit. The notion of desert seems not to apply to these cases.[1]

Rawls's view is, in a way, compelling. Inevitably, our efforts are aided by natural gifts, positional advantages, and sheer luck, so how much can we deserve? And if our very characters result from an interplay of these same factors, how can we (capitalists and workers alike) deserve anything at all?

Does Rawls leave no room for desert? Rawls's intent may have been narrower: simply to eliminate a rival to his difference principle as a test of the justness of basic

---

1. Rawls (1971) 104. Rakowski (1991, 112) sees the passage as an "uncontroversial assertion, which even libertarians such as Nozick accept." Scheffler (1992, 307) likewise calls the passage "uncontroversial." Hayek (1960, 94) says, "A good mind or a fine voice, a beautiful face or a skilful hand, and a ready wit or an attractive personality are in large measure as independent of a person's efforts as the opportunities or experiences he has had." Hayek insists it is neither desirable nor practicable to ask basic structure to distribute according to desert. Gauthier (1986, 220) says, "We may agree with Rawls that no one deserves her natural capacities. Being the person one is, is not a matter of desert," although Gauthier doubts that this fact has normative implications.

structure. Whatever he intended, though, his critique of desert has no such surgical precision. We know Rawls intended his two principles to apply only to society's basic structure, but his critique of desert is not similarly constrained, and cannot be constrained merely by stipulating or intending that it be so constrained. When Rawls says "the concept of desert seems not to apply" to cases where outcomes are influenced by natural advantages or by character, he is implicating the larger moral universe, not merely basic structure. In particular, he wants to say the larger moral universe contains nothing (beyond his own first principle) to stop his difference principle from being *the* test of basic structure's justness. If Rawls's attack on desert is warranted, then the skepticism he is justifying is of a global nature.[2]

Scheffler says "none of the most prominent contemporary versions of philosophical liberalism assigns a significant role to desert at the level of fundamental principle."[3] If so, I argue, then these prominent contemporary versions of philosophical liberalism are mistaken. In particular, there is an aspect of what we do to make ourselves deserving that, although not discussed in the literature, plays a central role in everyday moral life, and for good reason.

1. The "Big Bang" Theory

Nearly everyone would say people ought to get what they deserve. But if we ask *what* people deserve, or on what basis, people begin to disagree. A few will say we deserve things simply in virtue of being human, or being in need. Many will say we deserve reward for our efforts, or for the real value our efforts create. It is not necessary, and may not even be feasible, to produce a complete catalog of all possible desert-bases. Suffice it to say that the standard bases on which persons commonly are said to be deserving include character, effort, and achievement.[4]

What are we doing when we deem someone deserving, that is, when we acknowledge someone's character, effort, or achievement? Here is a suggestion: to judge Bob deserving is to judge Bob worthy. It is to judge that Bob has features that make a given outcome Bob's just reward.[5] Intuitively, although less obviously, to acknowledge that there are things Bob can do to be deserving is to acknowledge that Bob is a *person*: able to choose and to be responsible for his choices.[6] Something like this is implicit in normal deliberation about what a person deserves.

The skeptics' theory, in its most sweeping form, depicts desert in such a way that to deserve X, we not only must supply inputs standardly thought to ground a desert claim but also must be deserving of everything about the world, including its history,

---

2. Rawls sometimes says he is arguing not against desert per se but only against desert as a preinstitutional notion. I will return to this issue.

3. Scheffler (1992) 301.

4. Feinberg (1970, 58) coins the term "desert base" to refer to what grounds desert claims. The idea is that well-formed desert claims are three-place relations of the form "P deserves X in virtue of feature F."

5. See Sher (1987) 195. See also Narveson (1995) 50–51.

6. See Morris (1991).

that put us in a position to supply that input. In effect, the possibility of our being deserving ended with the big bang.

Recall Rawls's claim that a man's "character depends in large part upon fortunate family and social circumstances for which he can claim no credit."[7] Rawls repeatedly stressed, and thus evidently thought it relevant, that "even the willingness to make an effort, to try, and so to be deserving in the ordinary sense is itself dependent upon happy family and social circumstances."[8] Needless to say, we all have whatever we have partly in virtue of luck, and luck is not a desert maker. Every outcome is influenced by factors that are morally arbitrary. ("Arbitrary" has a negative connotation, but without further argument, we are entitled only to say luck is morally neutral or inert. That is how I use the term here.) However, does the supposition that *some* of an outcome's causal inputs are arbitrary entail that all of them must be?

Of course not. Everyone is lucky to some degree, but the more a person supplies in terms of effort or excellence, the less weight we put on the inevitable element of luck. In any case, there is a big difference between being lucky and being merely lucky. The bare fact of being lucky is not what precludes being deserving. Being *merely* lucky is what precludes being deserving, because to say we are merely lucky is to say we have not supplied inputs (the effort, the excellence) that ground desert claims.

To rebut a desert claim in a given case, we must show that inputs that *can* ground desert claims are missing in that case. On a nonvacuous conception of desert, there will be inputs that a person can supply, and therefore can fail to supply. In general, finding that X falls outside a category is interesting only if falling inside is a real possibility.[9]

A further point; there are infinitely many inputs that do not ground desert claims (luck, the big bang). So what? Skeptics say every causal chain has morally arbitrary links, but no one doubts that. The truly skeptical idea is that no chain has *non*arbitrary links. A skeptic says, "Even character, talent, and other internal features that constitute us as persons are arbitrary so long as they are products of chains of events containing arbitrary links. Every causal chain traces back to something arbitrary, namely the Big Bang. Therefore, nothing is deserved."[10]

Some causal chains work their way through features internal to persons; it would be strangely credulous for a skeptic unquestioningly to assume this does not matter. If a so-called skeptic says, "Character is arbitrary," then someone who

---

7. Rawls (1971) 104.
8. Rawls (1971) 74.

9. We entertained the idea that character is an accident of nature/nurture for which we deserve no credit. In some way, that must be true, but where does it end? Could I have had an altogether different character, or is there a point beyond which such a person would not have been me? Am I lucky I was born human when I could have been a seagull? (Is there a seagull out there that could have been me?) Would we be wrong to say luck is a matter of what happens to me, whereas my basic nature (the fact that I have my character rather than yours) did not *happen* to me—it *is* me?

10. See Brock's (1999) discussion in a subsection entitled "How can we deserve anything since we don't deserve our asset bases?" Those who reject the premise (that, to be a desert maker, an input must itself be deserved in turn) include Narveson (1995, 67), Sher (1987, 24), and Zaitchik (1977, 373).

is properly skeptical replies, "Compared to what?" We distinguish outcomes that owe something to a person's character from outcomes that do not. Desert makers, if there are any, are relations between outcomes and internal features of persons. We need not (and normally do not) assume anything about what caused those features.

Is it odd that we normally make no assumptions about a desert maker's causal history? What if we had been talking about features of nonpersons? Joel Feinberg observes: "Art objects deserve admiration; problems deserve careful consideration; bills of legislation deserve to be passed."[11] John Kleinig says the Grand Canyon deserves its reputation.[12] Such remarks are offered as small digressions, noted and then set aside, but they point to something crucial. We *never* say the Grand Canyon deserves its reputation only if it in turn deserves the natural endowments on which its reputation is based. We *never* question artistic judgments by saying, "Even the greatest of paintings were caused to have the features we admire. Not one painting ever did anything to deserve being caused to have those features." Intuitively, obviously, it doesn't matter.

Skeptics assume it does matter in the case of persons, but the assumption is groundless. To my knowledge, it has never been defended. As with nonpersons, when a person's internal features support desert claims, the support comes from appreciating what those features are, not from evidence that they are uncaused.

Some will say desert claims about paintings do not mean the same thing as desert claims about persons. Not so. The meaning is the same; what changes are the stakes. We do not need to reject claims about what paintings deserve to make room for our favorite principle of distributive justice; we need only reject claims about what *persons* deserve. This difference in what is at stake is why big bang theories are deployed only against desert claims made on behalf of persons. Stakes aside, though, big bang theories are as undefended for persons as for paintings.

Here, then, is where matters currently stand. Ordinary thought about desert would be a recipe for skepticism if it were true that ordinary practice presupposes that people deserve credit for doing X only when people in turn deserve credit for having the ability and opportunity to do X. However, because ordinary practice assumes no such thing, ordinary practice has no such problem. We are left with two options. First, we can say no one deserves anything, and that is what we will say *if* we assume we deserve credit for working hard only if we in turn deserve credit for being "destined" to work hard. The second option is to say we deserve credit for working hard not because we deserve to have been destined to work hard but simply because we did, after all, work hard. The latter is our ordinary practice.

Neither option is compelling. We are not forced to believe in desert; neither are we forced to be skeptics. We decide. We can ask whether we treat people more respectfully when we give them credit for what they do or when we deny them credit. Or we can ask what kind of life we have when we live by one conception rather than another. These are different questions, and not the only ones we could ask. Perhaps

---

11. Feinberg (1970) 55.
12. Kleinig (1971).

the answers all point in the same direction. Perhaps not. Sweeping skepticism is unattractive to most people, but there is no denying that skepticism is an option, and that some do choose to be skeptics.[13]

Refuting skeptics and answering "How can we deserve anything at all?" are different tasks. We can answer the question, but not by refuting skeptics. For those who want an answer—who *want* an alternative to skepticism—my objective is to make room within a philosophically respectable theory of justice for the idea that there are things we can do to be deserving.

So, when we consider how much sheer good luck we needed to get where we are today, it is natural for us to wonder, "Do I deserve this?" What does the question mean? If we translate the question as, "What did I do, at the moment of the Big Bang, to deserve this?" the answer is, "Nothing. So what?" If we translate the question as "What did I do, before being born, to deserve this?" the answer again is "Nothing. So what?" However, if we translate the question as "What did I *do* to deserve this?" then the question will have a real answer.

Also eminently sensible would be to ask, "What *can* I do to deserve this?" This question, too, will have an answer. The answer may be that, as it happens, there is nothing I can do, but that is not preordained. A theory that lets us ask and answer this question is a theory that lets the concept of desert be what it needs to be in human affairs: a message of hope that is at the same time life's greatest moral challenge. Such a theory acknowledges the existence of persons: beings who make choices and who are accountable for the choices they make.

In summary, a genuine theory of desert tells us what to look for when investigating what particular people have done. A genuine theory will not say what "big bang" theories say: namely, we need not investigate actual histories of particular people, since we know a priori as a perfectly general feature of human nature that no one deserves anything.

2. Deserving a Chance

Suppose we know what a person has to do to be deserving. Is there also a question about *when* a person has to do it? James Rachels says "what people deserve always depends on what they have done in the past."[14] David Miller says "desert judgments are justified on the basis of past and present facts about individuals, never on the basis of states of affairs to be created in the future."[15] Joel Feinberg says "if a person

---

13. Walzer (1983, 260) says, "Advocates of equality have often felt compelled to deny the reality of desert." In a footnote, Walzer says he means Rawls. Walzer sees Rawls's argument as supposing "the capacity to make an effort or to endure pain is, like all their other capacities, only the arbitrary gift of nature or nurture. But this is an odd argument, for while its purpose is to leave us with persons of equal entitlement, it is hard to see that it leaves us with *persons* at all. How are we to conceive of these men and women once we have come to view their capacities and achievements as accidental accessories, like hats and coats they just happen to be wearing? How, indeed, are they to conceive of themselves?"

14. Rachels (1997) 176.

15. Miller (1976) 93.

is deserving of some sort of treatment, he must, necessarily, be so in virtue of some possessed characteristic or *prior* activity."[16]

If we are not careful, we could interpret such statements in a way that would overlook an important, perhaps the most important, kind of desert-making relation. It is conventional that what we deserve depends on what we do, and that we deserve no credit for what we do until we do it. I now believe that there is a further academic gloss on this convention, though, namely that when we first receive (for example) our natural and positional advantages, if we have not already done something to deserve them, it is too late. We are born into our advantages by mere luck, and that which comes to us by mere luck can never be deserved.

This more specific academic gloss is what I reject. I said being merely lucky precludes being deserving. I did not say, and do not believe, that being merely lucky at t_1 precludes being deserving at t_2. In particular, we do not deserve our natural gifts at the moment of our birth, but that need not matter. What matters, if anything at all matters, is what we do after the fact.[17] Let me make a claim that may at first seem counterintuitive:

We sometimes deserve X on the basis of what we do after receiving X.

Upon receiving a surprisingly good job offer, a new employee vows to work hard to deserve it. No one ever thinks the vow is paradoxical. No one takes the employee aside and says, "Relax. There's nothing you can do. Only the past is relevant." But unless such everyday vows are misguided, we can deserve X on the basis of what we do after receiving X.

How can this be? Isn't it a brute fact that when we ask whether a person deserves X, we look backward, not forward? If we concede for argument's sake that we look back, we would still need to ask: back from where? Perhaps we look back from where we are, yet mistakenly assume we look back from where the recipient was at the moment of receiving X. If we look back, a year after hiring Jane, wondering whether she deserved the chance, what do we ask? We ask what she *did* with it. When we do that, we *are* looking back even while looking at what happened after she received X. From that perspective, we see we can be deserving of opportunities.[18] We deserve them by not wasting them—by giving them their due, as it were.[19]

16. Feinberg (1970) 48. Emphasis added.

17. In passing, there are desert bases that do not require action, such as when we say the Grand Canyon deserves its reputation. It deserves its reputation because of what it is, not because of what it did. I thank Neera Badhwar for noting the implication: being merely lucky only *sometimes* precludes being deserving.

18. I speak interchangeably of deserving a chance, being deserving of a chance, and being worthy of it. Sometimes, it is more natural to describe a person as being deserving of X rather than as deserving X, especially when the question concerns opportunity rather than reward. But this is a verbal point. If a student said "No one deserves anything, yet there is much of which people are deserving," we would think the student was making an obscure joke.

19. Is this a sufficient condition? No. If something is wrong with the opportunity, as when we have a chance to use stolen property, then not wasting the opportunity does not suffice to show we deserve it. We could say the same of standard theories about deserving rewards: when we know the reward is stolen property, qualifying for it does not suffice to show we deserve it. In the same way, we may think we establish

Therefore, even if we necessarily deserve no credit for what we do until after we do it, it does not follow—and indeed is not true—that if we have not already done something to deserve an opportunity by the moment we receive it, then it is too late. Imagine another case. Two students receive scholarships. One works hard and gets excellent grades. The other parties her way through her first year before finally being expelled for cheating. Does their conduct tell us *nothing* about which of them was more deserving of a scholarship?

Can we save the convention (that whether we deserve X depends entirely on what happens before we receive X) by saying the students' conduct is relevant only because it reveals what they were like before the award? No. When we look back at the expelled student's disgraceful year, our reason for saying she did not deserve her award has nothing to do with speculation about what she did in high school. Both students may have been qualified for scholarships qua reward. Or equally *un*qualified: suppose both were chosen via clerical error, and before that were equally destined for a lifetime of failure. The difference we care about here, and have reason to care about, concerns the subsequent performance, not the prior qualification. What grounds our conviction that one is more worthy of the scholarship qua opportunity is that one student gave the opportunity its due; the other did not. Again:

We sometimes deserve X on the basis of what we do after receiving X.

Needless to say, skeptics greet this conclusion with skepticism. Why? Part of the answer is that we learn as philosophers to focus on desert as a *compensatory* notion. The idea is, desert makers we supply before getting X put a moral scale out of balance, and our getting X rebalances the scale. To those who see desert as necessarily a compensatory notion, we deserve X only if X represents a restoring of moral balance. We deserve X only if we deserve it qua reward—only if our receiving X settles an account.

In ordinary use, though, desert sometimes is a *promissory* notion. Sometimes our receiving X is what puts the moral scale out of balance, and our subsequently proving ourselves worthy of X is what restores it. X need not be compensation for already having supplied the requisite desert makers. Sometimes it is the other way around. There are times when supplying desert makers is what settles the account.

In either case, two things happen, and the second settles the account. In compensatory cases, desert-making inputs are supplied first; responding with rewards settles the account. In promissory cases, opportunities are supplied first; responding with desert-making inputs settles the account. In promissory cases, a new employee who vows "I will do justice to this opportunity. I will show you I deserve it" is not saying future events will retroactively cause her receiving X to count as settling an account *now*. Instead, she is saying future events *will* settle the account. She claims not that she is getting what she already paid for but that she is getting what she *will* pay for.[20]

---

title to a previously unowned good by mixing our labor with it, without thinking that labor-mixing can give us title to what otherwise is someone else's property.

20. Feldman (1995, 70–71) argues that a soldier who volunteers for a suicide mission can deserve a medal in advance. (Feldman is still talking here about deserving rewards. He does not claim people deserve opportunities.) Jeremy Waldron and Fred Miller see forward-looking elements in Aristotle's discussion of

So why does James Rachels assert that "what people deserve always depends on what they have done in the past"?[21] Rachels says, "the explanation of why past actions are the only bases of desert connects with the fact that if people were never responsible for their own conduct—if strict determinism were true—no one would ever deserve anything."[22] Crucially, when he says, "past actions are the only bases of desert," Rachels is stressing "actions," not "past." What Rachels sees as the unacceptable alternative is not a theory like mine, but rather the view that people deserve to be rewarded for having natural endowments. He is thinking of past actions versus past nonactions, and is not considering whether actions postdating X's receipt might be relevant. That is why Rachels could see himself as explaining why "past actions are the only bases of desert" when he says, "if people were never responsible for their own conduct...no one would ever deserve anything." Notice that this argument in no way connects desert bases to events predating X's receipt. The argument connects desert to action, but not particularly to past action.[23]

Rachels also says, "People do not deserve things on account of their willingness to work, but only on account of their actually having worked."[24] There are reasons for saying this, and Rachels may be right when speaking of rewards. It appears analytic that rewards respond to past performance. However, rewards are not the only kind of thing that can be deserved. We sometimes have reason to say "She deserves a chance." We may say a young job candidate deserves a chance not because of work already done but because she is plainly a talented, well-meaning person who wants the job and who will throw herself into it if given the chance.

A more senior internal candidate for a job may be deserving in a different way: that is, worthy of reward for past performance. Yet, the idea that an inexperienced candidate can deserve a chance, for the reasons mentioned, is something most people find compelling. We can be glad they do, too, insofar as thinking this way leads them to give opportunities to people who are worthy in the promissory sense, that is, people who, when given a chance, give the opportunity its due.[25]

---

meritocracy in distributing political offices. Aristotle (*Politics* 3.12.1282b. 30) says, "When a number of flute players are equal in their art, there is no reason why those of them who are better born should have better flutes given to them; for they will not play any better on the flute, and the superior instrument should be reserved for him who is the superior artist." See Fred D. Miller (2001). Intriguingly, Waldron suggests a school might choose among candidates by comparing how meritorious the *school* would be if it hired one rather than another. See Waldron (1995) 573.

21. Rachels (1997) 176.
22. Rachels (1997) 180.
23. An important caveat: although Rachels and David Miller (1976) say what we deserve depends on what we did in the past, and never on the future, it would be anachronistic to interpret them as rejecting my proposition that we can deserve X in virtue of what we do after receiving X. At the time, it had not yet occurred to anyone to be for, or against, my proposition. My main aim here is not to defend the proposition against bitter enemies, but simply to introduce it as a possible position.
24. Rachels (1997) 185.
25. Not all true statements about what we deserve have the status of desert *claims*. Claims in the relevant sense imply correlative duties, such as the duty to give claimants what they deserve. Someone who says Jane did justice to her opportunity may be expressing a truth without meaning to be making a claim on Jane's behalf against anyone else.

If we say a job candidate deserves a chance, and then, far from throwing herself into the job, she treats it with contempt, that would make us wrong. The promissory aspect of desert will have failed to materialize. She had a chance to balance the account and failed. If she treats the job with contempt, then she supplies neither the performance nor even the good faith effort the hiring committee expected.

By contrast, if the candidate fails through no fault of her own, then we cannot hold it against her. And if her failure is simply a stroke of unforeseeable bad luck, then neither can the committee blame themselves for having chosen wrongly. They may say in retrospect that although the new employee failed to do justice to the opportunity, it was because she did not really get the opportunity the committee intended. By analogy, suppose we intend to give salt a chance to dissolve in water, but what we actually end up doing is giving salt a chance to dissolve in olive oil. If the salt fails to dissolve, we still insist the salt would have dissolved in water, given the chance.

The possibility of bad luck notwithstanding, the fact remains that we sort out applicants for a reason. In normal cases, the point is not to reward someone for past conduct but to get someone who can do the job. That is why, by the time we reach t_2, the question is not what she did before the opportunity but what she did with it. The question at t_2 need not and normally does not turn on what was already settled at t_1.

A note on examples. Realistic examples are complex, raising issues beyond those intended by the theorist who brings them up. In this case, real-world hiring committees must juggle several criteria, not all of them having to do with desert. Some points might be better illustrated by speaking of tenure and promotion committees, where decisions are more purely a matter of desert but where candidates have enough of a history that it is harder to sort out backward- versus forward-looking grounds for judging whether a candidate is deserving. Candidates often see their case as purely backward looking, but tenure committees do not. Tenure committees want to know that a candidate will not become deadwood—that past performance was not spurred mainly by a prospect of tenure qua reward. They want to be able to look back years later and say the candidate deserved tenure qua opportunity.

3. Refining the Promissory Model

To further clarify the nature of the promissory model, we should separate it into two elements. The first explains what we can say about Jane from the perspective of t_2. The second explains what we can say about her from the perspective of t_1.

> Element (a): A person who receives opportunity X at t_1 can be deserving at t_2 because of what she did when given a chance.
> Element (b): A person who receives opportunity X at t_1 can be deserving at t_1 because of what she will do if given the chance.

What does element (a) tell us? It tells us that it can be true at t_2 that the account has been settled. Jane supplied inputs that did justice to X. We need not suppose Jane supplied those inputs at t_1. When we call Jane deserving at t_2, as per element (a), we are not denying that she may have been merely lucky at t_1. All we are saying is that when Jane got the chance to prove herself worthy, she did so.

Element (a) concerns what Jane can do to be deserving at t_2 even if she was merely lucky at t_1. By contrast, element (b) concerns how Jane can deserve X at t_1 not as a reward for past performance but as an opportunity to perform in the future. In other words, element (b) concerns how a committee nonarbitrarily could select Jane in preference to some other candidate. Jane is choice-worthy if she is the sort of person who will do justice to the opportunity. She may be choice-worthy in virtue of past performance, but a search committee is not trying to *reward* past performance. They are trying to decide whether to count Jane's past performance as evidence that she will do justice to opportunity X—evidence that she *will* settle the account, given the chance.

There are various ways to formulate element (b). None is perfect. However, when we think of contexts like hiring decisions, it is natural to say a hiring committee is looking not merely for someone who theoretically can do the job, but for someone who *will* do the job given a chance, meaning she will do the job if we offer it to her, if she accepts it, if there is no unforeseen catastrophe, and so on. Our invocation of element (b) at t_1 is essentially a prediction that by the time we get to t_2, we will be in a position to invoke element (a). We are predicting that by t_2, Jane will have supplied the relevant desert-making inputs. However, we are not merely wagering on future performance. Rather, we are wagering that Jane has desert-making internal features that will translate into future performance, barring unexpected misfortune. We are judging that Jane is the kind of person who will do the job given the chance.[26]

Element (a) says that although desert requires a balance between what Jane gives and what Jane is given, Jane need not move first. Element (b) says Jane can deserve opportunity X (in the sense of being choice-worthy) before she does her part. Element (a), by contrast, pointedly does not say Jane can deserve X before doing her part. Element (a) stresses that *even if* Jane deserves X only after doing her part, it still does not follow that she has to do her part before receiving X.

Element (a) therefore is the essence of the promissory model. So far as our purpose is to challenge the ideas that we deserve X only if we deserve it as a reward for past performance, and that we cannot deserve X except in virtue of what we do before receiving X, we do not need element (b). We need some version of element (b) only insofar as we further seek to vindicate our ordinary practice—in particular our tendency to speak of candidates as deserving a chance in virtue of what they can and will do if we give them a chance.[27]

---

26. When we think a machine will perform well if we give it a chance, we do not say the machine deserves a chance. We may say "It is worth a try," but we do not mean the same thing when speaking of a person's character as when speaking of a machine's characteristics. I owe this point to Michael Smith.

27. David Miller comes as close as any philosopher ever has, to my knowledge, to endorsing element (b). Miller says there are insuperable obstacles to interpreting *jobs* as rewards for past conduct (1999a, 159). When we say someone deserves a prize, we standardly base our judgment on past or present performance, but when we are making hiring decisions, the best-qualified candidate, the one who deserves it, is the one who will perform it best, other things being equal (162). And "in the case of jobs past performance matters only as a source of evidence about a person's present qualities" (170).

I said there are various ways of formulating element (b), and none are perfect. In spelling out element (b), we could interpret choice-worthiness as a question of either what is true of the candidate or what the committee justifiably believes about the candidate.[28] There are pros and cons either way. We may sometimes have reason to distinguish evidence that Jane will do well from the fact (if and when it becomes a fact) that Jane will do well. What makes Jane choice-worthy in the metaphysical rather than the epistemological sense is the fact that she truly is the kind of person who (barring unforeseen catastrophe) would supply the requisite desert makers and thus become deserving at t_2 in the sense of element (a).

If a committee concludes that Jane is choice-worthy at t_1, then whether the committee judged correctly (that is, whether it truly picked the right person, as opposed to whether its members were justified in believing they picked the right person) remains to be seen. Is this a puzzle? If so, it is less a puzzle about desert and more a puzzle about prediction in general. Suppose at t_1 we say Jane will be married at t_2. Jane then gets married. In that case, events at t_2 have indeed settled the truth-value of a claim uttered at t_1. Does anyone find this puzzling? The future event does not backward-cause the prediction to be true; it simply settles that the prediction was true. Events at t_2 can settle the truth-value of a claim like "She'll get married, given a chance." They also can settle the truth-value of a claim like "She'll do justice to X, given a chance." There comes a time when we can say "You said she'd get married; it turns out you were right," or when a committee can say "We said she'd do justice to the opportunity; it turns out we were right." In either case, Jane settles what had been unsettled. Saying "She deserves X," meaning she will do justice to X given a chance, is no odder than saying "Salt is soluble," meaning it will dissolve in water given a chance.

Insofar as the idea that Jane deserves a chance at t_1 depends on whether Jane has relevant dispositional properties at t_1, and insofar as a test of this idea lies in the future, element (b) implies that life sometimes involves decision-making under uncertainty. Hiring committees judge which candidate is most worthy, with no guarantee that they are judging correctly.

When a committee judges at t_1 that Jane deserves a chance, they are placing a bet. They are judging her character. They may even transform her character, insofar as their trust may inspire her to become the kind of person they judge her to be. At t_1, though, it remains to be seen whether Jane is or will become that kind of person. Jane settles that later, in an epistemological sense, and perhaps (more intriguingly) in a metaphysical sense, too, insofar as she must decide, not merely reveal, whether she really is that trustworthy, that hardworking, and so on. The committee will have to wait and see. Since life truly is difficult in this way, we can be glad to have a theory that correctly depicts the difficulty—that does not make life look simpler than it is.[29]

---

28. Recall David Miller's (1976) claim that "desert judgments are justified on the basis of past and present facts about individuals." I can agree that the epistemological *justification* of desert claims is backward looking, because that is where the information is, while still holding that *truth makers* for some desert claims can lie in the future. (We would say the same of predictions in general.)

29. I thank Guido Pincione and Martín Farrell for their insight on this point.

In passing, what can the promissory model say about unsuccessful candidates, or more generally about people who lack opportunity? What if there are more deserving candidates than positions for them to fill? Element (a) is silent on questions about people who never get a chance, but element (b) can say about unsuccessful candidates roughly what it says about successful ones; namely, they may deserve X insofar as they, too, would have done justice to X, given a chance. *My theory does not say people who lack opportunities are undeserving.* (Recall the salt analogy. When salt fails to dissolve in olive oil, we do not conclude that salt is not water-soluble. We acknowledge that it never got the chance, perhaps adding that we still believe in salt's water-solubility, meaning we believe it would have dissolved in water given the opportunity.)

Also in passing, would I entertain a promissory theory of punishment? ("He may be innocent now, but if we put him in jail, he'll become the sort of person who belongs in jail.") No. We may view reward and punishment as two sides of the same compensatory coin, but there is no such parallel between opportunity and punishment. The transformative role of expectations (the fact that we tend to live up to them, or down, as the case may be) can justify the faith involved in granting an opportunity but cannot justify punishment.[30] If Jean Valjean wrongly is imprisoned and says, "Okay, if they treat me like a criminal, I'll act like one," this does not vindicate the wrongful punishment. Indeed, the fact that the punishment induces punishment-worthy behavior further condemns the punishment. By contrast, if Valjean later is rocked by a bishop's kindness and says, "Okay, if they treat me like a decent human being, I'll act like one," that *does* vindicate the bishop's kindness.[31]

According to my theory, there is something slightly misleading, or at best incomplete, in assessing a society by asking whether people get what they deserve. If desert matters, then often a better question is whether people do something to deserve what they get. Do opportunities go to people who will do something to be worthy of them?

My purpose here is to make room within a credible theory of justice for the idea that there are things we can do to be deserving. Specifically, we can deserve an opportunity. Moreover, whether we deserved an opportunity can depend on what we did with it. First, there are things we can do after the fact to balance the scale, making it fitting in retrospect that we got a chance to prove ourselves at t_1. Second, we can be choice-worthy even at t_1, insofar as a committee can see (or insofar as it is true) that we will do justice to the opportunity. The latter is not the core of my theory of desert, but it is a way of pushing the envelope and making sense of a central part of ordinary life.

---

30. George Rainbolt suggests that my promissory model may have a greater range of explanatory power than I give it credit for. In particular, if we have good reason to believe that a prisoner convicted of a violent crime is unrepentant and indeed intent on repeating his crime upon being paroled, that is a reason for not granting parole. It is a reason not only in the sense that society has a right to protect itself from a confirmed and unreformed violent criminal but also in the sense that the prisoner is undeserving of parole.

31. Jean Valjean is a character from Victor Hugo's novel *Les Misérables*.

4. Deserving and Earning

We commonly show our respect for what a person has achieved by saying "You deserved it" or "You earned it." The words "deserving" and "earning" are nearly interchangeable in ordinary use. There is a difference, though, and it will be useful to give the difference a bit more emphasis than it gets in ordinary use.

A paycheck is not earned until the work is done. Upon being hired, I will do what I need to do to earn the paycheck, but the future does not settle that I have earned the paycheck now. I have not earned it until I do the work. Thus, while we do speak of people as deserving a chance even before they supply the requisite inputs, we do not speak of people as having earned a paycheck prior to supplying requisite inputs.

Perhaps this is because what Jane deserves has more to do with her character, whereas what Jane has earned has more to do with her work. Jane's character can be manifest before she supplies the requisite inputs. Her work cannot similarly be manifest prior to supplying requisite inputs, since her work *is* the requisite input when the question concerns what she has earned. Jane can be deserving at t_1 in virtue of what she will do, if given a chance. To have earned a paycheck at t_1, though, she has to have done the work at t_1.

Therefore, that she *would* earn the check at t_2 is not relevant to what Jane has earned at t_1, even though—according to element (b)—it is relevant to whether she deserves a chance at t_1. Thus, the promissory model does not, at t_1, work for earning. There is no analog of element (b).

However, there is an analog of element (a). We acknowledged that I have not earned the paycheck until I do the work. Does that mean I can earn the check only if I do the work first, before the check is issued?

No! In everyday life, we do not doubt that a new but trusted employee, paid in advance, can earn the money after the fact. Money is paid at t_1, then what was not true at t_1 becomes true at t_2: namely, the scale is now balanced and money given at t_1 has been earned. It becomes true at t_2 that Jane did what she was paid to do.

Therefore, we cannot save the academic convention that desert is a purely compensatory notion by recasting it as a thesis about earning. It does not capture the concept of desert. It does not work for earning either.[32]

An unearned opportunity is an unearned opportunity, but though unearned, a person may yet do justice to it. That possibility often is what we have in mind when we say a person deserves a chance. To ignore that possibility is to ignore the possibility of redemption involved in working to do justice to an opportunity.

In a popular film about World War II, *Saving Private Ryan*, Captain Miller is fatally injured while rescuing Private Ryan. As Miller dies, he says to Ryan: "Earn it!" At that moment, neither character is under any illusions about whether Ryan

---

32. However, we might defend a version of Feldman's (1995) thesis in this way. The soldier awarded a medal in advance does not deserve it and has not earned it. (The medal is an award, not an opportunity. If it is deserved at all, it must be deserved qua award, which is to say it must be deserved along lines specified by the compensatory model.) Even so, it can make sense to honor the soldier now for what the soldier is about to do. Then, after the soldier makes the heroic sacrifice, it will make sense to speak of the soldier as having earned the medal.

earned the rescue. He did not, as they both know. Neither is Ryan choice-worthy in the sense of element (b), as they both know. (As the story goes, the reason High Command orders Ryan's rescue has nothing to do with Ryan's worthiness. Ryan's three brothers have just died in battle. The point of rescuing Ryan is to avoid having to send a telegram to Ryan's mother saying her entire family has just been wiped out.) Still, as both characters also know, that is not the end of the story, for it is now up to Ryan to settle whether Miller's sacrifice was in vain.[33] It is not too late for Ryan to try to redeem the sacrifice by going on to be as worthy as a person could be.[34]

If there is anything Ryan can do to earn the rescue, it will be at t_2, not t_1, as analogous to the promissory model's element (a). When Miller says "Earn it," he fully realizes that Ryan has not yet done his part. Ryan's rescue can never be deserved in the way a reward or prize is deserved. To be earned (deserved) at all, the rescue will have to be earned in the way advance salary is earned: that is, after the fact.

Fittingly, the film ends with a scene from decades later. An elderly Ryan visits Miller's grave. Anguished, Ryan begs his wife: "Tell me I've been a good man!" The implication: if Ryan has been a good man, then he has done all he could to earn the rescue that gave him a chance to be a good man. Notice that Ryan's story is neutral regarding the relevance of alternative desert bases. The elderly Ryan's wife may say the relevant basis is effort and thus that Ryan is deserving in virtue of having done all he could. Ryan himself may see achievement as the relevant basis, and conclude that despite his efforts he has not done nearly enough to be worthy of all the lives that were sacrificed to save his. The problem is general. If great sacrifices were made so as to put us in a position to flourish, we have to wonder whether there is anything we can do to be worthy of those sacrifices. The easy answer is that if we do all we can, we have done all anyone could ask. Yet, if we are reflective, we cannot help but think the easy answer sometimes is too easy, and that there is no guarantee that "doing all we can" will be enough.

Good luck cannot rob us of the chance to act in ways that make people deserving, although bad luck can, which is one reason bad luck is bad. For example, if Private Ryan is killed by a stray bullet within minutes of being rescued, then there is no fact of the matter about whether Ryan did justice to the opportunity to live a good life, since (in this scenario) he got no such opportunity. Bad luck robbed him of it.

In some ways, Ryan's situation is like a lottery winner's. If Miller hands Ryan a winning lottery ticket and says with his dying breath "Earn it," can Ryan earn it? No one would say Ryan has earned it at t_1;[35] but that is not the end of the story, because

---

33. Abraham Lincoln's Gettysburg Address, one of the most moving speeches ever made, gains its rhetorical power from precisely this point, speaking as it does of the unfinished work of those who died in battle, calling on us to make sure their "last full measure of devotion" shall not be in vain.

34. Here is another way of interpreting what Captain Miller means when he says "Earn it." Miller is saying Ryan owes it to the men who died to be as worthy as possible of their sacrifice. So interpreted, Miller's question invokes compensatory as well as promissory models. Going on to be as worthy as possible is the closest Ryan can come to giving the fallen soldiers what they deserve in recognition of their sacrifice. I owe this thought to an email exchange with Bas van der Vossen.

35. If the case were more like the kind of case covered by element (b), Captain Miller conceivably might say Ryan deserves the ticket. For example, suppose Miller needs to select someone from a list of applicants, and sees that Ryan would move mountains to prove himself worthy. In that case, deeming Ryan choice-worthy on that basis might be Miller's best-justified option.

even when a windfall is sheer luck, it is not only sheer luck. It is also a challenge, and as with most challenges, there is a right way of responding. Some day, there will be a fact of the matter regarding whether Ryan responded well.

Private Ryan's situation also is a bit like that of persons born with natural and positional advantages. We are not born having done anything to deserve advantages as rewards. So, a standard compensatory model has no resources to underwrite claims of desert at the moment of birth. At birth, we are merely lucky. (Neither is there any basis for deeming us choice-worthy, if choosing were even an issue.) Still, regarding our advantages, there is something we can do later on. We can do justice to them.

5. Grounding Desert

Are the two models, compensatory and promissory, truly models of desert? Does it matter? The main issue is not whether we use the same word when referring to those who did their best before receiving rewards and to those who did their best after receiving opportunities. In fact, we do, but the larger question is whether we are justified in thinking of desert claims as weighty in both cases.

I explained how in everyday life we grasp the concept of deserving a chance in virtue of what we did, or will do, with it. I would not appeal to common sense to justify our common-sense understanding, though. To justify, we look elsewhere. This section indicates (although only indicates) where we might look.

Part of what makes it difficult even to begin such a discussion is that in trying to justify, we risk trivializing. We risk seeming to ground a thing in considerations less important than the thing itself. That could be a problem when trying to justify a conception of justice. When assessing alternative conceptions of justice, we generally cannot settle the contest by appeal to yet another lofty but contested ideal of justice. However, if we appeal to something else—something other than (our conception of) justice—we are bound to be appealing to that which seems less important. But that is all right. We are not confusedly seeking the foundation of that which is itself foundational. We simply ask what can be said on the conception's behalf.

The Least Advantaged

Margaret Holmgren says justice "demands that each individual be secured the most fundamental benefits in life compatible with like benefits for all," and then adds, "the opportunity to progress by our own efforts is a fundamental interest."[36] Richard Miller concurs: "Most people (including most of the worst off) want to use what resources they have actively, to get ahead on their own steam, and this reflects a proper valuing of human capacities."[37]

On one view, the Rawlsian supposition that inequalities should be arranged to maximally benefit the least advantaged rules out the idea that people deserve more—and thus should get more—if and when and because their talents and efforts

---

36. Holmgren (1986) 274.
37. Richard Miller (2002) 286.

contribute more to society. Holmgren, though, notes that contractors in Rawls's original position would know (because by hypothesis they are aware of perfectly general features of human psychology) that people not only want to be given stuff; they want to be successful, and they want their success to be deserved. Accordingly, even contractors who are so grossly risk-averse that they focus only on the least advantaged economic class would still want to ensure that least advantaged people have an opportunity to advance by their own efforts. What would such contractors choose? Holmgren says, "Rather than focusing exclusively on the share of income or wealth they would receive, they would choose a principle of distribution which would ensure that they would each have this opportunity."[38]

Holmgren's claim seems incompatible with Rawls's difference principle, *if* we interpret the principle as Nozick interprets it, as a ground-level prescription for redistribution. In that case, the idea that Jane deserves her salary threatens to override our mandate to lay claim to her salary on behalf of the least advantaged. However, Nozick's way is not the only way to interpret the difference principle. Suppose we interpret the principle not as a mandate for redistribution but rather as a way of evaluating basic structure. That is, we evaluate basic structure by asking whether it works to the benefit of the least advantaged. On the latter interpretation, we choose among rules like "Try to give people what they deserve" and "Try to give the least advantaged everything" by asking which is best for the least advantaged in actual empirical practice.

The latter undoubtedly is the difference principle's canonical interpretation. Unfortunately, we naturally slip into thinking of bargainers as choosing a plan for redistribution. Rawls himself slips in this way when he says, "There is a tendency for common sense to suppose that income and wealth, and the good things in life generally, should be distributed according to desert.... Now justice as fairness rejects this conception. Such a principle would not be chosen in the original position."[39] The conclusion is right, but the argument leading to it is not. We can agree that such a principle would not be chosen, but the reason is because distributional principles per se are not on the menu. They are not even the kind of thing bargainers choose. Bargainers choose metalevel principles for evaluating principles like distribution according to desert.

Read in this canonical way, the difference principle, far from competing with principles of desert, can support the idea that people deserve a chance. The difference principle supports principles of desert if Holmgren is correct to say the least advantaged want and need the chance to prosper by their own merit. Likewise, the difference principle supports principles of desert if it is historically true that the least advantaged tend to flourish within, and only within, systems in which honest hard work is respected and rewarded. Such a system may be the best that unskilled laborers could hope for: best for them as wage laborers, as consumers of what other workers produce, as parents who believe their children deserve a chance, and perhaps also as people who may one day need the kind of safety net (private or public insurance)

---

38. Holmgren (1986) 275.
39. Rawls (1971) 310.

that only a booming economy can afford. Rawlsians and non-Rawlsians alike can see these considerations as weighty.

Utility

Likewise, utilitarians and nonutilitarians alike can care about consequences. Feinberg says, "The awarding of prizes directly promotes cultivation of the skills which constitute bases of competition."[40] Rawls says, "Other things equal, one conception of justice is preferable to another when its broader consequences are more desirable."[41] So, both Feinberg and Rawls can correctly insist that utility is not a desert maker, while also recognizing that (a) things that are desert makers (effort, excellence) can as a matter of fact make people better off, and that (b) making people better off is morally significant. Rachels adds,

> In a system that respects deserts, someone who treats others well may expect to be treated well in return, while someone who treats others badly cannot. If this aspect of moral life were eliminated, morality would have no reward and immorality would have no bad consequences, so there would be less reason for one to be concerned with it.[42]

In short, our ordinary notions of desert serve a purpose. One (if only one) way a society benefits people is by distributing fruits of cooperation in proportion to contributions to the cooperative effort. That is how societies induce contributions to begin with. Desert as normally understood is part of the glue that holds society together as a productive venture. Respecting desert as normally understood (respecting the inputs people supply) makes people in general better off. To be sure, it would be a misuse of terms to say Bob deserves a pay raise on the grounds that giving him a raise would have utility. We may say Bob deserves a raise because he does great work, does more than his share, and does it without complaint. We do not say giving Bob a raise would have utility. But if we ask why we should acknowledge that Bob is a great worker, a big part of what makes Bob's efforts worthy of recognition is that his efforts are of a kind that make us all better off. If we ask why Bob is deserving, the answer should be: Bob supplied the requisite desert makers. If we ask why we *care* whether Bob supplied inputs that make a person deserving, one answer would be: supplying those inputs makes Bob the kind of person we want our neighbors, our children, and ourselves to be, and makes us all better off to boot.

The point need not be to maximize utility so much as to show respect for customs and institutions and characters that make people better off. (Either way, desert tracks constructive effort rather than effort per se. Effort-tokens need not be successful, but they do need to be of a type that tends to produce worthy results.) If we are to do justice to individual persons, then when their individuality manifests itself in

---

40. Feinberg (1970) 80.
41. Rawls (1971) 6.
42. Rachels (1997) 190.

constructive effort, we had better be prepared to honor that effort, and to respect the hopes and dreams that fuel it.

Need

When we say "She deserves a chance," how does that differ from saying she needs a chance? "Deserves" suggests she has some realized or potential merit in virtue of which she ought to be given a chance, whereas "needs" suggests neither real nor potential merit. However, when we say "*All* she needs is a chance," that comes close to saying she deserves a chance. It comes close to saying she is the kind of person who will give the opportunity its due.

Nonetheless, whatever room we make for desert, the fact remains that people's needs matter, at least at some level.[43] In fact, I would go so far as to say that desert matters partly because needs matter. That Bob needs X is no reason to say Bob deserves X for the same reason that X's utility is no reason to say Bob deserves X. And if that is true, then need is not a desert base. But there are other ways for need to be relevant.

Suppose, for simplicity's sake, that the only way to deserve X is to work hard for X. In that case, by hypothesis, need is not at all relevant to whether Bob deserves X. By hypothesis, all that matters is that Bob worked hard for X. Still, even though by hypothesis need has nothing to do with our reason for thinking Bob deserves X, need remains a reason for *caring* about desert. One reason to give people what they deserve is that it renders people willing and able to act in ways that help them (and the people around them) to get what they need. Welfare considerations are not desert bases, but they can still provide reasons for taking a given desert maker seriously (e.g., for respecting people who work hard).

Dignity

When wondering whether a person did justice to an opportunity, we typically do not look back to events that occurred before the opportunity was received. I indicated how we might argue for this on consequentialist grounds. It may be a good thing on Kantian grounds, too. Although I will not press the point, there is something necessarily and laudably ahistorical about simply respecting what people bring to the table. We respect their work, period. We admire their character, period. We do not argue (or worse, stipulate as dogma) that people are products of nature/nurture and thus ineligible for moral credit. Sometimes, we simply give people credit for what they achieve, and for what they are. And sometimes, simply giving people credit is the essence of treating them as persons rather than as mere confluences of historical forces.

Part of the oddity in doubting whether Jane deserves her character is that Jane's character is not something that happened to her. It *is* her. Or if we were to imagine treating Jane and her character as separate things, then it would have to be Jane's character that we credit for being of good character, so the question of why Jane

---

43. I am agreeing here with, among others, Brock (1999, 166).

per se should get the credit would be moot. In truth, of course, it is people, not their characters, that work hard. Thus, if we say exemplary character is morally arbitrary, it is people, not merely character, that we are refusing to take seriously.

Martin Luther King once said, "I have a dream that my four children will one day live in a nation where they will not be judged by the color of their skin but by the content of their character."[44] This was a dream worth living and dying for. King did not dream his children would live in a nation where their characters would be seen as accidents for which they could claim no credit. King asked us to judge his children by the content of their character, not by its causes. That was the right thing for King to ask, because that is how we take characters (that is, persons) seriously.

If the characters of King's children are not taken seriously, they will get neither the rewards nor the opportunities they deserve. Especially by the lights of Rawls's difference principle, this should matter, for the least advantaged can least afford the self-stifling cynicism that goes with believing no one deserves anything. Neither can they afford the license for repression that goes with the *more* advantaged believing no one deserves anything.

These remarks indicate that the possibility of deserving a chance is not mere common sense. In the end, the bottom line is in part a practical question, somewhat amenable to empirical testing: which way of talking—about what people can do to be deserving—empowers people to make use of their opportunities?

6. Desert as an Institutional Artifact

To Feinberg, "desert is a natural moral notion (that is, one which is not logically tied to institutions, practices, and rules)."[45] Rawls denies that desert is natural in this sense, but concedes the legitimacy of desert claims as institutional artifacts. Thus, faster runners deserve medals according to rules created for the express purpose of giving medals to faster runners. Those who

> have done what the system announces it will reward are entitled to have their expectations met. In this sense the more fortunate have title to their better situation; their claims are legitimate expectations established by social institutions and the community is obligated to fulfill them. But this sense of desert is that of entitlement. It presupposes the existence of an ongoing cooperative scheme.[46]

---

44. Martin Luther King, August 28, 1963, Washington D.C. See King (1986).

45. Feinberg (1970) 56.

46. Rawls (1999, 89). In the 1971 edition, the final sentence reads: "But this sense of desert presupposes the existence of an ongoing cooperative scheme " (1971, 103). So the explicit assimilation of desert to entitlement came later. However, the next paragraph of the 1999 edition makes a further change that goes in the opposite direction, as if unaware of the change to the previous paragraph. Rawls says in that next paragraph that we do not deserve our social endowments, or even our character, "for such character depends in good part upon fortunate family and social circumstances in early life for which we can claim no credit. The notion of desert does not apply here. To be sure, the more advantaged have a right to their natural assets, as does everyone else" (1999, 89). The last sentence is a new addition, separating desert, which does not apply, from entitlement, which evidently does.

The idea is that at some point we will be in a position to define, then acknowledge, claims of desert; but such claims (1) will have no standing outside the context of particular institutional rules, and therefore (2) cannot bear on what rules we should have in the first place.[47]

Other senses of desert, though, are less closely tied to institutional structures. A medalist who trains for years deserves admiration in a way a medalist who wins purely on the strength of genetic gifts does not, even when the two are equally deserving of medals by the lights of the institutional rules. Likewise, athletes prove themselves worthy of their families' and coaches' faith by doing all they can to win, and by being role models in the process, even when institutional rules are silent on the relevance of such inputs.

Consider this case. Canadian sprinter Ben Johnson ran the fastest time in the 100-meter race at the 1988 Olympics. Did he deserve a gold medal? He did nothing to show that he deserved his genetic gifts, or his competitive character, or the excellence of his coaches. All he did was run faster than the competition, which on its face entailed that he deserved gold.

However, blood tests revealed that Johnson had taken steroids. Did it matter? Yes. The fact that he took steroids raised questions of desert, whereas the bare fact that Johnson had a background (he had genes; he grew up in an environment) did not. Being born in the wake of the big bang did not stop Johnson from deserving a medal, but there is a real question about whether taking steroids preempts inputs by which sprinters come to deserve medals. We may ask whether steroids are in fact banned. That is an institutional question. We also may ask whether steroids should be banned. That question is preinstitutional: its answer (1) does not turn on particular institutional rules, and (2) does bear on what rules we should have in the first place.

As noted, Rawls says those who do what the system announces it will reward are entitled to have their expectations met. Rawls insists the status of such expectations is an institutional artifact. He is right in one way and wrong in another. On the one hand, it is an institutional artifact that the winner is entitled to gold rather than platinum. On the other hand, it is a preinstitutional moral fact that if the system promises a gold medal to the winner, then the system ought to give the winner a gold medal.

Notice that the system need not announce an obligation to keep promises. It has that obligation regardless. Therefore, while many of the factors that go into determining entitlements may be institutional artifacts, this one is not.

Obviously, some desert claims carry moral weight as institutional artifacts. (It makes sense for a winner to claim to deserve a platinum medal only if that is what the system has led the winner to expect.) However, some claims do not merely happen to carry weight as institutional artifacts. They *should* carry weight as institutional artifacts because they carry weight preinstitutionally. It is a matter of indifference whether the system promises the winner gold or platinum. It is not a matter of indifference whether the system encourages excellence rather than corruption or incompetence. We see winning sprinters as deserving when we see their excellence as a product of years of ferocious dedication. If instead we thought the key to winning

---

47. Rawls (1971) 103.

was more drugs, we would not regard winners as deserving. This difference is not an institutional artifact. We see the cases differently even when a performance-enhancing drug is allowed by the rules.

Part of our reason for caring is that the race's point is to show us how excellent a human being can be. If we explain success in terms of steroids rather than in terms of features of persons that ground desert claims in a preinstitutional sense, the institution is not working. If the competition inspires impressionable viewers to take steroids rather than to develop their talents, the institution is not working. If one way of competing risks competitors' lives and sets a dangerous example for children who idolize them, while a version that bans steroids is healthier for everyone, then we have preinstitutional grounds for thinking it was right to establish, publicize, and enforce the ban, and that my compatriot Ben Johnson did not deserve a medal.[48]

7. The Limits of Desert

As mentioned earlier, this essay's purpose is to offer a nonskeptical conception of desert for those who wish to make room in a philosophically respectable theory of justice for the idea that there are things we can do to be deserving. (To be sure, not everyone does wish to make room for this idea.) Specifically, it is possible for Jane to deserve an opportunity. And whether Jane deserved an opportunity can depend at least partly on what she did with it. *It is crucial that the scales be balanced. It is not crucial that components of the balance be supplied in a particular order.* If X is conferred first, and the desert base is supplied later, that, too, is a balancing of the moral scale.

The import of the promissory model's element (a) is that what once was morally arbitrary need not remain so. The most valuable things we are given in life are opportunities, and the main thing we do to deserve them is to do justice to them after the fact. The import of element (b) is that this theory has room for the common-sense idea that people can deserve a chance. They can deserve a chance not because of what they have done but because of what they can and will do, if only we give them a chance.

We need to keep these conclusions in perspective, though. It is a core feature of my overall theory of justice that what I call "deserving a chance" is not the whole of desert. Desert is not the whole of justice. Justice is not the whole of morality. This part of a larger theory tells us to treat opportunities as challenges and to respect those who meet their own challenges in fitting ways, but this part *does not answer all questions*. It does not say what Wilt Chamberlain should have been paid, or what opportunities Wilt should have had. It answers one question: What can Wilt or anyone blessed by good fortune do to be deserving? Its answer is: when we look back on Wilt's career, wondering whether he deserved his advantages, we are not restricted to considering what he did before receiving them. What matters, if anything matters, is what he did with them.

---

48. This conclusion does not presuppose the promissory model. The possibility of preinstitutional desert is manifest even within the compensatory framework.

So, did Wilt Chamberlain do justice to the potential given to him by luck of the draw in the natural lottery?[49] One possible answer is that whether he did justice to his potential is no one else's business. Wilt is not indebted to anyone for his natural assets. He did not borrow his talent from a common pool. No account is out of balance merely in virtue of Wilt having characteristics that make him Wilt. Still, even if it is no one else's business whether Wilt does justice to his potential, the fact remains that one way or another, Wilt will do, or fail to do, justice to it.

Part of our reason for thinking it is Wilt rather than you or me who deserves credit for the excellence of Wilt's performance is that, as David Miller puts it, "the performance is entirely his."[50] Note that the issue is not whether the performance is Wilt's rather than the big bang's; the issue is whether the performance is Wilt's rather than some other person's. The question of whether to credit Wilt for his performance is never a question of whether Wilt caused himself to have his character and talent. Instead, the question is whether the character, talent, or other desert-making inputs are, after all, Wilt's rather than some other person's.[51]

If and when we applaud Wilt's effort, we imply that the credit is due to Wilt rather than to, for example, me. Why? Not because Wilt deserved the effort (whatever that means) or deserved the effort more than I did (whatever that means) but because the effort was Wilt's rather than mine. When we ask whether the effort is truly Wilt's, the answer sometimes is simply yes. Other times, we credit Wilt's coaches or parents for performances that contributed to Wilt's in tangible ways.[52]

Notice that giving credit is not a zero-sum game. We do not think less of Wilt when Wilt thanks his parents. Indeed, we think less of Wilt if he fails to give credit where credit is due. The credit due to Wilt's parents takes away from credit due to Wilt only if the implication is that the performance we thought was Wilt's was not really his. (Imagine Wilt, in an acceptance speech for an academic award, naively thanking his coaches and parents for writing all those term papers.)

Partly because giving credit is not essentially a zero-sum game, desert is not essentially a comparative notion. In particular, the models of desert developed here make room not for honoring those with advantages as compared to those without, but for honoring people who do what they can to be deserving of their advantages. These elements of a larger theory of justice ask whether a person has supplied the requisite desert makers, not whether the person has done more than someone else has. There are cases like the following:

49. I thank Paul Dotson and Peter Dietsch for discussions about what is involved in having status as a person.

50. Miller (1999a) 144.

51. Beitz says, "While the distribution of natural talents is arbitrary in the sense that one cannot deserve to be born with the capacity, say, to play like Rubinstein, it does not obviously follow that the possession of such a talent needs any justification. On the contrary, simply having a talent seems to furnish prima facie warrant for making use of it in ways that are, for the possessor, possible and desirable. A person need not justify the possession of talents, despite the fact that one cannot be said to deserve them, because they are already one's own: the prima facie right to use and control talents is fixed by natural fact" (1979, 138).

52. In this way, when we get to the bottom of desert, it turns out to presuppose a rudimentary conception of entitlement, or at least possession. We must have a sense of when a talent is mine and not Wilt's.

(a) Wilt Chamberlain has X and you have Y,
(b) Wilt did something to deserve X while you did something to deserve Y,
(c) X is more than Y, and yet (so far as desert is concerned),
(d) there is nothing wrong with X being more than Y, despite the fact that Wilt does not deserve "more than you" *under that description.*

In other words, the question about Wilt is not whether Wilt did something to deserve *more than you,* but whether Wilt did something to deserve *what he has.* Perhaps there was never a time when an impartial judge, weighing your performance against Wilt's, had reason to conclude that Wilt's prize should be larger than yours. All that happened is that Wilt did justice to his opportunity and you did justice to yours. Should we focus on the relation, or imagine there is one, between you and Wilt? Or should we focus on a pair of relations, one between what Wilt did and what Wilt has, and another between what you did and what you have? Perhaps neither focus captures the whole truth about justice, but the second focus (that is, on the pair of relations) is a focus on desert, where the first is a focus on something else, something more comparative, such as equality.

A central distributor, intending to distribute according to desert, would need to judge relative deserts and then distribute accordingly. Without a central distributor, the situation is different. If Wilt worked hard for his salary of X, while you worked hard for your salary of Y, there is something fitting in Wilt getting X and you getting Y. You each supplied desert-making inputs connecting you to your respective salaries. It might be impossible for a central distributor to justify judging that Wilt deserves so much more than you, but by hypothesis there was no such judgment.

Needless to say, Wilt deserves no credit for the economic system that attaches a given salary to his performance. On the other hand, he does not need to deserve credit for the system. He claims credit only for his performance. If it is Wilt rather than you who deserves credit for Wilt's performance, then it is Wilt rather than you who has a presumptive claim to the salary that the system (or more accurately, Wilt's employer) attaches to Wilt's performance.

You may doubt Wilt's profession should be paid so much more than yours, not because you think people in top professions are undeserving, but because you think there is a presumption against that much inequality.[53] You may think no amount of desert could be enough to overturn that presumption. You may be right. It would have to be argued within the context of a theory of equality, which reminds us that, as just noted, there is more to justice than desert, and more to desert than deserving a chance.

Our reasons to respect desert as normally understood also are reasons to respect desert's limits as normally understood. In particular, there are limits to what a society can do, and limits to what society can expect its citizens to do, to ensure that people get what they deserve. Thus, even something as fundamental as the principle that people should get what they deserve has limits.

---

53. Olsaretti (2004, 166–68) says theories of desert cannot easily justify inequality. She is right, not because theories of desert *fail* in their attempt to justify inequality, but because justifying inequality per se does not fall within their purview. Principles of equality may presuppose that inequality needs justifying, but principles of desert do not.

A just system works to minimize the extent to which people's entitlements fly in the face of what they deserve, but not at a cost of compromising people's ability to form stable expectations regarding their entitlements, and thus to get on with their lives in peaceful and productive ways. The point goes both ways, though, for desert in turn corrects the caprices of rightful entitlements, and that, too, is a good thing. For example, a proprietor may know her employee is entitled to a certain wage while also seeing that the employee is exceptionally productive and (in both promissory and compensatory senses) deserves a raise. If she cares enough about desert, she restructures her holdings (her payroll) accordingly, benefiting not only the employee but probably her company and her customers as well.

Think of the contrast this way: principles of entitlement acknowledge our status as *separate* agents. Principles of desert acknowledge our status as *active* agents.

A society cannot work without a "rule of law" system that secures people's savings and earnings, thereby enabling people to plan their lives.[54] Neither can a rule of law function properly in the absence of an ethos that deeply respects what people can do to be deserving.[55] Part of our job as moral agents is to do justice to opportunities embedded in our entitlements. It is in meeting that challenge that we make entitlement systems work.

This essay revises David Schmidtz, "How to Deserve," *Political Theory* 30 (2002): 774–99. Reprinted by permission of Sage Publications.

---

54. Waldron (1989).

55. What determines whether a given salary is a fitting response to desert-making inputs we supply? In the abstract, a theory of desert cannot say. Salaries are artifacts of systems of entitlement, and systems of entitlement are not pure responses to facts about what workers deserve. They also respond to notions of reciprocity, equality, and need, and to all kinds of factors (supply and demand) not directly related to matters of justice. Thus, the going rate for a type of work will not be determined by what a particular worker deserves, although whether a worker deserves to be paid the going rate will depend on whether she does something (supplies the expected desert-making inputs) to deserve it.

Some notions of desert are defensible by virtue of encouraging us to respect mutually advantageous systems of entitlement. Some notions of entitlement are defensible by virtue of empowering us to do something to deserve such opportunities as come our way. Which notion is more foundational? Out of context, there is no truth of the matter. In the context of aiming to justify a notion of desert, we must treat something else as foundational, if only for argument's sake. Likewise with entitlement. What we aim to justify defines the context and determines what can and what cannot be treated as foundational.

7

Moral Dualism

Chapter 4 argues that reflectively rational beings have reasons to be other-regarding and to have integrity. If the conclusion is true, does that answer the question "Why be moral"? It depends on whether having integrity and having concern and respect for others are ways of being moral. Common sense says they are, which counts for something, but (and this, too, is common sense) common sense is not infallible. This essay offers a theoretical framework for sorting out what parts of common sense morality warrant endorsement as genuinely moral.

1. The Formal Structure of a Moral Theory

My approach to moral theory begins by borrowing from H. L. A. Hart. Hart's legal theory distinguishes between primary and secondary legal rules.[1] Primary rules make up what we normally think of as the law. They define our legal rights and obligations. Secondary rules, especially *rules of recognition*, are rules we use to identify primary rules, that is, to determine what the law is. For example, among the primary rules in my neighborhood is a law saying the speed limit is 30 miles per hour. The secondary rule by which we recognize the speed limit is "Read the signs." Exceeding speed limits is illegal, but there is no further law obliging us to read signs that post the speed limit. So long as I stay within the speed limit, the police do not worry about whether I read the signs. In reading the signs, we follow a secondary rule, not a primary rule.

The central project in modern ethics (even more central than the "Why be moral?" issue) is to formulate a rule of recognition for morals. Utilitarianism's recognition rule is the principle of utility: X is moral if and only if X maximizes utility. The principle defines a family of moral theories rather than any particular member thereof. Replacing X with a specific subject matter produces different flavors of utilitarianism. Act-utilitarianism applies the principle of utility to actions. Act-utilitarianism's fully

---

1. Hart (1961) 89–93.

specified recognition rule—an act is right if and only if it maximizes utility—then translates directly into act-utilitarianism's single rule of conduct: maximize utility. Rule-utilitarianism applies the principle of utility to sets of action-guiding rules. The resulting recognition rule states that an action guide is moral if and only if following it has more utility than would following any alternative action guide.

Recognition rules are not ultimate rules of conduct; primary rules are not mere rules of thumb. Primary rules do not defer to the "ultimate" rules in cases of conflict. Again, consider the legal analogy. "Read the signs" may be the rule by which we recognize rules of the road, but if we found ourselves in a situation where obeying a speed limit would somehow prevent us from reading a traffic sign, that would not be enough to make the speed limit give way. It would not even begin to make the speed limit give way. The highway patrol judges our conduct by the rules of the road, and would be properly unimpressed if we said we violated the rules of the road out of commitment to a "higher law" bidding us to read the signs. Accordingly, the utility-maximizing set of primary rules *might* boil down to a single rule of conduct saying "Maximize utility." Then again, it might not. The general point: the action-guiding imperative, not the rule of recognition, is what guides action.

A moral *theory* consists of a recognition rule applied to a particular subject matter. Given a subject matter, a rule of recognition for morals specifies grounds for regarding items of that kind as moral. By "grounds" I do not mean necessary and sufficient conditions. In act-utilitarianism, the principle of utility presents itself as necessary and sufficient for an act's morality, but trying to contrive necessary and sufficient conditions is not the only way (and I think not the best way) to do moral theory. To have a recognition rule, all we need is what I call a *supporting* condition.

A *supporting condition* is a qualified sufficient condition, qualified in the sense of being a sufficient basis for endorsement in the absence of countervailing conditions. In different words, a supporting condition is sufficient to shift the burden of proof. (Analogously, in a court of law, certain kinds of evidence suffice, barring countervailing evidence, to establish legal liability.) Formulating recognition rules in terms of supporting conditions rather than attempting to specify necessary and sufficient conditions is one way of acknowledging intuitionist claims that we could never fully articulate all of the considerations relevant to moral judgment. We can allow for that possibility (without letting it stop us from doing moral theory) by formulating recognition rules in terms of supporting conditions—conditions sufficient to shift the burden of proof without ruling out the possibility of the burden being shifted back again, perhaps by considerations we have yet to articulate.

As an example of a supporting condition, we might say, along the lines of act-utilitarianism, that an act is right if it maximizes utility, barring countervailing conditions. In two ways, act-utilitarianism properly so-called goes beyond merely offering a supporting condition. First, it denies that there are countervailing conditions, thereby representing the principle of utility as a proper sufficient condition, not just a supporting condition. Second, act-utilitarianism says an act is right only if it maximizes utility, thereby representing the principle of utility not only as sufficient but also as necessary for an act's morality.

I do not think we will ever have a complete analysis of morality, any more than we will ever have a complete analysis of knowledge. We use such terms in a variety of related ways, and there is no single principle or any biconditional analysis to which our varying uses can all be reduced.² This is not an admission of defeat, though, for the important thing is not to find the one true principle but rather to look for principles that can form a backbone for a useful rule of recognition. Three points are worth highlighting, as follows.

(1) *A moral theory can range over more than one subject matter.* We devise moral theories to help us answer questions raised by the subject of individual choice and action, of course. Yet, we may also want to assess personal character.³ Or we may want to assess the morality of institutional frameworks within which people choose and act and develop their characters. These are distinct subject matters. So, different moral theories range over different subject matters. Also, a given theory may be monistic, ranging over only one, while ignoring or trying to reduce others, but pluralistic theories (pluralistic in virtue of ranging over more than one subject matter) are a real option.

(2) *A moral theory can incorporate more than one recognition rule.* There is nothing in the nature of morality to indicate that we should aim to answer all questions with a *single* recognition rule, because nothing in the nature of recognition rules suggests there cannot be more than one. Modern ethical inquiry is often interpreted (perhaps less often today than a few years ago) as a search for a single-stranded theory, that is, a single rule of recognition applied to a single subject matter, usually the subject of what moral agents ought to do.⁴ Perhaps Kant and Mill intended to promulgate single-stranded theories; friends and foes alike often take them to have done so. In any case, when interpreted this way, their theories can capture no more than a fragment of the truth.

The truth is that morality is more than one thing. A theory will not give us an accurate picture of morality unless it reflects the fact that morality has more than one strand. Thus, I would not try to derive all of morality from a single recognition rule.

---

2. Note that when scientists theorize, they are not trying to identify necessary and sufficient conditions. Instead, they seek general and illuminating explanations. Philosophical theorizing, insofar as it aims at specifying necessary and sufficient conditions, does not work by its own lights. I call it a folk theorem of analytic philosophy that all such theories have counterexamples. I also have heard philosophers say all scientific theories turn out to be false. A depressing thought, in a way, but here is a different perspective. A scientific theory aims to give people a different perspective: a map that improves on existing maps of the world by virtue of being more illuminating and less misleading. A map such as Newton's was a revelation for a given technological stage, but a time comes when such a theory no longer provides sufficiently accurate answers to some of our changing questions. For most purposes, I would not call Newton's theory false, because for most purposes, that would be neither the most illuminating nor least misleading way of understanding scientific progress. Chapter 7 summarizes some of the material in Schmidtz (2006) on the nature of moral theory.

3. Stocker says, "good people appreciate the moral world in ways which go beyond simply seeing what is to be done" (1990, 114).

4. I realize philosophers sometimes try too hard to distinguish themselves from their predecessors, leading them to caricaturize the history of philosophy as monolithically moving in a direction different from the one they themselves propose. I do think the convention within modern philosophy has until recently been to assume that the correct moral theory will be single-stranded, but I say this without meaning to slight moral philosophy's venerable pluralist tradition.

I once began an essay by noting that utilitarianism (which says rightness is determined by consequences) and deontology (which says it isn't) both express powerful insights into the nature of morality. "Doing as much good as one can is surely right. On the other hand, keeping promises is also right, sometimes even in cases where breaking them has better consequences."[5] The essay concluded on a grim note. "We have intuitions about morality that seem essentially embedded in theories that contradict each other. Something has to give."[6] This dilemma stumped me at the time, but I now realize that what can and should give is the assumption that morality is single-stranded. When we come to despair of finding the single property shared by all things moral, we can stop looking for essence and start looking for family resemblance. By abandoning the search for a single-stranded moral theory, we put ourselves in a position to notice that whether rightness is determined solely by consequences might depend on the subject matter.

(3) *A moral theory can be structurally open-ended*. Utilitarianism and deontology, or single-stranded interpretations thereof, purport to capture the whole truth about morality. By the lights of either theory, the other theory is a rival competing for the same turf. The theories are closed systems in the sense that, having incorporated one recognition rule, and claiming to capture the whole of morality with it, they have no room for others.

By contrast, from a more natural even if somewhat unconventional perspective, morality is an open-ended series of structurally parallel strands, each with its own recognition rule, each contributing different threads of morality's action guide. Any particular recognition rule has a naturally limited range, applying only to its own subject matter. No particular recognition rule pretends to capture the whole of morality, and so verifying that they do not do so does not refute the theory.

One might think we ought to look for the single recognition rule underlying all of morality, on the grounds that a theory with more than one recognition rule would violate the principle of parsimony. But such an objection oversimplifies the principle of parsimony. The question is not whether a theory is simpler in the beginning, but whether it is simpler in the end. Gracefully admitting the real complexity of morality at the outset can make for a simpler theory in the end. Thus, when astronomers stopped insisting that planetary orbits were circular, having only one focal point, and accepted the reality of elliptical orbits, which have two focal points, their theories became simpler, more elegant, and more powerful.

On my theory, morality has at least two focal points, maybe more than two. One part of morality focuses on *personal goals*, while a second part focuses on *institutional structures* that regulate the pursuit of personal goals in a social setting. The theory's two parts—I will call them strands—map a respectable portion of the terrain of morality.[7] They may not map all of it, but the theory has an open-ended structure so as to allow for that possibility. The two strands do not exclude each other. Neither

---

5. Schmidtz (1990b) 622.

6. Schmidtz (1990b) 627.

7. A good map, like a good theory, accurately represents the subject's most important general features. It does not try to capture fine details. See pt. 1 of Schmidtz (2006).

do they preclude the introduction of further strands: gaps in the theory can be filled by adding further recognition rules or further subject matters as necessary.

Or, we may take the lesson of the history of moral philosophy, and its endless dance of counterexamples, to be this: some of the knowledge on which moral judgment is based is *inevitably* tacit and could never be fully articulated. Even so, this need not stop us from pushing the articulation of morality's recognition rules as far as we can, acknowledging the inevitably tacit residue by allowing that the theory's recognition rules admit of countervailing conditions.

2. The Substance of Moral Dualism

I discussed the formal structure of a multistranded, open-ended moral theory. Here is one way of fleshing out the substance of such a theory. The theory depicted by figure 7.1 says a goal is moral if pursuing it is individually rational, whereas a constraint is moral if operating within it is collectively rational. Putting the two strands together, to be moral is to pursue individually rational goals within collectively rational constraints.

This is roughly the theory with which I began. I was not satisfied. More than once, I changed my mind about how the subject matters and recognition rules should be defined. I was not always sure why I was changing my mind, either. What should we expect of a theory? To what questions is a moral theory supposed to give answers?

Looking at the activity of theorizing itself, it appears to me that, as with other intellectual endeavors, we need some sense of a subject matter and of questions to which it gives rise before we can have any reason to devise theories about it. Long before we begin to formulate moral theories, we already classify certain issues as moral issues. Roughly speaking, when an issue is crucial to human flourishing in communities, and when human beings can make a difference regarding that issue, we tend to see it as raising moral questions, and thus as a subject calling for moral theory. In this sense, the subject matters of moral inquiry are (at least provisionally) a pretheoretical given.[8]

	Personal strand	Interpersonal strand
Generic recognition rule	Is X individually rational?	Is Y collectively rational?
Subject matter	X = personal goals	Y = interpersonal constraints
Fully specified recognition rule	A goal is moral if pursuing it is individually rational (subject to countervailing conditions)	A constraint is moral if pursuing goals within it is collectively rational (subject to countervailing conditions)

FIGURE 7.1. A multistranded moral theory.

---

8. Partly for this reason, I think a method of seeking "reflective equilibrium" is practically unavoidable in moral theorizing. I do not think of seeking reflective equilibrium as a metaprinciple or a moral theory or even a formal philosophical method, really. I think of it simply as a matter of remaining responsive

Accordingly, in constructing a moral theory, I wanted to apply recognition rules only to subjects that make us feel a need for moral theory in the first place. I began with the general idea of assessing the morality of personal goals (What goals should we pursue?) and interpersonal constraints (How should the interests of others constrain our pursuits?). My search for recognition rules for those two subject matters was guided by objectives not easily reconciled. A recognition rule must home in on a property with normative force, one that constitutes reason for endorsement. To complicate matters, the property's normative force must be independent of morality.[9] It must give us reasons for endorsement of an ordinary kind, ordinary in the sense of appealing to interests and desires. (If we said we recognize X as moral in virtue of its having the property of being moral, that would be circular. Our method of recognizing what is moral must not presuppose that we already recognize what is moral.) On the other hand, morality is, after all, what a recognition rule is supposed to be recognizing. The rule has to be a basis for endorsing something *as moral*, despite having a normative force that is not essentially moral.

By that standard, individual rationality fails to make the grade. However, we can reformulate the personal strand's recognition rule in terms of reflective rationality. As discussed in chapter 3, what I call reflective rationality is a standard means-end conception of rationality informed by a certain psychological profile. For Kate to be reflectively rational is for Kate to understand that the robustness of her self-regard is a variable. Indeed, it is a key variable in her preference function. Accordingly, Kate rationally takes steps to develop and enhance a healthy self-regard. Principally, she takes steps to give her life instrumental value, and one of the best ways of doing that is to make herself valuable to others, to be a force for good in her community, and to be esteemed by others. This strand of morality, personal morality, involves having something and *being* something worth living for. In short, a reflectively rational person asks not "What do I want to get?" so much as "What do I want to be?" The former does not wear moral significance on its sleeve; the latter does.

Second, we can contract the personal strand's subject matter, using its recognition rule to assess personal goals only in terms of their self-regarding effects. Some theorists would say that questions about how we treat others and how we treat ourselves, respectively, define the separate domains of morality and prudence. The distinction cannot be so simple, though, for matters of prudence often evoke reactions that have the character of moral judgment. It is an ancient and I think correct view that there are matters of right and wrong involved in how we treat ourselves. People sometimes say "You owe it to yourself to take better care of yourself," and when people say such things, they usually mean it literally. One may not violate anyone's

---

to that which is pretheoretical. In the context of a given subject matter, we assess candidate action guides (for example) by the light of our recognition rules. In turn, though, we assess our recognition rules by asking whether the action guides they yield are plausibly responsive to what pretheoretically seems important about that particular subject matter. I thank Thomas Pogge for discussions of this point.

9. Because collective rationality, for example, is not an essentially moral concept, it can provide a *fundamental justification* within the realm of morality and thus can form the backbone of a useful recognition rule for morals, whereas essentially moral concepts like justice, for example, cannot. (The term "fundamental justification" is from Morris [1988] and refers to justification within a domain by reference to standards independent of that domain.)

rights in the process of becoming addicted to crack cocaine, but one does waste a life. There is something wrong with wasting a life, even if the life wasted is one's own.[10]

The moral significance of things we do to ourselves sometimes is obscured by a persistence in the social sciences of an oversimplified conception of self-regard. There are at least two kinds of self-regard. For example, professional athletes sometimes play for pride, sometimes for money. In abstraction, playing for money is neither moral nor immoral. It all depends on how a person goes about it. Playing for pride, though—pushing oneself in pursuit of excellence rather than money—is a matter of character. We recognize a difference between using one's talents in a purely instrumental way and wanting to make the most of one's talents and opportunities—wanting not to waste them—as a matter of self-respect, a matter of integrity.

So, a test question: is being a mugger a moral way of making the most of one's talents? The answer is that this is not the right question. To capture the core reason why we cannot endorse being a mugger, we need to talk about how it affects others. If we argued that being a mugger is not reflectively rational, even if the argument was sound, we would be getting the right answer for the wrong reason. To be sure, being a mugger would not shape one's character in a reflectively rational way, but the core of what makes it wrong to be a mugger is not that wise men would find it unfulfilling, but that it violates interpersonal constraints. For that reason, we are well advised to apply reflective rationality only to the subject of how our pursuits affect ourselves. Aside from obligations to others that derive from obligations to ourselves, the subject of how we ought to treat others is something we leave for the interpersonal strand. (It is not always true, though, that a person morally ought to abide by morally justified constraints. See section 7.)

The final changes to the simple theory with which I started concern the interpersonal strand. Institutions affect human behavior, and their effect on human behavior is subject to moral assessment. If an institution makes people in general worse off, that is a decisive reason to reject it. If it makes people in general better off, that need not be a decisive reason to accept it, because there might be countervailing conditions. But although making people in general better off may not be decisive, few would deny that it is presumptively moral for an institution to make people in general better off. An interpersonal constraint is a moral constraint if it works through social structure in such a way as to serve the common good.

3. From the Concept to a Conception of the Common Good

I proposed that it is moral for an institution to serve the common good. Before we go farther, consider how mild a proposal this is. The proposal is not that serving the

---

10. In passing, my sense is that there are theorists who reject the neo-Aristotelian view that we have any duties to ourselves. There also are theorists who reject the neo-Lockean view that we are self-owners. Moreover, theorists who reject the latter view also tend to reject the former. This may not be a coherent combination, though, for if we are not self-owners but are instead owned by, say, the People, then what we do to ourselves is not a purely self-regarding matter, and therefore ought to be as much a moral question as what we do to anyone else.

common good is necessary for institutional morality. Neither would I propose it as a sufficient condition. Instead, the idea of serving the common good enters this theory as a supporting condition, a reason for concluding that an institution is moral, barring countervailing conditions. With that caveat, let us make the principle more precise.

Suppose we know that an institution makes literally everyone better off. That typically would be solid ground for saying it serves the common good and thus is presumptively moral. The trouble is that few if any institutions could pass that test. Insofar as we seek to make distinctions—to have grounds for endorsing some real-world institutions but not others—we need to look for something that provides broader, even if weaker, support.

As an alternative, suppose we know that an institution is making at least half the people it affects better off. Is that any reason to think of it as serving the common good? In fact, we would need information about what is happening to those who are not better off before we have any reason at all to see the institution as serving the common good. The principle is too weak.

Suppose we say, then, that an institution is moral if it makes over half of the people it affects better off and no one worse off.[11] (Perhaps some people are affected in some way but not in a way that makes them determinably better or worse off.) Although this principle gives us a genuine basis for endorsement, as far as it goes, it might be too restrictive. An institution (that makes most people better off) might be recognizably moral even though someone somewhere is worse off in some respect. For example, a pattern of generally improving opportunities for workers might be to a capitalist's disadvantage, insofar as it forces her to raise wages at her factory, but somehow this seems irrelevant to the morality of an institution that generally improves opportunities for workers.

To accommodate this possibility without opening the door to worsenings of all kinds, suppose we call it moral for an institution to make over half the people it affects better off, provided either that it makes no one worse off or else that the process by which it makes a few people worse off is *nonexploitative*. It seems consistent with serving the common good that a few are made worse off. However, if the institution makes the minority worse off as a *method* of making the majority better off, then the institution cannot without torturing the language be said to serve the common good.

So far, as defined here, an exploitative institution makes some worse off as a method of making others better off. However, when an institution empowers us to disarm would-be muggers, its purpose is to make muggers worse off as a method of making others better off. Do we want to say disarming muggers is a form of exploitation? No. Thus, a final refinement: an exploitative institution uses its targets as a resource. More concretely, exploitation makes some better off in virtue of the *existence* of targets. By contrast, disarming muggers does not make some better off in virtue of the existence of muggers, and therefore is not a form of exploitation.

---

11. One institutional arrangement is *Pareto-superior* to an alternative if it would make at least one person better off and no one worse off. I think we would have grounds for endorsing an institution that makes one person better off and no one worse off, but not for saying it serves the common good. The basis for endorsement discussed in the accompanying text is a strengthened version of Pareto-superiority, one that strikes me as more in keeping with the idea of serving the common good.

As a necessary condition for the morality of institutions, a prohibition of exploitation could be controversial. Why? Because if an institution does enough good for enough people, some people will want to endorse the institution as moral whether or not it is exploitative. (Consider a progressive tax system intended to make a majority better off at a minority's expense.) But the clause excluding exploitative methods does not function as a necessary condition for institutional morality; it functions as one part of a supporting condition. Making half the people better off becomes a reason for endorsement only in conjunction with a presumption that no one is made worse off, or more specifically that no one is worse off in virtue of being used as a resource.

When I proposed that an institution is moral if it makes over half the people it affects better off, the point of saying "over half" was to give the recognition rule an air of precision. We should reconsider that now, because, after all, such precision is artificial. To say "over half" is to impose a peculiar cutoff on our grounds for endorsement—peculiar because any precise cutoff whatsoever would be peculiar. Our grounds for moral endorsement are in fact not so precise, and are not subject to arbitrary cutoffs. For an institution to serve the common good is for it to make people in general better off, and there is no number that can appropriately be substituted for the notion of people in general, such that 51 percent means people in general but 49 percent does not. If making 51 percent better off gives us reason to endorse an institution, then making 49 percent better off usually will give us similar reason to endorse it.

Instead of there being a sharp separation between our having reason to endorse an institution and our not having reason to endorse it, there is a continuum. At one end, an institution benefits no one, and there is little reason to endorse it; at the other extreme, an institution benefits everyone, and there is little reason not to endorse it. As we move toward the latter extreme, we encounter institutions that make more and more people better off and that we have increasing reason to recognize as making people in general better off. A theory that pretends to give us a precise cutoff (between institutions that are recognizably moral and those that are not) is, in most cases, merely pretending. When a theory answers our questions about the morality of real world institutions by presenting us with spuriously precise cutoffs, it fails to take our questions seriously.[12]

This is not to deny that before we can say whether institutions make people better off, we need to know what counts as evidence that people are better off. Better off compared to what? What is the baseline? Should we say institutions serve the common good if people are better off than they would be in a hypothetical state of nature?

My suggestion is to look at how we answer such questions in the real world. No one begins by trying to imagine a hypothetical baseline array of institutions. It is

---

12. The objection here is to building precise cutoffs into recognition rules for moral institutions. I have no such objection to institutions themselves imposing arbitrary cutoffs that mark, for example, sixteen years as the age when it becomes legal to drive a car. In that case, the arbitrarily precise legal cutoff is subject to moral assessment, and might be recognizably moral (e.g., it might serve the common good) despite being somewhat arbitrary.

easier and more relevant to ask how particular institutions change actual lives. Does a given institution solve a real problem? It is no easy task to say whether a particular institution solves a real problem, thereby affecting people in a positive way. Nevertheless, we do it all the time. We have sophisticated ways of assessing whether rent controls or agricultural price support programs, for example, make people in general better off. We do not need to posit arbitrary baselines, either. It is enough to look at people's prospects before and after an institution's emergence, to compare communities with the institution to communities without it, and so on. These comparisons, and others like them, give us baselines, and such baselines are not arbitrary.[13]

In assessing institutions, we use any information we happen to have. Evidence that an institution is making people better off could come in the form of information that people who come in contact with the institution have higher life expectancies or higher average incomes, for example. No such measure would be plausible as an analysis of what it *means* to make people better off. But such measures are the kind of information we actually have. Therefore, such measures are the kind of information on which we base our decisions about whether to regard an institution as moral. More specific indices are surrogates for the idea of making people better off. Or, if you like, they are part of the common good's ostensive definition, in the sense that one way to make people better off, other things equal, is to increase their life expectancy; another way is to increase their income; and so on. (In case it does not go without saying, we need not require of a moral institution that its range of beneficial influence be universal, but the constraint against exploitation *is* universal. A nation can be moral in virtue of making citizens better off, but not if it exploits noncitizens in the process. A hospital can be moral in virtue of making patients and staff better off, but not if it serves patients by occasionally kidnapping visitors for use as unwilling organ donors.)

There is no obstacle to reformulating my proposed recognition rule by substituting more precisely defined evaluative criteria (like measuring impact on general welfare by looking at changes in median income), except that we would be in danger of confusing a measurement with the thing being measured. The substitution would invite gratuitous counterexamples, showing that institutions could satisfy such criteria without making people in general better off or that institutions might satisfy such criteria by exploitative methods. The idea of making people generally better off (without exploitation), imprecise though the idea may be, represents the true bottom line in our thinking about moral institutions. It is fine to gather information about changes in median income as a way of measuring whether people are better off, so long as we understand that median income is an imperfect measurement, morally important only insofar as it indicates that people in general are indeed better off. If we learn that, while median income rose, incomes well above the median did not rise

---

13. That is, we look at how institution X functions in its actual context, which means we take the rest of the institutional context as given. We have good reason to use this baseline not only because it tends to be the one baseline regarding which we have actual data but also because it is the baseline with respect to which institution X's functioning is of immediate practical significance. By this method, we can evaluate each part of the institutional array in turn. If (for some reason) we wanted to evaluate everything at once, we would need some other method.

and incomes below the median actually fell,[14] then we stop seeing evidence of rising median income as evidence that people in general are better off.

This section proposed that serving the common good, as the basis for a recognition rule for moral institutions, could be understood as making people in general better off without exploitation. One might feel that this proposal sets too low a standard, and that we should settle for nothing less than institutions that make literally everyone better off. Not so. To make people better off at all, we sometimes have to settle for institutions that make people better off in general. If the government said organ transplants were forbidden until hospitals become able to meet all demands for organ transplants, our prospects would be worse, not better.

Conversely, one might think the caveat on exploitation sets too high a standard, or perhaps the wrong kind of standard. If we truly want people to be better off, we should at least in principle accept exploitative methods of making people better off.

This might be plausible if we were talking about a subject matter other than institutions. It is a familiar idea that no prohibition of exploitation is built into the concept of utility maximization. Indeed, exploitation may well be utility maximizing in particular cases, thus commanding endorsement on act-utilitarian grounds. But exploitative *institutions* are not like exploitative *acts*. Exploitative institutions, like exploitative acts, can have utility in isolated cases, but an institution is not an isolated event. An institution's effect is a cumulative matter. Whether an institution makes people better off depends not on how it functions on one unusual day but on how it functions over its life span. Good results on one unusual day are not the test of an institution. The relevant concern is that, over time, an exploitative institution's overall record is increasingly likely to reflect exploitation's tendency toward bad results.

If an institution that gives its officers a license to exploit could be trusted to employ officers who use such methods only in unusual cases where the benefits would be great and widespread, the situation would be different. Indeed, we might say such institutions are moral after all. Exploitative institutions are costly in a general, ongoing way, though, and their costs tend to rise over time. Institutional power may be used for good, but, the fact remains that people who successfully compete for licenses to exploit will use such licenses for whatever purposes, good or bad, those people happen to have. When we institutionalize the power to pursue ends by exploitative means, we create a power that invites abuse. And inviting such abuse has a robust history of making people in general worse off, not better off.

Indeed, limiting opportunities for exploitation is a primary method by which institutions make people in general better off. Therefore, when a conception of serving the common good joins the idea of making people better off to the idea of operating by nonexploitative methods, the prohibition of exploitation is not merely a bit of deontology arbitrarily grafted onto the theory so as to save it from the worst excesses of utilitarianism. On the contrary, we are talking about institutions, and in that special context, a restriction against exploitation naturally follows from a consideration of how institutions make people better off. Thus, hard-core utilitarians should find that, when they apply the principle of utility to the subject matter of institutions, they can *derive* the same restriction on exploitation that is built into my conception of serving the common good. A constraint against exploitation is not derivable from principles of utility as such, but is derivable from principles of utility *applied to the subject of institutional structure*.

---

14. Suppose the range of incomes in a three-person economy goes from (5, 11, 14) to (3, 12, 14).

As an example of a legal structure that makes people better off by limiting opportunities for exploitation, consider constitutional limits on the scope of democratic decision-making. Unrestrained democracy pits shifting majorities against shifting minorities in ways that make shifting majorities better off. But this need not and often would not make most people better off. You could have a situation where every democratic *move* makes as many as two out of three people better off, even though every *pair* of moves makes as many as two out of three people worse off.[15] People tend to be better off when means of isolating minorities for ad hoc exploitation are unavailable.

Had I been trying to formulate a *necessary* condition for institutional morality, I would have been under more pressure to try to force convergence on a single conception of the general concept of serving the common good. But the idea of a supporting condition leaves room for the existence of families of conceptions each member of which provides a related kind of support for moral endorsement. For example, readers can interpret serving the common good in terms of universal benefit, maximum aggregate utility, or Pareto-superiority, or in terms of some precisely quantified statistical version (denominated in terms of life expectancy, for example) of the idea of making most people better off.

4. The Substance of Moral Dualism

The substance of *moral dualism* is that our question about what serves as a recognition rule for morals has at least two answers (see fig. 7.2). One answer is that

	Personal strand	Interpersonal strand
Generic recognition rule	Is X reflectively rational?	Is Y collectively rational?
Subject matter	X = goals, in terms of how their pursuit affects the agent's character	Y = constraints on conduct as embedded in social structure
Fully specified recognition rule	A goal is moral if pursuing it helps the agent to develop in a reflectively rational way (subject to countervailing conditions)	A constraint on conduct is moral if it works through social structure in a collectively rational way (subject to countervailing conditions)

FIGURE 7.2. Moral dualism's two strands.

15. Proof: let A, B, and C represent individual voters or classes of voters. Suppose A and B vote in favor of a measure that leaves each of them $1 richer and C $2 poorer. Then A and C vote in favor of a measure that leaves A and C each $1 richer and B $2 poorer. The pair of majority votes leaves B and C poorer and A richer. (And when we factor in things like lobbying costs, the zero-sum game becomes negative-sum.) Each vote made two out of three voters (or classes of voters) better off, but the pair of votes made two out of three worse off. Moreover, if A has the power to set the agenda for this voting mechanism, the outcome described here is just what we should expect. It would be a matter of routine.

structurally embedded constraints on personal conduct warrant endorsement if they are collectively rational, in the sense of making people in general better off by non-exploitative means. Another answer is that personal conduct warrants endorsement in terms of its self-regarding effects if it is reflectively rational, in the sense of helping the agent to develop and sustain a psychologically healthy character along lines discussed in chapter 4. There may be other answers, too.

One recognition rule says that, barring countervailing conditions, X is moral if it is reflectively rational. The other recognition rule says that, barring countervailing conditions, Y is moral if it is collectively rational. The former rule applies to *internal* effects—how agents affect themselves. The latter rule applies to structurally embedded constraints within which agents choose and act. It concentrates on *external* effects—how agents affect others. One strand focuses on matters of character, the other on how constraints function when externally imposed on people by formal and informal social structures. The interpersonal strand ranges over social structure in general, including all of the cultural, commercial, religious, political, legal, familial, and fraternal institutions and descriptive norms that affect how people deal with each other.

Applying these generic rules to their respective subject matters yields two fully specified rules of recognition. One rule recognizes, as moral, goals that help the agent develop and sustain a reflectively rational character. The other rule recognizes, as moral, constraints that function in a collectively rational way as embedded in social structure. The general idea, in plainer words, is that we owe it to ourselves to nurture a good character, whereas we owe it to others to abide by social norms that serve the common good.

The two recognition rules specify grounds for endorsement the force of which goes beyond any appeal they make to self-interest, but they transcend appeal to self-interest in different ways. Collective rationality goes beyond appeal to self-interest by being *impartial*. It is about serving the common good. Reflective rationality goes beyond appeal to self-interest by being an *idealization* of self-interest. It is about character and ends that make life worth living, not occurrent desires. Reflective rationality does not essentially require impartiality.[16] Moral dualism thus makes room for agents to pursue their own projects within morality's interpersonal constraints, but the point is to make room for an idealization of self-interest—the kind of self-interest we might hope to instill in our children—not for self-interest as such.

I know from experience that some readers will feel more comfortable classifying the interpersonal strand as a kind of rule-utilitarianism. So I want to be clear about how far we stretch the familiar label when we call the interpersonal strand rule-utilitarian. One simple difference is that the interpersonal strand does not purport to be the whole of morality. A more subtle and complex difference is that the interpersonal strand does not ask us to search the universe of logically possible sets of action-guiding rules. It does not ask us to adopt the action guide that would lead us to produce more utility than we would produce by following any alternative action guide. It does not ask us to adopt the action guide that would have the most utility if

---

16. It may contingently require impartiality, given facts about human psychology.

adopted by everyone. Unlike the personal strand, and unlike any other moral theory I know of, the interpersonal strand does not ask us to idealize at all. Instead, it asks us to look around at existing formal and informal constraints and to respect those that here and now are *actually working* through social structure in such a way as to make people in general better off.

The interpersonal strand ties moral obligations to the content of social structure existing right now. It does not do so blindly, though. It ties only one strand of morality to existing social structures, and *only* insofar as such structures serve the common good without exploitation.

5. "Why Be Moral?" and the Plural Perspective

Before going further, let me fill in some of the metaethical background. I aim here to say more about recognition rules, in particular, what they are supposed to be recognizing. In the process, I aim to say more about what kind of reason a moral reason is. It is hard even to begin, but I have found it useful to start by asking what is being questioned when a person asks "Why be moral?" I answer as follows. First, when asked in earnest, "Why be moral?" is a question about something that matters. Second, the question "Why be moral?" matters despite the fact that the person who asks the question patently is not presuming that being moral matters to people from their first-person-singular perspectives. Whether people have first-person-singular reasons to be moral is precisely what is being questioned. Thus, the implicit urgency has some other source.

It stems, I say, largely from the fact that we care about morality from a first-person-plural perspective. My endorsement begins to look like characteristically moral endorsement when grounded in the thought not that *I* have reason for endorsement but that *we* have reason for endorsement. While endorsement as rational need not go beyond the first person singular, *moral* endorsement at a minimum goes beyond first person singular to first person plural.[17]

The next thing to say is that the transcending of the singular perspective involved in moral endorsement cannot go much farther than this. If moral endorsement involves taking a plural perspective, then we can imagine how being moral could be disadvantageous for you or me and yet we could still have reason to endorse being moral. Consider that many theorists now offer cooperating in a prisoner's dilemma as a paradigm case of being moral.[18] While disadvantageous from an I-perspective,

---

17. There is truth in Thomas Nagel's thesis (1986 or 1991) that individuals inhabit both personal and impersonal points of view. The distinction between first-person-singular and first-person-plural perspectives, though, borrowed from Gerald Postema (2007, see also 1995), captures that truth in terms that seem a bit more concrete and more firmly rooted in everyday experience. Note that the idea that to endorse something as moral is to endorse it from a plural perspective does not beg the question against egoist or otherwise individualist theories. I might endorse a sufficiently refined egoism not only for me but for you, too, and not only because it is best for me but because it is best for you, too. In short, I can from a plural perspective endorse our tending our respective gardens. Again, to belabor a distinction that I know from experience to be not obvious, recognition rules are not rules of conduct. Rules of conduct are what we look at. Recognition rules are what we look *with*.

18. See especially Gauthier (1986).

cooperating remains rational in the sense of being to our advantage from a we-perspective. It is from a plural perspective that, in a prisoner's dilemma, we find something irrational about individual rationality. When you and I each decide not to cooperate, I am doing the best I can, given your noncooperation, and you are doing the best you can, given mine, and yet *we* are not doing the best we can. However, if being moral were pointless not only from a singular perspective but from a plural perspective as well, then it would be pointless, period. No one would ask "Why be moral?" because no one would care whether the question has an answer. In fact, though, while being moral need not be prudent from a singular perspective, part of the essence of being moral is that we have reason to endorse it from a plural perspective.

One difference between moral versus legal reasoning is that questions about how we recognize morality are hard to separate from questions about whether we have reason to endorse it. Morality's recognition rules pick out the extension of "moral" just as the law's recognition rules pick out the extension of "legal." Morality's recognition rules, however, pick out X as moral by homing in on properties that, from a plural perspective, give us reason to endorse X. We sometimes can discern the rules of the road by reading the signs. We sometimes can discern the applicable law simply by looking it up. Analogously, we might sometimes discern what is moral simply by consulting what we (correctly) take to be a moral authority. But in formulating a theory about what makes something moral, we are seeking to identify truth *makers*. So, although recognition rules serve an epistemological role, they serve that role by tracking moral ontology. Moreover, to play their epistemological role in a moral agent's life, recognition rules have to be *usable* truth makers. A theory's recognition rules, then, must direct us to look for a kind of truth; moreover, they must direct us to look for a truth we are capable of finding.[19]

The question "Why be moral?" that we inherited from Plato is a question about the relation between two kinds of telos—between what matters to us as individuals and what matters to us as a group. Morality, as we (like Plato) conceive of it, matters to us from a first-person-plural perspective, and this is why we care whether "Why be moral?" has an answer.

If, *per impossible*, morality did not matter from our plural perspectives, then neither would it matter whether morality could be reconciled with our singular perspectives. In different words, both Socrates and Glaucon care from a plural perspective about Glaucon's being moral. They treat it as up in the air whether morality can be reconciled with Glaucon's singular perspective, yet there is some perspective, some other perspective, from which it is not up in the air. They *want* the answer to be that morality is reconciled with Glaucon's singular perspective. Analogously, we care about whether people cooperate in a prisoner's dilemma. It is in the interest of both players to decline to cooperate, so from their singular perspectives, it makes no sense to be trying to convince them to cooperate. What makes sense of *caring* whether they cooperate is that there is a different perspective, a plural perspective, from which cooperating will make them better off.

---

19. I thank Philip Pettit for pressing me on this point at a meeting in Buenos Aires organized by Horacio Spector and Guido Pincione.

This takes us to one place where satisfactory moral theorizing becomes really difficult. Unfortunately, while the scope of a person's I-perspective is more or less fixed (encompassing the person's own interests and preferences), the we-perspective does not have fixed borders, making it hard to characterize the we-perspective with any precision. It should go without saying, though, that the plural perspective is no mere fiction. (It is not for nothing that natural languages have words like "we" and "us" for plural self-reference.) When I speak of the we-perspective, I have in mind not the sort of perspective you and I take when we identify ourselves as fellow Mets fans, but rather the particular perspective we take when we worry about the question "why be moral?"

That perspective usually does not encompass the whole world.[20] If I see that my mowing the lawn will hamper your efforts to write your book, then my taking a we-perspective involves identifying with you as a member of the group of people who will be affected by my mowing the lawn. If I see that mowing the lawn will adversely affect people in a faraway country (because they anxiously await your book), then my taking a we-perspective involves identifying with them as well. The scope of my we-perspective expands and contracts along with my awareness of whose interests are at stake.[21] This does not mean I should not mow the lawn. We could not live together if we did not allow ourselves the latitude to impinge on each other in various ways. Your latitude may not serve my ends, and mine may not serve yours, but what is relevant from the plural perspective is that *our* latitude serves our ends.

This, then, is the normative status of morality's recognition rules. Being recognized as moral has normative force because, when morality's recognition rules pick out X as moral, they do so by recognizing that we have reason to endorse X from a plural perspective. Note that this is a characterization of the perspective from which we formulate recognition rules. Whether *being* moral essentially involves taking a plural perspective is a separate question. (Do morality's rules of conduct include an injunction to take a plural perspective? No, not any more than the rules of the road include an injunction to read the signs.)

Consider the following objection. Kate has reason from a plural perspective to endorse Disneyland. "We'll have a lot of fun there. Nearly everyone does," she says to her friends. Yet, though Kate endorses Disneyland from a we-perspective, she is endorsing it not as moral but as, say, amusing. To endorse something as moral is

---

20. Geoffrey Sayre-McCord (1994) addresses this issue. The original version of this essay went to press before Geoff's article appeared, but the ideas in this paragraph are similar enough to his to make me wonder whether I got them from him. In any case, I thank Geoff for wonderfully illuminating conversations on such topics over a period of years.

21. The scope of my plural perspective will not always coincide with the scope of yours, which is one reason why we sometimes disagree about what is moral. Discussing our differences often helps us extend our perspectives in ways that bring them into alignment, though, so disagreement that can be traced to differences in perspectival scope need not be intractable. If you convince Kate that her we-perspective until now has failed to encompass the interests of members of other races, for example, then she will broaden her perspective accordingly. Or if she willfully refuses to do so, then her kind of we-perspective reveals itself to be quite unlike the perspective I am attributing to people who earnestly ask the question "Why be moral?"

to endorse it from a plural perspective, but not everything endorsed from a plural perspective is thereby endorsed *as moral*.

I agree with the objection. Certainly, we should not equate endorsing Disneyland from a plural perspective with endorsing Disneyland as moral. What then is the plural perspective's role in moral theory? From a plural perspective, we do not pick out maxims (for example) as moral. Still less do we pick out Disneyland as moral. Instead, we pick out a *criterion for assessing* maxims, given that maxims are subject to moral assessment.

Now, if something is a lot of fun for almost everyone, why is that not a property that we have reason to endorse from a plural perspective? Or if being a lot of fun is such a property, then what distinguishes endorsing something as fun from endorsing it as moral? To understand what is going on when we theorize about morality, or about anything, really, we must grasp a crucial fact: it is not a recognition rule's job to circumscribe its own subject matter. Any theory whatsoever starts by taking a subject matter as given. We begin with an intuitive understanding that subjects giving rise to moral questions include (roughly speaking) things that bear on human flourishing in communities, regarding which human action can make a difference. (Let me stress that I do not offer intuitions as recognition rules for morals. Intuition enters here as a source of questions, not as a tool for answering questions.)

Accordingly, "X is moral if X is a lot of fun" is not a recognition rule for morals because, when applied to any of the specific subject matters over which *moral theories* range, the property of being fun is not a reason for endorsement from a plural perspective. We do not in fact recognize "being fun" as reason to endorse capital punishment or promise keeping or any of the subjects that normally raise moral questions. The recognition rules I propose for the subjects over which moral theories range are the two specified earlier.

To summarize, a recognition rule like the principle of utility could embody a genuine reason for endorsement from a plural perspective and still fail to exclude Disneyland as a subject for moral assessment. However, it is not incumbent on recognition rules to have the internal resources to limit their subject matters. We test a purported recognition rule not in abstraction but rather as applied to a pretheoretically given subject matter.

I have no theory to tell me what the subject matters of moral assessment are; on my theory, again, that is a *pre*theoretical question. I have only a sense that morality and moral assessment concern what makes it possible for human beings to flourish together. Given this pretheoretical understanding of the general character of the subject matters of moral assessment, amusement parks are not among morality's subject matters, but *institutions* are. Thus, Disneyland is subject to moral assessment not as an amusement park but rather as an institution that affects people.

6. Morality's Ultimate Foundation

I used reflective rationality as a basis for a generic recognition rule on the grounds that being reflectively rational serves people's ends. Reflective rationality thus has normative force whether or not we recognize it as moral. Accordingly, as a recognition rule, it is not question begging. Is reflective rationality something we have reason to endorse from a plural perspective? Not necessarily. It depends on the subject matter. When we look at how people treat themselves, though, and especially at how their pursuits affect their characters, reflective rationality does indeed matter to us from a plural perspective. We do approve of people treating themselves in a reflectively rational way, and for good reason; namely, we care about them. We care about them not just as means to our ends or even each other's ends but as ends in themselves. We try to raise our children to be reflectively rational not only because we care about how they treat others but also because we care about how they treat themselves. We approve of people developing in a reflectively rational way, at least insofar as the question before us concerns how people should treat themselves. As a recognition rule, reflective rationality is on its strongest ground when applied to the subject of how people should treat themselves.

In abstraction, the idea of collective rationality is at risk of collapsing into act-utilitarianism, with all its attendant controversy. (If we were obligated to search logical space for constraints to impose upon ourselves, we might conclude we should constrain ourselves to do all and only that which maximizes aggregate utility.) But I narrowed the subject matter to externally imposed constraints, assessed in terms of how they actually function as embedded in social structure here and now. This distanced my interpretation of collective rationality from any traditional form of utilitarianism, putting it on stronger albeit narrower ground as a reason for endorsement. Thus was born moral dualism.

As a crude generalization, we *discover* interpersonal morality's action-guiding content by learning how social structures around us are functioning. We *create* personal morality's action-guiding content by settling on ends that shape our lives and characters, giving us a sense of having and being something worth living for. Interpersonal constraints are out there, whether or not we ever discover them, but personal morality really is personal. It is only after we embrace a reflectively rational goal as our own that it begins to dictate what we should do.

Moral dualism's recognition rules pick out parts of common-sense morality that serve our ends from a plural perspective and thus are not merely moral as the term is commonly understood but are independently shown to warrant endorsement. Reflectively rational character and collectively rational institutions command our endorsement from a first-person-plural perspective even when they fail to motivate from a first-person-singular perspective, and one of the marks of a moral reason is that it engages us in this way. When applied to suitable subject matters, moral dualism's recognition rules identify parts of common-sense morality as warranting endorsement on grounds that go beyond matters of occurrent desire to concerns crucial to human well-being and to a concept of the good life for human beings living together.[22]

22. Louden accepts this, as far as it goes, but does not think moral inquiry is limited to subjects that are crucial to our well-being in communities. He writes: "Whatever is within our control is (subject to the usual excusing conditions) a possible object of moral assessment. My natural eye color is not a fact for moral assessment; my diffidence may well be" (1992, 20). I would not disagree, but neither would I insist that moral inquiry's scope is this broad. For my purposes, it does not matter exactly how broad the scope of moral inquiry can be, so long as the subject matters over which moral dualism ranges fall within moral inquiry's scope.

I do not know whether moral dualism's two recognition rules are morality's ultimate foundation. Asking whether they are is like asking Charles Darwin whether the theory of natural selection is biology's ultimate foundation. The real question is whether the theory serves the purpose for which it was devised, namely, to illuminate its subject matter. Does the theory of natural selection explain the origin of species? Not necessarily, but if it does, then it serves its purpose. Does moral dualism identify reasons for endorsement from a plural perspective? Not necessarily, but if it does, then it serves its purpose.

Moral dualism's recognition rules are fundamental enough to support endorsement, and that is what matters. We could try to reduce matters of character to matters of serving the common good, or vice versa. We could try to reduce both to variations on some third and even more basic theme. We might even succeed. But neither rule's status as a supporting condition depends on whether we can reduce it to something else. When we get to either rule, we get to something that, applied to an appropriate subject matter, supports endorsement. We do not need to reduce either rule to anything more fundamental.

We need not look for grounds that are *unique* in supporting endorsement. There are other ways to map the moral terrain. Some may be just as illuminating and just as resistant to counterexamples. So be it. We need not discover the terrain's one true map. There are truths about how our choices affect our characters, and truths about how well our social structures serve our collective ends; therein lie genuine and related grounds for endorsement. These truths may not be our only grounds for endorsing parts of common-sense morality as genuinely moral, but the grounds they provide are real. Our grounds for endorsement must be real; they need not be uniquely so.

7. The Two Strands Form a Unified Theory

My aim now is to argue that moral dualism's two strands belong together; they really are parts of the same theory. First, they help to determine each other's *content*. Second, they help to determine each other's *limits*. This section explains how the common good is defined in terms of reflective rationality and, conversely, how reflective rationality as a recognition rule has a countervailing condition defined in terms of collective rationality. The next section explains what happens when moral goals clash with moral constraints.

I defined the common good in common-sense terms, that is, in terms of making people in general better off. With a single-stranded utilitarian theory of the right, there would be little more to say. We would be more or less at a dead end, needing to look beyond the theory for a conception of goodness. In contrast, since moral dualism has two distinct recognition rules, they can look to each other rather than beyond the theory. For example, we can look to the personal strand for ideas about what social structure is supposed to accomplish. Specifically, we can define collective rationality as the property of being conducive to the flourishing of people in general as reflectively rational agents. The theory's two strands are therefore connected via their recognition rules, since both incorporate conceptions of rationality, one of which is defined in terms of the other. (See fig. 7.3.)

	PERSONAL STRAND	INTERPERSONAL STRAND
GENERIC RECOGNITION RULE	Is X reflectively rational? *helps define* →	Is Y collectively rational?
SUBJECT MATTER	X = goals, in terms of how their pursuit affects the agent's character	Y = constraints on conduct as embedded in social structure
FULLY SPECIFIED RECOGNITION RULE	A goal is moral if pursuing it helps the agent to develop in a reflectively rational way	A constraint on conduct is moral if it works through social structure in a collectively rational way
	(subject to countervailing conditions)	(subject to countervailing conditions)

FIGURE 7.3. Defining collective rationality.

It does not go both ways. I would not define reflective rationality in terms of collective rationality. Reflective rationality does have a kind of definitional link to collective rationality, though. Namely, as the personal strand's recognition rule, reflective rationality is subject to countervailing conditions that get their content from the interpersonal strand. Specifically, moral goals must be pursued within moral constraints. Kate's goal of going to medical school and becoming a surgeon may be reflectively rational, but the morality of her goal does not give her license to raise tuition money by fraudulent means. (See fig. 7.4.)

We now have two definitional links between moral dualism's recognition rules. By definition, collective rationality involves helping individuals to flourish as reflectively rational beings (fig. 7.3). In turn, reflective rationality's countervailing conditions are defined in terms of collective rationality (fig. 7.4).

There are contingent links as well. As chapter 4 argues, being a reflectively rational agent in a social context involves nurturing respect and concern for others, establishing honest rapport with others, and living peacefully and productively

	PERSONAL STRAND	INTERPERSONAL STRAND
Generic recognition rule	Is X reflectively rational? *helps define* →	Is Y collectively rational?
Subject matter	X = goals, in terms of how their pursuit affects the agent's character	Y = constraints on conduct as embedded in social structure
Fully specified recognition rule	A goal is moral if pursuing it helps the agent to develop in a reflectively rational way	A constraint on conduct is moral if it works through social structure in a collectively rational way
	(subject to countervailing conditions) ← *helps define*	(subject to countervailing conditions)

FIGURE 7.4. Defining the personal strand's countervailing conditions.

within one's community. It involves becoming an important part of one's community and thereby having more to live for. In these ways, matters of collective rationality enter the personal strand not only (by definition) through reflective rationality's countervailing conditions but also (as a psychological contingency) through reflective rationality itself, insofar as caring about the common good is contingently part of being reflectively rational in a social setting.

Contingent links between reflective and collective rationality are secured not only by the psychological tendency of reflectively rational agents to want to play a role in a collectively rational community but also (from the other direction) by the economic and sociological tendency of a collectively rational community to make room for reflectively rational pursuits (see figure 7.5).

The most novel feature of the interpersonal strand is that constraints are assessed in terms of how they affect behavior when imposed from outside. Because the constraints impose themselves from outside rather than from within, they serve the common good only insofar as they have the actual effect of inducing people to serve the common good. Moral social structures create incentives and opportunities such that individually rational agents, reflective or not, normally have reasons to act in ways that serve the common good.

We should not think of either strand as independently specifying a sufficient condition for something being moral. No single strand speaks for morality as a whole. If a goal's choice and subsequent pursuit help Kate to sustain a reflectively rational character, then the goal is moral by the lights of the personal strand. If Kate pursues that goal within constraints imposed by collectively rational social structure, then her pursuit is moral by the lights of the interpersonal strand. To be moral, period, her choice and subsequent pursuit must pass both tests (and maybe other tests as well, if morality has more than these two strands).

In terms of their action-guiding function, then, the two strands are complementary parts of a unified theory. In concert, they converge on an action guide that says something about both ends and means: one should pursue reflectively rational ends

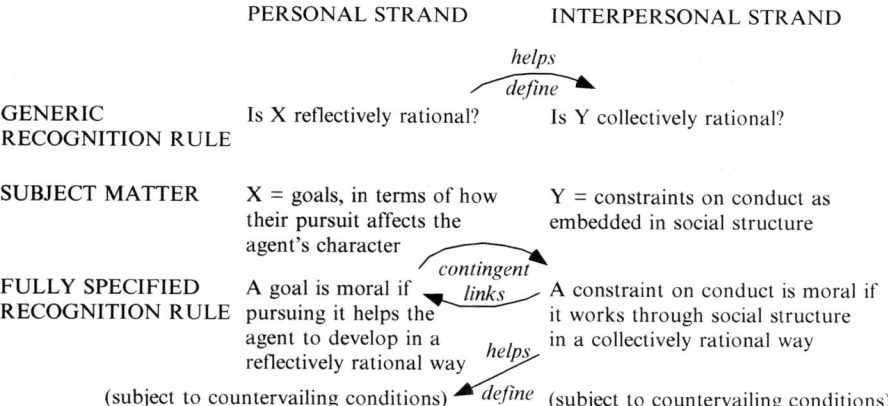

FIGURE 7.5. Contingent links between moral goals and moral constraints.

via means permitted by collectively rational social structures. Morally, one seeks to make oneself a better person—a person with more to live for—within constraints imposed by social structures that serve the common good.

8. The Two Strands Can Come into Conflict

Here is an issue that, I think, arises for anyone trying to live morally, and thus arises for anyone trying to theorize about moral life. The problem is easy to see and articulate for moral dualism, though, which I consider a plus rather than a minus. The issue is that morality is more than one thing, and morality's pieces can come into conflict.

Structurally embedded interpersonal constraints are moral in virtue of making people in general better off in normal cases, and moral agents pursue reflectively rational goals within those constraints. Matters are not always this simple, though. Like reflective rationality as applied to personal goals, collective rationality as applied to interpersonal constraints admits of countervailing conditions. Suppose you have a medical emergency on your hands. You are bleeding badly, and the most straightforward way of getting to a doctor involves parking illegally, on a street where parking laws serve the common good. My remarks in the previous section on how the strands intertwine, and my conclusion that they constitute a unified theory, may seem to suggest they cannot yield conflicting guidance. True? Are the strands really so neatly woven together?

If we insist there can be no conflict between collectively rational constraints and reflectively rational goals, we have two alternatives. We can say *moral* parking laws incorporate exemptions for bleeding motorists as a matter of course, which seems false (unless we want to say no real-world parking laws are moral). Or we can say that if the laws really are moral, then we must never break them, not even to save our lives, and that, too, seems false.

The theory (and our lives as moral agents) would be simpler if we could insist that moral social constraints never conflict with urgent personal goals. Realistically, though, the harmony between moral goals and structurally embedded moral constraints is contingent rather than necessary. Normally, moral social structures help people flourish as reflectively rational agents. It can sometimes be reflectively rational, though, even for people who appreciate and respect moral social structures, to react in ways that are not "by the book." Moral constraints usually trump—they constrain—moral goals, but there can be exceptions. Municipal parking regulations, for example, have normative force, insofar as they constitute an institution that generally serves people's ends. Yet, parking regulations can have this normative force without entailing that people have decisive reasons to conform to those regulations in a given case. The kind of moral force that real-world regulations have, when they have any, cannot preclude the possibility of cases where people have decisive reasons to disregard pertinent regulations and, for example, park illegally in an emergency. Moral regulations give reasons for action in normal cases, but it is in the nature of the reasons provided that they will not always be decisive.

It does not follow from this that parking regulations are moral in some cases but not in others. Regulations may tell us to do what turns out to be perverse in a given case, but that does not make the *regulations* perverse. On the contrary, if we tried to tweak the contours of a parking regulation so as to allow us to do all and only that which would serve the common good, no matter how abnormal the circumstances, the resulting modified system is bound to be decidedly more perverse in other ways. Like it or not, an optimal system—a system that functions cleanly and simply, making it easy for people to understand what is required in normal cases—occasionally will forbid actions that would have served the common good.[23]

In some cases, constraints embedded in institutional structures come into conflict with each other. Thus, in a medical emergency, a doctor's obligation to obey collectively rational parking laws can come into conflict with the collectively rational constraints embedded in his or her code of professional conduct.[24]

Moral constraints also can conflict with the dictates of morality's personal strand. For example, one's reflectively rational promise to be on time to see one's child perform in a school play can, through no fault of one's own, come into conflict with one's professional obligations or with one's obligation to observe collectively rational traffic laws. (Of course, we can owe it to ourselves or to our families, patients, and colleagues to do what we can to avoid circumstances that generate conflicts.)[25] The fact that a given pursuit is reflectively rational is not enough to override constraints that work through social structures to serve the common good. On the other hand, if a reflectively rational pursuit is important enough on its own terms, that can make it a matter of collective rationality as well. After all, collective rationality ultimately is a matter of what makes people better off as reflectively rational agents. In situations of conflict, morality's interpersonal constraints normally trump personal goals, but moral agents should realize that forcing people to ignore overwhelmingly important moral goals is no part of a moral social structure's purpose. Acknowledging this, presiding judges within an institutional framework can consider mitigating circumstances on a case-by-case basis. This is how legal structures should work, because a legislature that tried to deal with all possible peculiar cases before they happened would not work as well as a legislature that relies on courts to recognize mitigating circumstances as they arise.

This is also how individual conscience should work. Parking regulations become morally irrelevant to, say, a person seeking medical attention for a seriously injured family member. More precisely, their *action-guiding function* becomes morally irrelevant. We might appreciate that the regulations have moral force even while realizing they should not guide our actions in a medical emergency. Under the circumstances, a person of conscience breaks regulations, perhaps with regret but without reluctance.[26] It would not serve the common good and thus would not be moral for social structure

---

23. As Coleman puts a similar point, "rules are incapable of being perfectly fine-tuned. Sometimes rules will include within their domain cases that fall outside their set of background reasons, and they will exclude others that fall within that set. These characteristics are a function of rule generality. Thus, rules are necessarily under- and over-inclusive with respect to the sets of reasons that support or ground them" (1991, 710).

24. See Baier (1958) 193.

25. There may also be conflicts best seen as conflicts between the interpersonal strand and some third strand of morality.

26. For more on act-evaluations that are not action-guiding, see Stocker (1990, chap. 4).

to force us to ignore overwhelmingly important personal goals or overwhelmingly important interpersonal constraints embedded in other social structures.

So, while it is essential to morality's interpersonal constraints that they mesh both with each other and with morality's personal strand in normal cases, interpersonal constraints can clash with each other or with reflective rationality in abnormal cases. Just as personal goals must defer to interpersonal constraints in normal cases, so interpersonal constraints must defer to personal goals in some abnormal cases. Naturally, some constraints are less deferential than others. To make a constraint against mugging give way, a case would have to be otherworldly—the stuff of fiction rather than of real life—both in terms of its consequences and in terms of the agent being unrealistically sure of the consequences.[27]

9. A Pluralism That Won't Collapse

Single-stranded theories dominated modern moral philosophy partly due to a widespread view that multistranded theories are inevitably beset by conflict between strands. Moreover, so the story goes, conflicts are resolvable only by some overarching principle of adjudication. The overarching principle will be the theory's real and only fundamental recognition rule. Thus, some theorists would say there is instability in theories proposing more than one recognition rule. With a little pushing, all such theories collapse into single-stranded theories.

Perhaps enough has been said by now to show why this view is mistaken when it comes to moral dualism. Moral social structures impose constraints that can conflict with reflective rationality, but the two strands can settle their disputes without having to resort to outside arbitration. In normal cases, the personal strand defers to the interpersonal strand, because flouting rules of collectively rational institutions normally would not help an agent to develop and sustain a reflectively rational character.

In extraordinary cases, however, our reflectively rational goals can become overwhelmingly important. Reflectively rational people have reasons to comply with moral social structures in normal cases, but to comply with moral parking laws in

---

27. Recall that the interpersonal strand is not an idealization. It does not ascribe to agents a duty or even a right to maximize utility, except within externally imposed constraints of moral institutions. So, one standard sort of objection to utilitarianism is that mugging could be utility-maximizing in some possible world. That objection is a nonissue for moral dualism. (Is there a possible world in which mugging as we know it serves the common good without using anyone as a mere resource? I doubt it.)

Still, there is a problem here for the theory as I have so far developed it. The interpersonal strand commands us to respect norms that serve the common good without exploitation, which is not the same as commanding us not to exploit. A closely related idea: when it comes to mugging, the issue is not simply about respecting norms but about respecting the individuals whose rights are protected and to some degree defined by the norms. My tentative response is that the interpersonal strand is explicitly an answer to the question of what we owe others. This part of morality is interpersonal, not impersonal. The point of respecting the norms that exist between us is to respect each other, not the norms per se. So, if we have so far observed a norm of not being the first to attack, then our respecting that norm is a form of mutual respect. It is not merely derivatively respectful of each other. Rather, it is a tangible embodiment of our mutual respect. I called this a tentative response because, although it parsimoniously responds to the objection, there may well be better responses that involve introducing a third strand.

a situation in which one is in danger of bleeding to death would not be reflectively rational. In such cases, the personal strand cannot defer, but the interpersonal strand can, and it has good reason to do so. Moral social structures do not try to change us in such a way that we would rather die than double-park. The attempt to command such blind allegiance would not be collectively rational.

For example, a rule against shouting in libraries is moral because it makes people generally better off by nonexploitative means. The constraint makes us better off in virtue of how it channels behavior in normal cases. The constraint does not spell out what we should do in literally every possible contingency. Library patrons generally are better off with simple norms, and the fact of their being generally better off with simple norms gives simple norms their moral force. Shouting in a library might be reflectively or even collectively rational in a given case, but that by itself is not enough to undermine the morality of a prohibition that (by enabling patrons to count on peace and quiet) remains collectively rational as an ongoing norm.

If you notice smoke pouring from the vent, though, the situation is so far from the norm that normal constraints no longer apply. When smoke is pouring from the vent, background conditions that give the norm its ongoing utility, and thus its moral force, can no longer be taken as given. As a general rule, we have a duty not to yell "Fire!" in a library, but like other rules, this one has countervailing conditions, such as the circumstance of there being an actual fire.

Note that there is no direct appeal here to the plural perspective as an overarching moral principle. Instead, as in normal cases, the plural perspective is the perspective from which we identify reasons for endorsement; it is not itself a reason for endorsement. Having identified collective rationality as grounds for endorsing social structures as moral, we conclude that a rule against disturbing fellow patrons, grounded in considerations of collective rationality, reaches its natural limit when the building is on fire. The only kind of rule against disturbing library patrons that could be considered collectively rational is a rule that is understood not to apply when you notice smoke pouring from the vent.[28]

Likewise, it would run counter to interpersonal morality for a government to hire police to run down and handcuff drivers who double-park in a desperate attempt to avoid bleeding to death, even though laws forbidding double-parking are morally justified.

This is how moral dualism explains the occurrence and resolution of moral conflict. There is no need—there is not even room—for an overarching principle of adjudication. Moral dualism's two strands provide the source of each other's countervailing conditions. Conflict between the two strands is the source of the personal strand's countervailing conditions in *normal* cases, and is the source of the interpersonal strand's countervailing conditions in *abnormal* cases (see figure 7.6).

The latter point is the puzzle's final piece; we have characterized the theory's recognition rules, its subject matters, and now its main countervailing conditions as well. Reflective rationality is defined exogenously.[29] Collective rationality is defined

---

28. I thank Geoff Sayre-McCord for especially helpful discussions of this and related points.
29. See chapters 2, 3, and 4 here.

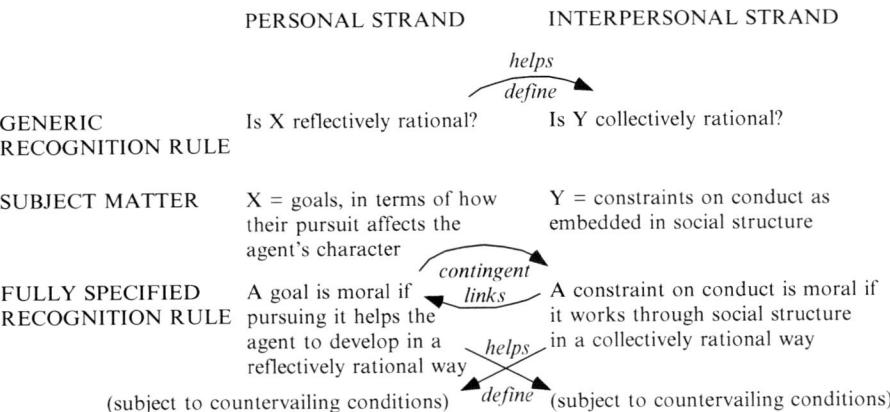

FIGURE 7.6. Defining the interpersonal strand's countervailing conditions.

in terms of reflective rationality. Personal morality's limits are defined in normal cases by the constraints of interpersonal morality. And interpersonal morality's limits are likewise defined in abnormal cases by considerations of reflective rationality so overwhelmingly important that obeying a moral constraint would defeat the constraint's purpose, which is to help people flourish as reflectively rational beings in a social context.

In passing, it can be obvious what to do when the library is on fire, or when one needs to double-park to save one's life, but it is not always obvious how to resolve conflicts. We saw that the two strands can conflict, and can resolve conflicts without outside arbitration, but it is also true that morality does not give us precisely articulated rules of conduct. (To be moral is less about having all the answers and more about being keenly aware that the test has begun.)[30] That lack of precisely articulated guidance can be especially daunting in cases where morality's strands conflict. In real life, moral agents need to exercise judgment.

Chapter 2 argues that there can be underdetermined rational choice—cases where rationality dictates simply picking something and getting on with one's life. Similarly, there may be cases of underdetermined moral agency—cases where we cannot avoid violating one collectively rational constraint or another, or cases of such unique importance that we are not sure whether we are really bound by constraints that in normal cases are collectively rational. There is no handy rule by which we discern the bright line between emergency and nonemergency cases. Indeed, the bright line may not exist; the boundary between the two categories may instead be a gray area with no definite answer, let alone a definite procedure for identifying the answer. If there are cases in which it never becomes clear which course of action is morally best or morally required, then we have no choice but to pick something and get on with our lives as moral agents.

30. See Schmidtz (2001a).

The other thing to say is that legislators create bright lines when framing laws, and it can be moral for them to do so. For the sake of argument, suppose we abstract from morally justified constraints imposed on us by institutions. Imagine that, in this abstract situation, there is no definitive moral answer to the question of what we should do when we need to choose between killing one person and letting five people die. Even so, legislators can make sure the question has a definitive albeit arbitrary *legal* answer. An arbitrarily drawn bright legal line might then present itself to us as a morally justified constraint, justified because it serves the common good to have some bright line or other rather than none. Thus, not all moral constraints are timeless. They can be born with changing laws and social norms, and they can pass away.

One final test question. Suppose you notice other people littering. Lots of other people are littering. Littering, it turns out, is not illegal, and no one else seems to care. Are you obligated not to litter? Intuitively, no, but what does moral dualism say?[31] By hypothesis, there is no formal norm you are bound to respect. Neither is there any informal norm. On its face, then, the interpersonal strand does not require you not to litter. Once you recognize that littering is a disgusting thing to do, though, the personal strand does require you not to litter, as a matter of self-respect. It may also encourage you to support any campaign with a reasonable chance of raising public awareness. There is more detail here than is apparent in the simple intuition that we should not litter, but it seems to me that this is a case where moral dualism does not need a third strand. Two strands encompassing "Person" and "Polis" are enough.

10. Conclusions

Some of this essay's most fundamental conclusions were stated near the beginning. First, a moral theory can range over more than one subject matter. Second, a moral theory can incorporate more than one recognition rule. Third, a moral theory can be structurally open-ended, constituted by strands that leave room for adding further strands or for accepting that some of our moral knowledge may be irremediably inarticulate.

As an example of a two-stranded theory, I adapted a notion of collective rationality to the task of assessing interpersonal constraints in terms of how they function when embedded in social structure. I adapted a notion of eudaimonist rationality to the task of assessing personal goals in terms of how they affect an agent's character. Moral dualism is the theory or partial theory that emerges when we apply this pair of principles to their respective subject matters.

I considered how conflict between the strands is resolved using conceptual resources internal to the two strands, thus showing how the two strands weave together to form a unified whole in the absence of an overarching principle of adjudication. The analysis permits the theory to be open-ended. Those who want to make

---

31. I thank Jason Brennan for the question. Littering is my example. Brennan's more intriguing and complex example concerns the morality of voting when you have reason to believe you exhibit the same defects as typical voters.

the analysis of morality more complete can add other subject matters and apply other recognition rules, as necessary.[32]

At the action-guiding level, the content of moral dualism is not especially novel. If the theory's substantive implications were really novel, that probably would be a good reason to reject it. The formal structure, though, is novel, so far as I know.

This material was originally published in *Rational Choice and Moral Agency* (Princeton, N.J.: Princeton University Press, 1995). Copyright David Schmidtz.

---

32. If we do need a third strand, though, moral dualism's two strands conceivably may not be part of the most effective way of dividing the moral terrain into three parts. Incompleteness per se is no reason to abandon the two strands, but the emergence of a simpler alternative would be.

8

Separateness, Suffering, and Moral Theory

What I call the Singer principle has an awkward consequence. Section 1 explains the principle. Section 2 explains the problem. The problem tells us something about the nature and limits of morality and moral theorizing, as later sections explain.

1. The Singer Principle

In his essay "Famine, Affluence, and Morality" (1972), after describing the famine in East Bengal around 1971, Peter Singer says,

> I shall argue that the way people in relatively affluent countries react to a situation like that in Bengal cannot be justified; indeed, the whole way we look at moral issues—our moral conceptual scheme—needs to be altered, and with it, the way of life that has come to be taken for granted in our society.
>
> In arguing for this conclusion I will not, of course, claim to be morally neutral. I shall, however, try to argue for the moral position that I take, so that anyone who accepts certain assumptions, to be made explicit, will, I hope, accept my conclusion.
>
> I begin with the assumption that suffering and death from lack of food, shelter, and medical care are bad.... Those who disagree need read no further.
>
> My next point is this: if it is in our power to prevent something bad from happening, without thereby sacrificing anything of comparable moral importance, we ought, morally, to do it. By "without sacrificing anything of comparable moral importance" I mean without causing anything else comparably bad to happen, or doing something that is wrong in itself, or failing to promote some moral good, comparable in significance to the bad thing that we can prevent. This principle seems almost as uncontroversial as the last one. It requires us only to prevent what is bad, and not to promote what is good, and it requires this of us only when we can do

it without sacrificing anything that is, from the moral point of view, comparably important.[1]

Here, then, is what I call the Singer Principle (SP):

SP: If it is in our power to prevent something bad from happening, without thereby sacrificing anything of comparable moral importance, we ought, morally, to do it.

The Singer principle has weaker and stronger forms. Its weaker form lets us rewrite "anything of comparable importance" as "anything significant." Its stronger form requires us to interpret the original phrase literally. Singer acknowledges that SP's uncontroversial appearance is deceptive. If SP were acted upon, even in its *weaker* form, our lives would be very different. The Singer principle's *strong* version, though, requires "reducing ourselves to the level of marginal disutility," by which Singer means "the level at which, by giving more, I would cause as much suffering to myself or my dependents as I would relieve by my gift. This would mean, of course, that one would reduce oneself to very near the material circumstances of a Bengali refugee." Singer adds, "I should also say that the strong version seems to me to be the correct one."[2]

The Singer principle has an implication that a moral principle should not have.

2. The Singer Principle Cannot Be Right

Here is what I have in mind. If we interpret SP from a straightforwardly utilitarian perspective, it would seem to be calling on us to ship food and money to wherever people need it more than we do.[3] Is that a problem? Not from a utilitarian perspective. It will conflict with some of our intuitions about the limits of our obligations to others, but utilitarians are accustomed to biting that bullet.

The Symmetry Problem

But what about toxic waste? Might shipping toxic waste to wherever it will do the least harm fall into the category of preventing something bad without causing anything comparably bad? Yes, of course. It may even be the rule rather than the exception that our own backyards will not be the best possible place to store toxic waste.

Both exporting goods and exporting bads could prevent something bad without sacrificing anything of comparable importance. If this leaves us realizing that SP, as seen through a utilitarian lens, is not the whole story of morality when it comes to exporting bads, we may infer that we have no good reason to regard it as the whole story for exporting goods either. Whatever we build into our theories to acknowledge

---

1. Singer (1972) 230–31.

2. Singer (1972) 241.

3. If we do not presume to flesh out the principle in utilitarian terms, then what it calls for becomes wide open.

that our right to export bads is more limited than a simple utilitarian story would suggest—acknowledging the separateness of persons, say—is likely to limit the obligation (and perhaps the right) to export goods at the same time that it limits the right (and perhaps the obligation) to export bads.

Before pursuing this, I want to mention a further awkward consequence SP has when combined with Singer's position on animal equality.[4]

Species Equality

Not every utilitarian shares Singer's concern about animals. It is a separate decision where to locate the boundaries of moral concern, and the location of boundaries normally is not dictated by the principle one adopts for guiding decisions within those boundaries.

The Singer principle requires us to prevent bad whenever we can do so without sacrificing anything comparably important. The Singer principle's strong form, interpreted in a sufficiently narrow way (that is, ignoring the suffering of animals), requires us to reduce ourselves to something approaching the circumstances of a Bengali refugee if Bengali refugees are the worst-off people we can help. However, if Singer were right that human and animal suffering are comparably important, then what SP actually requires would have little to do with Bengali refugees. Animals everywhere are dying from easily preventable thirst or hunger, and from easily preventable diseases. If we let nature take its course, the best that many animals can hope for is that their throats will be torn out by predators before they starve: not exactly merciful, but at least quicker. However, we could prevent that, too. In short, there are animals by the millions, perhaps billions, whose circumstances are worse than those of Bengali refugees. The Singer principle (conjoined to species equality) entails no obligation to Bengali refugees. On the contrary, SP's strong form, conjoined to species equality, requires us to "reduce ourselves to a level of marginal disutility" defined by the material circumstances not of Bengali refugees but of the worst-off animals we can help. (If we humans were "utility monsters" compared to other animals, utilitarianism would require us to favor humans in our investment decisions, but Singer does not believe we are, and neither do I.)

3. But How Can SP Be Wrong?

Yet, SP is a plausible idea about how we ought to respond to suffering (including animal suffering). I want to say SP can't be wrong as a *reason for action* (something approaching a supporting condition, to borrow a term from chapter 7). On my view, SP is telling us to do the best we can, which is uncontroversial, as Singer says. There is always reason to do the best we can. Having identified any given course of action X as the best we can do, our reason for doing X is that we believe X is, after all, the best we can do. To have picked out X as the best we can do is by that very fact to have seen some reason to do X.

    4. Singer (1990).

I am not claiming, though, that SP is a *comprehensive* account of our reasons for action. Why not? Briefly (the next section elaborates), many of our reasons for action in this world stem from the fact that this world is not what game theorists call a "parametric" world. Instead, ours is a strategic world: other agents respond to what we have done and also to what they anticipate from us. To give one of the simplest and most amply confirmed examples, players respond in one way to a strategy of unconditional cooperation, and respond quite differently to a strategy of tit for tat. The Singer principle must be, if not abandoned, at least interpreted in light of this fact. When suitably interpreted—that is, when interpreted as a strategy whose consequences will be a function of what happens when implemented in a strategic world—SP will not have the implications Singer says it has regarding how much we should contribute, when, or even why.[5]

A second concern, related but in any case the sort of concern we might express qua moral philosophers rather than qua game theorists, is that sometimes the best response to value is to respect it rather than to promote it. There comes a time for doing the best we can, which is to say there comes a time for SP or something like it. When? John Stuart Mill seemed to think SP, or something like it, would be required in only one case in a thousand.[6] However, it is hard to see any resources in Mill's utilitarianism to so limit the scope of SP's application. Many readers in the aftermath of twentieth-century utilitarianism dismiss Mill's claims as pandering to common opinion, an unconvincing disavowal of his theory's patently radical nature. But Mill was neither a stupid man nor a man overly concerned to ally himself with the prejudices of his day. So, perhaps he saw something that got lost in the shuffle of twentieth-century utilitarianism's development as a simple-minded decision procedure.

The following section develops these two concerns.

4. Respecting versus Promoting[7]

Elaborating the Game Theoretic Point

TRAGIC COMMONS: a baby is drowning in the pool beside you. You can save the baby by a process that involves giving its family $100. If you do not save it, it will die. You save the baby. A crowd begins to gather. Seeing what you have done, two onlookers throw their babies into the pool. The babies will drown unless you give each of their families $100. More onlookers begin to gather, waiting to see what you do.

I am not saying our world is like TRAGIC COMMONS. I would say, though, that TRAGIC COMMONS is a world we have no good reason to want to live in. And one way to make our world more like TRAGIC COMMONS is to embrace SP. Moreover, people do react to opportunities, including opportunities presented by the predictable actions and/or commitments of other people. Which is to say, our world is a strategic

---

5. Singer circa 1998 is alive to such complications. See his thoughtful "Darwin for the Left," in Singer (2000).

6. Mill (1979).

7. This section revises material from Schmidtz (2000).

world. (Substitute "dictator" for "onlooker" in TRAGIC COMMONS. May we *assume* our world is nothing like that? Anyone committed to getting actual good results will assume no such thing but will instead investigate, one case at a time, how dictators and the rest of us actually react to incentives.)

TRAGIC COMMONS illustrates one kind of type-token issue.[8] In TRAGIC COMMONS, the token-benefit is a saved life, but this token-benefit is wildly misleading as a characterization of your action's real consequences. The token-result of your action is a saved life, but the type-result is an escalating catastrophe. Knowing that foreign aid has a history of driving such wedges between token-benefits and type-disasters, I now get a letter asking me to participate in what may or may not be another commons tragedy in the making. I have to make a decision. Does morality require me to accept a theorist's or professional fund-raiser's all-too-predictable assurance that if we turn on the financial spigots in response to problems and turn them off in response to solutions, we'll eventually have fewer problems and more solutions?[9]

To whatever extent we take responsibility for other people as well as ourselves, our actions are encouraging people to depend on us rather than on themselves. Act-utilitarianism usually would not permit members of group A opportunistically to arrange circumstances so that the act-utilitarian commitments of group B require group B to support group A, but unless the members of group A, too, are committed act-utilitarians, that will not stop them from doing it. Theories often have implications other than ones they formally acknowledge. A theory can stipulate an action guide and an intended result. But a theory cannot stipulate that following its action guide will have its intended result, for that is an empirical matter. So it is with maximizing utility. One can say that trying to maximize utility actually tends to maximize utility, but saying it does not make it so. A simple maximizing strategy may tend to lead to the best possible outcome for beings like us in situations like ours. Then again, it may not. It has no history of doing so.

Elaborating the Moral Theoretic Point

The Singer principle is a suggestion about how to go about *promoting* value. However, promoting value is not the only concern if either (1) value itself is not the only concern, or (2) being moral sometimes is, as mentioned earlier, a matter of *respecting* rather than promoting value. Under what conditions might respecting value conflict with promoting it? Here are two notorious philosophical thought experiments.

> TROLLEY: a trolley is rolling down a track on its way to killing five people. If you switch to another track on which there is only one person, you will save five and kill one.

---

8. As analytic philosophers use these terms, a *type* is a general category, whereas a *token* is a particular instance of the more general category. For example, there are many blue shirts in the world. The one I am wearing is a token of the general type.

9. One need not be an ideologue to be a skeptic about foreign aid. Foreign aid's actual history appalls Brian Barry as much as it does me. See Barry (2005, chap. 3). See Schmidtz (2007) for a response.

Most people say you ought to switch tracks and kill one to save five. Compare this to:

> HOSPITAL: five patients are dying for lack of suitable organ donors. A UPS delivery person walks into the hospital. You know she is a suitable donor for all five patients. If you kidnap her and harvest her organs, you save five and kill one.[10]

People have a different intuition here. Among students (and U.S. congressional staffers, at whose workshops I sometimes lecture) that I informally poll, almost everyone responds to HOSPITAL by saying you cannot kidnap and murder people, period. Not even to save lives. On a trip to Kazakhstan, I presented the cases to an audience of twenty-one professors from nine post-Soviet republics. They said the same. Why? Are the cases really so different? How?

TROLLEY tells us numbers matter. Although HOSPITAL seems to have TROLLEY's logical structure, it leads us to a different conclusion. Why? The literature discusses several differences, but one difference I have not heard mentioned is this: HOSPITAL tells us that sometimes what matters is being able to trust others to respect us as separate persons. Hospitals cannot exist, and more generally we cannot live well together, unless we can trust each other to acknowledge that we all have lives of our own. HOSPITAL shows we sometimes get the best result—a community of people living well together—not by aiming at a result so much as by being trustworthy, so people can plan to deal with us in mutually beneficial ways.

To a cartoon utilitarian thinking about TROLLEY, all that matters is numbers. But in a more realistic institutional context like HOSPITAL, we intuitively grasp a more fundamental point. Namely, if we don't take seriously rights and separate personhood, we won't get justice; in fact, *we won't even get good numbers*. This is why I said morality sometimes is about respecting value, not because value does not matter, but precisely because it does.

Acts versus Practices

A consequentialist theory needs to treat some topics as beyond the reach of utilitarian calculation. Rights can trump (not merely outweigh) utilitarian calculation even from a broadly consequentialist perspective. Why? Because, from a consequentialist perspective, results matter, and because, as an empirical matter, there is enormous utility in being able to treat certain parameters as settled, as not even permitting case-by-case utilitarian reasoning.

Unconstrained maximizers, by definition, optimally use any resources to which they have access, including their neighbors' organs. To get good results in the real

---

10. It generally is understood that the trolley conductor is not using the lone victim as a mere means of saving five. The victim in TROLLEY simply is in the wrong place at the wrong time, unlike the victim in HOSPITAL, who in effect is being hunted down for use as a mere resource. The seminal article on this point probably is Foot (1967). Foot argues persuasively against attaching too much weight to the idea of double effect, but see the discussion of acts and omissions in Spector (1992). For a classic discussion of HOSPITAL-type cases, see Thomson (1976). See also chapter 7 on exploitation.

world, though, we need to be surrounded not by unconstrained maximizers but by people who respect rights, thereby enabling us to have a system of expectations and trust, which allows us together to transform our world into a world with greater *potential* (a world where delivery companies are willing to serve the hospital). When we cannot count on others to treat us as rights-bearers with separate lives, we are living in a world of lesser potential.

John Stuart Mill famously observed that it is better to be a dissatisfied Socrates than to be a satisfied pig.[11] Of course, it is better to hit an optimum than not, other things equal. On the other hand, Mill's insight is that other things are not equal. If our choice is between making the best of a low-potential situation versus falling short of making the best of a high-potential situation, we may prefer to fall short, and be a dissatisfied Socrates. Mill, wanting his society to operate as high as possible in utility space, considered it more important to live in a world with a higher ceiling than to make sure every action hits the ceiling. Mill was right.

All optimizing is done relative to a set of constraints and opportunities. Some of our constraints may be brute facts about the external world, but most will be to some extent self-imposed; some will reflect our beliefs about what morality requires. (We have limited time to spend looking for an apartment, limited money to spend on dinner, and there are things we will not do for money.)[12] We may be constrained not to murder—constrained both by choice and by external factors such as the presence of Joe's bodyguard. If other people can count on us not to murder them, new possibilities open up—opportunities people would not otherwise have. In contrast, if people *cannot* rely on us not to murder them, then our murderous act may be as good as possible under the circumstances—it may hit the utility ceiling, but the ceiling itself will be lower than it would have been had murder been ruled out. (Someone who says a true utilitarian will take all that into account is saying a true utilitarian cares not so much about consequences of acts as about consequences of practices that permit some acts and not others, thereby enabling citizens to make some kinds of plans rather than others. I agree. My point is that a true utilitarian in that sense is not an act-utilitarian.)

When doctors embrace a prohibition against harvesting organs of healthy patients without consent, doctors give up opportunities to optimize—to hit the ceiling—but *patients* gain opportunities to visit doctors safely. They gain a world with a higher ceiling. Such utility comes from doctors refusing even to ask whether murdering a patient would be optimal.

But what if your doctor really could save five patients by murdering one? Would not a rule letting your doctor do it, just this once, be the rule with the best consequences? Compare this to a question Rawls asked: in baseball, batters get three strikes, but what if there were a case where, just this once, it would be better if a batter had four?[13] Rawls's crucial and neglected insight is that this question presumes to treat "three strikes" as a rule of thumb, to be assessed case by case. Rules of thumb

---

11. *Utilitarianism*, chap. 2.
12. See chapter 2.
13. See "Two Concepts of Rules," in Rawls (1999b).

are "rules made to be broken." But in baseball, "three strikes" is a rule of practice, not a rule of thumb. If an umpire were to allow a fourth strike in an exceptional circumstance, baseball would not be able to go on as before.

"Rule of thumb" utilitarians may say, and even believe, they respect the rule against murder, yet they treat whether to obey as a question to decide case by case. By contrast, "rule of practice" utilitarians decline even to *ask* about the utility of particular actions in particular cases. Facing a case where violating a rule would have more utility, rule-of-practice utilitarians say, "Our theory sorts out alternative practices, like three strikes versus four, by asking which has more utility as the kind of practice that even *umpires* have no right to evaluate case by case. Our theory *forbids* us to consider consequences in a more case-specific way. We need not say why—the theory says what it says, and letting that be the end of it would be fine—but if we wanted to defend the theory rather than merely specify it, we would say our being forbidden to consider case-specific consequences has better consequences. For one thing, it gives other people the option of rationally trusting us."

What do we think about a case like HOSPITAL where we are certain no one will ever know what we've done, therefore certain that our action will not undermine trust? Perhaps it does not matter, since I am not speaking of a world where we can be certain it will never occur to UPS Inc. to wonder what is happening to all the delivery personnel they keep sending to our hospital. Suffice it to say, real-world morality has the shape it does in part because real-world uncertainty is what it is.

Some utilitarians find it a mystery why morality would incorporate any constraints beyond a requirement to do whatever maximizes the good.[14] But from an institutional perspective, there is no mystery. Moral institutions constrain the good's pursuit because the good is pursued by individuals. If the good is to be realized, then institutions—legal, political, economic, and cultural institutions—must get the constraints right, so as to put individuals in a position to pursue the good in a manner conducive to the good's production in general.

There are parallels between rational agents and moral institutions in terms of how they operate in the face of real-world complexity. For example, individuals adopt satisficing strategies in pursuit of particular goals. They impose constraints on local goals so as to bring their various goals into better harmony with each other, thereby making life as a whole go as well as possible.[15] Likewise, moral institutions get the best result not so much by aiming at the best result as by imposing constraints on individual pursuits so as to bring individual pursuits into better harmony with each other. Institutions (hospitals, for example) serve the common good by leaving well enough alone—creating opportunities for mutual benefit, then trusting individuals to take advantage of them. That is how (even from a utilitarian perspective) institutions have a moral mandate to serve the common good that does not collapse into a mandate for ordinary moral agents to maximize utility.

In effect, there are two ways institutional utility is based on trust. First, people have to be able to trust their society to treat them as rights-bearers. Second,

---

14. See Kagan (1989) 121–27. Scheffler (1982, 129), expresses similar skepticism, despite departing from utilitarianism in other respects.

15. See chapter 2.

society must in turn trust people to use the opportunities they have as rights-bearers within society.

A reflective consequentialist morality is not about one versus five, nor even about costs versus benefits. It is about how we need to live in order to be glad we are neighbors. It's about getting on with our lives in a way that complements rather than hinders our neighbors' efforts to get on with theirs. It accepts constraints on optimizing in order to have a higher ceiling.

Acts aren't the important thing in the long run. They are not the main variable on which long-run utility depends. The ceiling itself is the main variable. An optimizer on the ground in Bangladesh can do only so much. What Bengalis need is not to optimize or be surrounded by (or fed by) optimizers so much as to live in a society with a Western-style ceiling: a society where people (men *and* women, people of all religions, all castes, and so on) have the opportunity and the responsibility to do what meets needs: that is, to produce. If we care about people meeting needs on a global scale, our task is to throw ourselves not into meeting needs but into encouraging processes by which people meet needs. Such encouragement, I surmise, would never involve or even be compatible with reducing ourselves to the material circumstances of a Bengali refugee.

Postscript on Trolley Problems

Experimental psychologists have demonstrated repeatedly that their subjects' intuitions regarding such things as probability and logical implication become increasingly unreliable as the experimental context becomes more abstract or unworldly. In the face of such findings, why would moral philosophers continue to treat intuitive moral reactions to bizarre thought experiments as if such intuitions were reliable? I see no good reason; their teachers did it, so they do it. I am glad Singer seldom partakes of this tradition.[16] I seldom do as much thought-experimenting as I am doing here. I am glad I did it in Kazakhstan, though. Here's why.

Wherever I go, whether my audience consists of local students, congressional staffers, or post-Soviet professors, when I present the trolley case and ask them whether they would switch tracks, about 90 percent will say "There has to be another way!" A philosophy professor's first reaction is to say "Please, stay on topic. I'm trying to illustrate a point here! To see the point, you need to decide what to do when there is no other way." When I said this to my class of post-Soviet professors, though, they spoke briefly among themselves in Russian, then two of them quietly said (as others nodded, every one of them looking me straight in the eye), "Yes, we understand. We have heard this before. All our lives we were told the few must be sacrificed for the sake of many. We were told there is no other way. What we were told was a lie. There was always another way."

They were right. The real world does not stipulate that there is no other way. (Have you, or anyone you know, ever been in a situation like TROLLEY, literally

---

16. I wonder how Singer feels about SHALLOW POND, after which this essay's TRAGIC COMMONS is patterned; authors today are still writing on SHALLOW POND, often without knowing it began life in an article of Singer's (1972).

needing to kill one to save five? Why not? Have you been unusually lucky?) In any case, I now see more wisdom in the untutored insight that there has to be another way than in what TROLLEY originally was meant to illustrate. As Rawls and Nozick (in different ways) say, justice is about respecting the separateness of persons. We are not to sacrifice one person for the sake of another.[17] If we find ourselves seemingly called upon to sacrifice the few for the sake of the many, justice is about finding another way.[18]

5. Ethical Theory in an Ethical Life

Is it *important* to reject the argument that SP can require us to export bads? An all-the-way-down utilitarian should yawn, saying, "So what? Utilities may or may not add up that way in the real world. If they do, so be it. It's not as if recommending that we move bads to wherever they do the least harm is an embarrassment for the theory. What's the problem?"

Would we feel uncomfortable in reacting to the symmetry problem by saying "So what?" I would (and I *am* uncomfortable, insofar as we do in fact export bads). What is the source of my discomfort? Something like this: people have lives of their own. Exporting bads (when we do so without recipients' consent—the *real* recipients, not just their governments) would treat recipients as mere means rather than as separate agents with lives of their own.

Singer is a smart, skilled philosopher. He may say, "So what?" He may say something more clever. No doubt Singer could respond in an interesting way to the species equality problem, too. Among analytic philosophers, the bare fact that Singer can give a good account of himself in philosophical debate is too predictable to be interesting.

My main reason for raising the symmetry and species equality problems (especially the latter) is not to prove I can "spot the fallacy" but simply to reflect on how to take human nature into account when doing moral philosophy. I do not mean to be pointing out a mistake when I observe that what fires Singer's imagination changes from time to time. Sometimes, what fires Singer's imagination is information that there are laboratories where animal experiments are being conducted that have little point and where, even if the research were important, the animals are suffering unnecessarily. Sometimes Singer is gripped by reports of human famine. Sometimes what grips Singer is how animals are treated on factory farms. Singer is normal. He does one thing for a while, then moves on. Moving on is human. It is not a mistake. It is not immoral. Singer is not obliged to commensurate his projects—to show that a moral imperative to spend his days exactly as he does is derivable from SP. He does not need to show that his positions on species equality and on SP fit nicely together.

---

17. I insert the word "actively" here to distinguish Rawls and Nozick from utilitarians who say not rescuing people amounts to sacrificing them, so that at any given moment, we are sacrificing everyone who would not have died if individually or collectively we had acted differently.

18. Hampton (1993) argues that the moral argument against sacrificing one person for the sake of another applies to self-sacrifice as well.

Animal liberation and famine relief are different projects, as are euthanasia, abortion, and so on. Moreover, not everything that matters to Singer is a *project*. Henry Spira was a friend rather than a project of Singer.[19] *Friend* is something to be rather than something to do.[20]

Selective Focus

> FAST PAIN RELIEF: There is a button you could push. If you push it, all sentient life will painlessly vanish from existence. You will, of course, minimize suffering in the process.

FAST PAIN RELIEF shows that minimizing suffering is not the only thing that matters. Neither is it always what matters most.[21]

What FAST PAIN RELIEF leaves open is whether minimizing suffering matters a lot, or relatively little, in the cosmic scheme of things. We need not settle this, because suffering could matter quite a lot without it being true that we ought to spend quite a lot of our lives working to put an end to it. Let me approach the point obliquely, beginning with a story. Environmental activist Paul Watson, founder of the Sea Shepherd Society, confronted a Japanese fishing fleet in 1982 and negotiated a halt to a netting process that was killing dolphins. During the discussion, a fisherman asked Watson which is of more value, the life of a dolphin or a life of a human?

> I answered that, in my opinion, the life of a dolphin was equal in value to the life of a human. The fisherman then asked, "If a Japanese fisherman and a dolphin were both caught in a net and you could save the life of one, which would you save?"
> All the fishermen in the room smirked. They had me pegged for a liberal and felt confident that I would say I would save the fisherman, thus making a mockery of my declaration that humans and dolphins are equal. I looked about the room and smiled. "I did not come to Japan to save fishermen; I am here to save dolphins."[22]

There is power in Watson's response. It is no mere philosophical inconsistency. We can learn from it. It is a pivotal feature of our moral psychology that when we focus on something, it takes on added moral significance to us. We can call it *selective focus*.[23] A lot of people are consumed by one burning issue or another, and sometimes

---

19. See Singer's moving tribute to his friend in Singer (2000).
20. The next two sections revise Schmidtz (2000).
21. This subsection and the one that follows revise Schmidtz (2000).
22. Watson (1995).
23. Human beings, including Singer, are what Elijah Millgram (personal correspondence, June 2005) has called serial hyperspecializers. What Millgram has in mind is that humans adapt to ecological niches by adapting software, not hardware, and the flexibility of human software permits exquisitely refined adaptation: to niches for such organisms as Antarctic nature photographer, corporate merger lawyer, or animal rights activist. Moreover, that flexibility persists to some extent, such that humans retain the capacity to colonize new niches. Individual humans do not pursue only one project, although they may be gripped by one main project at any given time. One of the problems with a project such as that SP suggests—the project of making sure that no one in the world is worse off than oneself—is that the project

make the mistake of thinking everyone ought to be consumed by the same issue. In fact, we freely choose to be consumed by one issue rather than another. Singer may think what he has chosen to focus on is the thing on which we are all obliged to focus, but it only looks that way to someone already focusing on the same thing. Paul Watson was telling the fishermen that although he might be committed to seeing humans and dolphins as equals, he was not obliged to be preoccupied by that particular commitment. He was committed to *respecting* humans and dolphins alike, but not to giving them equal time when deciding how to plan his life.

Paul Watson believes in fighting injustice. Does that commit him to fighting injustice wherever he finds it? Not at all. There is injustice everywhere. Is Watson committed to fighting whichever injustice currently is firing the imagination of Peter Singer? Not at all. That's not what Watson is here for. Like Singer, Watson decides for himself where to make his stand, as do we all.[24]

Western Civilization: What Makes It Work

Distant problems are types of which there are innumerable tokens. Local emergencies are simply tokens. If one falls in your lap today, you can be fairly sure there won't be another in your lap tomorrow. You help, and that's the end of it. Life goes on.

When professional fund-raisers exhort us to help relieve famine, they talk about token-cost (without using that name), going into some detail explaining how a hundred-dollar donation can change a recipient's life. Yet, it is no particular token of the type "starving person" they have in mind. It is the type itself, and famine relief's type-cost is not small. If we embrace the duty to relieve famine in the way Singer says we should, life does not just go on.

Singer himself rightly stresses that pious talk is not enough. "What is the point of relating philosophy to public (and personal) affairs if we do not take our conclusions seriously? In this instance, taking our conclusion seriously means acting upon it."[25]

Can Singer's conclusion be taken seriously in this sense?[26] Singer gives the impression that he is not keen on Western civilization. Having endorsed SP in its strong form, Singer adds,

> Even if we accepted the principle only in its moderate form, however, it should be clear that we would have to give away enough to ensure that the consumer society, dependent as it is on people spending on trivia rather than giving to famine relief, would slow down and perhaps disappear entirely. There are several reasons why this would be desirable in itself.[27]

---

cannot be brought to a state of satisfactory completion. There never comes a time to move on to the next project, and so serial hyperspecializers (including Singer) cannot possibly take SP as seriously as Singer says they should, and their lives would be grossly unlivable if they were seriously to try.

24. I argue that we can and do deliberate about our ends, even our final ends, in chapter 3.

25. Singer (1972) 242.

26. Zell Kravinsky takes SP seriously. He has given away nearly everything he owned, including a kidney, and feels unquenchable guilt over not yet having given away the other one. See Parker (2004).

27. Singer (1972) 241.

Desirable. Desirable *in itself*. We might have expected that Singer would classify the collapse of Western society as a cost, albeit an acceptable one. Evidently not. Singer calls it desirable in itself, and seems to find it so obviously desirable that the "several reasons why" need not be mentioned. And if this is the moderate principle's predictable result, what happens if we follow the strong principle Singer favors? What else disappears along with consumer society? Books? Presumably. Art? Presumably. By the lights of SP, spending *time* on "trivia" is no more allowable than spending money on it.

Theorists need to acknowledge, though, that moral theorizing isn't a game you win by having the most demanding theory. How much should we give? Singer's theory gives a simple answer: more. (Singer himself typically calls for lesser sacrifices in his popular writing, but his theory does not license him to ask for less, except in the sense that the theory licenses him to maximize utility by pretending that from his utilitarian perspective people can buy a clean conscience with a limited sacrifice.) To get something we can take seriously in Singer's sense, we must do better than that.

Peter Unger imagines a world in which

> whenever well-off folks learn of people in great need, they promptly move to meet the need, almost no matter what the financial cost. So, at this later date, the basic needs of almost all the world's people will be met almost all the time.... What's more, should any of these descendants find herself facing such preventable suffering as now actually obtains, she'd devote almost all her energy and resources toward lessening the suffering.[28]

I doubt that Unger's vision is even coherent. It has the following logic. The productive output of the Western world is put up for grabs. A worldwide competition ensues. And the way for a country's leaders to win the competition for that output is to have a population that needs (or seems to need) it more than anyone else. But if we devote almost all our energy and resources to meeting such need, *then how do we get to be so well off*? Where does Unger think prosperity comes from in the first place?

Imagine what our community would be like if a lot of us did as Unger asks. There were about five thousand people in Humboldt, the nearest town when I was growing up on a farm in Saskatchewan. Suppose we farmers gave up that part of our crop that we would have cashed in to buy movie tickets. If we do that, the Towne Theater goes out of business. No big deal, perhaps. The handful of employees seek work elsewhere. Maybe they find work at the Princess or Lucky Cafes. Fine, but we also stop exchanging grain for burgers at the café, instead sending that part of our crop abroad. The cafés close, over a dozen people are out of work, and we exceed Humboldt's ability to find work for them.

Unger says we would not have nice cars and homes.[29] We sacrifice that part of our crop that would have bought new cars. Fine. Car dealers and their employees are out of work. *They* no longer send money to Bangladesh; neither do they buy trivia from local shops, so furniture and clothing shops close, defaulting on their business

---

28. Unger (1996) 20.
29. Unger (1996) 145.

loans. Their employees stop making mortgage payments, and of course, they stop sending money to Bangladesh. Banks start foreclosing on houses, relieving occupants of the obligation to liquidate their houses in service of famine relief. There is no one to buy the houses, though, so the banks close, too.

Those able to leave Humboldt do so, becoming refugees themselves, searching for a community that has not yet succumbed to Unger's call to prevent suffering. So, Singer was right that obeying SP would result in our reducing ourselves to the circumstances of a Bengali refugee. It would do little for Bangladesh in the long run, but would have the result for Western civilization that Singer calls desirable in itself.

Singer would allow that we have to keep doing our part to maintain our incomes so that we remain able to send money overseas. But in the foregoing thought experiment, the problem is not that we aren't working but that we aren't *consuming*, which is to say, we aren't sustaining other people's work. We aren't *doing* business, so we aren't *sustaining* business. It is the lack of business—our declining to spend time and money on trivia—that shuts down the theater and the coffee shop. Moreover, the experiment is not merely a thought experiment. Historically, with few exceptions, this is how thoroughly communal societies crash, unless they switch to some other way of doing business.[30]

Singer says we need a "Darwinism of the left."[31] I agree. No doubt we would disagree on what such a view would imply. We might agree, though, with an observation recently made by David Miller. Miller reflects that if someone in France were getting far better health care than Miller was getting in England, Miller's first instinct would be to suspect that France has a better system and England ought to consider adopting it, not that resources ought to be transferred from France to England so as to reduce inequality.[32] Why? Because the aim of Miller's egalitarianism is to improve life prospects, not to equalize them. Miller's credentials as a spokesperson for the Left are beyond question, and the point he makes here is more or less Darwinian. That is, the thing to do with failed social systems is not to *subsidize* them but to *replace* them with something having a history of working.

We must of course remain (or become) humbly aware that revolutions imposed by alien cultures and philosophies have no history of working. Nothing we do will have only the effects we intend. The only course of action with a history of helping people in the long term is whatever enables them to take responsibility for their own futures (and of course, even that is no guarantee). I cannot pretend to know all that this implies about what is the most humane policy for dealing with the Indian subcontinent. One implication, though, is that we have no duty, and indeed no right, to react as if the problem were simple, as if the problem were simply like that of a neighbor's baby who had the bad luck to fall into a swimming pool. The system and its problems have a logic, and any real solution will involve inventing or (more likely) evolving a system with a different logic.

    30. See chapter 11 for several exceptions to this historical rule and also for some explanation of why this general rule is, after all, the rule.

    31. Singer (2000).

    32. David Miller (1999a).

6. The Nature of Moral Theory

Perhaps we need not reject SP. It may suffice to understand what SP is. The impossibility of living by SP (of living the kind of life we would want for anyone we care about) should lead us to reconsider what theories are and what they have to do with living a moral life. I wish here to reflect on what to do about the apparent fact that SP is intuitively an important part of our lives, yet unacceptable as a moral theory, at least insofar as a moral theory is supposed to specify necessary and sufficient conditions for being moral.

In my view, SP is a piece of a theory, nothing more. Moreover, theories are maps, not attempts to specify necessary and sufficient conditions.[33] We begin with a terrain (a subject matter) and with questions about that terrain. Our questions spur us to build theories—maps of the terrain—that articulate and systematize our answers. To know how to reach Detroit, we need one kind of map. To know how to be a good person, we need another map. Note that *maps* do not tell us where we want to go. (This is equally true of scientific theorizing. For example, to those who want to understand nature in secular terms, Darwinism is a serviceable map. It does not explain everything, but it explains a lot. Creationists reject Darwinism, though. Why? Not because it *fails* to help them understand the origin of species in secular terms, but precisely because it succeeds. They have a different destination; understanding themselves in secular terms is not what they want.) Our questions predate our theorizing, and are our reasons to theorize in the first place. In different words, moral theorizing primarily is for those who aim to be moral. It is when we aim to be moral that we make moral theory the kind of map we have reason to consult.

Theories Are Abstractions

A map of Detroit is an artifact, an invention. So is a map of morality. When we look at a theory's way of representing morality, we are tempted to say, "Real world morality does not really look like that." But Detroit does not look like the map either. A map of Detroit is stylized, abstract, simplified. It otherwise would fail as a map. Yet a map can be accurate, in the sense that it does not mislead. A given map will have ample detail for some purposes; for other purposes, it will be oversimplified.

A map is not itself reality. It is at best a serviceable representation. A theory likewise is a more or less serviceable representation of a terrain. A theory cannot be more than that.

Fine Detail Is a Means to an End

When we construct a map, we leave out details that would merely confuse users. Fine detail is not an end in itself. We do not try to show the current location of every stalled car on the side of the road, and we do not call a map false when it omits such

---

33. I thank Jenann Ismael and quite a few other people over the years for helpful and enjoyable conversations about theories as maps. This section revises portions of pt. 1 of Schmidtz (2006).

details. The question is whether users honestly wanting to follow directions would be led astray.

Road maps would be better in the sense of allowing more detail if we printed them on 10-square-meter sheets rather than the roughly 1-meter sheets we use today. What does that tell us? It tells us that road maps are functional artifacts. We design and create them for a purpose. Their purpose limits how accurate they can be, limits how detailed they can be, limits how much information they can represent. Moral theories are the same. We could "blow them up" in an effort to make them correspond exactly to the moral terrain they are supposed to represent. At some point, though, loading in more detail causes users to lose sight of the forest for the trees. There also is a limit to how much detail a finite mapmaker can possibly anticipate needing to represent. Giving someone directions to your house is not an exact science. It is an art. We get better at it with practice, but still it takes wisdom and judgment. It makes sense to say one thing for daylight hours and another thing to a person who will be navigating at night. We have no reason to expect any set of instructions to be apt for all contexts. It does not help to tell someone to look for Starbucks if that person has never been outside rural China before and has no idea what Starbucks is. Likewise, in 1990, it may help to tell a driver to turn left at Starbucks, yet the same instruction becomes useless in 2008 when there is a Starbucks on nearly every corner.

Comprehensive Scope Is a Means to an End

Existing theories tend to be like maps of the globe: a striving for comprehensive scope—for a principle or set of principles that covers everything. Real moral questions, though, often are more like questions about getting to campus from the airport. When we want to get to campus, a map of the globe does not help. It is not even relevant.

Local maps do not say how to reach all destinations. Yet, though noncomprehensive, they almost always are what we want when we want a map. Why? Because they provide the detail we need for solving problems we actually have. The distant perspective from which we view the whole globe of morality is a perspective from which the surface looks smooth. Principles we stretch to cover the globe fail to make contact with the valleys of moral life. They do not help people on the ground to make moral decisions.

Theories Have Counterexamples

Typically, a counterexample's point is to show that a theory is not algorithmic: we could follow the letter of a theory and still arrive at the wrong destination. But we can consider it a folk theorem of analytic philosophy that *any* theory simple enough to be useful, including SP, has counterexamples. (This folk theorem is a simple theory. Therefore, if correct, it has counterexamples.)

Counterexamples are warnings, telling us theories should not be trusted blindly, any more than a map should be trusted blindly in the face of signs warning that the bridge ahead is washed out. Even simple travel instructions require interpretation, judgment, and experience. (Carbury said the turn was after "about a mile." Have we gone too far? Is that the gas station he told us to watch for?) There is virtually no such thing as simply following instructions.

Theories Say What to Do in Context C,
Not That We Are in Context C

Like it or not, we apply theories, not merely follow them. We can put it like this: When we formulate *rules*, we try to formulate instructions agents can follow, but when we formulate *principles* rather than rules, we are not even trying to formulate instructions agents can simply follow. (The idea of following is comforting, seeming to relieve us of responsibility, whereas *applying* a theory requires good faith, wisdom, and experience, and leaves little room for doubt about who is choosing and who is responsible for the consequences.) Those who want principles of justice to be "idiot-proof" have the wrong idea about what a theory can do.

If your destination is the campus, a city map may tell you to turn left at First and Broadway, but by itself an ordinary map cannot tell you what to do right now unless you already know from experience and observation that you are at the corner of First and Broadway. An ordinary road map does not come with a red X saying "You are here." Ordinary maps depend on a user to know where he or she is, and where he or she wants to go.

Theories are like ordinary maps in that respect. Even if a theory says unequivocally that principle P applies in context C, one still needs to decide whether one's current situation is enough like C to make P applicable. Unequivocal though principle P may be, one still needs wisdom and experience to judge that the time for principle P has come.

Different Destinations Call for Different Maps

Our purposes change. We seek answers to new questions, calling for a new map. A map of the city is for one purpose; a map of the solar system is for another. Likewise, a theory that maps a public official's duties may be quite different from a theory that maps a parent's duties. Note that if we have more than one purpose, we may need more than one map, *even if* there is only one ultimate reality. (My theory that theories are like maps is a theory: a way of systematizing and articulating how I see the activity of theorizing. The activity of theorizing is the reality; my "map theory" is my attempt to describe that reality. If my "map theory" is correct, it will have the limitations maps tend to have.)

When Maps Overlap, They Can Disagree. So What?

Suppose I have two maps, and they disagree. I infer from one that I should take the freeway; the other says the freeway is closed. If I discard one, I make disagreement vanish, but that doesn't solve the problem. Disagreement is informative, telling me I need to pay attention. I cannot trust any map blindly. So, when maps are imperfect, there are worse things than having more than one. If I notice that they disagree, I check whether one is out of date, or consult a local resident. If I see grains of truth in incompatible theories, must I discard one for the sake of consistency? No, not if theories are maps.

Theories Are Compromises

When we theorize, we seek to render what we know simple enough to be understood, stated, and applied. If we try verbally to describe every nuance of morality's complexity, we get something so unwieldy that it may not appear to be a theory at all. If instead we try to simplify, homing in on justice's essence, we get incompleteness or inaccuracy. The task is like trying to represent three-dimensional terrain in two dimensions. Mapmakers projecting from three dimensions onto two can accurately represent size or shape, but not both. Mercator projections depict lines of longitude as parallel, representing shapes more or less accurately but at a cost of distorting relative size. Greenland looks as big as Africa but in fact is one-fourteenth its size. Goode's Homolosine is better at representing individual continents, at a cost of depicting the world as a globe whose surface has been peeled like an orange.

Like other theories, utilitarianism is rather like a Mercator projection. It has an equator around which its implications seem intuitively accurate, and poles around which its exclusive emphasis on consequences seems wildly distorted.

In short, mapmaking, like theorizing, is a messy activity. Mapmakers choose how to represent worlds, and there is no perfect way of representing three-dimensional truth in two dimensions. Moral theorists choose how to represent complex thoughts in simple words, and there is no perfect way of representing in words everything we believe.

Yet, this is not a skeptical view! There remains an objective truth that the map can represent (or fail to represent) in a helpful way. Regardless of whether partisans of Mercator and Peters projections ever settle which representation best serves a particular user's purposes, there will remain a three-dimensional truth of the matter.

It need not be a skeptical view in the arena of moral theorizing either. We choose to believe one moral theory rather than another, and there is no obvious way to prove that those who choose differently are wrong. However, the same is true of road maps. A road map cannot point us in the right direction until we choose a destination. We do not get our destination *from* the map. We bring it *to* the map. There are reasons for choosing one destination (for wanting to be one kind of person, say, or live in one kind of society) rather than another, but we do have to choose.[34]

Articulating the Code

When hiking in the Tucson mountains, I can tell the difference between a pincushion cactus and a hedgehog cactus. I *see* the difference even while doubting I can state the difference. If I try to state the difference, my statement will be incomplete, or

---

34. Do we wish that moral theories were *less* like road maps in this sense? Do we instead want a theory to be a *treasure* map, identifying X as the spot at which every agent *must* aim on pain of being irrational? Why? I thank Chris Freiman, Kevin Vallier, and Jason Brennan for helpful discussion.

will have counterexamples. Our ability to track ethical norms similarly exceeds and precedes our ability to articulate the norms being tracked. Indeed, if being able to track X presupposed verbal skills we develop only in graduate school, then X could not function in society as moral norms must.

Any code one can articulate is no more than a rough summary of wisdom gleaned from experience, that is, wisdom about where one has been. Our articulated wisdom will be useful going forward, since the future will be somewhat like the past. Yet, the future will be novel, too. No code is guaranteed to anticipate every contingency, which is to say, no formula (so far) unerringly prescribes choices for all situations. (The theorists I know do not expect their theories to tell them what grade to assign, how to vote when the hiring committee meets, or whether to cancel class.)

Consider what may be a simpler issue. Can a code tell investors when to buy and sell stocks? Market analysts look at histories of price fluctuations and see patterns. Patterns suggest formulas. Occasionally someone markets a formula, offering proof that the formula would have predicted every major price movement of the last fifty years. Investors buy the formula, which promptly fails to predict the next major move. My point is that many phenomena are codifiable—exhibiting a pattern that, after the fact, can be expressed as a formula—but that does not mean the formula will help us make the next decision.

So, when business majors in ethics courses ask for "the code" the following of which is guaranteed to render all their future business decisions beyond reproach, we may have little to say, even if we think such a code is, in principle, out there awaiting discovery. Business majors tend to understand stock markets well enough to know they can expect only so much from a stock-picking code. Responsibility for exercising judgment ultimately lies with them, not with any code. Some of them have not done enough moral philosophy to know they likewise can expect only so much from a moral code. But we can tell them the truth: philosophers are in the business of articulating principles, not rules and not codes. Moral wisdom is less like knowing answers to test questions and more like simply being aware that the test has begun (and that every day is a new test).

Moral theorizing doesn't necessarily have a global focus. Morality is about what should guide us, given that our focus (yours, mine, Paul Watson's, Peter Singer's, everyone's) inevitably is a *focus*—something that does not cover everything. A humanly rational morality is one that can help people live well together, given that neither we nor the people around us are going to consider everything. A conception of morality that induces us to internalize negative externalities (roughly, to avoid having our existence be a net cost to anyone else) is both psychologically realistic and empirically effective: conformity to such a morality is something we can and do reasonably expect from anyone with some real degree of moral motivation. Conforming to such a morality also enables people to live well together, to prosper individually, and to develop a significant capacity to make their society a better place for other people as well as for themselves. This is the kind of morality we find predominating in prosperous societies, and this is no fluke. I also think the ethos of prosperous societies is more a cause than an effect of prosperity. Not everyone believes morality makes a difference, but I do, and so does Singer.

7. Conclusion

I argued that SP lends as much weight to exporting bads as to exporting goods, to the point of marginal disutility. If SP is not the only consideration that bears on the question of whether to export bads, it is not the only consideration that bears on exporting goods either. (Singer could concede that foisting negative externalities on innocent people without consent falls into the category of "wrong in itself" that he accepted from the start as a sort of catchall category for counterexamples to SP. Fair enough. I will not try to develop the idea that there is something analogously "wrong in itself" with exporting goods, but I do think tragic commons is a real problem for SP in a strategic world like ours. We need not settle whether it is wrong in itself to treat one's productive capacities as mere means to aggregate ends.)

I noted that SP conjoined to species equality does not direct us to relieve famine in Bangladesh so long as rescuable animals are in greater need. I do not believe in species equality, but my point is not to fault Singer for either part of the conjunction that has this implication. Rather, my point is that Singer has more than one project, and is not obliged to fit them all together. Neither logic nor any conception of the good life requires that all our values and projects fit together to make sense as precipitates of a single principle. Singer is not wrong to care about things other than famine relief, and to spend most of his life on them. Neither are we. (At the risk of belaboring the obvious, this is not an ad hominem argument. To say of a theory that its inventor should be able to live by it is to criticize the theory, not the inventor.)

I said SP can't be right; then I asked: but how can it be wrong? The Singer principle is not quite right, but rejecting it does not seem quite right either. I suggest that the apparent dilemma is an artifact of a mistaken assumption about the nature of moral theorizing. The mistaken assumption is that the point of moral theorizing is to identify necessary and/or sufficient conditions for being moral, when in fact the point of moral theorizing is the same as the point of any other kind of theorizing, namely to draw a map. The Singer principle is a suggestion about how we might find our way around the terrain of morality.

Singer's theory is simple, and that is not a problem. It has counterexamples, and that is not a problem. The only problem comes when we treat SP as something more than a way of articulating an understanding about one facet of morality. The Singer principle is a piece of a map. It cannot be more than that. No principle can be more than that.

Previously unpublished. Copyright David Schmidtz. Forthcoming in Jeffrey Schaler, ed., *Singer under Fire* (Chicago: Open Court, 2009).

9

Diminishing Marginal Utility

I have elsewhere discussed synergies between meritocracy, humanitarianism, and equal treatment.[1] This essay examines a well-known argument about an alleged synergy between equal shares and utility, grounded in the idea of diminishing marginal utility. The argument does not work.

1. On the Utility of Equal Shares

Thomas Nagel believes that from an impersonal standpoint, if we were picking principles of just distribution from an impartial perspective, we would have to favor radical egalitarianism.[2] Yet, Nagel realizes, principles of equality are not the only principles we might adopt if we were to consider matters impartially. In particular, utilitarianism embodies its own brand of impartiality, and not everyone would agree that the imperative to equalize matters more than imperatives to maximize utility or to meet basic needs.

Nagel, however, believes that resolving theoretical tensions between equality and utility is moot. Egalitarianism and utilitarianism diverge in theory. As a practical matter, though, they converge in virtue of the phenomenon of diminishing marginal utility (DMU). As R. M. Hare puts it, the DMU of wealth and consumption means that approaches toward equality tend to increase total utility.[3] Edwin Baker argues that, if wealth has DMU, then "a partial redistribution of income would maximize the total of individual utilities."[4] Therefore, "at least a limited intervention to increase equality will always be justified under utilitarian principles."[5] Abba Lerner says: "total

---

1. Schmidtz (2006) pt. 4.

2. Nagel (1991) 65.

3. Hare (1982) 27. One who anticipates my rebuttal is Narveson (1997) 292. See also Narveson (1994) 485.

4. Baker (1974) 45.

5. Baker (1974) 47.

satisfaction is maximized by that division of income which equalizes the marginal utilities of the incomes of all the individuals in the society."[6] Lerner infers: "If it is desired to maximize the total satisfaction in a society, the rational procedure is to divide income on an egalitarian basis."[7]

Consider that we have a hierarchy of needs.[8] Food could be our first priority, even though satisfactions we pursue only after getting enough to eat are greater than anything we get from food. Therefore, what has first priority and what has highest utility need not coincide. (When I got up this morning, eating breakfast came before writing, on my list of priorities, but at the end of the day, the thing I remember as the day's highlight was the writing, not the breakfast.) Theorists tend to assume such cases are atypical, though.

Suppose it is rational from a personal standpoint for Jane Poor not to patronize the arts with money she needs for groceries. Does it follow that it also is rational from an *impersonal* standpoint for a community not to patronize the arts with money that could have been spent on groceries? If we put ourselves in Jane Poor's shoes, eating first and patronizing the arts later seems rationally imperative. What if impartiality is more a matter of stepping into *no one's* shoes? In that case, we see that hunger relief is not the only impersonal value; it is unclear that the world would be a better place if, say, resources that went into building the pyramids and the Parthenon had instead gone into soup kitchens.

Again, though, most philosophers assume equality and efficiency go hand in hand, and that from an impartial perspective this is a reason to favor equality. Broome refers to the argument as "the standard utilitarian argument for equality."[9] Nagel says:

> Even if impartiality were not in this sense egalitarian in itself, it would be egalitarian in its distributive consequences because of the familiar fact of diminishing marginal utility. Within any person's life, an additional thousand dollars added to fifty thousand will be spent on something less important than an additional thousand added to five hundred—since we satisfy more important needs before less important ones. And people are similar enough in their basic needs and desires so that something roughly comparable holds between one person and another.[10]

Nagel says we satisfy more important needs before less important ones. Not quite. We satisfy more *urgent* needs first, but the most urgent need is not necessarily most important. Nevertheless, DMU is, as Nagel says, a familiar fact. We have all seen cases of one person turning to another and saying, "Here. You need this more than I do." We can all imagine contexts where such words seem not only intelligible but true.

This does not mean, however, that we should join Nagel and others in thinking that DMU resolves the apparent tension between equality and efficiency. In fact, the

---

6. Lerner (1970) 28.
7. Lerner (1970) 32.
8. See the seminal work of the psychologist Maslow (1970). See also Schmidtz (2006) chap. 5.1.
9. Broome (1991) 176.
10. Nagel (1991) 65.

tension is real. Further, the tension exists not only in spite of DMU, but sometimes *because* of it.

Whether we should take this as a critique of utilitarianism or of egalitarianism is a matter of perspective. The point here is not to refute egalitarianism, or utilitarianism, but to show that DMU does not reconcile them and, under conditions often assumed to secure their reconciliation, can even worsen the tension between them.

2. Premises

Harry Frankfurt believes the DMU argument is unsound, for it is grounded in false premises. As Frankfurt sees it, the DMU argument assumes that:

> the utility provided by or derivable from an nth dollar is the same for everyone, and it is less than the utility for anyone of dollar (n - 1).... It follows that a marginal dollar always brings less utility to a rich person than to one who is less rich. And this entails that total utility must increase when inequality is reduced by giving a dollar to someone poorer than the person from whom it is taken.[11]

Frankfurt thinks there are two false premises here. First, it is not true that the utility of money invariably decreases at the margin. Second, individuals are not alike; nor is there any reason to suppose their utility functions are alike. Thus, interpersonal utility comparisons are problematic. Different people get differing satisfaction from wealth, such that a marginal dollar could be more satisfying to a rich person than to a poor person. We could add that, third, even if the argument were sound, the bureaucracies we set up to undertake egalitarian redistribution tend to be wasteful. Fourth, even if the costs of redistribution are manageable, there can be incentive problems: redistribution can rob both rich and poor of the incentive to work. From a utilitarian perspective, such costs are at least relevant.

These four responses have some merit, no doubt, but this chapter asks what happens when (1) marginal utilities smoothly diminish; (2) all are known to have the same utility function, so interpersonal comparisons are easy; (3) redistribution is costless; and (4) there are no problems regarding incentives to work. I will show that even in this pristine environment, where the utilitarian case is most straightforward, we have a situation where transferring a dollar from someone who needs it less to someone who needs it more can be unjustified from a strict utilitarian perspective.

Frankfurt says it follows from the premises of the standard utilitarian argument for equality that a marginal dollar always brings less utility to a rich person than to one who is less rich. Let us accept this for argument's sake. This, adds Frankfurt, entails that "total utility must increase when inequality is reduced."[12]

Not so. To see why not, suppose two people, Joe Rich and Jane Poor, have identical and smoothly declining marginal utility functions. For the sake of simplicity, suppose the only good whose distribution is at issue is corn. We take as given, then,

---

11. Frankfurt (1987) 25.
12. Frankfurt (1987) 25.

that a marginal unit of corn is worth less to a corn-rich person than to a corn-poor person.

Suppose Poor has zero units of corn, whereas Rich has two units. Further, suppose that to have one unit of corn is to have enough to eat, while two units of corn is more than Rich would want. Perhaps having a unit of corn is a matter of life and death. Or perhaps, without corn, Rich and Poor would survive by eating something awful, which they simply could not bring themselves to do if they could eat corn instead. In any case, consuming the first unit has high marginal utility for Rich and Poor alike, while consuming a second unit has low marginal utility. It is easy to see how someone might conclude that total utility increases when we transfer a unit from Rich to Poor, then go on to conclude that the DMU argument for egalitarian redistribution is, at least here, airtight.

3. The Argument

But is it airtight? If it is *possible* that transferring a unit from Rich to Poor in this pristine environment does not maximize utility, then the alleged entailment fails. Note that we are not trying to prove it *never* maximizes utility to redistribute from people with low marginal utility to people with high marginal utility. To defeat the entailment claim, we need only show that it is not *necessarily* maximizing to make such a transfer.

Given one unit of corn, Jane Poor puts it to its highest valued use, namely immediate consumption. Joe Rich, having already consumed a unit and thus being satiated for the moment, invests the corn in something less urgent by Rich's own lights. Poor eats the corn, whereas Rich, having eaten enough, has nothing better to do with his surplus than to plant it.

For a person with one unit, consumption is overwhelmingly the highest valued use of that unit. For a person with two units, consumption is overwhelmingly the highest valued use of the first unit; due to the diminishing utility of consumption, production is the second unit's highest valued use. Thus, if Joe Rich's second unit is transferred to Jane Poor, both units are consumed. If Joe Rich retains the second unit, one unit is consumed and one is planted.

In figure 9.1, C* is the point at which a person with that much corn would rather plant additional corn than eat it. In the story of Rich and Poor, C* equals one unit. Because of diminishing (that is, downward-sloping) marginal utility of consumption, production becomes a higher valued use as wealth (measured on the horizontal axis as units of corn) rises.[13]

---

13. Figure 9.1. generalizes the argument of the text. In the particular example, C* = 1 unit of corn. As a picture of that example, figure 9.1 is a static snapshot of a dynamic multiperiod model in which, if we redistribute in accordance with DMU in period 1, each party consumes one unit by hypothesis. If the utility of consuming a unit equals U, then total utility for period 1 is 2U, and zero thereafter, because no units remain to put into production. By hypothesis, both Rich and Poor are without corn for all subsequent periods.

If we do not redistribute corn in period 1, Rich consumes 1 unit and plants the second, so total utility of corn consumption for period 1 is 1U. Suppose the productive yield of planted units is 2 + e units, so Rich can consume 1 unit each period and still have more seed corn than in the previous period. After

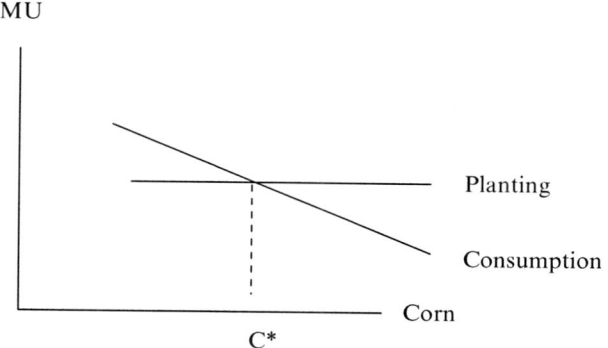

FIGURE 9.1. Marginal utility of corn: planting versus consuming.

Note that production's tendency to become more desirable relative to consumption is a general consequence of consumption's DMU, and not an artifact of an odd example. The general conclusion: if a community does not have people out so far on their utility curves that they have nothing better to do with marginal units of corn than to plant them, the community faces stagnation at best.

Therefore, unequivocal utilitarian support for egalitarian redistribution is not to be found in the idea that consumption has DMU. This result in no way depends on questioning the premises of the DMU argument. On the contrary, the argument is *grounded* in DMU. Contra Nagel, it does not follow from positing DMU that if everyone counts the same, then a more equal distribution will be a better distribution. A society that takes Joe Rich's second unit and gives it to Jane Poor is taking that unit away from someone who, from his perspective, has nothing better to do than plant it and giving it to someone who, from her perspective, does have something better to do with it. That sounds good, but in the process, the society takes seed corn out of production and diverts it to current consumption, thereby cannibalizing itself.

4. Responses

A. The Argument Assumes a Philosopher's Conception of Utility

The concept of aggregated interpersonal utility used by Hare and Nagel and Frankfurt, which gets the argument going in the first place, has largely disappeared

---

two periods, total consumption utility = 2U, that, is, 1U consumed during each of the two periods so far, with $1 + e$ now in production. After three periods, total consumption utility = 3U, with $1 + 2e + e^2$ now in production, and so on. Eventually, the leverage of the e's mounts. By the time we reach a period where accumulating increments of e add up to over a unit of corn, Rich is in a position to give or sell or lend (for example) $1 + e$ units of corn to Poor. Now Poor also has a surplus and nothing better to do with it than to become a producer. After that point, the utility of consumption accumulates at a rate of two units, indefinitely, while on the production side, the e's continue to mount.

from economic discourse. Kenneth Arrow says that in economics, "the utilitarian approach is not currently fashionable, partly for the very good reason that interpersonally comparable utilities are hard to define."[14]

B. The Argument Assumes a Dynamic Model

With that caveat about the argument's premises, however, Arrow judges the argument to be valid. "In the utilitarian discussion of income distribution, equality of income is derived from the maximization conditions if it is further assumed that individuals have the same utility functions, each with diminishing marginal utility."[15] Arrow is not the only Nobel laureate economist who considers the argument valid. Paul Samuelson reasons that if people are all roughly the same, "so that their utilities can be added, then the dollars gained by the rich do not create so much social welfare or total utility as the dollars lost by the poor."[16] Elsewhere, Samuelson says, "If each extra dollar brings less and less satisfaction to a man, and if the rich and poor are alike in their capacity to enjoy satisfaction, a dollar taxed away from a millionaire and given to a median-income person is supposed to add more to total utility than it subtracts."[17]

Undoubtedly, Arrow and Samuelson would respond by saying they did not mean to suggest that the DMU argument would hold in a world of production. They presumably would deny being surprised by the result obtained here, saying they were implicitly if not explicitly assuming that the stock of utility-generating goods is fixed.

I accept this response. *If* the DMU argument were treated as relevant only to worlds without production, the argument would be valid, or near enough. Unfortunately, many people, and possibly Arrow and Samuelson, too, reason as follows. If the DMU argument's strongly egalitarian conclusions do not quite follow in a world of production, what presumably does follow is a suitably weakened version of those same egalitarian conclusions. Not so. In a world of production, DMU can weigh *against* egalitarian redistribution rather than for it, depending on the details of initial endowments and production functions.

C. The Argument Assumes That Production's Marginal Utility Is NOT Decreasing

Figure 9.1 represents the marginal utility of planting as a horizontal line, which we can interpret as constant returns to scale. Under that assumption, there will exist a point C* where DMU weighs against rather than in favor of egalitarian redistribution. (The main point of holding constant other variables, such as production's marginal utility, is that it lets us focus on how consumption's DMU can be the change that leads to production becoming a use valued relatively higher at C*.) Had we instead assumed increasing returns to scale, representing the marginal product of

---

14. Arrow (1971) 409.
15. Arrow (1971) 409.
16. Samuelson (1973) 409.
17. Samuelson (1973) 423.

planting as a rising curve, the same conclusion would follow, for C* would still exist. Suppose we assume decreasing returns to scale, thus representing planting's marginal product as a falling curve. If production's marginal utility is downward-sloping, a point C* will exist just in case the production line's slope is gentler than the consumption line's slope (that is, just in case there comes a point when Joe Rich has eaten so much that he'd rather bury an additional unit than eat it).[18] And so long as there is a point C*, there is a range where a person is better off planting. If so, then whether consumption's DMU weighs for or against egalitarian redistribution will depend on where we are on the curve, that is, whether we are to the left or to the right of point C*.

In any case, I do not assume that production exhibits DMU; nor do I assume otherwise (except for purposes of drawing fig. 9.1). My quarrel is with the idea that *consumption's* DMU necessarily weighs in favor of egalitarian redistribution.

D. What if We Combine the Utilities of Production and Consumption?

Acknowledging the losses that occur in the course of transferring wealth, Nagel says that, nonetheless, "the rate at which marginal utility diminishes is so rapid that it will still have egalitarian consequences even in many cases in which the better off stand to lose more resources than the worse off stand to gain."[19] In figure 9.1, though, the DMU of consumption for Joe Rich *grounds* the argument against redistribution.

For this argument to work, the marginal utility of consumption for Rich must diminish rapidly enough to dip below the marginal utility of planting by the time Rich allocates his last unit. Otherwise, there will be no point C* at which productive activity becomes relatively attractive. In that case, since Rich's last unit is destined for consumption, it makes utilitarian sense to transfer that unit to someone whose marginal utility of consumption is higher.

So, let me stress that my argument is not against redistribution in general but against assuming that, from a utilitarian perspective, consumption's DMU necessarily weighs in favor of egalitarian redistribution. Neither am I arguing against taxation for the sake of capital investment. Such investments would have to be assessed on their productive merits. Programs aimed at subsidizing the education of poor children could be a wise investment in a society's future. But DMU does not and cannot carry the argumentative weight in such cases.

Redistribution could enhance productivity by putting corn in the hands of people who otherwise would have no chance to become productive, but then we would no longer be redistributing from Rich to Poor; we would be redistributing corn not to poor recipients per se but rather to recipients better positioned to put extra units to productive use. Such recipients may tend to be people who already have C* units of corn, so that they will have the luxury of putting our grants to productive use. Such redistribution could go from the rich to the poor, or from the poor to the middle

---

18. The point will be to the right of the y-axis if the C-line starts out above the P-line and then falls to meet it. Otherwise, if even the first unit is, improbably, better planted than consumed, C* will be on the y-axis.

19. Nagel (1991) 65.

class. Or, imagine a middle class with more than enough to eat but not enough to invest optimally. Combining the utilities of planting and eating could suggest a case for transferring wealth away from this class in *both* directions—to poor consumers with less to eat, and (other things equal) to rich producers better positioned to exploit economies of scale.

E. The Argument Assumes Jane Poor Discounts Future Periods

I assumed both Joe Rich and Jane Poor would consume their first unit and plant a second unit, if only they had a second. I stipulated that if they had one unit, they could not bring themselves to forgo its consumption. Suppose, contrary to my stipulation, Jane Poor is not starving or otherwise in need of a unit for immediate consumption. She would invest rather than consume even her first unit of corn, if she had one, for the sake of her future.[20] This case would not be a counterexample to the thesis that we maximize utility by transferring goods to consumers for whom the goods have the highest utility.

The counterexample I offered is a different case, in which a unit's donor has no higher-valued use than to put the unit into production, but where, *because of consumption's DMU*, the unit's recipient (even if the recipient is identical to the donor except for possessing fewer units) does have a higher-valued use, namely immediate consumption.

5. Conclusion

The implications of consumption's DMU are consistently egalitarian only in a model without production. In a world without production, a downward-sloping marginal utility function represents marginal wealth as increasingly frivolous consumption. Utility is maximized in this world by giving resources to those for whom resources have the most utility.

In a world of production, this does not follow. In a world of production, DMU of consumption implies less reason to consume and, relatively speaking, more reason to invest. In this world, it is an open question whether utility is maximized by transferring resources to those for whom those resources have the most utility. Utility may instead be maximized by transferring resources to those who will use them in the most productive way.[21]

The practical implication, from a utilitarian perspective is that goods that can be invested in production should not be transferred as if they were nothing more than consumption goods.

There is a purpose served by model-simplifying assumptions, but assuming away production possibilities is not like ignoring steps in the utility curve. Ignoring

---

20. I thank Kate Johnson for suggesting this objection, and for several enjoyable conversations about what to make of it.

21. Needless to say, perverse incentive effects of paying people to *look* needy also afflict institutions that pay people to *look* productive. The latter problem is not unusual in large corporations.

steps simplifies the truth. When we ignore production, though, we do not merely simplify; we ignore *the* prerequisite for meeting needs in the real world.

This essay revises David Schmidtz, "Diminishing Marginal Utility and Egalitarian Redistribution," originally published in a special issue on liberalism, guest edited by Jan Narveson, of *Journal of Value Inquiry* 34 (2000): 263–72. Reprinted by permission of Kluwer Academic Publishers and Springer Science and Business Media.

10

Guarantees

People have accidents. They get old. They eat too much. They have bad luck. And sooner or later, something will be fatal. It would be a better world if such things did not happen, but they do. There is no use arguing about it. What is worth arguing about is whether it makes for a better world when people have to pay for other people's misfortunes and mistakes rather than (or as well as) their own.

Misfortune and mistakes aside, it is sometimes said that, even in the ordinary course of events, people should not have to pay for basic human needs. There is no use arguing about that, either. Someone, after all, has to pay. The question is who. Edwin Baker says,

> If the practices of the society indicate that certain things are necessary in order to be a full member, then the community must assure the provision of these things to all who are expected to be part of the community. Anything less would not be a convincing basis from which to argue that he ought to join, that he ought to accept the request to be obligated. Or to put it in different terms, it would be an insult for a person to have to do without those things.[1]

Is that true? Baker leaps straight from the premise that certain things are necessary to the conclusion that the community must assure their provision. However, the "insult" of having to do without "those things" is not the same as the "insult" of having to do without guaranteed provision of those things at someone else's expense. Even if the value of the goods themselves is beyond question, the value of the guarantee is not. After all, the guarantee does not mean the goods are free. What it means is that someone else has to pay.

This essay is about guarantees. It is about trying to ensure that no one ever loses. It is about trying too hard. This essay is also about what actually happens in the absence of guarantees. How do people respond when left to fend for themselves, with no guarantee that their needs will be satisfied at someone else's expense?

---

1. Baker (1974) 52.

Do they cooperate, voluntarily coming together to pool resources, share risks, and help each other in times of trouble? If they do, then to that extent they are accepting responsibility for their welfare as a group rather than as individuals. Are they making a mistake? It depends. Collective responsibility is not a problem in and of itself, and individual versus collective responsibility is not the crucial distinction.

1. Individual versus Collective Responsibility: Not the Real Issue

More crucial is a distinction between *internalized* and *externalized* responsibility. In general, we say a decision has a (negative) external or spillover effect when someone other than the decision-maker ends up bearing some of the decision's costs. A factory deciding to dump wastes into a river, leaving them to be dealt with by people who live downstream, is a classic example. When I speak of responsibility being externalized, I have something similar in mind. Responsibility is externalized when agents are able to foist responsibility on someone else—responsibility for cleaning up the messes they find themselves in, whether the mess results from mistake, misfortune, or (in the case of the factory) business as usual.

This contrast between internalized and externalized responsibility—taking responsibility for meeting one's own needs versus foisting such responsibility on others—does not neatly track the contrast between individual and collective responsibility. Some forms of collective responsibility help to internalize responsibility. They have a history of enabling people to take responsibility for themselves as a group and consequently have been important contributors to human welfare. My thesis is that a society is trying too hard when, to avoid the prospect of leaving individuals to "sink or swim," it issues guarantees that not only collectivize responsibility but externalize it at the same time—that not only help decision-makers spread costs among themselves but also help them pass costs onto third parties without consent.

2. Joint Responsibility

My brother Jim smoked two packs of cigarettes a day. He died of lung cancer at the age of thirty-nine. I sometimes think anyone who ever sold Jim a cigarette ought to be in jail, but Jim blamed himself. He did not need to guess at what role he played in his impending death, either. He knew beyond reasonable doubt. Untangling joint responsibility may be an intractable problem in theory. It can look that way to theorists. In practice, figuring out whom to blame is a matter of daily routine in any court of law.

But this essay is not about whom to blame. It is about institutional settings that make people more likely to take responsibility. *Holding* people responsible involves assigning blame or credit. When I speak of *taking* responsibility, I use the term in a different way. To take responsibility is to accept a cluster of challenges: to plan your future, to deal with your own mistakes as best you can, to deal with other people's mistakes as best you can, to make the best of your good luck, and your bad luck as well.

Internalizing responsibility, then, also is a cluster of things. In particular, it involves being committed to working for a living. (It need not involve working for wages. Homemakers and subsistence farmers work for a living.) It does not preclude cooperation or mutual aid, though. More generally, we internalize responsibility when we take responsibility for the future. We need not take credit for the past. We internalize responsibility when we take responsibility for making use of our opportunities. We need not take credit for the existence of those opportunities. We internalize responsibility when we see our problems as our problems; we need not see them as our fault.

Internalizing responsibility is not a matter of courts sorting out how much to blame Jim and how much to blame tobacco companies for Jim's death. It is more a matter of courts doing what they can (1) to make tobacco companies take a more proactive responsibility for the consequences of their actions, and (2) to make people like Jim do the same, so as to save people like Jim from tobacco companies, and also from themselves. In turn, citizens internalize responsibility when they face the world of tangled joint causation as it is, and do not rely on courts to save them from themselves.

How, then, can institutions help? It would be easy to oversimplify obstacles facing institutions that would lead people to internalize responsibility. The big oversimplification, though, lies in supposing that we do not need to internalize responsibility—that a cure for poverty lies in taking wealth from those who create it and giving it to those who do not. Causation is indeed complex, so we should not be surprised if and when simply handing out other people's money fails to do much good.

Some people think social conditions partly determine whether people take responsibility. I agree. I have stressed the point. I have heard it said that when people fail to take responsibility, it is not entirely their fault. And if it is not entirely their fault, then they should not be punished for it. Therefore, society (that is, other people who are not even partly at fault) ought to pay. That conclusion does not follow, but in any case, the real implication is hard to miss: if institutions determine whether people take responsibility, then we should *favor* institutions that lead people to take responsibility.

3. Static and Dynamic Perspectives

I have come to see that there are two fundamentally different perspectives on questions of justice in distribution and in production. From a static perspective, we see society as a snapshot, and what is wrong with the picture is that some people have unmet needs while others have plenty. The question defining the static perspective is how do we get needed resources to needy people? How can we help those the system has left behind? From a more dynamic perspective, though, society is a process by which one snapshot evolves into another. The question defining the dynamic perspective is, which institutions make people less likely to need help in the first place?

From a static perspective, our task is to rearrange the resources visible in the snapshot, frame by frame. From a dynamic perspective, our task is to nurture the processes that produce the resources, and thereby produce better snapshots in the future. From a dynamic perspective, we worry about the consequences of rearranging resources for purposes other than the purposes for which producers are producing them. When we worry about that, we appear from a static perspective to be willfully out of touch. We are talking about history or economic theory, perhaps, but not about the real world. The real world is the snapshot.

To people who see things from a purely static perspective, it will seem that people who take a dynamic perspective want people to suffer. Why else would people hesitate to rearrange resources? Those who see things from both perspectives, though, see a complex dance of incentives, opportunities, evolving culture, and fragile personal values. They see that many things happen when we reshuffle resources, and that not all of them are good.

What should be our top priority—to clean up messes, or to prevent them? Which is the key to reducing the amount of mess in the world? I am not against cleaning up messes, but I do want to say that if we focus on the first task and ignore the second, we miss the point of encouraging people to take responsibility for their own welfare. Encouraging people to take responsibility can help many of the people who need help right now, but that is not the main reason for such encouragement. The main reason is that when people take responsibility, they are less likely to need help in the first place.

When I refer to the static perspective as static, I mean no insult. I mean only to suggest that an exclusively static perspective is not enough. A static perspective looks at how things are, while a dynamic perspective looks at how things change. Each perspective is legitimate in its own way. The suffering we see from a static perspective is, after all, really there. Unfortunately, there are things we do not see from a static perspective. We do not see long-term progress. We do not see what causes long-term progress. Those things are abstract. They lack the visceral urgency of the crises of the day. But they are no less real.

If it is only from a static perspective that we fully appreciate the problems, it is only from a dynamic perspective that we fully appreciate what it takes to solve them.

4. How to Make Sure the Poor Are Left Behind

Some theorists look at those who are left behind, and all they see, to invoke another familiar metaphor, is the part of the glass that remains empty. We have to look at the part of the glass that has been filled, though, to see the point of internalizing responsibility. The people who take responsibility are the people who fill the glass.

If the degree of internalization now in place has not filled the glass to the brim, some people conclude that internalization has failed. They say we need something else, usually something that, in my eyes, involves punching holes in the glass. Danziger and his colleagues estimate that every $1 in U.S. welfare transfers causes a reduction of 23 cents in the amount of labor that recipients contribute to the economy.[2] Is the number correct? I do not know, but I am confident that any institution that has such a result is not good for people. Not good for recipients. Not good for

---

2. Danziger, Haveman, and Plotnick (1981) 1020.

their neighbors. My view is, if you want a full glass, then you want institutions that lead people to live and interact in ways that fill the glass.

President Clinton presumably wanted to help fill the glass in 1993 when he tried to appropriate $17 billion for a program he predicted would create five hundred thousand jobs. From a static perspective, it was an obvious response to problems visible in the current frame. Suppose Clinton's numbers were correct. That would amount to $34,000 (in 1993 dollars) for every job created. How many jobs would be created if that much money were left in the hands of those who produced it? Five hundred thousand? A million?

All we know for sure is that, after the appropriation was denied, the unemployment rate fell. By August 1996, it had fallen to 5.1 percent. The unemployment rate for African American males over age twenty fell to 8.1 percent.[3] No minority ever was more notoriously left behind than African Americans, yet their unemployment rate was lower than the *overall* unemployment rates of Germany (10 percent), Italy (12.2 percent), France (12.5 percent), and Spain (22.9 percent).[4] Fifteen million new jobs were created between the end of 1992 and July 1997.[5]

Market society is sometimes described as a tide that lifts all boats. In many ways, the metaphor is apt. It reminds us that the key to prosperity in market society is to produce what other people value. Profits normally are not made at other people's expense. People get rich when they market the light bulb, telephone, or computer not because such inventions make people worse off but because they make people better off.

People tend to see human commerce as a zero-sum game—a game in which wealth is redistributed but not created. If society were a zero-sum game, though, we would be born in caves. Our teeth would fall out before we turned thirty, and we would die soon thereafter, as our ancestors did when human society was in its infancy. We fare better than that today because human commerce is not zero-sum. There is a tide. It is lifting boats. In principle, it could lift them all.

What I do not like about the metaphor is its suggestion that the tide lifts us all unconditionally or indiscriminately. There are tides in market society that lift virtually all boats, of course. Market society gave us telephones and light bulbs, and few of us would be better off without them. Nevertheless, as a general rule, material progress does more for some people than for others. The tide lifts the boats it touches; the rest are left behind. They are not left living in caves, but still they are left behind, at least in relative terms.

---

3. Bernard Baumohl, John Greenwald, Joseph R. Szczesny, Adam Zagorin. "Too Many Jobs?" *Time*, Sept. 16, 1996, 68.

4. Thomas K. Grose, "Labor, Social Costs Taking Toll on Governments," *USA Today*, Sept. 19, 1996, 1–2B. There are several ways to explain (or explain away) these numbers. Grose says, "Laws in many European countries, including Germany, Italy, and France, make it all but impossible to fire people. So companies don't hire—they invest in equipment instead" (2B). Gary Becker says the European picture is worse than the numbers suggest, for new jobs in Europe tend to be temporary or casual, owing to the difficulty of firing regular staff. Moreover, in Europe, "those out of work for more than a year now account for one-third of the unemployed" (1996, 101).

5. In 1993, the unemployment rate was 6.9 percent. As of July 1997, it had dropped to 4.9 percent. U.S. Bureau of Labor Statistics, at http://www.bls.gov/cps/prev_yrs.htm

Why are they left behind? To see why the tide does not touch everyone, we need to see why it touches anyone. If we try to force the tide to lift everyone, without understanding how the tide works, we are likely to end up with more poverty rather than less, a few decades down the road. The first question, then, is not why some people still live in caves, but rather, why doesn't everyone? Why is there such a thing as material progress in the first place?

The basic answer is that progress occurs because people produce. People perceive a need. They take responsibility for meeting it. And in meeting perceived needs, they produce things of value. Their productivity creates and constitutes the tide of material progress. That explains in the most general terms why there is a tide, and why some people are lifted by it. The tide tends to lift people when they contribute to it. The tide is not an external force. People who contribute are not merely *lifted* by the tide; they *are* the tide.

Unfortunately, those who do not produce do not contribute to the tide. They are not part of the tide. And the tide tends to leave them behind. The tide tends to offer less to those who, sometimes through no fault of their own, fail to produce what other people value.

People in market societies view poverty as an aberration, but it became unusual only recently, and only in some countries. People sometimes make an extraordinary claim about what market society can afford. They claim that market society is so rich that (to provide guarantees against ever being poor, say) it can afford to become a nonmarket society—a society whose central government is licensed to distribute according to need. Or, if we cannot afford to convert the whole society to a nonmarket system, surely we can create enclaves within which people are sheltered from the imperative to produce something of value and can instead acquire money simply by needing it. Obviously, such enclaves can and do coexist with market society, but not without cost. While people are sheltered from the tide (that is, from the need to contribute to it), the tide is leaving them and their children behind. If the enclaves' inhabitants find themselves living like victims of a third-world economic disaster, and if their children are no more ready to participate in market society than suddenly free citizens of the former Soviet Union, what do we conclude? If we look only at the snapshot, it will seem obvious: we need bigger enclaves.

If we truly want to help our fellow citizens, though, we should stop to remind ourselves that the overwhelming majority of them are contributors. They are not being left behind. They do not need our help. We should try not to change that. Above all, we should avoid disrupting economic processes in virtue of which ordinary citizens of market societies do not need our help.

Welfare programs, though, sometimes seem highly disruptive. They seem not to encourage people to take responsibility. In the U.S., out-of-wedlock births have risen by over 600 percent since 1960. They now represent over 30 percent of the total. (Japan's illegitimacy rate, by comparison, is 1.1 percent.)[6] Thirty percent of out-of-wedlock births are to teenagers. Sixty percent are to women who were teens when they began bearing out-of-wedlock children.[7] Several studies suggest that incentive

---

6. Nechyba (1997).

7. Tanner (1996) 70–71.

structures of programs like the now-defunct Aid to Families with Dependent Children (AFDC) made the problem worse.⁸

However, even if AFDC initially caused the problem, it does not follow that simply shutting down AFDC would make the problem disappear.⁹ The current problem is not merely a matter of perverse incentives but also a matter of transformed values and attitudes—a transformed sense of responsibility—and no one can think the transformation is easy even to understand, let alone undo.¹⁰ We have experimented with externalized responsibility on a massive scale, without what scientists would consider an adequate experimental control.

In some cases, the experiments were self-conscious attempts to encourage dependency. There was a time when journalist Richard Elman could say in all seriousness,

> Perhaps when all our poor have been made dependent upon government and assured of stability and decency, liberty, and justice, we will be able to worry about how they work out their psychic destinies without seeming like hypocrites. In the meantime, data that the American poor are not yet dependent accumulates.¹¹

Elman concludes that "we of the rising middle class must somehow dispel our own myth that we are not dependent and do not wish to become dependent. We must try to create even more agencies of dependency."¹²

And so it was. In 1966, New York City mayor John Lindsay appointed Mitchell Ginsberg as his social services commissioner.

> Ginsberg organized his staff to go out and recruit more people on to the welfare rolls. Using federal funds, they set up some 200 storefront centers in the city to recruit new welfare clients.... The new commissioner both raised payments and eliminated eligibility background checks—people qualified for welfare on their own say-so.... New York City's welfare population barely grew between 1945 and 1960. But between 1960 and 1965, it grew by more than 200,000 to a total of 538,000. It then ballooned to a staggering 1,165,000 in 1971—larger than the total populations of 15 states and more than double the size of the state's second largest city, Buffalo. Amazingly, the explosion occurred amid a great economic boom and declining black male unemployment.¹³

As I said, we do not have an experimental control. We know only so much about what happens to people and to their children when they go on welfare. We do not know

---

8. For example, Lundberg and Plotnick (1995).

9. The passage of the Personal Responsibility and Work Opportunity Act in 1996 limited lifetime eligibility for benefits to a total of five years. Since then, teen pregnancy rates have been dropping. Different sources offer different numbers and different explanations, but all sources seem to agree that the drop has been large and steady in every state, and that teen birth rates had already begun to drop by 1991. The most reputable (albeit least decipherable) source is probably the National Center for Health Statistics. See *http://www.cdc.gov/nchs/fastats/teenbrth.htm*. Other readily available internet sources include the Guttmacher Institute, PhysiciansForLife.org, and the Annie E. Casey Foundation.

10. Nechyba (1997).

11. Elman (1966) 198.

12. Elman (1966) 300.

13. Siegel (1996) 14, 16.

what would have become of them if they had relied on themselves and on each other instead. And we do not know what will happen if we throw them off welfare now, a few years after encouraging them to get on. Intuitively, though, we do know that it is a mistake to rescue children from the prospect of growing up poor by putting them in a situation where they grow up not knowing what being productive (or feeling the self-respect that goes with it) would even be like. The cure is worse, much worse, than the disease.

Some say welfare programs encourage (or even require) people to drop out of the workforce.[14] Is it true? Robert Goodin concludes that they do not, at least not in a major way.[15] Yet, on Goodin's own account, citing the aforementioned Danziger study and describing it as a "masterly synthesis," Goodin admits that "the major U.S. income transfer programs, all taken together, are probably responsible for a total reduction of work hours by recipients amounting to 4.8 percent of total work hours for all workers in the U.S."[16] Obviously, though, as Danziger and his colleagues warn readers, "the percentage of reduction in work *per transfer recipient* implied by this estimate is substantially larger than 4.8 percent."[17] Transfer recipients account for only a small part of the overall work force, so for that small group to be pulling the entire workforce down by 4.8 percent, the effect within that small group has to be huge. Danziger and his colleagues estimated that "AFDC reduces work effort of the average recipient by roughly 600 hours per year."[18] If the Danziger estimate of six hundred hours was anywhere near true, AFDC recipients were dropping out with a vengeance.[19] (One might object that AFDC recipients are not typical members of the workforce. Indeed this is the whole point. Something about being an AFDC recipient went hand in hand with at least a 30 percent decrease in work effort, if Danziger et al. are right, given that a year's worth of full-time work is no more than 2000 hours.)

The financial gap between people who accept responsibility for themselves and people who do not cannot help but grow over time (and the gap in self-esteem will grow along with it). The only way to fully share in society's growing wealth is to fully participate in the process that makes wealth grow.

If we wanted to guarantee that the poor would be left behind, here would be the way to do it: teach them that their welfare is someone else's responsibility.

5. Need-Based Distribution

If we suppose that the point of the welfare state is to help poor people prosper, what role does that suggest for need-based distribution? From a static perspective, the

14. Mead (1986).
15. Goodin (1988) 235.
16. Goodin (1988) 233.
17. Danziger et al. (1981) 998. Emphasis added.
18. Danziger et al. (1981) 997.
19. Why do they drop out? There is no simple explanation, but Tanner, Moore, and Hartman (1995, 27) calculated that AFDC payments, together with food stamps and associated benefits, were the equivalent of (in 1995 dollars) a pretax hourly wage of $14.76 in New York, $12.45 in Philadelphia, $11.35 in Baltimore, and $10.91 in Detroit, based on a forty-hour work week.

answer is obvious. Need-based distribution meets needs. Or is that not as obvious as it sounds? Need-based distribution is meant to meet needs, but how well does intent match reality? The record of twentieth-century attempts to distribute according to need is not encouraging. Although there is a place for need-based distribution, we should neither exaggerate this place nor jump to conclusions about how centralized or bureaucratic the administration of such distribution ought to be. It would be a fallacy to assume that those who object to need-based distribution by a central bureaucracy do not care about need. Some think instead that need-based distribution (especially by a central bureaucracy) is not what people need.

Goodin knows that need-based distribution is not the only way to meet needs, but he observes, "What a straightforward redistribution would accomplish in an instant, supply-side policies would accomplish only in due course."[20] Goodin has a point. To borrow a proverbial metaphor, giving someone a fish accomplishes in an instant what teaching the person to fish accomplishes only in due course. What constitutes "due course"? We certainly want to know. However, it misconceives the nature of free society to think that, within it, poor people have no choice but to wait patiently for wealth to "trickle down."[21] There was a time in the nineteenth century when poor people found it hard to afford the price of health care. They did not wait for the "long term." They got together and solved the problem.

6. How Friendly Societies Solved the Problem

If we honestly sought to identify social arrangements with a history of helping people to become self-supporting, would we find that collective responsibility has a history of failure, while individual responsibility has a history of success? Not exactly. Certainly, the prosperity of any society depends substantially on the ability of its culture and institutions to inculcate expectations of individual responsibility. Just as certainly, though, some ways of collectivizing responsibility can be and have been important contributors to economic and cultural development. Certain kinds of collective responsibility, it turns out, are compatible with a culture of personal initiative and accountability.

Francis Fukuyama says, "the United States has never been the individualistic society that most Americans believe it to be; rather, it has always possessed a rich network of voluntary associations and community structures to which individuals have subordinated their narrow interests."[22] Fukuyama is right. Institutions of collective responsibility per se are nothing new.

They have taken a new shape, though. Collective responsibility once manifested itself primarily in family-based and community-based norms that sustained neighborhoods and a rich network of mutual aid and thus made crucial contributions to social welfare. Today, collective responsibility is a concept we associate with a distant bureaucracy. It has been externalized. People we never meet decide what

---

20. Goodin (1988) 271.
21. I thank Dan Russell for discussions of this point.
22. Fukuyama (1995) 29.

to deduct from our paychecks and how to spend it. It has become commonplace to accuse the welfare state of eroding norms of individual responsibility by encouraging dependence, but that may not be the worst of it; in some ways the welfare state also undermined our sense of *collective* responsibility. David Green says that, in recent times, "socialists have not seen the good person as someone who gave his own time and energy in the service of others, but as the individual who demanded action by the state at the expense of other taxpayers."[23]

In his 1996 State of the Union address, President Bill Clinton said we can't go back to the time when people were left to fend for themselves. But what time was that? Perhaps he had in mind the time before Franklin Roosevelt's New Deal. Were people in fact left to fend for themselves? If so, what actually happened? Did people roll over and die? Did they thrive as hermits, in the manner of Robinson Crusoe? Or did they get together with neighbors and figure out how to solve their problems? Perhaps Clinton is right; it may be impossible to go back to such a time. I suppose no one knows for sure. What I do know is that it is a false dichotomy to suppose the only alternative to the welfare state is everyone fending for themselves. (The dichotomy is too obviously false for anyone to endorse it explicitly, but endorsing it implicitly is so commonplace that no one bothered publicly to make note when Clinton did it in 1996.)

As in many other countries, there once flourished in England organizations known as "friendly societies" that, according to Green, historically share with trade unions an older kind, a self-help kind, of collectivist philosophical underpinning.[24]

> Through the trade unions workers would win the wages necessary to sustain a decent existence, and through the friendly societies they would organize their own welfare services—social insurance, medical care, even housing loans. The profit motive, too, was to be supplanted: in the factory by the mutuality of the workers' co-op; and in retailing by the co-op store. Not all of these working-class hopes were realized, but the friendly societies, the trade unions, and the co-op stores were successful and offered a fraternal alternative to the sometimes cold world of commercial calculation. Particularly striking is the success of the friendly societies, whose social insurance and primary medical care schemes had attracted at least three-quarters of manual workers well before the end of the nineteenth century. Until the 1911 National Insurance Act every neighborhood of every town was dotted with friendly society branches, each with their own doctor, who had usually been elected by a vote of all the members assembled in the branch meeting.[25]

How expensive was participation in such societies? Access to club medical care was inexpensive to the point of being an outrage to the organized medical profession. David Beito writes that in America in 1900, a lodge member "could acquire a physician's care for about two dollars a year; approximately a day's wage for a laborer at the time."[26] Green and Cromwell report that in Australia in the 1830s and 1840s,

23. Green (1993) 3.
24. Green (1985) 1, 4–5.
25. Green (1985) 1.
26. Beito (1997) 580.

fees charged by private doctors were sometimes over 10 shillings per visit—well beyond the means of most people. By 1869, friendly societies had emerged, providing medical service at a rate of 10 shillings per *year* for members, plus an additional 10 shillings per year for a member's wife and children. To win election to a post as club doctor, candidates offered competitive rates, submitted to questioning by the assembled members regarding their training and experience, and offered perks such as free house visits within 3 or 4 miles of the lodge.[27]

How widespread was participation in such societies? Green estimates that "at least 9 million of the 12 million originally included in the National Insurance scheme were already members of friendly societies offering medical care."[28] Moreover, between friendly societies, provident dispensaries (which provided need-based subsidized care), private charity, regular insurance, fees for service (which competition from friendly societies eventually forced down to levels that average workers could afford), and—as a last resort[29]—the Poor Law, universal coverage had, for all practical purposes, been achieved. "No one, therefore, went without some sort of primary medical care."[30]

How adequate was the care such societies provided? Green reports disputes between the societies and the organized medical profession over the societies' refusal to exclude wealthy members; means-testing would have been contrary to the principle that all joined on equal terms.[31] The fact that there was an issue over wealthy members using the service suggests that the quality of service must have been reasonably good—good enough that rich people in significant numbers wanted access to it.[32]

For what it is worth, the friendly societies were a remedy for exploitation as well. When there are multiple providers of relevantly similar services, people who dislike terms offered by one provider can look elsewhere. No provider, nor any coalition of providers, was in a position to dictate terms to clients. The friendly societies decentralized collective responsibility for medical care without turning it into a strictly individual responsibility. Individually and collectively, they gave people a range of choices at prices that almost anyone, even then, could afford.

Unfortunately, as Fukuyama says,

> the growth of the welfare state accelerated the decline of those very communal institutions it was designed to supplement. Welfare dependency in the United States is the most prominent example: Aid to Families with Dependent Children, the depression-era [1935] legislation that was designed to help widows and single

27. Green and Cromwell (1984) 76–80.
28. Green (1985) 95.
29. England's Poor Law Amendment Act of 1834 sought to limit access to (and desirability of) government poor relief, so as to ensure that it would indeed be treated as a last resort. The general idea was that the standard of living made possible by public assistance ought to be less desirable than that available to the humblest of self-supporting laborers. See Himmelfarb (1994) chap. 4.
30. Green (1985) 179.
31. Green (1985) 19–21.
32. A royal commission assigned to investigate whether the poor were systematically deterred from joining friendly societies found that in 1901–2, "registered friendly society membership was highest in rural areas where wages were lowest" (Green, 1993, 68).

mothers over the transition as they reestablished their lives and families, became the mechanism that permitted entire inner-city populations to raise children without the benefit of fathers.[33]

Also helping to make friendly society medical services redundant were benefit packages provided by employers. Meanwhile, physicians' guilds hated the friendly societies, correctly believing that friendly societies gave medical consumers the bargaining power they needed to prevent effective price collusion by doctors. By the early 1900s, such guilds had become a powerful political force, especially when they joined forces with for-profit insurance companies (who likewise recognized friendly societies as an obstacle to higher profits). Together, they played an active and highly visible role in the friendly societies' decline. In England, they were a major influence on the process of amending early drafts of the 1911 National Insurance Act so as to make the final legislation as prejudicial as possible to the friendly societies.[34]

Similar forces were at work in the United States. David Beito reports that doctors who worked for lodges

> faced forfeiture of membership or, just as seriously, a boycott. In 1913, for example, members of the medical society in Port Jervis, New York vowed that if any physician took a lodge contract they would "refuse to consult with him or assist him in any way or in any emergency whatever." In this instance, and many others, boycotts extended to patients as well. One method of enforcement was to pressure hospitals to close their doors to members of the guilty lodge.[35]

Their demise notwithstanding, friendly societies seem to have had many of the features that we wish our health care system had today. They also provided services like old-age pensions, unemployment insurance, life insurance, workmen's compensation, day care, and so on, at the same time serving as a form of community association. Is it realistic to suppose that friendly societies in the twenty-first century could emulate their earlier success?[36] Realistically, they could never be like they were, simply because they would be responding to needs that are not the same as the needs of nineteenth-century lodge members. Times change. Conditions that contributed to an institution's history of success may no longer be operative, and we may not realize that until after we try and fail to replicate its success in another

33. Fukuyama (1995) 313–14.

34. The Act made it compulsory for male workers earning less than a certain income to purchase government medical insurance. Panels and committees staffed by representatives of doctors' guilds and insurance companies were established to regulate the benefits provided by local friendly societies. The fees of local doctors were subsequently established by the committees rather than by the societies, and as a result more than doubled within two years of the Act's passage (Green, 1985, 113). It is also interesting that, in some respects, the Act hardly even pretended to be providing national insurance. For example, the Act made no provision for the care of widows and orphans because the insurance companies felt that such provision would make it harder to sell life insurance (Green, 1993, 99).

35. Beito (1997) 30.

36. Given the lack of modern actuarial and accounting techniques, it is easy to imagine how nineteenth-century friendly societies could have run into financial difficulties. Yet, none of them, to my knowledge, ever appealed to financial hardship as a reason for refusing to provide promised benefits.

time and place.³⁷ But all that says is that policy-makers, too, have to live without guarantees. It is no reason not to explore alternatives, especially alternatives that have histories of success.

In any case, friendly societies show how responsibility can be successfully collectivized. Medical savings accounts and privatized pension plans can help people to internalize, by helping them individualize, responsibility for their health care and their retirement. Friendly societies are a distinct alternative, allowing people to internalize responsibility in a collective form.

7. The Possibility of Political Disarmament

There are reasons why people voluntarily seek to join groups that collectivize responsibility. Certain forms of collective responsibility help to spread risk, for example.³⁸ For some people, sharing is intrinsically desirable, and understandably so. It is intrinsically a form of community. Theda Skocpol defends the welfare state;³⁹ she is skeptical about mutual aid societies on the grounds that the former institution has woven into it a pattern of sharing (to use Skocpol's apt phrase) while the latter does not. I see exactly the opposite. What is woven into the welfare state is a pattern of transfer, not a pattern of sharing. It is mutual aid societies, not welfare programs, that are knit together by a pattern of sharing. It is not true that where the welfare state goes, community spirit flourishes. Nor is it true, to say the least, that authentic community spirit was dead before fifty years of expanding federal programs gradually brought authentic community back to life.

According to Robert Goodin, the welfare state is a form of institutionalized altruism. "Fraternal feelings and generalized altruism thus constitute at least the historical core of the communitarian case for the welfare state."⁴⁰ Goodin is right to say that some communitarians have appealed to this sort of argument. Anticommunitarians could argue, alternatively, that the welfare state obliterates fraternal feelings, and that this is a good thing. It enables people to move to the anonymous big city rather than remain financially tied to a thick community of small-town relatives.

In any case, fraternal feeling is possible in a small group, but when we institutionalize altruism on a national scale, the possibility of genuine community is precisely what we give up.⁴¹ At present, the welfare state's actual operation plainly provides more occasion for mutual resentment than for fraternal feeling.⁴² By giving people

---

37. As recently as the 1960s, though, the Taborian Hospital of Mound Bayou, Mississippi, provided basic medical coverage for as little as $30 per year, according to Beito (1999).

38. There is some evidence, though, that the advantages of communal management as a form of collective responsibility tend to decrease as an economy matures. See chapter 11.

39. In conversation following my presentation of a draft of this essay at the University of Chicago, April 18, 1996.

40. Goodin (1988) 78.

41. I thank James Buchanan for this point.

42. I am surprised that "corporate welfare" does not provoke more resentment than it does, from all sides of the political spectrum, but that is a topic for another essay.

the right to extract benefits from productive ventures without making contributions to them, the welfare state turns individual productivity into a commons problem, and commons problems have a robust history of turning people against each other, turning them into what communitarians call "social atoms." Commons problems isolate and alienate people because they leave people feeling too vulnerable to each other—too easily, pervasively, and uncontrollably liable for costs of other people's overconsumption and underproduction.

A peaceful community is one in which people have no reason to fear each other. A community in which people hold blank checks on each other's incomes is a community in which that condition is not met. If we want a system that nurtures fraternal feeling, we have to start by acknowledging that compulsory deductions from paychecks do nothing of the kind. Rightly or wrongly, more than a few taxpayers feel victimized by the welfare state. Rightly or wrongly, more than a few beneficiaries feel the same way. (Taking it as given that they are entitled to be given whatever they need, some beneficiaries consider it an insult that they could be viewed as needing so little. I admit that this attitude seemed more common in Canada when I was growing up than it seems in the U.S. today.) The upshot is that the welfare state balkanizes people. It externalizes responsibility, and in the process does the opposite of fostering a sense of community. What we need are ways of bringing people together that are (in their own eyes) in their common interest, so that they may come together willingly. We have to look for ways that enable people to live peaceful and productive lives, pursuing their own projects in such a way as to make themselves better off by making the people around them better off.

When an activist government takes itself to be a player with a license to do whatever it takes to win, people do not know what to expect from it. Or, to the extent that they do know, their own interests lie in trying to get the government to play for them rather than against them, which results in a channeling of resources into the negative-sum game of maximizing the extent to which government plays for their side. In contrast, voluntarily assumed responsibility, whether individual or collective, reduces the extent to which people constitute threats to each other. It is a form of political disarmament.

8. Progress

In any society, there really are people who cannot look after themselves, and there really are people who choose not to look after themselves. We rightly evaluate any society by asking how good it is to live there. The answer will depend in part on what happens to people who cannot, or in any case do not, take care of themselves.

I think we drastically exaggerate the importance of solving the problem in the short term, which has led us to create programs that obliterate the very social capital that was already solving the problem in the long term—namely, forms of mutual reliance that do not presume we owe each other a living but instead treat self-reliance as the default responsibility. So much of what we do in the policy arena seems aimed not at solving problems so much as at proving that our hearts are in the right place.

Within a nation's population, Goodin observes, there is "much productive potential; but to bring out that productive potential, people must be healthy, educated, well fed, etc. The welfare state guarantees that such basic needs are met.... That the welfare state contributes in this way to economic efficiency is pretty well indisputable."[43] Guarantees? I only wish it actually were true that children of welfare recipients are guaranteed, or even *tend*, to be healthy, educated, and well fed. Nevertheless, in Western market society more generally, children today are healthier, better educated, and better fed than children were a century ago. Someone must be doing something right. Looking at the long run, it is obvious the poor have not been getting poorer.[44] American graduate students, for example, are poor. Their incomes place most of them squarely in America's bottom quintile. (The country's poorest adult age bracket consists of those aged eighteen to twenty-four, for obvious reasons. Many are in school. Most of the rest are in entry-level jobs.) Yet most own a telephone, a microwave oven, a radio, a toothbrush, a closet-full of factory-made clothing, even an automobile. All have access to flush toilets, and most incredibly, computers. As recently as a century ago, these amenities and thousands of others would have been rare if not inconceivable for people in the bottom quintile. In 1900, the average life expectancy was 47.3 years in the United States. By 2004, it had risen to 77.8 years.[45] I suspect the increase in life expectancy would be even more dramatic if we compared only people in the bottom quintile for income. I am not suggesting that everyone in the bottom quintile has a lifestyle as comfortable as that of graduate students.[46] The point, rather, is that people in the middle of the bottom quintile are spectacularly wealthy compared to people in the same relative position a hundred years ago. We could show that by comparing today's students to nineteenth-century students (with similar family backgrounds), by comparing today's manual laborers to nineteenth-century manual laborers, and so on.

There are people, though, who find it offensive to compare the snapshots of today to the snapshots of a century ago. The comparison will seem complacent to those who think the only things that really matter are problems they see in snapshots of today. To them, the fact that things are far better than they were a century ago does not matter. I tried to explain the vitriolic nature of debates concerning the welfare state by positing two kinds of perspectives, static and dynamic. One of this essay's themes is that the world looks very different from the two perspectives. People who

---

43. Goodin (1988) 237.

44. For some discussion of short-run trends, see Schmidtz (2006) pt. 4.

45. U.S. Department of Health and Human Services (2006) table 27; www.cdc.gov/nchs/data/hus/hus06.pdf#027

46. Many readers of previous versions of this essay have hated my use of graduate students as an example of what it is like to be in the bottom quintile. I am not saying everyone in the bottom quintile lives like a student. My point is merely that we all have more reliable impressions about what it is like to be in the bottom quintile than we can get from Charles Dickens novels or even from newspapers. All of us know people, and most of us have at one time been people, who live on bottom quintile incomes. Admittedly, students and retired people make up a substantial portion of the bottom quintile, and of course many of these people have resources far beyond their bottom quintile incomes. Many other people, though, really do live on bottom quintile incomes, and since most of us know some such people, we can get some indication of how deprived they are by looking at them, or asking them.

take the static perspective sometimes think that those who see things differently are indifferent to suffering, and in some cases they are probably right. People who take a dynamic perspective sometimes think that those who see things differently must simply hate it when a society's institutions enable people to prosper, and in some cases they, too, are probably right.

Another theme is that the extent to which a society is peaceful and prosperous depends on the extent to which responsibility is internalized, that is, on the extent to which people bear the cost of their own mistakes and misfortunes, and are not made to bear the cost of other people's mistakes and misfortunes without consent. At the same time, certain social arrangements for collectivizing responsibility have a history of making people better off—specifically, those that avoid externalizing responsibility in the process of collectivizing it. Internalizing responsibility is a form of political disarmament. As with literal disarmament, it is a recipe for peace and prosperity.

A third theme is that, although we all want guarantees, their hidden cost is high. Systematically rewarding productive effort helps people internalize responsibility and thus helps make for a peaceful and productive society. It is in response to a lack of guarantees that people take responsibility for their own welfare and for the welfare of those they care about. Like it or not, a lack of guarantees has been one of the great engines of human progress.

A fourth theme is that although the direct approach to meeting needs is the most obvious, it is not always the best. Could a welfare safety net be packaged in such a way that people would willingly pay for it? It would have to avoid treating those who work for a living as mere means to the ends of those who do not. It would have to serve the ends of both those who support it and those supported by it. It would have to institutionalize reciprocity rather than free riding. Is that possible?

The answer is that such schemes are not only possible; they have a long history. The history of friendly societies is a history of people producing and paying for their own guarantees. Friendly societies never were perfect, and never would be, but in many countries they have a history of doing what a welfare safety net is supposed to do, and doing it increasingly well over time as they evolved in response to consumer demand.

I conclude that there are reasons for endorsing certain forms of group responsibility but that the best arguments for group responsibility are bad arguments for the welfare state as a set of institutions for administering that responsibility. The welfare state undertakes to offer people the wrong kind of guarantee, namely a guarantee that externalizes responsibility. It is a better world when people come together of their own free will to share each other's burdens. It is a worse world when people can foist the cost of their misfortunes and misadventures on others without consent.

This essay revises David Schmidtz, "Guarantees," *Social Philosophy and Policy* 14 (1997): 1–19. I thank Cambridge University Press for permission to reprint. I thank Robert Goodin, along with series editor Ray Frey and Cambridge editor Terry Moore, for all the work they put into the book (Schmidtz and Goodin 1998) that grew out of this article. Several paragraphs here are from the book rather than from the original article.

PLANET

11

The Institution of Property

The evolution of property law is driven by an ongoing search for ways to internalize what economists call externalities: positive externalities associated with productive effort and negative externalities associated with misuse of commonly held resources.[1] If all goes well, property law enables would-be producers to enjoy the benefits of productive effort. It also enables people to insulate themselves from external costs associated with activities around the neighborhood. Property law is not perfect. To further reduce external costs that neighbors might otherwise impose on each other, people resort to nuisance and zoning laws, regulatory agencies, and so on, all with a view to supplementing and perfecting the critical role that property law plays in minimizing external costs.

Philosophers speak of the ideal of society as a cooperative venture for mutual advantage. To be a cooperative venture for mutual advantage, though, society must first be a setting in which mutually advantageous interaction is possible. In other words, borrowing a term from game theory, society must be a positive-sum game. What determines the extent to which society is a positive-sum game? This essay explains how property institutions convert negative-sum games to positive-sum games, setting the stage for society's flourishing as a cooperative venture.

The term "property rights" is used to refer to a bundle of rights that could include rights to sell, lend, bequeath, and so on. In what follows, I use the phrase to refer primarily to the right of owners to exclude nonowners. Private owners have the right to exclude nonowners, but the right to exclude is a feature of property rights in general rather than the defining feature of private ownership in particular. The National Park Service claims a right to exclude. Communes claim a right to exclude nonmembers. This essay does not settle which kind or which mix of public and private property institutions is best. Instead, it asks how we could justify *any* institution that recognizes a right to exclude.

---

1. A negative externality or external cost is a cost (of a decision or transaction) paid by bystanders who were not consulted and whose interests were not taken into account. A transaction may also, analogously, create positive externalities, that is, have external benefits.

1. Original Appropriation: The Problem

The right to exclude presents a philosophical problem. Consider how full-blooded rights differ from mere liberties. If I am at liberty to plant a garden, that means my planting a garden is permitted. That leaves open the possibility of you being at liberty to interfere with my gardening as you see fit. Thus, mere liberties are not full-blooded rights. When I stake a claim to a piece of land, though, I claim to be changing other people's liberties—canceling them somehow—so that other people no longer are at liberty to use the land without my permission. To say I have a right to the land is to say I have a right to exclude.

From where could such rights come? There must have been a time when no one had a right to exclude. Everyone had liberties regarding the land, but not rights. (Perhaps this does not seem obvious, but if no one owns the land, no one has a right to exclude. If no one has a right to exclude, everyone has liberties.) How, then, did we get from each person having a liberty to someone having an exclusive right to the land? What justifies original appropriation, that is, staking a claim to previously unowned resources?

To justify a claim to unowned land, people need not make as strong a case as would be needed to justify confiscating land already owned by someone else. Specifically, since there is no prior owner in original appropriation cases, there is no one from whom one can or needs to get consent. What, then, must a person do? Locke's idea was that any residual (perhaps need-based) communal claim to the land could be met if a person could appropriate it without prejudice to other people, in other words, if a person could leave "enough and as good" for others.[2] This so-called Lockean Proviso can be interpreted in many ways, but an adequate interpretation will note that this is its point: to license claims that can be made without making other people worse off.

We also should consider whether the "others" who are to be left with enough and as good include not just people currently on the scene but latecomers as well, including people not yet born. John Sanders asks, "What possible argument could at the same time require that the present generation have scruples about leaving enough and as good for one another, while shrugging off such concern for future generations?"[3] Most theorists accept the more demanding interpretation. It fits better with Locke's idea that the preservation of humankind (which includes future generations) is the ultimate criterion by which any use of resources is assessed. Aside from that, we have a more compelling defense of an appropriation (especially in environmental terms) when we can argue that there was enough left over not just for contemporaries but also for generations to come.

Of course, when we justify original appropriation, we do not in the process justify expropriation. Some say institutions that license expropriation make people better off; I think our histories of violent expropriation are ongoing tragedies for us all. Capitalist regimes have tainted histories. Communist regimes have tainted histories.

---

2. See Locke (1960) chap. 5. Locke sometimes uses other locutions, such as "as much and as good."

3. Sanders (1987) 377.

Indigenous peoples have tainted histories. Europeans took land from Algonquin tribes, and before that, Algonquin tribes took the same land from Iroquois tribes. We may regard those expropriations as the history of markets or governments or Christianity or tribalism or simply as the history of the human race. It makes little difference. This essay discusses the history of property institutions, not because their history can justify them, but rather because their history shows how some of them enable people to make themselves and the people around them better off without destroying their environment. Among such institutions are those that license original appropriation (and not expropriation).

2. Original Appropriation: A Solution

Philosophical critics of private property often have claimed that justifying original appropriation is the key to justifying private property, frequently offering a version of Lockean Proviso as the standard of justification. Part of the Proviso's attraction for such critics was that it seemingly could not be met. Many critics conclude that the Proviso is, at least in the case of land appropriation, logically impossible to satisfy, and thus that (private) property in land cannot possibly be justified along Lockean lines.

The way Judith Thomson puts it, if "the first labor-mixer must literally leave as much and as good for others who come along later, then no one can come to own anything, for there are only finitely many things in the world so that every taking leaves less for others."[4] To say the least, Thomson is not alone:

> "We leave enough and as good for others only when what we take is not scarce."[5]
>
> "The Lockean Proviso, in the contemporary world of overpopulation and scarce resources, can almost never be met."[6]
>
> "Every acquisition worsens the lot of others—and worsens their lot in relevant ways."[7]
>
> "The condition that there be enough and as good left for others could not of course be literally satisfied by any system of private property rights."[8]
>
> "If the 'enough and as good' clause were a necessary condition on appropriation, it would follow that, in these circumstances, the only legitimate course for the inhabitants would be death by starvation... since *no* appropriation would leave enough and as good in common for others."[9]

And so on. If we take something out of the cookie jar, we *must* be leaving less for others. This appears self-evident. It has to be right. But it isn't right, for two reasons.

---

4. Thomson (1990) 330.
5. Fried (1995) 230n.
6. Held (1980) 6.
7. Bogart (1985) 834.
8. Sartorius (1984) 210.
9. Waldron (1976) 325.

A. Appropriation Is Not a Zero-Sum Game

First, it is hardly impossible—certainly not logically impossible—for a taking to leave as much for others. We can at least imagine a logically possible world of magic cookie jars in which, every time you take out one cookie, more and better cookies take its place.

Second, the logically possible world I just imagined is the sort of world we actually live in. Philosophers writing about original appropriation tend to speak as if people who arrive first are luckier than those who come later. The truth is, first appropriators begin the process of resource creation; latecomers get most of the benefits. Consider America's first permanent English settlement, the Jamestown colony of 1607. (Or, if you prefer, imagine the lifestyles of people crossing the Bering Strait from Asia twelve thousand years ago.) Was their situation better than ours? How so? They were never caught in rush-hour traffic jams, of course. For that matter, they never worried about being overcharged for car repairs. They never awoke in the middle of the night to the sound of noisy refrigerators, leaky faucets, or even flushing toilets. They never wasted a minute at airports waiting for delayed flights. They never had to change a light bulb. They never agonized over the choice among cellular telephone companies. They never faced the prospect of a dentist's drill; after their teeth fell out, in their thirties, they could subsist for a while on liquids. Life was simple.

Philosophers are taught to say, in effect, that original appropriators got the good stuff for free. We have to pay for ugly leftovers. But in truth, original appropriation benefits latecomers far more than it benefits original appropriators. Original appropriation is a cornucopia of wealth, but mainly for latecomers. The people who got here first literally could not even have imagined what we latecomers take for granted. Our life expectancies exceed theirs by several *decades*.

Original appropriation diminishes the stock of what can be originally appropriated, at least in the case of land, but that is not the same thing as diminishing the stock of what can be owned.[10] On the contrary, in taking control of resources and thereby removing those particular resources from the stock of goods that can be acquired by original appropriation, people typically generate massive increases in the stock of goods that can be acquired by trade. The lesson is that appropriation typically is not a zero-sum but a positive-sum game. As Locke himself stressed, it creates the possibility of mutual benefit on a massive scale. It creates the possibility of society as a cooperative venture.

The point is not merely that enough is produced in appropriation's aftermath to compensate latecomers who lost out in the race to appropriate. The point is that being an original appropriator is not the prize. The prize is prosperity, and latecomers win big, courtesy of those who arrived first. If anyone had a right to be compensated, it would be the first appropriators.

---

10. Is it fair for latecomers to be excluded from acquiring property by rules allowing original appropriation? Sanders (1987, 385) notes that latecomers "are *not* excluded from acquiring property by these rules. They are, instead, excluded from being the first to own what has not been owned previously. Is *that* unfair?"

B. The Commons before Appropriation Is Not Zero-Sum Either

The second point is that the commons before appropriation is not a zero-sum game either. Typically it is a negative-sum game. Let me tell two stories. The first comes from the coral reefs of the Philippine and Tongan Islands.[11] People once fished those reefs with lures and traps, but then began bleach-fishing, which involves dumping bleach into the reefs. Fish cannot breathe sodium hypochlorite. Suffocated, they float to the surface, where they are easy to collect.[12]

The problem is, the coral itself is composed of living animals. The coral suffocates along with the fish, and the dead reef is no longer a viable habitat. (Another technique, blast-fishing, involves dynamiting the reefs. The concussion produces an easy harvest of stunned fish and dead coral.) Perhaps your first reaction is to say people ought to be more responsible. They ought to preserve the reefs for their children.

But that would miss the point, which is that individual fishermen lack the option of saving the coral for their children. Individual fishermen obviously have the option of not destroying it themselves, but what happens if they elect not to destroy it? What they want is for the reef to be left for their children; what is actually happening is that the reef is left for the next blast-fisher down the line. If a fisherman wants to have anything at all to give his children, he must act quickly, destroying the reef and grabbing the fish himself. It does no good to tell fishermen to take responsibility. They are taking responsibility—for their children. Existing institutional arrangements do not empower them to take responsibility in a way that would save the reef.

Under the circumstances, they are at liberty to not destroy the reef themselves, but they are not at liberty to do what is necessary to save the reef for their children. To save the reef for their children, fishermen must have the power to restrict access to the reef. They must claim a right to exclude blast-fishers. Whether they stake that claim as individuals or as a group is secondary, so long as they actually succeed in restricting access. One way or another, they must have, and must effectively exercise, a right to restrict access.

The second story comes from the Cayman Islands.[13] The Atlantic Green Turtle has long been prized as a source of meat and eggs. The turtles were a commonly held resource and were being harvested in an unsustainable way. In 1968, when by some estimates there were as few as three to five thousand left in the wild, a group of entrepreneurs and concerned scientists created Mariculture Ltd. (sold in 1976 and renamed Cayman Turtle Farm) and began raising and selling captivity-bred sea turtles. In the wild, as few as one-tenth of 1 percent of wild hatchlings survive

---

11. Chesher (1985). See also Gomez, Alcala, and San Diego (1981). For a recent discussion of some of the legal issues pertaining to domestic conflicts between the fishing industry and the tourism industry's efforts to protect reefs with federal marine protected areas, see Craig (2008).

12. J. Madeleine Nash, "Wrecking the Reefs," *Time*, Sept. 30, 1996, 60–62, says fishermen currently pump 330,000 pounds of cyanide per year into Philippine reefs.

13. I thank Peggy Fosdick at the National Aquarium in Baltimore for correspondence and documents. See also Fosdick and Fosdick (1994).

to adulthood. Most are seized by predators before they can crawl from nest to sea. Cayman Farm, though, boosted the survival rate of captivity-bred animals to 50 percent or more. At the peak of operations, they were rearing over a hundred thousand turtles. They were releasing 1 percent of their hatchlings into the wild at the age of ten months, an age at which hatchlings have a decent chance of surviving to maturity.

In 1973, commerce in Atlantic green turtles was restricted by the Convention on International Trade in Endangered Species (CITES) and, in the United States, by the Fish and Wildlife Service, the Department of Commerce, and the Department of the Interior. Under the newly created Endangered Species Act, the United States classified the Atlantic green turtle as an endangered species, but Cayman Farm's business was unaffected, at first, because regulations pertaining to commerce in Atlantic green turtles covered only wild turtles, implicitly exempting commerce in captivity-bred animals. In 1978, however, the regulations were published in their final form, and although exemptions were granted for trade in captivity-bred animals of other species, no exemption was made for turtles. The company could no longer do business in the United States. Even worse, the company no longer could ship its products through American ports, so it no longer had access via Miami to world markets. The Cayman Farm exists today only to serve the population of the Cayman Islands themselves.[14]

What do these stories tell us? The first tells us that we do not need to justify failing to preserve the commons in its pristine, original, unappropriated form, because preserving a pristine commons is not an option. Leaving our environment in the commons is not like putting our environment in a time capsule as a legacy for future generations. There are ways to take what we find in the commons and preserve it—to put it in a time capsule—but before we can put something in a time capsule, we have to appropriate it.[15]

C. Justifying the Game

Note a difference between justifying *institutions* that regulate appropriation and justifying particular *acts* of appropriation. Think of original appropriation as a game and of particular acts of appropriation as moves within the game. Even if the game is justified, a given move within the game may have nothing to recommend it. Indeed, we could say (for argument's sake) that any act of appropriation will seem arbitrary

---

14. As later sections stress, privatization may be a key to avoiding commons tragedies, but it is not a panacea. In this case, there was concern that the farming of turtles would spur demand, and that rising demand would lead to rising prices, which would mean an increased poaching pressure on wild populations. This is unlikely. As a rule, the prices of scarce wild animals do not rise when people begin bringing to market large quantities of farm-bred alternatives. One more likely danger, though, is that large-scale farms (salmon farms, cattle farms, etc.) breed disease and put wild as well as domestic populations at risk. As with any other new industry, there are always unanticipated problems and newly emerging externalities that need to be contained. See Davis (2007).

15. A private nonprofit organization, the Nature Conservancy, is pursuing such a strategy. Although not itself an original appropriator, it has acquired over a billion dollars' worth of land in an effort to preserve natural ecosystems. Note that this includes habitat for endangered species that have no market value.

when viewed in isolation, and some will seem unconscionable. Even so, there can be compelling reasons for an institutional framework to recognize property claims on the basis of moves that would carry no moral weight in an institutional vacuum. Common law implicitly acknowledges morally weighty reasons for not requiring original appropriators to supply morally weighty reasons for their appropriations. Carol Rose argues that a rule of first possession, when the world is notified in an unambiguous way, induces discovery (and future productive activity) and minimizes disputes over discovered objects.[16] Particular acts of appropriation are justified not because they carry moral weight but because they are permitted moves within a game that carries moral weight.

Needless to say, the cornucopia of wealth generated by the appropriation and subsequent mobilization of resources is not an unambiguous benefit. Commerce made possible by original appropriation creates pollution, and other negative externalities as well. Further, there may be people who attach no value to the increases in life expectancy and other benefits that accompany the appropriation of resources for productive use. Some people may prefer a steady-state system that indefinitely supports their lifestyles as hunter-gatherers, untainted by the shoes, tents, fishing rods, and safety matches of Western culture. If original appropriation forces such people to participate in a culture they want no part of, then from their viewpoint, the game does more harm than good.

Here are two things to keep in mind, though. First, as I said, the commons is not a time capsule. It does not preserve the status quo. For all kinds of reasons, quality of life could drop after appropriation. However, pressures that drive waves of people to appropriate are a lot more likely to compromise quality of life when those waves wash over an unregulated commons. In an unregulated commons, those who conserve pay the costs but do not get the benefits of conservation, while overusers get the benefits but do not pay the costs of overuse. An unregulated commons is thus a prescription for overuse, not for conservation.

Second, the option of living the life of a hunter-gatherer has not entirely disappeared. It is not a comfortable life. It never was. But it remains an option. There are places in northern Canada and elsewhere where people still live that way. As a bonus, those who opt to live as hunter-gatherers retain the option of participating in Western culture on a drop-in basis during medical emergencies, to trade for supplies, and so on. Obviously, someone might respond, "Even if the hunter-gatherer life is an option now, that option is disappearing as expanding populations equipped with advancing technologies claim the land for other purposes." Well, probably so. What does that prove? It proves that, in the world as it is, if hunter-gatherers want their children to have the option of living as hunter-gatherers, then they need to stake a claim to the territory on which they intend to preserve that option. They need to argue that they, as rightful owners, have a right to regulate access to it. If they want a steady-state civilization, they need to be aware that they will not find it in an unregulated commons. They need to exclude oil companies, for example, which would love to treat northern Canada as an unregulated commons.

16. Rose (1985).

When someone says appropriation does not leave enough and as good for others, the reply should be "compared to what?" Compared to the commons as it was? As it is? As it will be? Often, in fact, leaving resources *in the commons* does not leave enough and as good for others. The Lockean Proviso, far from forbidding appropriation of resources from the commons, actually requires appropriation under conditions of scarcity.

Removing goods from the commons stimulates increases in the stock of what can be owned and limits losses that occur in tragic commons. Appropriation replaces a negative-sum with a positive-sum game. Therein lies a justification for social structures enshrining a right to remove resources from the unregulated commons: when resources become scarce, we need to remove them if we want them to be there for our children. Or anyone else's.

3. What Kind of Property Institution Is Implied?

I have defended appropriation of, and subsequent regulation of access to, scarce resources as a way of preserving (and creating) resources for the future. When resources are abundant, the Lockean Proviso permits appropriation; when resources are scarce, the Proviso requires appropriation. It is possible to appropriate without prejudice to future generations. Indeed, when the burden of common use begins to exceed a resource's ability to renew itself, leaving the resource in the commons is what would be prejudicial to future generations.

Private property enables people (and gives them an incentive) to take responsibility for conserving scarce resources. It preserves resources under a wide variety of circumstances. It is the preeminent vehicle for turning negative-sum commons into positive-sum property regimes. However, it is not the only way. Evidently, it is not always the best way, either. Public property is ubiquitous, and it is not only rapacious governments and mad ideologues who create it. It has a history of evolving spontaneously in response to real problems, enabling people to remove a resource from an unregulated commons and collectively take responsibility for its management. The following sections, discussing research by Martin Bailey, Harold Demsetz, Robert Ellickson, and Carol Rose, show how various property institutions help to ensure that enough and as good is left for future generations.

A. The Unregulated Commons

An unregulated commons need not be a disaster. An unregulated commons will work well enough so long as the level of use remains within the land's carrying capacity. However, as use nears carrying capacity, there will be pressure to shift to a more exclusive regime. For a real-world example of an unregulated commons evolving into a regime of private parcels as increasing traffic began to exceed carrying capacity, consider economist Harold Demsetz's classic account of how property institutions evolved among indigenous tribes of the Labrador peninsula. As Demsetz tells the story, the region's people had, for generations, treated the land as an open-access commons. The human population was small. There was plenty to eat. Thus, the pattern of exploitation was within the land's carrying capacity.[17] The resource maintained itself. In that situation, the Lockean Proviso, on the previously discussed interpretation, was satisfied. Original appropriation would have been permissible, other things equal, but it was not required.

With the advent of the fur trade, though, the scale of hunting and trapping activity increased sharply. The population of game animals began to dwindle. The unregulated commons had worked for a while, but now the tribes were facing a classic "tragedy of the commons."[18] The tragedy of the commons is one version of a more general problem of externalities. In this case, the benefits of exploiting the resource were internalized but the costs were not, and the arrangement was no longer viable. In response, tribe members began to mark out family plots. The game animals in question were small animals like beaver and otter that tend not to migrate from one plot to another. Thus, marking out plots of land effectively privatized small game as well as the land itself. In sum, the tribes converted the commons in nonmigratory fur-bearing game to family parcels when the fur trade began to spur a rising demand that exceeded the land's carrying capacity. When demand began to exceed carrying capacity, that was when the Lockean Proviso came not only to permit but to require original appropriation.

One other nuance of the privatization of fur-bearing game was that although the fur was privatized, the meat was not. There was still plenty of meat, so tribal law allowed people to hunt for meat on each other's land. Unannounced visitors could kill a beaver and take the meat, but had to leave the pelt, prominently displayed to signal that they had eaten and had respected the owner's right to the pelt. The new customs went to the heart of the matter, privatizing what had to be privatized, and leaving intact liberties people had always enjoyed with respect to other resources where unrestricted access had not yet become a problem.

B. The Communal Alternative[19]

We can contrast the unregulated or open-access commons with communes. A commune is a restricted-access commons. In a commune, property is owned by the group rather than by individual members. People as a group claim and exercise a right to exclude. Typically, communes draw a sharp distinction between members and nonmembers, and regulate access accordingly. Public property tends to restrict access by time of day or year. Some activities are permitted; others are prohibited.

Ellickson believes a broad campaign to abolish either private property or public and communal property would be ludicrous. Each kind of property serves social

---

17. This was not true everywhere. I have seen places where tribes hunted bison by stampeding whole herds over the edge of a cliff. (The Blackfoot name for one such place translates as "head-smashed-in buffalo jump.") So I accept Dukeminier and Krier's warning against forming "an unduly romantic image of Native American culture prior to the arrival of 'civilization.' There is considerable evidence that some American Indian tribes, rather than being natural ecologists who lived in respectful harmony with the land, exploited the environment ruthlessly by overhunting and extensive burning of forests" (1993, 62).

18. Hardin (1968) 1243. The cases described in previous sections are examples of the "tragedy of the commons," where unregulated access to a resource results in overuse by a population of users who lack the effective right to exclude other users and thus whose only rational alternative is to jump in and overuse while they can. See also Schmidtz and Willott (2003).

19. This essay discusses Ellickson's article in some detail. While I take little credit for the ideas in the next few sections, any errors are presumably mine.

welfare in its own way. Likewise, every ownership regime has its own externality problems. Communal management leads to overconsumption and to shirking on maintenance and improvements, because people receive only a fraction of the value of their labor, and bear only a fraction of the costs of their consumption. To minimize these disincentives, a commune must monitor production and consumption activities.

In practice, communal regimes can lead to indiscriminate dumping of wastes, ranging from piles of unwashed dishes to ecological disasters that threaten whole continents. Privately managed parcels also can lead to indiscriminate dumping of wastes and to various other uses that ignore spillover effects on neighbors. One advantage of private property is that owners can buy each other out and reshuffle their holdings in such a way as to minimize the extent to which their activities bother each other. But it does not always work out so nicely, and the reshuffling itself can be a waste. There are transaction costs. Thus, one plausible social goal would be to have a system that combines private and public property in a way that reduces the sum of transaction costs and the cost of externalities.

4. Local versus Remote Externalities

Is it generally best to convert an unregulated commons to smaller private parcels or to manage it as a commune with power to exclude nonmembers? It depends on what kind of problem the property regime is supposed to be solving. In particular, not all problems are of equal scale; some are more local than others. As a problem's scale changes, there will be corresponding changes in which responses are feasible and effective. An individual sheep eating grass in the pasture is what Ellickson and Demsetz would call a *small* event, affecting only a small area relative to the prevailing parcel size. If the commons is being ruined by small events, there is an easy solution: cut the land into parcels. We see this solution everywhere. If we can divide the land into parcels of a certain size, such that the cost of grazing an extra sheep is borne entirely by the individual owner who decides whether to graze the extra sheep, then we have internalized externalities and solved the problem. If we divide the pasture into private parcels, then what a particular sheep eats on a particular owner's pasture is no one else's concern. The grass is no longer a common pool.

For better or worse, events come in more than one size. For the sake of example, suppose six parcels are situated over a pool of oil in such a way that, via oil wells, each of the six owners has access to the common pool. The more wells individual owners sink, the more oil they can extract, up to a point. As the number of wellheads goes up, oil pressure per wellhead declines. Not only is the reserve of oil ultimately fixed, but the practically extractable reserve eventually begins to decline with the number of wells sunk. Past a point, we no longer have a situation in which what individual owners do on their property is of no concern to other owners.

Instead, the six owners become part of a *medium* event, a kind of problem that neighbors cannot solve simply by putting up fences. This kind of problem occurs when an event is too large to be contained on a single parcel, or does not have a precise and confined location, or migrates from one location to another. For one reason or another, the event is large enough that its effects spill over onto neighboring parcels.

In an unfenced commons, there is in effect only a single parcel, so the words "small," "medium," and "large" would refer simply to the radius over which the effects of an event are felt, that is, small, medium, or large parts of the whole parcel. In a regime that has been cut into smaller parcels, the more interesting distinction is between a small event that affects a single owner, a medium event that affects immediate neighbors, and a large event that affects remote parts of the community. When land is divided into parcels, whether an event is small, medium, or large will depend on the size of the parcels. Whether a regime succeeds in internalizing externalities will depend on whether it succeeds in carving out parcel sizes big enough to contain those events whose effects it is most crucial to internalize. In effect, if an individual owner's parcel size could be increased without limit, any event could be made "small."[20]

Ellickson says private regimes are clearly superior as methods for minimizing the costs of small and medium events. Regarding small events, the first point is that the external effects of small events are by definition vanishingly small. Neighbors do not care when we pick tomatoes on our own land; they do care when we pick tomatoes on their communal plot. In the former case, we are minding our own business; in the latter, we are minding theirs. (In effect, there are no small events on communal land. Everything we do affects our neighbors. Even doing nothing at all affects our neighbors, given that we could instead have been helping to tend the communal gardens.) The second point regarding small events concerns the cost of monitoring. To internalize externalities, whatever the property regime, owners must be able to monitor other would-be users and misusers. On a private parcel, though, it is only boundary crossings that need monitoring; guard dogs and motion sensors can handle that. By contrast, the monitoring needed in a commune involves evaluating whether workers are just going through the motions, whether they are taking more than their share, and so on. In sum, "detecting the presence of a trespasser is much less demanding than evaluating the conduct of a person who is privileged to be where he is."[21] Thus, the external cost of small events is lower on private parcels, and monitoring, while still required, is relatively cheap and relatively nonintrusive in a parcelized regime.

The effects of medium events tend to spill over onto one's neighbors, and thus can be a source of friction. Nevertheless, privatization has the advantage of limiting the number of people having to be consulted about how to deal with the externality, which reduces transaction costs. Instead of consulting the entire community of communal owners, each at liberty with respect to the affected area, one consults a handful of people who own parcels in the immediate area of the medium event. A further virtue of privatization is that disputes arising from medium events tend to be left in the hands of people in the immediate vicinity, who tend to better understand local conditions and thus are in a better position to devise resolutions without harmful unintended consequences. They are in a better position to foresee the costs and benefits of a medium event.[22]

20. I have modified this discussion from that of the original essay, borrowing what first appeared in "Reinventing the Commons" (revised as chapter 12 here). I thank Elizabeth Willott for helpful discussions of the small/medium distinction.

21. Ellickson (1993) 1327.

22. Ellickson (1993) 1331.

When it comes to large events, though, there is no easy way to say which mix of private and public property is best. Large events involve far-flung externalities among people who do not have face-to-face relationships. The difficulties in detecting such externalities, tracing them to their source, and holding people accountable for them are difficulties for any kind of property regime. It is no easy task to devise institutions that encourage pulp mills to take responsibility for their actions while simultaneously encouraging people downstream to take responsibility for their welfare, and thus to avoid being harmed by large-scale negative externalities. Ellickson says there is no general answer to the question of which regime best deals with them.

Large events will fall into one of two categories. Releasing toxic wastes into the atmosphere, for example, may violate existing legal rights or community norms. Or, such laws or norms may not yet be in place. Most of the problems arise when existing customs or laws fail to settle who (in effect) has the right of way. That is not a problem with parceling land per se but rather with the fact that key resources like air and waterways remain in a largely unregulated commons.

So, privatization exists in different degrees and takes different forms. Different forms have different incentive properties. Simply parceling out land or sea is not always enough to stabilize possession of resources that make land or sea valuable in the first place. Suppose fish are known to migrate from one parcel to another. In that case, owners have an incentive to grab as many fish as they can whenever the school passes through their own territory. Thus, simply dividing fishing grounds into parcels may not be enough to put fishermen in a position to avoid collectively exceeding sustainable yields. It depends on the extent to which the sought-after fish migrate from one parcel to another, and on continuously evolving conventions that help neighbors deal with the inadequacy of their fences (or other ways of marking off territory). Clearly, then, not all forms of privatization are equally good at internalizing externalities. Privatization per se is not a panacea, and not all forms of privatization are equal.

There are obvious difficulties with how private property regimes handle large events. The nature and extent of the difficulties depends on details. So, for purposes of comparison, Ellickson looked at how communal regimes handle large events.

5. Jamestown and Other Communes

The Jamestown Colony was North America's first permanent English settlement. It began in 1607 as a commune, sponsored by the London-based Virginia Company. Land was held and managed collectively. The colony's charter guaranteed to each settler an equal share of the collective product regardless of the amount of work personally contributed. Of the original group of 104 settlers, two-thirds died of starvation and disease before their first winter. New shiploads replenished the colony; the winter of 1609 cut the population from five hundred to sixty. Colonist William Simmons wrote, "It were too vile to say (and scarce to be believed) what we endured, but the occasion was only our own for want of providence, industry, and government, and not the barrenness and defect of the country, as is generally supposed."[23] In 1611,

---

23. Haile (1998) 340.

career soldier Thomas Dale (appointed by Governor Thomas Gates to administer martial law) arrived to find living skeletons bowling in the streets, waiting for someone else to plant the crops.[24] The settlers' main food source consisted of wild animals such as turtles and raccoons, which they hunted and ate by dark of night before neighbors arrived to demand equal shares.[25]

Colonist George Percy wrote that bad water accounted for many deaths, but most of the deaths were from "meere famine."[26] Archeologist Ivor Hume writes with wonder: "The James Fort colonists' unwillingness or inability to work toward their own salvation remains one of American history's great mysteries."[27] Newly arriving ship's crew members caught 7-foot sturgeon and oysters the size of dinner plates, and left their fishing gear with the colonists. How could colonists starve under such circumstances? Moreover, "Percy's recognition that bad water was the cause of many deaths leaves one asking why, then, nothing was done to combat its dangers. That foul water was bad for you had been known for centuries."[28]

In 1614, Thomas Dale (by now governor) had seen enough. He assigned 3-acre plots to individual settlers, which reportedly increased productivity at least sevenfold. (What colonist Captain John Smith actually said was "When our people were fed out of the common store, and laboured jointly together, glad was he could slip from his labour, or slumber over his taske he care not how, nay, the most honest among them would hardly take so much true paines in a weeke, as now for themselves they will doe in a day.")[29] The colony converted the rest of its land holdings to private parcels in 1619.[30]

24. The word chosen by eyewitness George Percy was not *skeletons* but "anatomies" (Haile, 1998, 507). Eyewitness Ralph Hamor refers to Thomas Dale arriving at Jamestown, where "the most company were, amid their daily and usuall workes, bowling in the streetes." Dale declared martial law, conscripting these people to repair their buildings, plant corn, etc. (Hume 1994, 298).

25. As reported by CNN News, Sept. 13, 1996, on the occasion of the original fort's excavation.

26. Hume (1994) 159.

27. Hume (1994) 160.

28. Hume (1994) 160. Hume adds: "Although considering the geology of Jamestown Island, it would have been fruitless to try to reach sustained freshwater by digging wells, they were not to know that—but nobody even tried!" (161). Upon visiting the Jamestown excavation in 2007, I saw new diggings indicating that the colonists had indeed tried to dig a well, but Hume's point still holds. When the well project failed, the colonists seemed to give up. Just as inexplicably, they seem to have torn down sections of the fort to use as firewood, even though eyewitnesses described the edge of the forest as "within a stone's throw." Apart from the need for firewood, the forest should have been cut back anyway so as to secure the fort's perimeter.

29. Quoted by Ellickson (1993) 1337. After visiting Jamestown in 2007, talking to four history buffs who work there, and reading scholarly work published since the first version of this essay (including Haile's extraordinary collection of eyewitness accounts), I now suspect that several factors exacerbated the communal charter's corrosive incentive effects. First, the Virginia Company intended to make a profit, so eventually skimming the produce of the colony was precisely the point. The colonists resented having been misled about how difficult life would be, and the idea of working harder than required for their own subsistence, largely to profit the lying fat cats who had put them in their plight to begin with, was intolerable. Second, the colonists wanted to go home, and had the idea that they could win a deadly game of chicken. The idea, as reported by a horrified Thomas Dale, was: "We will weary out the Company at home in sending us provisions, and then, when they grow weary and see that we do not prosper here, they will send for us home. Therefore let us weary them out" (Haile, 1998, 779).

30. Under the new "Headright" system, settlers were given 50-acre plots, plus an additional 50 acres for each servant in their employ. So, they planted tobacco, harvested a crop, and used the money to return

Why go communal in the first place? Are there advantages to communal regimes? One advantage is obvious. Communal regimes can help people spread risks under conditions where risks are substantial and where alternative risk-spreading mechanisms, like insurance, are unavailable. The Virginia Company was sending settlers to a frontier where, without help, something as simple as a sprained ankle could be fatal. The only form of insurance available was, in effect, mutual insurance among the settlers, backed up by their ability to work overtime for less fortunate neighbors. But as communities build up capital reserves to the point where they can offer insurance, they tend to privatize, for insurance lets them secure a measure of risk spreading without having to endure the externalities that tend to afflict communal regimes.

A communal regime might also be an effective response to economies of scale in large-scale public works that are crucial in getting a community started. To build a fort, man its walls, dig wells, and so on, a communal economy is an obvious choice as a way of mobilizing the teams of workers needed to execute these urgent tasks. But again, as these tasks are completed and community welfare increasingly comes to depend on small events, the communal regime gives way to private parcels. At Jamestown, Plymouth, the Amana colonies, and Salt Lake, formerly communal settlers "understandably would switch to private land tenure, the system that most cheaply induces individuals to undertake small and medium events that are socially useful."[31] (The legend of Salt Lake says that the sudden improvement in the fortunes of once-starving Mormons occurred in 1848, when God sent seagulls to save them from plagues of locusts, at the same time they coincidentally were switching to private plots. Similarly, the Jamestown tragedy sometimes is attributed to harsh natural conditions, as if those conditions suddenly changed in 1614, multiplying productivity sevenfold while Governor Dale coincidentally was cutting the land into parcels.)

Of course, the tendency toward decentralized and individualized forms of management is only a strong tendency and, in any case, there are trade-offs. For example, what would be a small event on a larger parcel becomes a medium event under more crowded conditions. Loud music is an innocuous small event on a ranch but an irritating medium event in an apartment complex. Changes in technology or population density affect the scope or incidence of externalities. The trend, though, is that as people become aware of and concerned about a medium or large event, they seek ways of reducing the extent to which the event's cost is externalized. Social evolution is partly a process of perceiving new externalities and devising institutions to internalize them.

Historically, the benefits of communal management have not been enough to keep communes together indefinitely. Perhaps the most enduring and successful communes in human memory are the agricultural settlements of the Hutterites, dating back to sixteenth-century Austria. They migrated to the Dakotas in the 1870s, then to Canada (to avoid compulsory military service during World War I). North

---

to England to recruit new servant/settlers. The recruiter collected the new settler's 50-acre grant. The new settler got transport to Virginia and some portion of the 50 acres, in return for working the recruiter's land for a few seasons while learning the essential skills. Recruiters thus began to cobble together large plantations, new recruits in turn became recruiters themselves, and Virginia's tobacco economy began to gallop.

31. Ellickson (1993) 1342.

American Hutterite communities now contain around forty thousand people (mostly on the Canadian prairies). Hutterites believe in a fairly strict sharing of assets. They forbid radio and television, to give one example of how strictly they control contact with the outside world.

Ellickson says Hutterite communities have three special things going for them:

1. *A population cap*: when a settlement reaches a population of 120, a portion of the community must leave to start a new community. The cap helps them retain a close-knit society.
2. *Communal dining and worship*: people congregate several times a day, which facilitates an intense monitoring of individual behavior and a ready avenue for supplying rapid feedback to those whose behavior deviates from expectations.
3. *A ban on birth control*: the average woman bears ten children (the highest documented fertility rate of any human population), which more than offsets the trickle of emigration.[32]

We might add that Hutterite culture and education leave people ill-prepared to live in anything other than Hutterite society, which accounts for the low emigration rate.

Ellickson discusses other examples of communal property regimes. But the most pervasive example of communal ownership in America, Ellickson says, is the family household. American suburbia consists of family communes nested within a network of open-access roadways. Family homes tacitly recognize limits to how far we can go in converting common holdings to individual parcels. Consider your living room. You could fully privatize, having one household member own it while others pay user fees. The fees could be used to pay family members or outside help to keep it clean. In some respects, it would be better that way. The average communal living room today, for example, is notably subject to overgrazing and shirking on maintenance. Yet we put up with it. No one charges user fees to household members. Seeing the living room degraded by communal use may be irritating, but it is better than treating it as one person's private domain.

Some institutions succeed while embodying a form of ownership that is essentially collective. History indicates, though, that members of successful communes internalize the rewards that come with that collective responsibility. In particular, they reserve the right to exclude nonmembers. A successful commune does not run itself as an open-access commons.

6. Governance by Custom

Many commons (such as our living rooms) are regulated by custom rather than by government, so saying there is a role for common property and saying there is a

---

32. Seth Mydans, "Hmong Refugees Import a Near Record Birthrate," *New York Times*, August 27, 1989, http://query.nytimes.com/gst/fullpage.html?sec=health&res=950DE7 D91631F934A1575BC0A96 F948260.

role for government management of common property are two different things. As Ellickson notes, "group ownership does not necessarily imply government ownership, of course. The sorry environmental records of federal land agencies and Communist regimes are a sharp reminder that governments are often particularly inept managers of large tracts."[33] Carol Rose tells of how, in the nineteenth century, public property was thought to be owned by society at large. The idea of public property often was taken to imply no particular role for government beyond whatever enforcement role is implied by private property. Society's right to such property was held to precede and supersede any claim by government. Rose says: "Implicit in these older doctrines is the notion that, even if a property should be open to the public, it does not follow that public rights should necessarily vest in an active governmental manager."[34] Sometimes, rights were held by an "unorganized public" rather than by a "governmentally organized public."[35]

Along the same lines, open-field agricultural practices of medieval times gave peasants exclusive cropping rights to scattered thin strips of arable land in each of the village fields. The strips were private only during the growing season, after which the land reverted to the commons for the duration of the grazing season.[36] Thus, ownership of parcels was usufructuary, in the sense that once the harvest was in, ownership reverted to the common herdsmen without negotiation or formal transfer.[37] The farmer had an exclusive claim to the land only so long as he was using it for the purpose of bringing in a harvest. The scattering of strips was a means of diversification, reducing the risk of being ruined by small or medium events: small fires, pest infestations, and so on. The postharvest commons in grazing land exploited economies of scale in fencing and tending a herd. The scattering of strips also made it harder for a communal herdsman to position livestock exclusively over his own property, thus promoting more equitable distribution of manure (i.e., fertilizer).[38]

According to Martin Bailey, the pattern observed by Rose and Ellickson also was common among aboriginal tribes. That is, tribes that practiced agriculture treated the land as private during the growing season, and often treated it as a commons after the crops were in. Hunter-gatherer societies did not practice agriculture, but they, too, tended to leave the land in the commons during the summer when game was plentiful. It was during the winter, when food was most scarce, that they privatized. The rule among hunter-gatherers is that where group hunting's advantages are considerable, that factor dominates. But in the winter, small game is relatively more abundant, less migratory, and evenly spread. There was no "feast or famine" pattern of the sort one expects to see with big-game hunting. Rather, families tended to gather enough

---

33. Ellickson (1993) 1335.
34. Rose (1986) 720.
35. Rose (1986) 736.
36. Ellickson (1993) 1390.
37. For an excellent discussion of the issue of adverse possession, see Rose (1985). A "usufructuary" right is an entitlement that persists only so long as the owner is using an item for its customary purpose. For example, you establish a usufructuary right to a park bench by sitting on it, but you abandon that right when you leave.
38. Ellickson (1993) 1390.

during the course of the day to get themselves through the day, day after day, with little to spare.³⁹

Even though this pattern corroborates my own general thesis, I confess to being a bit surprised. I might have predicted that it would be during the harshest part of the year that families would band together and throw everything into the common pot in order to pull through. Not so. It was when the land was nearest its carrying capacity that they recognized the imperative to privatize.

Customary use of medieval commons was hedged with restrictions limiting depletion of resources. Custom prohibited activities inconsistent with the land's ability to recover.⁴⁰ In particular, the custom of "stinting" allowed the villagers to own livestock only in proportion to the relative size of their (growing season) land holdings. Governance by custom enabled people to avoid commons tragedies.⁴¹

Custom is a form of management unlike exclusive ownership by individuals or governments. Custom is a self-managing system for according property rights.⁴² For example, custom governs rights-claims you establish by taking a place in line at a supermarket checkout counter. Rose believes common concerns often are best handled by decentralized, piecemeal, self-managing customs that tend to arise as needed at the local level. So, to the previous section's conclusion that a successful commune does not operate as an open-access commons, we can add that a successful commune does not entrust its governance to a distant bureaucracy.

7. The Hutterite Secret

I argued that the original appropriation of (and subsequent regulation of access to) scarce resources is justifiable as a mechanism for preserving opportunities for future generations. There are various means of exclusive control, though. Some internalize externalities better than others, and how well they do so depends on the context. There is no single form of exclusive control that uniquely serves this purpose. Which form is best depends on what kind of activities are most prevalent in a community at any given time. It also depends on the extent to which public ownership implies control by a distant bureaucracy rather than by local custom.

As mentioned earlier, I have heard people say Jamestown failed because it faced harsh natural conditions. But communal (and noncommunal) settlements typically face harsh natural conditions. Jamestown had to deal with summer in Virginia. Hutterites deal with winter on the Canadian prairie. It is revealing, not misleading, to compare Jamestown to settlements that faced harsher conditions more successfully. It also is fair to compare the two Jamestowns: the one before and the one immediately following Governor Dale's mandated privatization. What distinguished the

---

39. Bailey (1992).
40. Rose (1986) 743.
41. Of course, no one thinks governance by custom automatically solves commons problems. Custom works when local users can restrict outsider access and monitor insider behavior, but those conditions are not always met, and tragedies like those discussed earlier continue to occur.
42. Rose (1986) 742.

first Jamestown from the second was not the harshness of the former's natural setting but rather the thoroughness with which it prevented people from internalizing externalities.

Michael Hechter considers group solidarity to be a function of (1) the extent to which members depend on the group, and (2) the extent to which the group can monitor and enforce compliance with expectations that members will contribute to the group rather than free ride upon it.[43] On Hechter's analysis, it is unsurprising that Hutterite communal society has been successful. Members are extremely dependent, for their upbringing leaves them unprepared to live in a non-Hutterite culture. Monitoring is intense. Feedback is immediate. But if that is the Hutterite secret, why did Jamestown fail? They, too, were extremely dependent on each other. They, too, had nowhere else to go. Monitoring was equally straightforward. Everyone knew who was planting crops (no one) and who was bowling (everyone). What was the problem?

The problem lay in the guarantee embedded in Jamestown's charter. The charter entitled people to an equal share regardless of personal contribution, which is to say it ensured that individual workers would be maximally alienated from the fruits of their labors—that they would think of their work as disappearing into an open-access commons.

Robert Goodin says: "Working within the constraints set by natural scarcity, the greatest practical obstacle to achieving as much justice as resources permit is, and always has been, the supposition that each of us should cultivate his own garden."[44] However, Jamestown's charter did not suppose that each of us should cultivate his own garden. It supposed the opposite. Colonists abided by the charter, and starved. Only a few years later, with a new charter, colonists were tending their own gardens, and thriving.

We should applaud institutions that encourage people to care for each other. But telling people they are required to tend someone else's garden rather than their own does not encourage people to care for each other. It does the opposite. It encourages spite. The people of Jamestown reached the point where they would rather die, bowling in the street, than tend the gardens of their free-riding neighbors, and die they did.

This essay revises David Schmidtz, "The Institution of Property," *Social Philosophy and Policy* 11 (1994): 42–62. Reprinted by permission of Cambridge University Press. 1.

---

43. Hechter (1983) 21.
44. Goodin (1985, 1). Goodin and I debate the issue at length in Schmidtz and Goodin (1998).

12

WITH ELIZABETH WILLOTT

Reinventing the Commons

An African Case Study

Political scientist Elinor Ostrom writes that, over generations,

> Swiss and Japanese villagers have learned the relative benefits and costs of private-property and communal-property institutions related to various types of land and uses of land. The villagers in both settings have chosen to retain the institution of communal property as the foundation for land use and similar important aspects of village economies.[1]

Lest we think this institution must be merely a vestige of a more "primitive" culture, Ostrom adds:

> One cannot view communal property in these settings as the primordial remains of earlier institutions evolved in a land of plenty. If the transaction costs involved in managing communal property had been excessive, compared with private-property institutions, the villagers would have had many opportunities to devise different land-tenure arrangements.[2]

History is full of examples of people converting communally held land into private parcels.[3] How often do people voluntarily move the other way? Not often. On our most recent trip to South Africa, though, we were surprised to find a constellation of economic, ecological, and cultural forces leading landowners voluntarily to convert private parcels into commons.[4]

---

1. Ostrom (1990) 61.
2. Ostrom (1990) 61
3. For several examples, see Ellickson (1993).
4. For what it is worth, we were in Africa on other business, namely to meet Ian Whyte at Kruger Park. Ian was preparing an essay for a textbook we were editing. What we report here was not what we

212   PLANET

This essay treats South Africa's Sabi Sand Game Preserve as a case study of incentives and pressures that lead people to switch from one land ownership regime to another, in this case from private to communal management.

1. Pressure for Change from Private Ranchers

What is now the Sabi Sand Game Preserve was once a patchwork quilt of privately owned ranches. Many tried at some point to raise cattle, but ranching was never profitable. Hoof-and-mouth disease was a problem. The soil is not rich. Water is not plentiful. Predators abound.[5] The local customer base is limited and cash poor, and getting perishable products to distant markets is not easy. Before the development of malaria prophylactics, no one wanted to live there during the wet season. Under the circumstances, ranchers were open to new ideas about how they might use their land.

The new idea: game preserves. According to Lambrechts, "the most expensive rangeland in South Africa is the Sabi Sand Game Reserve." Lambrechts estimates that the value of "privately owned wildlife habitat has increased by as much as 2500%

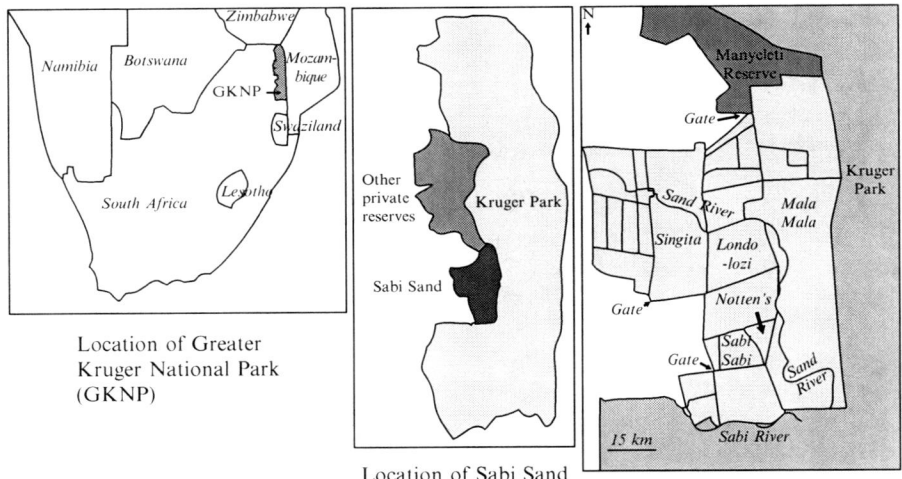

FIGURE 12.1. Maps of South Africa, Greater Kruger National Park, and Sabi Sand.

---

were expecting. We did not conduct interviews as we would have done had we been expecting from the start to find ourselves in the middle of an experiment in the conversion from private to communal land management. We did, however, follow up with telephone and email correspondence and have since found evidence that similar processes of converting private rangeland to jointly managed game preserves are not uncommon in southern Africa.

5. "In the early 1900s attempts were made to substitute Mala Mala's wildlife with cattle farming. A losing battle with lions and a constant struggle with wildlife, diseases and drought soon proved that it was not a viable option." Greenlife South Africa, African Safari website, www.e-gnu.com.

during the last 20 years."[6] A Price Waterhouse study of game reserves in Zimbabwe in 1994 said wildlife utilization could return 11 percent on capital, compared to just 1 percent for cattle ranching.[7]

Although a given rancher might have seen this coming, it would have been hard for him to tap the tourism market on his own.[8] First, there is the "shopping mall" factor. While it may seem optimal for a single business to capture the entire demand for tourist amenities, businesses often do better in the company of other businesses, even direct competitors, because in concert they represent a more salient destination for potential customers. Second, there is a cost-savings issue. There is a grain of truth in the cliché that "good fences make good neighbors," but erecting and maintaining fences is costly. David Evans, business manager of Mala Mala, Sabi Sand's largest resort, says one factor leading to the formation of Sabi Sand was "the economy of scale of a larger community. Our 53 miles of fencing is substantially less than were we to be individually fenced. This is an enormous cost savings. So too is the issue of entrance gates, security at such gates, a single administrative structure, a common voice with authorities, etc."[9] Similar economies of scale rationalized medieval Europe's open-field agricultural practices.[10] The institutions on their face have nothing in common, so we were stunned to find so similar a logic in their emergence and persistence.

Some of the forces driving the emerging commons in Sabi Sand are historically unique, although not uncommon in contemporary sub-Saharan Africa. First, the physical scale of individual ranches was not ideal for tourism. Customers do not fly across the ocean to see something resembling a zoo. They want open space. They want their wildlife wild, not "potted." They want to see animals fending for themselves in a natural ecosystem, born to the land rather than stocked by owners. The kind of customer who flies to Africa wants reality, not the programmed experience of an amusement park. Second, the scale of the ranches was wrong for the animals. A parcel size optimal for a cattle ranch is too small for African megafauna. An elephant spends 80 percent of its life, day and night, eating. Adult elephants can eat 500 pounds of forage per day. They need room. As we explain below, even Kruger National Park, massive as it is, is not a self-contained ecosystem. In short, the parcels were scaled for cattle ranching. To succeed as commercial game preserves, the parcels had to get bigger.

2. Pressure for Change from Kruger Park

Immediately to Sabi Sand's east is its massive neighbor, Kruger National Park. Sabi Sand is approximately 250 square miles (65,000 hectares). Kruger Park is about

---

6. Lambrechts (1995) 39.

7. Krug (2001). In addition to ecotourism, wildlife uses include safari hunting, subsistence hunting for meat, and live game sales of meat and skins.

8. To the best of our knowledge, all of the owners were male.

9. David Evans, personal communication, June 4, 2003.

10. Ellickson (1993) 1390.

8,000 square miles (2 million hectares). Fences separated Kruger Park and Sabi Sand since 1961. People at Sabi Sand say the fence was never their idea, and people at Kruger Park say the same.

Ian Whyte is the chief scientist in charge of large herbivore management at Kruger Park.[11] According to Whyte, the fence was mandated by the Animal Health Department, known then as Veterinary Services, to control the spread of disease from wildlife to livestock. Some of the owners of Sabi Sand and nearby Timbavati, though, had already dispensed with cattle and had been managing their land as private game reserves since the 1950s, and in some cases longer.[12] According to Evans, Sabi Sand Wildtuin (Afrikaans for "wild place") formed as a conservation body with a written constitution in 1950. As interest in cattle waned, the members of Sabi Sand began collectively to agitate for removal of the fences. Whyte and other Kruger Park officials were sympathetic, because the larger the area, the closer it comes to being a self-contained ecosystem and the easier it is to manage.

There were two catches. First, for public relations purposes, commercial hunting had to be prohibited before the private preserves could become part of Greater Kruger National Park. Second, to satisfy the Animal Health Department, cattle had to be separated from wildlife areas.[13] Commercial hunting in Sabi Sand ended by 1986, so the hunting issue was moot. In addition, by that time, no livestock remained within Sabi Sand, so a boundary fence to Sabi Sand's west could serve the quarantine purpose originally served by the fence to Sabi Sand's east, between it and Kruger Park.[14] There was little cattle ranching to the west of Sabi Sand, but the preserve and the park had other reasons to erect the new fence to the west: to deter poachers, and protect villagers from big cats and from crop-raiding animals such as hippo, rhino, and elephant. Meanwhile, Sabi Sand and Kruger Park were free to take down the fence between them and did so in 1993.[15]

3. Results

Sabi Sand, as part of Greater Kruger Park, is now a single, constitutionally governed management unit. Although individual parcel ownership is retained, restrictions are significant. An executive committee, consisting of eleven elected members, meets every three months. There is an annual meeting to which each of the thirty-six properties sends a voting representative.[16] Each property has one vote, but votes are weighted according to the size of the property the vote represents. Parcels can be sold. They can be inherited. However, they cannot be developed for uses other than

---

11. Whyte, incidentally, is coauthor of the birdwatcher's canonical field guide for the region.

12. Krug (2001) 24.

13. Ian Whyte, personal communication (May 7, 2003).

14. Gavin Hulett (warden of Sabi Sand), personal communication, June 2, 2003.

15. Krug (2001, 24) reports this as 1994, but in correspondence, Ian Whyte confirms the 1993 date. Whyte notes, in Krug's defense, that Krug was relying on Whyte, who inaccurately reported the date as 1994 in his thesis.

16. Hulett, personal communication, June 2, 2003.

as part of a wildlife preserve. Gavin Hulett, Sabi Sand's warden, says parcels cannot be subdivided into portions smaller than 856 hectares. Parcels smaller than that exist but were created before the subdivision restriction was added to the constitution.[17]

The number of guest "beds" per resort is restricted to one per 150 hectares (just under two beds per square mile).[18] By limiting the number of beds—that is, the number of guests—Sabi Sand controls overall traffic on the land. Each owner, although constrained in terms of numbers of customers, freely decides what clientele he wishes to attract. Some resorts are extravagant; others are rustic. Most decisions about how to do business remain matters of private choice. Customers who prefer going without electricity and enjoying blissfully quiet evenings by candlelight at a relatively moderate price go to a place like Notten's Bush Camp. Customers wanting world-renowned luxury, with a full bar, refrigerator, "his and hers" bathrooms, and a private swimming pool with each cottage, go to a place like Singita Private Game Reserve or Mala Mala Game Reserve. Each resort finds its own niche and clientele. Managers regard each other with respect, privately voicing philosophical differences about the proper way to experience the bush but not regarding themselves as competing for the same pot of money.

Each resort offers two Land Rover safari tours per day—one at dawn, one at dusk.[19] Other than this, animals are left in peace. Land Rovers routinely leave their home resorts, touring neighboring lands for the sake of a change of scenery (and sometimes in response to hot tips from neighbors about special sightings—see "Matters of Scale" below). This requires a neighbor's invitation, and presupposes reciprocity, but understandings regarding mutual access arise easily enough among neighbors. Pairs of neighbors need not involve other owners in day-to-day negotiations that interest only the pair of them.

Resorts profit by showing animals in seemingly wild habitat, so each resort is motivated to preserve the land. By keeping its own land attractive to wildlife, a resort maintains its stock of wildlife and acts as a good neighbor, making sure it has something to offer in exchange for reciprocal access rights. There is little room for free riding.

Management of wildlife is unobtrusive. The Preserve does not feed animals.[20] Feeding makes animals dangerously and unattractively tame. However, individual

---

17. Hulett, personal communication, June 2, 2003. Interestingly, on details like this we often found discrepancies. One source said subdivisions were not allowed, another that properties could not be subdivided into parcels of less than 2,000 hectares. Most owners don't need to know most of the fine details on such matters, since most are not planning to subdivide.

18. Hulett, personal communication, June 2, 2003. There is an extra bed tax if the number of beds exceeds one per 150 hectares. As with the rules of subdivision, different owners had slightly different versions—all consistent with the idea that it should not be easy for a resort to regularly exceed carrying capacity in guests. Since the constitution can change, and is changing, the legal details are less important to most managers and resorts than that the practices of other resorts be sensible. So their memory of the "rules" is likely to be inexact.

19. The animals are most active around dawn and dusk, so this practice makes sense.

20. We have read of one exception, in the mid-1980s, concerning a female cheetah that wounded her foot in a poacher's trap. Five cubs relied on her. By agreement of Sabi Sand owners, she was temporarily fed so these six rare animals could survive. See Seijas and Vorhies (1989).

owners are free to make sure their water holes do not run dry. Ecologically, the institution seems to work (but see "Ongoing Problems" below). Lambrechts says the private preserves to Kruger Park's west "contain virtually the full spectrum of wildlife that occurred in the area during historic times. The contribution of the three largest and oldest collaborative nature reserves (i.e., the Sabi Sand, Timbavati, Klaserie) to nature conservation is evident."[21] Our personal experiences confirmed that the diversity of wildlife at Sabi Sand is astounding.

4. Why Reinvent the Commons?

To explain why Sabi Sand's property institutions evolved as they did, we discuss in general terms why communal regimes evolve into private ones. We then apply the same logic to questions about why Sabi Sand went the other way. Then we discuss problems that owners of Sabi Sand face as a consequence of going communal. We discuss how successful communes historically faced analogous problems, and found analogous solutions.

Why People Privatize

The trend toward land privatization is driven by a collision of economic and ecological forces. Private ownership of land often is the best way to prevent overgrazing. An unregulated commons is a recipe for economic and ecological waste. As the level of use exceeds the land's carrying capacity, the land will be degraded.[22] When access to a pasture is unregulated, an individual herd owner has little incentive or opportunity to conserve the pasture. Regardless of what an individual herd owner does, the resource is being depleted by unlimited numbers of unregulated users. Accordingly, private ownership often is offered as the solution to the tragedy of the commons. Private ownership gives an owner a right to exclude. By conferring a right to exclude, the system gives an owner the opportunity to conserve a resource.

Harold Demsetz's case study of the emergence of private property institutions on the Labrador peninsula shows that people are capable of seeing when they have a commons problem and of responding with judicious institutional change. In that case, people only privatized what had to be privatized to solve the particular commons tragedy at hand.

One lesson of Sabi Sand is that the point of changing only what needs changing goes both ways. When private owners have reasons to switch to a form of collective management and cannot institute more sweeping changes by force, they do not fix what "ain't broke." Needing to achieve consensus, their changes tend to be conservative, communizing only what needs to be communal to solve the problem. In creating

---

21. Lambrechts (1995) 39.

22. The concept of carrying capacity is somewhat problematic. It points to something real, because there really are limits to what the land can support. On the other hand, such limits are not fixed. Carrying capacity is somewhat fluid, and is a function of many variables. Whether Kruger Park can carry fifteen thousand elephants, for example, depends on whether we want to leave room for rhinos, which is not simply an ecological issue.

Sabi Sand Preserve, what needed to be communal was land management, for reasons mentioned earlier. There was no need to share Land Rovers or guests. Communal management's advantages are limited, so at Sabi Sand, communal management was implemented in a judiciously limited way.

Matters of Scale

As noted in chapter 11, Ellickson and Demsetz categorize as small, medium, or large the ways different activities affect neighbors. As also noted, if an individual owner's parcel size can be increased without limit, any event can be made "small." In the case at hand, a single owner could have purchased all of Sabi Sand and run the preserve as a single large business. In that limiting case, all events within the reserve would be small in the technical sense, with externalities fully internalized. Given two dozen owners who had no interest in selling, though, the situation required the sort of cooperation that characterizes medium-event management.

Sabi Sand's owners continue to manage their property as a set of privately owned parcels, in the sense that is relevant for responding to small and medium problems. Neighbors are expected to handle their own affairs and to negotiate with each other on matters of common concern. Individual resorts have problems of their own (i.e., small problems) or problems in concert with immediate neighbors (i.e., they jointly face medium problems). In order to make decisions in the easiest and most informal way, neighbors minimize how many owners are involved in any given decision. They let small events remain small and avoid turning medium events into large ones.

In particular, allowing a neighbor's guests to tour one's property benefits both neighboring owners and their guests. The degree of cooperation in this matter is impressive. If a neighbor has just seen a pride of lions run down a wildebeest, he will treat his own guests to the spectacle, at the same time contacting one or two neighbors by walkie-talkie to let them know he will drive off in a few minutes and they are welcome to take a look. This is made easier by the fact that all Land Rovers are presumed to be touring at the same time. If access is negotiated between immediate neighbors rather than at the preserve level, owners retain rights to regulate access on an ad hoc basis. Neighbors form agreements more readily and fall out of agreement when that is appropriate. Incentives to cooperate and opportunities to coordinate are retained. Thus the tendency to bureaucratize is minimized.[23]

Patterns of Successful Communal Management

Privatization is one, but only one, solution to the tragedy of the commons. Many medieval commons lasted, nontragically, for hundreds of years. Ostrom describes a Swiss commons whose written records date back to the thirteenth century. Cattle are privately owned but graze in communal highlands in the summer. People grow private crops on individual plots in the valleys, intending to use part of their crops

---

23. Individual partners face a trade-off when decision-making falls to the group as a whole: they gain a measure of control to the extent that other partners need to get their consent before doing anything, and lose control to the extent that they, too, need to get consent before doing anything.

to sustain their cattle over the winter. The basic limit on communal summer grazing is that owners can send only as many cattle to the highland meadows as their private parcel can sustain over the winter, with fodder grown during summer.[24]

The arrangement solves the central problem of how to prevent overgrazing: how to govern decisions regarding herd size. Allowing individual owners freely to decide whether to add to their individual stock is above all what governors of a commons cannot do. To avoid tragedy, governors of a common pasture manage the overall livestock population, based on their estimate of the pasture's overall carrying capacity. To manage overall numbers, communal managers constrain individual decision-making. There are several ways of doing so. Managers can allow a given owner to graze cattle on common land only in proportion to (1) how much hay he produces, (2) what proportion of the land belongs to him, or (3) the number of shares he owns in the cooperative.

Whatever institutions people create must be able to respond to change. Suppose people discover some way to increase crop yields in the valley, increasing their ability to produce winter fodder. As a consequence, the valley's winter carrying capacity rises, but the highland's summer carrying capacity does not. In that case, the rule tying summer grazing rights to winter feeding capacity no longer works; it has become a prescription for summer overgrazing. Managers of the highland meadow will need to change the rule for allocating grazing rights.

Ostrom writes:

> All of the Swiss institutions that used to govern commonly owned alpine meadows have one obvious similarity—the appropriators themselves make all major decisions about the use of the common property resource.... Thus, residents of Törbel and other Swiss villages who own communal land spend time governing themselves. Many of the rules they use, however, keep their monitoring and other transactions costs relatively low and reduce the potential for conflict.[25]

The lesson is twofold: Successful commons are (1) flexible, and (2) under local control. Rules sometimes need to change in response to circumstances, and local people know what needs changing locally.[26]

Of Sheep and Ecotourists

In the medieval commons, land was held in common. Individual members remained, in a sense, private businessmen—private owners of their livestock. The parallel with Sabi Sand is that a basic resource, land and its wildlife, is managed as a common unit while the business per se remains private. Each individual business within Sabi Sand has its own "flock" of guests. Thus, the analog at Sabi Sand of privately owned but communally grazing sheep is the customer, not the wildlife. In the medieval case,

---

24. Ostrom (1990) 61.

25. Ostrom (1990) 65.

26. Ostrom (1990) 62. In some cases, the recorded history of these legal arrangements and their changes dates back to the 1200s.

sheep graze the land, and owners profit on a per sheep basis. At Sabi Sand, customers "graze" on wildlife (and other features of the land), and owners profit on a per customer basis.

In the Swiss commons, "no citizen could send more cows to the Alp than he could feed during the winter."[27] Similarly, no partner in Sabi Sand unilaterally decides how many customers to "graze" on the preserve. The problems differ in detail, but the logic is the same. Partners recognize an imperative to avoid commons tragedies and do so by taking the option of overgrazing out of the hands of individual partners. In the case of Sabi Sand, this means executive committee decisions about carrying capacity—in particular, the land's capacity to carry guests without long-term degradation. On the medieval common, this meant deciding when overgrazing would affect flocks to the point where a head of sheep would be worth less. The parallel at Sabi Sand is the point at which overgrazing by guests will begin to reduce a prospective customer's desire to visit Sabi Sand.

5. Keys to Success

Ostrom lists keys to long-term survival of any common pool resource. Among them:

1. Boundaries are well defined, both physically and in terms of people. The resource is clearly delimited. Insiders who do have rightful access are clearly distinguished from outsiders who do not.
2. Rules are sensitive to local conditions.
3. Users get involved in monitoring each other.
4. Users generally can participate in modifying operational rules.[28]

Sabi Sand's owners faced many of the same problems as communal herd owners of medieval Europe and developed many of the same solutions. According to economist Wolf Krug, the reasons for the success of private reserves include efficient monitoring of wildlife stocks; well-trained staff; and high levels of investment in antipoaching measures.[29] Although Krug speaks of the contributions a well-trained staff can make to the success of private reserves, we should not confuse training with professional certification. Many of the people at Sabi Sand with whom we talked acknowledged invaluable contributions by natives who grew up in the bush. A bush-savvy local staff helps maintain connections with local villagers, which minimizes poaching. If a manager learns that the impala snared a few days ago was eaten by a desperately poor family, it affects how the case is handled. The manager can decide to look the other way, hoping the trespass is limited by the inherent limits of the particular poacher's need. In contrast, poaching a rhino for its horn is a declaration of war; if the reserve does not defend itself from those seeking rhino horns for international

---

27. Ostrom (1990, 62), citing Netting (1976) 135, 139.
28. Ostrom (1990) 61.
29. Krug (2001) 25.

markets, it will be overrun. So some poaching of small game by neighboring villagers is tolerated, but Sabi Sand's perimeter is designed to minimize the costs of excluding and monitoring would-be poachers while maximizing the area for wildlife and wildlife observation.

There is no fence at the boundary with Kruger Park or with Manyeleti Preserve, a private reserve to Sabi Sand's north that is also part of Greater Kruger National Park (see fig. 12.1). A perimeter fence remains or was installed on other boundaries. Main roads at times follow this perimeter. Visitors are exposed to a minimum of fences and traffic while on safari, thereby enhancing the safari experience. Land alongside the fence and road also serves as a firebreak—it is cleared and sometimes burned. The fence is hardly impenetrable, but getting through it takes work. The clearing of perimeter land, together with strategic placement of roads, makes trespass easier to spot; breaches of the fence are likely to be spotted by the next vehicle coming along the road. The perimeter road thus reduces trespass and poaching.

The main boundary road is packed dirt, suitable for rental cars and wide enough to leave room for passage of oncoming traffic. Narrow internal roads branch from the main boundary road, allowing access to individual resorts. These may be shared by a few neighbors. The main purpose of sharing is to minimize the land that roads consume, but sharing also facilitates contact among neighbors. There are also internal tracks suitable for Land Rovers, so that there is limited off-track movement. However, the land here evolved to withstand elephants and can handle occasional Land Rover use. We saw a mild degree of visible degradation in 2001 (flattened grass and shrubs) but were told it was from elephants, not Land Rovers. The animals themselves often use the roads, though; walking along the road is easier and quieter than wading through thickets. Roads thus minimize wear and tear on the land by providing established trails not only for vehicles but also for megafauna.

Although hunting is banned at Sabi Sand, if an animal is seriously injured, it can be killed.[30] If there is time, a veterinarian is consulted before the animal is killed; if not, a veterinarian certifies after the killing. We asked one resort manager whether the hunting ban was absolute or whether a wealthy would-be hunter could get away with bribing a particular owner or tour guide to look the other way. The manager said no resort would ever risk that. If discovered, there would be legal penalties, and there would be little chance of avoiding discovery, given the constant observation of neighbors. The system thus discourages defection.

Regular scheduling of Land Rover tours, at dawn and dusk, means animals know when Land Rovers are coming, owners know when they are expected, and everyone knows something is wrong if Land Rovers are heard when or where they shouldn't be. Everyone knows they should never hear gunshots.[31] So monitoring becomes simpler. As one manager said, "There are too many eyes and ears to make illegal hunting much of an option." Indeed, guests pay to be the eyes and ears! The cost of internal

---

30. Hulett, personal communication, June 2, 2003. Hulett reports one exception. In 2001, a male cheetah broke its leg. Unable to hunt, it would have died. Since cheetah are endangered, and since it could still serve in the cheetah gene pool, this cheetah was sent to the De Wildt Cheetah Breeding Station.

31. Poachers often hunt with snares, though, not rifles. Snare hunting is quiet, uses only inexpensive materials, and does not require a lot of time on the part of the poacher. It is also a ghastly way for an animal to die.

monitoring often is the downfall of communal managers, but at Sabi Sand, internal monitoring is part of the package that resorts are selling.

Knowledge is a prerequisite for successfully managing the preserve's ecosystem. Day-by-day observations supplemented by high technology such as remote sensing or aerial photography can help managers gauge an ecosystem's long-term viability. To do this well, one wants collaboration between bush-savvy people and high-tech scientists. Note that hiring people who know and love the land is not enough. Also needed are employees who know and love people—who can run resorts and interact well with villagers outside the park. The preserve needs to understand its customer base, so it needs to understand marketing and sociology.

Different resorts use different strategies for catering to guests, hiring staff, and long-term monitoring of wildlife. Some of these strategies will work, some will not. But the temporary failure of one resort need not jeopardize the whole preserve. Failure of one resort can remain a small event. Resorts that do not adequately monitor ecosystem sustainability may (perhaps quickly) become less profitable, but they need not take the rest of Sabi Sand down with them. Conversely, if they have a new idea, they need not wait for everyone else to be convinced. They can go ahead and experiment, and if the experiment goes well, other owners can imitate. The system at Sabi Sand has room to evolve and thus to endure.

6. Problems External to Sabi Sand

Several obstacles limit private investment in sub-Saharan wildlife conservation. There are perverse economic and political incentives as well as difficult legal and social problems to overcome. For example, the South African government subsidizes cattle ranching, while the European Community guarantees quotas of imported beef at above-market prices.[32] It is hard to imagine the South African government subsidizing cattle ranching to a point where Sabi Sand would be tempted to abandon ecotourism in favor of cattle. Still, people elsewhere are making a living as ranchers. Subsidies keep them in business when market price signals otherwise would tempt them to turn their land over to wildlife conservation.

Problems also arise from the lack of an appropriate legal framework, especially a lack of secure property rights, for the wildlife business. The problem is most acute in Zimbabwe, but as managers of Sabi Sand are aware, there is no guarantee that such problems will not spill over into South Africa. The manager at Singita said his family fled political oppression and civil war in Zimbabwe when he was a child. Just before we visited Singita in 2001, some of his Zimbabwean cousins needed to flee to relative safety in South Africa with only one suitcase each. With that kind of uncertainty, people may choose not to make long-term investments, such as developing the kind of infrastructure necessary to profitably convert from ranching to game preservation.

Evans says that at present, Sabi Sand is facing claims of people who say they were there first and that they were displaced. Evans says current owners can (with

---

32. Krug (2001) 32.

one exception) trace their claims back to Crown grants in 1869. Moreover, it is generally acknowledged that the area was only sparsely and intermittently inhabited before then on account of the prevalence of malaria. The law allows claims for reparation going back only to 1913. Thus, Sabi Sand appears to be on solid legal ground. Still, the law is only as solid as a ruling party's respect for it. Most of Sabi Sand's owners trust the current regime, but history has not been kind to Africa. Like all Africans, Sabi Sand's owners know that things can change with little warning.

A third kind of problem involves social pressures created by international wildlife groups and restrictions on international trade in wildlife products, which reduce a reserve's profit opportunities. When hunting is not allowed, not even to control overpopulation, profits drop. When ivory sales are banned, profits drop. When trade in meat and other wildlife products is not allowed, profits drop. One lesson of wildlife conservation efforts in Africa is that we can go too far trying to preserve nature sans people. Unable to profit from wildlife because they were blocked by animal rights groups that were insufficiently sensitive to local ecology (including human ecology), rural people who could have made a living from wildlife instead drive wildlife off their land to make room for (relatively unprofitable) crops and cattle.[33]

Evans notes that Mala Mala is storing ivory, rhino horn, and other wildlife products, collected from animals that died on its land, pending the lifting of CITES bans on the trade of such products.[34] Evans argues that the ban ought to be lifted, perhaps on the condition that revenue from sales be used to acquire additional land for wildlife reserves.[35]

We have discussed political and economic problems external to Sabi Sand. There are ecological reasons why legislators would want to solve them. Lambrechts says that as of 1993, the Transvaal region had about 2.5 million hectares of national and provincial parks and 4 million hectares of private reserve. The latter figure is over 17 percent of the region's total land area.[36] Given other pressing problems, such as AIDS, illiteracy, and unemployment, little prospect exists for devoting further government resources to biodiversity. At the very least, private conservation is complementing governmental efforts.

There are also economic reasons for solving these problems. Private wildlife preserves such as the properties of Sabi Sand often are primary employers. Mala Mala properties, owning over a quarter of the land within Sabi Sand, has three lodges, which Lambrechts estimates employ a staff of 220, of whom 190, with an estimated 2,000 dependents, come from surrounding rural communities. Lambrechts adds:, "Although accurate figures are impossible to obtain, the number of individuals employed within the private sector wildlife industry in Transvaal is estimated at 12,000, with 100,000 dependents."[37]

33. Bonner (1993); a relevant excerpt is reprinted in Schmidtz and Willott (2002) 306–19.

34. David Evans, personal communication, June 2, 2003.

35. Evans, personal communication, June 2, 2003.

36. Lambrechts (1995) 38, table 1. The former Transvaal Province has since been split into the Limpopo (or Northern), Northwest, Gauteng, and Mpumalanga provinces.

37. Lambrechts (1995) 39. Spenceley and Seif (2003) estimate that Sabi Sabi Resort employs sixty local villagers, who support 460 residents of the village (Huntingdon, population sixty-five hundred) located just outside Sabi Sand; Sabi Sabi Resort is only one of many employers in Sabi Sand.

7. Sabi Sand's Internal Problems

Greater Kruger Park is home to several endangered species, including rhinoceros and cheetah. The rhinoceros is threatened by an overabundance of elephants, since elephants consistently outcompete the rhinoceros for forage. Elephants are bigger, smarter, and socially organized in a way that is beyond the rhinoceros. There is a bit of a biological mystery here. Accurate records from Kruger National Park and elsewhere in southern Africa indicate elephant populations increase roughly 5–7 percent per year in the absence of human killing.[38] What can account for these high rates of increase? Why isn't everything else in Africa (or for that matter, in other parts of the world historically populated by elephants and their ancestors) already extinct? What normally controls elephant populations?

In North America, humans are what we call an exotic or introduced species. Large human populations have been in North America for perhaps twelve thousand years. We typically see nature as something separate from humans and as something that would carry on nicely but for human interference. That may be true in North America, but it is not true in Africa. Elephants appeared in Africa about 5 million years ago.[39] So did humans.[40] Humans and elephants coevolved. Humans have hunted elephants since before humans and elephants evolved to become what they are today.

Elephants are too big, too smart, and too well-organized for a feline predator, even a lion, to have much chance of taking a baby elephant, unless a herd is disrupted. We have no evidence of elephants ever being routinely hunted by any species other than humans. Just as in North America, where exterminating wolves and cougars caused deer and elk populations to explode, so, too, in parts of Africa where hunting by humans was stopped, elephant populations exploded. Without its keystone predator, any ecosystem is unstable. We can let natural processes control impala populations, but if we ask why we cannot likewise let natural processes control elephant populations, the answer is that, when it comes to elephants, hunting by humans *is* the natural process, or the closest thing to it. In Africa there is no such thing as humans simply "letting nature be."

How much damage could humans in Africa do before acquiring guns? More than one might imagine. Just as some Native Americans hunted bison by stampeding herds over cliffs, there is evidence that *Homo erectus* hunted elephants by stampeding whole herds into swamps.[41] Note that elephant herds consist entirely of females and their young. Since the introduction of firearms, trophy hunters have hunted the

---

38. A minimum 5 percent increase is reported in an internal memorandum (Joubert 1996). Kruger National Park's elephant population was increasing at an average of 7–8 percent annually, according to Butler (1998) 76.

39. Jackson (1982) 15.

40. Michael D. Lemonick, and Andrea Dorfman. "Up from the Apes: Remarkable New Evidence Is Filling in the Story of How We Became Human," *Time*, August 23, 1999, 50.

41. Johanson and Edey (1981, 73). F. Clark Howell discovered evidence of *Homo erectus* living in Spain and hunting elephants as long as four hundred thousand years ago. He found large numbers of elephant fossils, together with evidence of fires used to stampede them, and stone tools used to butcher them.

more solitary bulls. Before firearms, stampede-style hunters took out whole herds, in effect taking out multiple generations of breeding-age females at a stroke. This incredible selection pressure may help to explain how such an incredible animal as the elephant could evolve and persist, eating as prodigiously and reproducing as prolifically as as it does, without driving itself and its ecosystem into oblivion.

The Kruger Park area may never have had many elephants or people. Elsewhere in Africa, pictographs record evidence of ancient elephant hunting. By contrast, of 109 shelters containing rock art so far discovered in Kruger Park, only one depicts elephants. This suggests there were elephants in what is now Kruger Park somewhere between 7000 BCE and 300 CE, but they may have been rare.[42] Since the park's formation in the early 1900s, elephant populations have increased. In the 1960s, scientists and rangers estimated the park's carrying capacity to be about seven thousand elephants. Culling began in 1972 to maintain the elephant population between 6,800 and 7,200. Even at the peak of poaching, during the 1980s, culling was needed to stabilize elephant numbers.[43] In response to pressure from animal rights groups, the culling stopped in 1995. There were 7,200 elephants at the time. Today there are 10,500;[44] and it is visibly apparent that the Park cannot sustain them indefinitely. If a park has few elephants, then adding a few promotes biodiversity. If a park already has too many, adding more reduces biodiversity. A maximum elephant population is not compatible with maximum biodiversity.

One key ecological role of elephants is to keep forests in check and maintain open savanna. Adult male elephants will push over four or five trees per night and nibble on the roots. At high numbers, instead of keeping forests in check, elephants destroy too many trees and endanger other flora and fauna, including rhinoceros. Mpalo Setshwantsho was our guide in Botswana's Okavango Delta in 1999. He had been working as a guide for eighteen years and had lived in the neighborhood of the delta his whole life. When we asked him whether he had seen major changes in the delta in his lifetime, he said there are more animals now. He also said there are fewer trees. In Chobe National Park, as elephant populations rose, woodland vegetation decreased from 60 percent coverage to 30 percent between 1962 and 1998.[45] In 1999, Aari Schreiber, a Kruger Park section ranger who manages roughly a quarter of the park, told us that if all elephants were removed, Kruger Park would need twenty years to recover from elephant damage done since 1995.

42. Whyte (2002).

43. Kobus Krüger was among a handful of rangers who took responsibility for putting an end to the poaching, at great personal risk. He spent days and weeks on his own in the bush, without fire and without radio contact, tracking and apprehending poachers. Kobus was also one of the rangers principally responsible for the culling. He was famous for his marksmanship, and it takes a superb marksman to hit an elephant's brain with a single shot from an AK-47 rifle while standing on a helicopter platform. But Kobus loves animals as much as anyone we have ever met, and the task of shooting elephants was literally the stuff of nightmares.

44. Whyte and Fayrer-Hosken (forthcoming). This is Ian Whyte's estimate as of 2003. Whyte estimates that at this size, 735 elephants would have to be culled each year to stabilize the population. If the population base were smaller, fewer elephants would need to be culled.

45. Mosugelo et al. (2002). For more on destruction of woodlands by elephants, see Whyte, van Aarde, and Pimm (1998).

Kruger Park gave away as many elephants as it could—140 as of 1999, when we first visited there—but not many people want to own an African elephant, and not many can be trusted with the responsibility. (Indian elephants are cuter, smaller, and more docile, and are the kind found in circuses and most zoos.) The cost of translocation is also prohibitive. Ian Whyte estimated the cost of moving eleven hundred elephants to adjacent land in Mozambique at 15 million rand ($2 million).[46]

Moving elephants turns out also to be a sociological problem. In their normal social setting, juveniles are kept in check by older males. Juvenile males translocated without their educational support groups have in some cases become delinquents: harassing rhinoceros and other animals, and sometimes humans, too.

Kruger Park has a problem with elephant overpopulation, a problem that, because of pressure from animal rights groups, it cannot readily solve. When the factor that prevents an ecosystem from being stable is that it lacks a keystone predator, merely enlarging the ecosystem will not solve the problem. Ultimately, something must play the role of that missing predator. The park is not a viable ecosystem in the long run unless something is done about the elephants, which is also to say the private reserves that now form part of Greater Kruger are not ecologically viable unless something is done. Adding more land does no more than buy time during which other solutions may emerge.

One approach is to develop a method of birth control suitable for elephants. Personnel of Kruger National Park, in conjunction with other scientists, have been investigating several methods. The first test of hormone-based birth control, analogous to the human birth control pill, was technically successful, insofar as females did become temporarily sterile. However, the method failed, because bulls thought the treated females were in estrus and continually harassed them, causing them to panic and leave their young unprotected and unfed. The test was stopped for humane reasons.[47]

Another method currently is being tested. Zona pellucida proteins, which normally surround the egg, are injected into female elephants. The resulting immune response in the female creates proteins (antibodies) that bind to the egg, thereby preventing sperm from fertilizing the egg. Females are thus temporarily rendered sterile. Since this method does not directly affect hormone levels, it has not led to the same problem as the initial method. So far, no side effects are known, although there has not yet been enough time for social side effects to manifest.[48]

46. Whyte, personal communication (2001).

47. Butler (1998) 53. See also Fayrer-Hosken et al. (2000).

48. McComb et al. (2001). If conditions are good, a cow may have eight calves in her life, of which half could be expected to be female. Herds are matriarchal and are led by the oldest female, typically a postmenopausal female in her fifties. Females remain in the herd for their whole lives. (Males leave at puberty.) The herd is thus an extended family consisting of the old matriarch and several generations of her and perhaps her younger sisters' female offspring. If a contraception program aimed to stabilize elephant numbers, each cow would theoretically have only two offspring. How would that affect the herds? Given standard probabilities, about half the matriarchs would have one daughter. A quarter would have two. A quarter would have two sons, thus no daughters. A female having two sons would thus find her sons leaving at puberty, leaving her with no herd over which to be a matriarch. She would be the end of the matrilineal line. If, like half of all females by hypothesis, she has no sisters, or if her one sister has no daughters, then she is the end of her mother's line as well. Again, given standard probabilities, twenty-five

There is a logistical problem, too. To stabilize populations, approximately 70 percent of breeding females would need to be under treatment at any one time. In Kruger Park alone, this means thousands of female elephants. Animals require repeated dosages. Each animal would need to be individually radio-collared or tagged in some way. This expense would be astronomical. However, it might be feasible on private preserves with larger staffs and smaller numbers of elephants.

What is the situation in Sabi Sand? Before the removal of the fence in 1993, there were sixty elephants in Sabi Sand. The trend since then is as follows:

1993	1994	1995	1996	1997	1998	1999	2000	2001	2002
60	116	202	202	311	429	497	531	601	757

This trend is obviously worrisome. Kruger Park's carrying capacity traditionally is estimated to be a little less than one elephant per square mile. In 2002, the population density within Sabi Sand rose to three per square mile. Plants that elephants most favor became rarer in Kruger Park but proliferated in Sabi Sand, while elephants were mostly absent. That may be why elephants are migrating to Sabi Sand. Ian Whyte guesses Sabi Sand's elephant population density will return to something like Kruger's when elephants damage Sabi Sand to the same degree that they have damaged Kruger Park since 1995, when the culling stopped.[49] Presumably, Sabi Sand does not want to go down that road. There may come a day when the moratorium on elephant culling at Kruger Park will force Sabi Sand's managers to put the fences back up again.

One solution to the overpopulation problem that would also raise revenue would be to run the game preserves as part-time hunting lodges, as many were run in the past. In 1999, we visited Khami Game Preserve in Zimbabwe. At the time, Khami operated as a hunting lodge one month of the year and as a no-hunting game preserve for the other eleven. Although this option is ethically or politically unacceptable to some people, it would have advantages over current alternatives, insofar as it is technologically and financially feasible. Indeed, unlike the alternatives, hunting would generate income that could be plowed back into communities and conservation efforts. The bottom line is that whatever policy Sabi Sand adopts, it will have to help local people make a living if it is to be sustainable.

8. Conclusion

Looking at principles derived from the study of long-enduring commons, it becomes clear that wherever possible, people let small events remain small. This is evident at

---

out of sixty-four females would have no granddaughters. So it is not merely numbers within a generation that would be thinned out. Also declining would be the number of generations per herd. Would remnant females, no longer having young to tend and thus losing their central reason to constitute themselves as a herd—or, for that matter, to live at all—want to join another herd, helping to raise a small number of offspring to which they are not closely related? Would remnant females be welcome in another female's herd? Is it *obvious* that limiting population this way would be more humane than culling?

49. Sabi Sand is being monitored. Tree damage increased considerably, and bull elephants were responsible for 92 percent of uprooted trees in the area studied (Hiscocks, 1999).

Sabi Sand, where individual resorts profit from making good decisions, suffer from making bad decisions, and neighbors learn from example.

Ellickson summarizes:

> The agricultural activities for which there were efficiencies of scale—harvesting, fencing, shepherding—were performed jointly on commonly accessible land according to explicit bylaw or implicit contract ("the custom of the manor"). The small agricultural events that lacked returns to scale—planting, weeding, thinning —were stimulated through the direct material incentives of private land ownership.[50]

Thus, at Sabi Sand, activities for which there are efficiencies or necessities of scale—managing wide-ranging megafauna, fencing, securing legal rights to river water—are performed jointly. Another key characteristic of long-enduring commons is their ability to change as required. Sabi Sand sometimes needs to modify its rules and customs to meet new ecological, financial, social, and political challenges. Being an organized group committed to building a sustainable preserve puts Sabi Sand's owners in a better position to address larger challenges. Being privately owned resorts gives owners an incentive to take individual responsibility for smaller ones.

This essay revises one originally published in *University of California at Davis Law Review* 36 (2003): 203–32. Copyright 2003 by David Schmidtz and Elizabeth Willott and the Regents of the University of California. All rights reserved. Reprinted by permission. Elizabeth Willott is a Lecturer in the Entomology Department and a member of the Institute for Study of Planet Earth at the University of Arizona.

---

50. Ellickson (1993) 1391.

13

Natural Enemies

An Anatomy of Environmental Conflict

For many who live in modern cities, nature is a haven, a refuge from an urban jungle. The frustrations of the city make it easy to feel nostalgia for a simple life that never was: days spent hiking in the Grand Canyon, nights spent curled up by the fireplace after a hot shower and something nice from the refrigerator.

But nature is not a national park, as people who make their living in its midst are aware. My ancestors emigrated from Germany to North America in the 1850s, settling in Minnesota and Saskatchewan. Like most settlers, they had mixed feelings about nature.[1] Beautiful it may have been, but it was not the innocuous beauty that city dwellers find in art galleries. Nature was wild, literally. It could be kind. It could be indifferent. Or it could be an appalling enemy, a promise of hard life and sudden death. My mother lost a brother to diphtheria. A mile down the road, her uncle watched his whole family, a wife and three children, die of diphtheria in the space of three days. She grew up on a farm that got virtually no rain for a stretch of ten years in the 1930s.[2] She once told me, "You'd see black clouds boiling on the horizon. If you didn't know better you'd think the rain was finally coming. But it wasn't rain. When you got up in the morning everything would be covered by a carpet of dust. Sometimes it was a carpet of grasshoppers." For many of the world's people today, nature remains as it was for my ancestors—red in tooth and claw. It comes in the night to kill their children.[3] No hot shower. No refrigerator.

---

1. I thank Don Scherer for his insights on how attitudes toward nature have changed over the centuries. See also Hargrove (1979).

2. I was the fifth of six children, and the first to be born into a house with running water and an indoor toilet. Before then, our family got through the summer on melted snow. (It snowed a lot in Saskatchewan, and people used water sparingly.)

3. Malaria, for example, is transmitted by mosquitoes. When my ancestors were landing in New Orleans in the 1850s, malaria was widespread as far north as the Great Lakes. See Ackerknecht (1945). Malaria remains endemic in many tropical and even temperate regions. When I visited Zambia in 1999, I met a young woman who told me that like everyone else in her village, she contracted malaria two or three times per year.

Western civilization has given me the luxury of being an environmentalist. I am insulated against nature, and this insulation gives me the luxury of no longer needing to see nature as a threat. Unfortunately, not everyone is so insulated, and thus not everyone is in a position to join me in treating wilderness preservation as an urgent priority. Therein lies a source of conflict, a kind of conflict that is bad for the environment and that we cannot resolve unless we understand that it is not like other kinds of conflict.

The following sections describe three kinds of environmental conflict, concentrating on a subtle but crucial contrast between conflicting values and conflicting priorities.[4] I discuss what it takes to avoid, manage, and resolve these kinds of environmental conflict. I discuss the contingent connection between environmental conflict resolution and environmental justice. Finally, I argue that economics can help us understand how to resolve environmental conflict. While we need not (and should not) attempt to reduce all values to economic values, we do need to understand that there is a certain logic to the working of economic systems. To ignore the logic of human economy is to ignore the logic of human ecology and thus to ignore the logic of any ecology in which humans play a role. Anyone who truly cares about the environment would not do that.

1. Three Kinds of Environmental Conflict

I will treat as basic a kind of conflict in which people simply find themselves in each other's way. I will refer to this as *conflict in use*. Conflict in use manifests itself in traffic jams, figuratively or literally. A pattern of overall use results in congestion, such that people trying to use a resource end up interfering with each other. Conflict in use is resolved by institutions that literally or figuratively direct traffic, such as a system of property rights that lets people know who has the right of way when their intentions put them on a collision course. Such institutions help people avoid, manage, and resolve conflict when they facilitate orderly use of a common resource, when they facilitate orderly removal of resources from the commons, and when they help people cope with *externalities*, including new externalities that emerge as property regimes evolve. Property regimes can be a kind of public good if and when they solve commons problems and induce overall patterns of sustainable use.

Some environmental conflicts, though, cannot be addressed merely by settling on a system of property rights. In particular, some of our most serious conflicts concern what should be property in the first place. Thus, there is a second kind of conflict that ultimately is a matter of conflicting *values*. Should Masai tribes be allowed to own and sell elephants as if elephants were pieces of property? One thing to be said on behalf of conferring such rights is that it would give the Masai reason to protect elephants against poachers.[5] However, some would say turning elephants into

---

4. I use the term "environmental conflict" to refer to conflict in which at least one party has concerns about the environmental impact of the other party's projects.

5. Such schemes seem to have had that effect in places where they have been tried. For a number of case studies describing the successes and failures of attempts to turn wildlife to the advantage of local economies in developing countries, thereby turning local economies to the advantage of wildlife, see Western (1994).

a commodity is another way of destroying them. Even when it does not literally destroy the elephants, it still destroys what elephants stand for in the minds of those who cherish the idea of nature wild and free. This is not a conflict we can resolve by deciding who owns the resource. The parties disagree on whether anyone has the right to regard elephants as a resource in the first place.

Environmentalists sometimes distinguish between anthropocentric (i.e., human-centered) and biocentric (i.e., nature-centered) orientations toward nature. *Conservationists* care about nature in an anthropocentric way, saying nature should be used wisely. *Preservationists* care about nature in a biocentric way, saying that, although we (like any living creature) cannot avoid using nature, nature nevertheless has moral standing independent of its utility for humans.[6] A preservationist will say some ecosystems or species should be left to evolve according to their own lights, as free as possible from human interference. We should not think of wilderness as a mere resource. Wilderness commands reverence; mere resources do not. We may call this clash a case of contested commodification. It exemplifies the second kind of conflict: conflict in values.

There is a third kind of environmental conflict: conflicting *priorities*. We misunderstand this kind of conflict if we see it simply as another case of conflicting values. The difference is that people's immediate goals can be incompatible even when their values are relevantly similar. International conservation groups raise money by pledging to fight for preservationist "no use at all" policies. Sometimes, though, farmers do not join in pursuing cosmopolitan environmentalist goals because they cannot afford to.

This kind of conflict could occur even among people who all feel precisely the same way about where elephants should rank in our hierarchy of values. To give a crude illustration, suppose we all agree that our children outrank elephants, but elephants outrank chess sets carved out of ivory. Even so, we could come into conflict when North Americans denounce hunting elephants to acquire ivory for carving chess sets, while Africans defend the practice because ivory revenues are feeding their children. Although both sides have the same values, they do not face the same cost. For one side, no elephant hunting means no ivory chess sets; for the other, no elephant hunting means no children.

Subsistence farmers for whom getting enough food is a day-by-day proposition can have priorities that differ from ours not because their values are different but precisely because their values are the same. This kind of conflict originates not so much from a difference of values as from a difference in which values people can afford to pursue under their differing circumstances.

Moreover, there is an additional problem, a feature of real-world conflict that some preservationists fail to appreciate. In parts of Africa, the dilemma for

---

6. Some people equate preservationism with environmentalism. This essay uses "environmentalist" to refer equally to conservationists and preservationists. I agree with Norton (1991, 12–13) that it is easy to exaggerate the distinction's practical importance. Norton finds it tempting to insist on reaching a verdict regarding which side is right, but ultimately argues on behalf of an integrated approach to valuing nature, and a consensus-building approach in the policy arena. Our diverse values need not stop us from agreeing on what we realistically can accomplish. Indeed, most of us have both conservationist and preservationist sympathies.

subsistence farmers is this: if they cannot commodify elephants (by selling ivory, hunting licenses, or photo safaris), then they will have to push elephants out of the way to make room for livestock or crops. In the abstract, exploiting elephants may seem obviously wrong, but it stops being obvious after one spends time in rural Africa, and sees that when rural people cannot exploit elephants in some fashion, their only alternative is to convert elephant habitat into farmland.

Whether we like it or not, elephants will not survive except by sharing the land with people, which means their long-term survival depends on whether people can afford to share. Realistically, at least in parts of Africa where this kind of conflict is extreme, threatened species will have to contribute to the local economy if they are to have any hope of survival. Thus, according to Brian Child, "wildlife will survive in Africa only where it can compete financially for space. The real threat to wildlife is poverty, not poaching."[7] With equal bluntness, Norman Myers says: "In emergent Africa, you either use wildlife or lose it. If it pays its own way, some of it will survive."[8]

And please understand: coexisting with elephants is costly. We are not talking about animals one looks at through a pair of binoculars, at a safe distance, while vacationing at a national park. Elephants are an integral part, and a dangerous part, of everyday life. Although we (my wife and I) knew this at an intellectual level, such knowledge left us unprepared when the time came to learn it from experience. In July 1999, we arrived at Oddballs' Camp in Botswana's Okavanga Delta in an airplane just big enough for three passengers. (The wings of the plane were reinforced with duct tape.) The airstrip was dirt. As we landed, baboons and warthogs scattered before us. The person who planned to meet us was late because, while walking to the airstrip from the camp, he had to detour around a herd of Cape buffalo, reputedly among the most dangerous animals in the world. After a fifteen-minute walk through the marsh, we arrived at the campground.

That night, we slept with the sound of baboons howling in the foreground and lions roaring in the background. We were awakened around four o'clock in the morning by what sounded like trees being shaken by a gale-force wind. I got up and found myself standing in the open air right next to a 12-foot elephant. It had been pressing its forehead against a *lala* palm, whipping it back and forth (thereby making the sound that woke us up) to shake down the fruit higher up. Tiring of that, the elephant had torn the whole tree out of the ground and was taking an experimental munch at the roots. (The elephant knew I was there, and it may have deliberately avoided letting the tree fall on us. Some elephants are considerate in that way. Some aren't.)

Elephants rarely sleep and there usually were a couple of them roaming the campground. It is important to grasp that these elephants were not pets. The camp did not adopt them. There was nothing domestic or cute about them. They were magnificent by day and literally breathtaking by night. They were there because despite everyone's efforts to keep elephants out of camp, the bottom line is that if an elephant takes an interest in something inside camp, it is coming in, and there is nothing anyone can do to stop it. (We were told that the day before we arrived, a couple of

7. Child (1993) 60.
8. Myers (1981) 36.

the older bulls had gotten tired of looking at all that lush vegetation on the inside of the electrified campground fence, and so had conspired to push one of the younger, smaller bulls through the electric fence, and had been foraging in the campground since.) Our experience makes for a great story and an unforgettable visit, but imagine spending your whole life that way, going to bed not knowing what will be left of your crop or garden or house or children when you get up in the morning.

Again, even people who embrace environmentalist values will act contrary to those values when they cannot afford to act in accordance with them. There are times when conflict is a matter of conflicting priorities.[9]

2. Ideals, Compromise, and Stewardship

To some extent, a philosopher's job is to say how the world ought to be in the grand scheme of things. It is an honorable job. However, whereas environmental ethics is a study of ideals, environmental conflict resolution is the art of compromise in a world that is not a blank canvas. Conflict mediation typically involves trying to help negotiate win-win solutions.

Sometimes the negotiation is between people who would not both win in a more perfect world. Often, though, conflicts are not clashes between good and evil. When we try to stop people from burning the rain forest, the situation may be a conflict of *values* between us and evil condominium developers burning forests for the sheer thrill of raping the planet. However, it is as likely to be a conflict of *priorities* between us and displaced farmers who just want to feed their children. If we understood each other, we might have no quarrel whatsoever with each other's values, and might well have taken each other's side if circumstances had been different. We often have no reason at all to be trying to win by making our adversary lose.

In choosing our priorities, we sometimes need to be sensitive not only to our own values but to other people's as well, sometimes even when we do not care about other people's values. Why? Because we cannot *decide* that people will act according to our view of what is best for Gaia. People decide for themselves. We have to ask what their values are, what their priorities are, and what could lead people with such values and priorities to act in environmentally benign ways.

The most basic principle of conflict resolution is that mediators should try to get people to focus on their *interests*, not their *positions*.[10] In other words, it is better if negotiation does not turn into a contest of wills (drawing lines in the sand, as they say) but instead revolves around the actual problem, as defined by actual benefits that might be realized if negotiation leads to agreement.

Consider what this implies for the familiar idea that we are not owners of the land so much as stewards of it. If we see ourselves as stewards, then we see ourselves as obliged to care for the land on behalf of future generations. But if we are to take our stewardship role seriously, we need to understand that honest stewardship is a commitment to environmental interests, not environmentalist positions.

9. Of course, the different kinds of conflict are not mutually exclusive. They can occur together.
10. See Fisher and Ury (1991).

Commitment to interests sometimes mandates compromise on positions. It sometimes requires negotiation. Sometimes, what people call values are dressed-up positions that have little to do with any real interests. We make a huge mistake if we equate what is bad for our enemies (corporations, economists, ranchers, Republicans, Western patriarchy, whatever) with what is good for the environment.

Mark Sagoff says government regulations have expressive and symbolic value. I agree with Sagoff that "regulation expresses what we believe, what we are, what we stand for as a nation."[11] Nevertheless, we need to be careful not to endorse a regulation merely because of what it symbolizes. If we want to make sure a law does not undermine a value in the course of symbolizing it, we must stop to ask what sort of behavior the law will induce when put in place.[12] Otherwise, when we glorify a regulation's symbolic value, we glorify the taking of environmentalist positions at the expense of environmental interests. We will be doing exactly what experience in the theory and practice of conflict resolution tells us to avoid.

My father was a farmer. When I was eight years old, a pair of red foxes built a den and raised a litter in our wheat field. I can remember watching Dad on his tractor in the late afternoon, giving the foxes a wide berth, leaving that part of our field uncultivated that year. He protected the den because he could afford to (and even then, I admired him for it). If there had been a law prohibiting farming on land inhabited by foxes, analogous to laws that prohibit logging in forests inhabited by spotted owls, then Dad would have had to make sure his land was not inhabited by foxes. Which is to say, Dad probably would have killed them. Although he loved them, he would not have been able to afford to let them live.

3. A Lesson for Environmental Ethics

Environmental philosophers often talk about environmental justice, but almost never talk about environmental conflict resolution. This is unfortunate. From a mediator's perspective, progress requires negotiation and compromise. Moreover, achieving acceptable and stable compromise can be more important from an environmental perspective than getting it right in some idealized sense that abstracts from political realities. Where the world can go from here is constrained by the histories of stakeholders and by a plurality of values. Mediators deal with the situation as it is.

The practical relevance of environmental ethics depends on our ability to do likewise. We need to think about conflict, not merely about how the world ought to be in the grand scheme of things. If humanity were a decision-making entity, and if its component parts had no interests of their own, this entity might rationally decide to prune itself back, amputating overgrown parts for the sake of the whole, thereby leaving more room for wildlife. In Africa, though, and in the developing world more generally, if people manage to protect their land and wildlife, it will be because doing

---

11. Sagoff (1988) 16.

12. In passing, we also need to accept that what we stand for as a nation differs from what any of us *wants* us to stand for as a nation. The things nations stand for are a product of ongoing piecemeal compromise. We do well not to glorify the expressive value of such compromised ideals.

so is in their interest, not because doing so is in the interest of "the whole." If we fail to treat them as players with interests of their own, we will be our own worst enemies.

In formal terms, philosophy of law distinguishes between procedural and substantive justice. *Substantive* justice is, roughly, a property of outcomes. It is about people (or any entities with moral standing) receiving what they are due. *Procedural* justice is about following fair procedures: procedures intended to be impartial. When philosophers discuss justice, they typically have one or another notion of substantive justice in mind (some vision of how stuff would be distributed in an ideal world). In large measure, though, conflict mediation tends to involve seeking justice in a procedural sense.

Perhaps mediators should and do seek to ground negotiations in principles of substantive justice as well. I am not a mediator and have no direct practical experience with institutions of conflict mediation, so it is hard for me to say. What I can say with confidence is that philosophers need to do their part to complete the circle. What I have in mind is that while mediators are trying to ground their practice in a sound theory, we could do our part by trying to ground our theories in the requirements of sound practice. If we say our philosophical principles ought to be put into practice, then we implicitly, if not explicitly, are warranting those principles as compatible with sound practice. However, when we make no effort to ground our theories in requirements of sound practice, it is fraudulent to recommend our theory to practitioners. In that case, if and when practitioners respond by ignoring us, they will be doing the right thing.[13]

4. Economics as Ecology

Conflict in priorities often is not only an environmental conflict. Often, perhaps typically, it is an economic conflict, too—a conflict rooted in differing economic circumstances—and it will not be resolved as an environmental conflict unless it also is resolved as an economic conflict.

Unfortunately, people who embrace ecological reasoning often reject that very reasoning as applied to human ecology. Environmentalists tend to be pretty far left of center, and they tend to think of economics as a tool of their enemies. It is not only ecofeminists and deep ecologists who tend to reject economics out of hand; even more mainstream philosophers such as Eugene Hargrove sometimes flatly reject what they call "the economic approach to nature preservation."[14] This attitude may sometimes be apt. I am an economist as well as a philosopher, but I, too, reject the

---

13. I can't defend a particular conception of substantive justice here, but let me suggest what sort of conception could count as completing the circle. Consider a principle that people ought to take responsibility for environmental consequences of their own actions: not just legally relevant consequences as determined by some regulatory agency, but real consequences, to the honest best of people's ability to ascertain them. In short, people ought to take responsibility for internalizing externalities. I believe such a principle is intuitively just. I also believe that promulgating this principle as a principle of justice could help mediators resolve real-world conflicts in a principled way. (As far as I know, the connection between internalizing externalities and being substantively just has not been explored in the literature. But see Schmidtz [2006].)

14. Hargrove (1989) 210.

economic approach, insofar as "economic approach" refers to trying to reduce all values to economic values.[15]

However, rejecting economic value-reductionism and ignoring the real-world logic of economic systems are two different things. In cases of conflicting priorities, ignoring the economic approach to understanding the logic of human interaction is bad for the environment.[16] If in that sense we are not taking an economic approach, then we are not taking a genuinely ecological approach either. We need to pay attention to the logic of human ecology, lest we stand rightly accused of not truly caring about ecology at all. Murray Bookchin offers what he calls "social" ecology as an alternative to "deep" ecology.[17] In Bookchin's terms, my point is that if we are serious about promoting deep ecology's values, then we must be equally serious in working with social ecology's logic.

Like economic reasoning, ecological reasoning is reasoning about equilibria and perturbations that keep systems from converging on equilibria. Like economic reasoning, ecological reasoning is reasoning about competition and unintended consequences, and the internal logic of systems, a logic that dictates how a system responds to attempts to manipulate it. Environmental activism and regulation do not automatically improve the environment. It is a truism in ecology, as in economics, that well-intentioned interventions do not necessarily translate into good results. Ecology (human and nonhuman) is complicated, our knowledge is limited, and environmentalists are themselves only human.

Intervention that works with the system's logic can have good consequences. Even in a centrally planned economy, the shape taken by the economy mainly is a function not of the central plan but of how people respond to it, and people respond to central plans in ways that best serve their purposes, not the central planner's. Therefore, even a dictator is in no position simply to decide how things are going to go. Ecologists understand that the same point applies in their own discipline. They understand that an ecology's internal logic limits the directions in which would-be ecological engineers can take it.

Within environmental philosophy, most of us have come around to something like Aldo Leopold's view of humans as plain citizens of the biotic community.[18] As Bryan Norton notes, the contrast between anthropocentrism and biocentrism obscures the fact that we increasingly need to be nature-centered to be properly human-centered; we need to focus on "saving the ecological systems that are the context of human cultural and economic activities."[19] If we do not tend to what is good for nature, we will not be tending to what is good for people either. As Gary Varner puts it, on purely anthropocentric grounds we have reason to think biocentrically.[20]

15. See Schmidtz (2001b).

16. Of course, it can be bad for people, too. Ramachandra Guha (1989) rails against those who assume that so long as they are "cutting edge radicals" they are ipso facto champions of the world's oppressed poor and thus are relieved of any responsibility for gathering real information concerning the effect their policy proposals would have on the world's oppressed poor.

17. Bookchin (1988).

18. Leopold (1966) 240.

19. Norton (1991) 252.

20. Varner (1998) 129.

I completely agree. What I wish to add is that the converse is also true: on purely biocentric grounds, we have reason to think anthropocentrically. We need to be human-centered to be properly nature-centered, for if we do not tend to what is good for people, we will not be tending to what is good for nature either. From a biocentric perspective, preservationists sometimes are not anthropocentric enough. They sometimes advocate policies and regulations with no concern for values and priorities that differ from their own. Even from a purely biocentric perspective, such slights are illegitimate. Policy-makers who ignore human values and priorities unlike their own will, in effect, be committed to mismanaging any ecology in which those ignored values and priorities play an integral role.

Africans seem to understand, and in some cases they have been able to structure their policies so as not to slight the priorities of rural people who pay the price of coexisting with the wildlife. They understand that rural people must also benefit from coexisting with wildlife if wildlife is to survive. For example, consider Zimbabwe's Communal Areas Management Program for Indigenous Resources (CAMPFIRE).

Shortly after Zimbabwe gained political independence in 1980, its Department of National Parks and Wildlife Management concluded that conventional agricultural practices were ecologically and economically unsound throughout much of Zimbabwe. (The soil is not right, and there is not enough water.) The best use of the land was as a reservoir for wildlife. The department also realized that the problem would not be solved unless it were handed over to the local people. So, the department created CAMPFIRE. They surveyed community areas, assessed wildlife populations, and came to conclusions about what sort of numbers could be considered surplus game. They then gave local communities a nearly free hand in deciding what to do with the surplus.

Local communities were granted authority to cull herds, sell hunting permits, or set up tourist ventures, and after 1992 they were allowed to keep 80 percent of the money. (The rest goes to wildlife management and rural district administration.) They put some of that money in a fund for compensating farmers when lions take their goats or elephants trample their crops, which defuses much of the resentment of wildlife. In some districts, rangers periodically hunt impala and sell meat to local villagers at a price that covers the cost of the hunt, making villagers less dependent on cattle as a source of protein. The issue is not just money but self-sufficiency. Decisions are made in the village square. In that setting, people have more knowledge, more understanding, more voice. There is less room for corruption.[21]

Eventually, enough money was coming in from hunting that villagers turned their land over to wildlife rather than grazing cattle. This is crucial, because the

---

21. A note of caution: there are programs in southern Africa that call themselves community-based but merely gesture at sharing revenue and at granting communities authority to set local policy. Such programs do not work (Songorwa, 1999). "The foundation of community empowerment lies in devolution of management decisions to the local level. Just giving the communities economic resources from wildlife is not CAMPFIRE. In CAMPFIRE, the concept of community empowerment means actually giving the community the power to decide on the allocation of these resources" (Matzke and Nabane, 1996, 73).

bigger threat to wildlife tends to be cattle, not hunting.[22] Cattle crowds out wildlife. (Actually, pastoral herds are one problem; farms and ranches are another. Nomadic Masai herdsmen compete with wildlife for space and water, but at least they do not cut off migration routes by erecting fences or otherwise defending their turf.)

Villages (directly or through tour guides) sell elephant hunting licenses. Hunters pay as much as $30,000 for the privilege—a lot of money in a country where the per capita annual income is around $2,000. As of 1999, when I was Zimbabwe, there were thirty-seven such districts, occupying well over half of the country (and containing 56 percent of the country's population), and much of the land in those districts was reserved for wildlife. (There is an unspeakably sad ending to this encouraging tale, though. Zimbabwe has become one of the world's most brutal dictatorships, its economy shattered. Zimbabwe is currently locked down. Little news escapes, but I fear CAMPFIRE has not survived the carnage. So-called war veterans were authorized first to resettle the lands of evicted white farmers. Having eaten everything they could find on once-productive farms, these people are now rumored to be settling in the national parks, presumably poaching the wildlife.)

In any case, CAMPFIRE allowed hunting. It did not treat animals as if they had rights. Yet, in Zimbabwe, it was CAMPFIRE that protected the wildlife, not People for the Ethical Treatment of Animals. It was CAMPFIRE that respected the priorities of the local people—that seemed to understand the practical priority of what Murray Bookchin calls social ecology—and thus it was CAMPFIRE that offered some hope for the long-run survival of Zimbabwe's wildlife.

5. Conclusion

Those who embrace economic values and those who embrace preservationist values are not natural enemies. If we want other people's actions (or our own, for that matter) to be environmentally benign, we must understand and work with human ecology. Environmentalists need to avoid thinking of economics as the enemy, because that antipathy interferes with understanding how to resolve conflicting priorities in environmentally benign ways.

In cases of conflicting priorities, we need to think about people first, if we care about people, or even if we do not. If we care about wildlife, we need to accept that

---

22. What about the morality of sport hunting? Is it something a sane person would do? Winston Churchill once shot a rhinoceros, but failed to kill it. The wounded rhino charged. The hunting party opened fire. The rhino kept coming into a hail of bullets, swerving aside at the last moment before more bullets finally brought it down. Churchill later wrote that, even in the midst of the charge, "there is time to reflect with some detachment that, after all, we it is who have forced the conflict by an unprovoked assault with murderous intent upon a peaceful herbivore; that if there is such a thing as right and wrong between man and beast—and who shall say there is not?—right is plainly on his side" (1908, 17).

I grew up on a farm, in a family of hunters, but I never joined in. I loved to shoot at targets, but I never killed sentient beings for fun. Perhaps you feel the same way. And yet, we should hesitate before concluding that regular tourism is benign whereas hunting is destructive. Actually, tourism may do more damage than hunting relative to the money it brings in. Why? Because, dollar for dollar, hunting needs less infrastructure than does regular tourism. Hunters in jeeps do not use water and do not demand wilderness-fragmenting highways the way tourist hotels do.

wildlife will survive to the extent that people who have to live with it are better off taking care of it. Requiring subsistence farmers to cooperate in putting the interests of wildlife before (or even on a par with) their own is not a winning strategy for helping the wildlife. We need their cooperation, and the terms of cooperation will have to address not only our interest in preserving wildlife but also their interest in being able to live with it.

Wildlife will survive only if people can afford to share the land. If they cannot share, then they will not share, and the wildlife will disappear.

This essay revises David Schmidtz, "Natural Enemies," *Environmental Ethics* 22 (2000): 379–408. Reprinted with permission of the journal.

14

Are All Species Equal?

Species egalitarianism is the view that all living things have equal moral standing. To have moral standing is, at a minimum, to command respect, to be more than a mere thing. Is there reason to believe that all living things have moral standing in even this most minimal sense? If so—that is, if all living things command respect—is there reason to believe that they all command *equal* respect?

I will try to explain why members of other species command our respect but also why they do not command equal respect. The intuition that we should have respect for nature is one motive for embracing species egalitarianism, but we need not be species egalitarians to have respect for nature. Indeed, I will question whether species egalitarianism is even compatible with respect for nature.

1. Respect for Nature

According to Paul Taylor, anthropocentrism "gives either exclusive or primary consideration to human interests above the good of other species."[1] The alternative to anthropocentrism is biocentrism, and it is biocentrism that, in Taylor's view, grounds species egalitarianism:

> The beliefs that form the core of the biocentric outlook are four in number:
> (a) The belief that humans are members of the Earth's Community of life in the same sense and on the same terms in which other living things are members of that community.
> (b) The belief that the human species, along with all other species, are integral elements in a system of interdependence....
> (c) The belief that all organisms are teleological centers of life in the sense that each is a unique individual pursuing its own good in its own way.
> (d) The belief that humans are not inherently superior to other living beings.[2]

---

1. Taylor (1983) 240.
2. Taylor (1986) 99. See also Taylor (1981).

Taylor concludes: "Rejecting the notion of human superiority entails its positive counterpart: the doctrine of species impartiality. One who accepts that doctrine regards all living things as possessing inherent worth—the *same* inherent worth, since no one species has been shown to be either higher or lower than any other."[3]

Taylor does not call this a valid argument, but he thinks that if we concede (a), (b), and (c), it would be unreasonable not to move to (d), and then to his egalitarian conclusion. Is he right? For those who accept Taylor's three premises (and who thus interpret those premises in terms innocuous enough to render them acceptable), there are two responses. First, we may go on to accept (d), following Taylor, but then still deny that there is any warrant for moving from there to Taylor's egalitarian conclusion. Having accepted that our form of life is not superior, we might choose instead to regard it as inferior. More plausibly, we might view our form of life as noncomparable. We simply do not have the same kind of value as nonhumans. The question of how we compare to nonhumans has a simple answer: we do not compare to them. We are not equal. We are not unequal. We are simply different.

Alternatively, we may reject (d) and say that humans are indeed inherently superior but that humans' superiority is a moot point. Whether humans are inherently superior (that is, superior as a form of life) does not matter much. Even if humans are superior, the fact remains that within the web of ecological interdependence mentioned in premises (a) and (b), it would be a mistake to ignore the needs and the telos of the other species referred to in premise (c). Thus, there are two ways of rejecting Taylor's argument for species egalitarianism. Each, on its face, is compatible with the respect for nature that motivates Taylor's egalitarianism in the first place.

These are preliminary worries, then, about Taylor's argument. Taylor's critics have been harsh—perhaps too harsh. After building on some criticisms while rejecting others, I explore some of our reasons to have respect for nature and ask whether they translate into reasons to be species egalitarians.

2. Is Species Egalitarianism Hypocritical?

Paul Taylor is among the most intransigent of species egalitarians, yet he allows that human needs override the needs of nonhumans. In response, French argues that species egalitarians cannot have it both ways. French perceives a contradiction between the egalitarian principles Taylor officially endorses and the unofficial principles Taylor offers as the real principles by which we should live. Having proclaimed that we are all equal, French asks, what licenses Taylor to say that, in cases of conflict, nonhuman interests can legitimately be sacrificed to vital human interests?[4]

Good question. Yet, somehow Taylor's alleged inconsistency is too obvious. Perhaps his position is not as blatantly inconsistent as it appears. Let me suggest how Taylor could respond. Suppose I find myself in a situation of mortal combat with an enemy soldier. If I kill my enemy to save my life, that does not entail that I regard my enemy as inherently inferior (i.e., as an inferior form of life). Likewise, if I kill a

---

3. Taylor (1981) 217.
4. French (1995) 44. See also James Anderson (1993) 350.

bear to save my life, that does not entail that I regard the bear as inherently inferior. Therefore, Taylor can, without hypocrisy, deny that species egalitarianism requires a radically self-effacing pacifism.

What, then, does species egalitarianism require? It requires us to avoid mortal combat whenever we can, not just with other humans but with living things in general. On this view, we ought to regret finding ourselves in kill-or-be-killed situations that we could have avoided. There is no point in regretting the fact that we must kill in order to eat, though, for there is no avoiding that. Species egalitarianism is compatible with our having a limited license to kill.

What seems far more problematic for species egalitarianism is that it seems to suggest that it makes no difference *what* we kill. Vegetarians typically think it is worse to kill a cow than to kill a carrot. Are they wrong? Yes, according to species egalitarianism. In this respect, species egalitarianism cannot be right. I believe we have reason to respect nature. However, we fail to give nature due respect if we say we should have no more respect for a cow than for a carrot.

3. Is Species Egalitarianism Arbitrary?

Suppose interspecies comparisons are possible. Suppose the capacities of different species, and whatever else gives living things moral standing, are commensurable. In that case, it could turn out that all living things are equal, but that would be quite a fluke.

Taylor says a being has intrinsic worth just in case it has a good of its own. And Taylor thinks even plants have a good of their own in the relevant sense. They seek their own good in their own way. As mentioned earlier, Taylor defines anthropocentrism as giving exclusive or primary consideration to human interests above the good of other species. So, when we acknowledge the ability to think as a valuable capacity, and acknowledge that some but not all living things possess this valuable capacity, are we giving exclusive or primary consideration to human interests? Probably not. Is there something wrong with noticing that there are valuable capacities that not all living things possess? Put it this way: if biocentrism involves resolving to ignore the fact that cognitive capacity is something we value—if biocentrism amounts to a resolution to value only those capacities that all living things share—then biocentrism is as arbitrary and as question-begging as anthropocentrism.

It will not do to defend species egalitarianism by singling out a property that all living things possess, arguing that this property is morally important, then concluding that all living things are therefore of equal moral importance. The problem with this sort of argument is that, where there is one property that provides a basis for moral standing, there might be others. Other properties might be possessed by some but not all living things, and might provide bases for different kinds or degrees of moral standing.

Obviously, Taylor knows that not all living things can think, and he would not deny that the capacity for thought is valuable. What he would say, though, is that it begs the question to rank the ability to think as *more* valuable than the characteristic traits of plants and other animals. Taylor himself assumes that human rationality is on a par with, for example, a cheetah's foot-speed: no less valuable, but no more valuable either.[5] In this case, though, perhaps it is Taylor who begs the question. The difference between the foot-speed of chimpanzees and cheetahs is at least arguably a difference of degree, while the difference between the intelligence of a chimpanzee and the intelligence of a carrot is something else: a difference in kind. Chimpanzees are very smart. Carrots, in contrast, are not merely a lot less smart. Carrots are not smart at all. They do not even make it into the same category.

Here, though, is the more telling point. Anthropocentrists might argue, against Taylor, that the good associated with the ability to think is superior to the good associated with a tree's ability to grow and reproduce. Could they be wrong? Let us suppose they are wrong. For argument's sake, suppose the ability to grow and reproduce is *superior* to the ability to think. Wouldn't that mean trees are superior to chimpanzees? No. The point is not that chimpanzees have one singular virtue, the ability to think, while trees have another singular virtue, the ability to grow and reproduce. Rather, both trees and chimpanzees share one virtue: they can grow and reproduce. They are both teleological centers of life, to use Taylor's phrase. But chimpanzees have a second virtue as well: they can think.

Of course, it is more complicated than this, for in fact both trees and chimpanzees have innumerable capacities. The crucial point, though, is this. Although both trees and chimpanzees are teleological centers of life, and we can agree that this is valuable, and that trees and chimpanzees share equally in this particular value, we cannot infer that trees and chimpanzees have equal value. We are entitled to conclude only that they are of equal value so far as being a teleological center of life is concerned.[6] From that, we may of course infer that *one* ground of our moral standing (i.e., that we grow and reproduce) is shared by all living things. Beyond that, nothing about equality even suggests itself. In particular, it begs no questions to notice that there are grounds for moral standing that humans do not share with all living things.

None of this presumes that the unshared capacity for thought is more valuable than the shared capacity for reproduction. In this argument, it does not matter which has more value. It matters only that the capacity for thought has *some* value.

4. Speciesism and Social Policy

Peter Singer and others talk as if speciesism—the idea that some species are superior to others—is necessarily a kind of bias in favor of humans and against nonhuman animals. (Singer has no problem with being "biased" against plants.) This is a mistake. If we have more respect for chimpanzees than for mice, then we are speciesists, no matter what status we accord to human beings. But we *should* have more respect for chimpanzees than for mice, shouldn't we? Or if not, then shouldn't we at least have more respect for chimpanzees than for carrots?

---

5. Taylor (1981) 211.

6. For a similar critique of Taylor from an Aristotelian perspective, see Anderson (1993) 348. See also Lombardi (1993).

Suppose we take an interest in how chimpanzees rank compared to mice. Perhaps we wonder what we would do in an emergency where we could save a drowning chimpanzee or a drowning mouse but not both. More realistically, suppose we conclude we must do experiments involving animals (because, let's say, there is no other way to develop an effective treatment for an otherwise catastrophic disease) and now we have to choose which animals. Whichever we use, the animals we use will die. We decide to use mice. Then a species egalitarian says, "Why not use chimpanzees? They're all the same anyway, morally speaking, and you'll get more reliable data." Wouldn't that sort of egalitarianism be monstrous? I say yes, and I expect that Singer would agree. But if we believe (with Taylor) all living things are equal, or even if we think only (with Singer) that all animals are equal, then *why not* use the chimpanzee instead of the mouse?

In reality, chimpanzees are, morally speaking, the wrong *kind* of animal to experiment on when researchers could get by with mice. To that extent, speciesism is closer to the moral truth than is species egalitarianism. Moreover, although in philosophy we tend to use science fiction examples, the situation just described is an ordinary problem, every day, in the scientific community. Suppose researchers had to choose between harvesting the organs of a chimpanzee or a brain-damaged human baby. Peter Singer says we cannot have it both ways. He argues that if the ability to think makes the difference, then the brain-damaged infant commands no more respect than a chimpanzee, and may indeed command less. Singer concludes that if we need to use one or the other in a painful and/or lethal medical experiment, and if it does not matter which one we use so far as the experiment is concerned, then we ought to use the brain-damaged child, not the chimpanzee.[7]

Does this seem obvious? It should not. Actually, Singer appears to be the one trying to have it both ways here. The mistake here is subtle, but it is, nevertheless, a mistake. Singer does not reject speciesism so much as what he considers to be a bad kind of speciesism. If we claimed that the rightness of eating beef has to be settled individual cow by individual cow, it would be Singer who would insist that cows are the wrong *kind* of thing for us to be eating, and that we need a policy governing our exploitation of cows as a species. Yet, when Singer criticizes those who exalt the value of rationality, he says rationality is relevant to justification only at the individual level.

Some speciesists are impressed with humanity's characteristic rationality. They say this characteristic justifies respect for humanity, not merely for particular humans who exemplify human rationality. Other speciesists such as Singer are more impressed with the ability to feel pain. They say this ability justifies respecting cows in general, not just those individual cows that have proven they can feel pain.

Singer is indeed a speciesist of the latter kind. Singer has to agree that if most chimpanzees have morally important characteristics that most mice lack, we do not need to compare individual chimpanzees and mice on a case-by-case basis in order to have a moral justification for passing laws that stop researchers from using chimpanzees in their experiments when mice would do just as well. It is Singer who would insist that researchers cannot be allowed to decide on a case-by-case basis

---

7. Singer (1990) 1–23. See also Johnson (1991) 52.

whether to use mice or chimpanzees or defective people in their experiments, when turnips would do just as well. Likewise, it is Singer who wants to insist that individual consumers should not decide on a case-by-case basis whether to eat cows or turnips—rather, they ought to quit eating cows, period. In the medical research policy area, what we actually do, and rightly so, is ignore Singer's point that some animals are smarter than some people, and instead formulate policy on the basis of characteristic features of the species. And if Singer objects to the policy we choose, it will not be because our policy is based on features of the species. His objection will be that we used the wrong feature. He will say the feature we ought to have used is the ability to feel pain.

Of course, some chimpanzees lack characteristic features in virtue of which chimpanzees command respect as a species, just as some humans lack characteristic features in virtue of which humans command respect as a species. Just as obviously, some chimpanzees have cognitive capacities superior to those of some humans. But when it comes to questions of practical policy, such as we face when trying to formulate policy regarding animal experimentation, whether every human being is superior in every respect to every chimpanzee is beside the point. The point is that we can, we do, and we must make policy decisions on the basis of our recognition that turnips, mice, chimpanzees, and humans are relevantly different types.

5. Equality and Transcendence

Even if speciesists are right to see a nonarbitrary distinction between humans and other living things, though, the fact remains that claims of superiority do not easily translate into justifications of domination.[8] We can have reasons to treat nonhuman species with respect, regardless of whether we consider them to be on a moral par with *Homo sapiens*.

What kind of reasons do we have for treating members of other species with respect? We might have respect for chimpanzees or even mice on the grounds that they are sentient. Even mice have a rudimentary point of view and rudimentary hopes and dreams, and we might well respect them for that. But what about plants? Plants, unlike mice and chimpanzees, do not care what happens to them. It is literally true that they could not care less. So, why should we care? Is it even possible for us to have any good reason, other than a purely instrumental reason, to care what happens to plants?

When we are alone in a forest, wondering whether it would be fine to chop down a tree for fun, our perspective on what happens to the tree is, so far as we know, the only perspective there is. The tree does not have its own. Thus, explaining why we have reason to care about trees requires us to explain caring from our point of view, since that (we are supposing) is all there is. In that case, we do not have to satisfy *trees* that we are treating them properly; rather, we have to satisfy ourselves. So, again, can we have noninstrumental reasons for caring about trees—for treating them with respect?

8. This is effectively argued by Anderson (1993) 362.

One reason to care (not the only one) is that gratuitous destruction is a failure of self-respect. It is a repudiation of the kind of self-awareness and self-respect we can achieve by repudiating wantonness. So far as I know, no one finds anything puzzling in the idea that we have reason to treat our lawns or living rooms with respect. Lawns and living rooms have instrumental value, but there is more to it than that. Most of us have the sense that taking reasonable care of our lawns and living rooms is somehow a matter of self-respect, not merely a matter of preserving their instrumental value. Do we have similar reasons to treat forests with respect? I think we do. There is an aesthetic involved, the repudiation of which would be a failure of self-respect. (Obviously, not everyone feels the same way about forests. Not everyone feels the same way about lawns and living rooms, either. But the point here is to make sense of respect for nature, not to argue that respect for nature is in fact universal or that failing to respect nature is irrational.) If and when we identify with a redwood, in the sense of being inspired by it, having respect for its size and age and so on, then as a psychological fact, we really do face questions about how we ought to treat it. If and when we come to see a redwood in that light, subsequently turning our backs on it becomes a kind of self-effacement. The values we thereby fail to take seriously are *our* values, not the tree's.

So, I am saying the attitude we take toward gazelles (for example) raises issues of self-respect, insofar as we see ourselves as relevantly like gazelles. Here is a different and complementary way of looking at the issue. Consider that lions owe nothing to gazelles. Therefore, if we owe it to gazelles not to hunt them, it must be because we are *unlike* lions, not (or not only) because we are *like* gazelles.

Unlike lions, we have a choice about whether to hunt gazelles, and we are capable of deliberating about that choice in a reflective way. We are capable of caring about the gazelle's pain, the gazelle's beauty, the gazelle's hopes and dreams (such as they are), and so forth. If we do care, then in a more or less literal way, something is wrong with us—we are less than fully, magnificently, human—if we cannot adjust our behavior in light of what we care about. And if we do not care, then we are missing something. For a human being, to lack a broad respect for living things and beautiful things and well-functioning things is to be stunted in a way.

Our coming to see members of other species as commanding respect is itself a way of transcending our animal natures. It is part of our natures unthinkingly to see ourselves as superior, and to try to dominate accordingly; our capacity to see ourselves as equal is one of the things that makes us different. (It may be one of the things that makes us superior.)[9] Coming to see all living things as equal may not be the best way of transcending our animal natures—it doesn't work for me—but it is one way.

Another way of transcending our animal natures and expressing due respect for nature is simply to not bother to keep score. This way is, I think, better. It is more respectful of our own reflective natures. It does not dwell on rankings. It does not insist on seeing equality where a more reflective being simply would see what is

---

9. When the Cincinnati Zoo erected a monument to the passenger pigeon, Aldo Leopold expressed a related thought. "We have erected a monument to commemorate the funeral of a species.... For one species to mourn the death of another is a new thing under the sun.... In this fact...lies objective evidence of our superiority over the beasts" (1966, 116–17).

there to be seen and would not shy away from respecting what is unique as well as what is common. Someone might say we need to rank animals as our equals so as to be fair, but that appears to be false. I can be fair to my friends without ranking them. Imagine a friend saying, "I disagree! In fact, failing to rank us is insulting! You have to rank us as equals!" What would be the point? Perhaps my friends are each other's equals (in some respect?). Even so, we are left with no need at all to *rank* them as equal. For most purposes, it is better for them simply to be the unique and priceless friends that they are. Sometimes, respect is simply respect. It need not be based on a pecking order.

Children rank their friends. It is one of the things children do not yet understand about friendship. Sometimes, the idea of ranking things, even as equals, is a child's game. It is beneath us.

6. Respect for Everything

Thus, a broad respect for living or beautiful or well-functioning things need not translate into equal respect. It need not translate into universal respect, either. Part of our responsibility as moral agents is to be somewhat choosy about what we respect and how we respect it. I can see why people shy away from openly accepting that responsibility, but they still have it.

We might suppose speciesism is as arbitrary as racism unless we can show that the differences are morally relevant. This is, to be sure, a popular sentiment among animal liberationists such as Peter Singer and Tom Regan. But are we really like racists when we think it is worse to kill a dolphin than to kill a tuna? The person who asserts that there is a relevant similarity between speciesism and racism has the burden of proof: go ahead and identify the similarity. Is seeing moral significance in biological differences between chimpanzees and mice anything like seeing moral significance in biological differences between races? I think not.

To be sure, burden of proof, crucial though it is to many philosophical arguments, is a slippery notion. Do we need good reason to exclude plants and animals from the realm of things we regard as commanding respect? Or do we need reason to *in*clude them? Should we be trying to identify properties in virtue of which a thing forfeits presumptive (equal) moral standing? Or does it make more sense to be trying to identify properties in virtue of which a thing *commands* respect? The latter seems more natural to me, so I am left supposing the burden of proof lies with those who claim we should have respect for all living things. I could be wrong.

But even if I am right, I would not say this burden is unbearable. One reason to have regard for other living things has to do with self-respect. (As I said earlier, when we mistreat a tree that we admire, the values we fail to respect are our values, not the tree's.) A second reason has to do with self-realization. (As I said, exercising our capacity for moral regard is a form of self-realization.) Finally, at least some species seem to share with human beings precisely those characteristics that lead us to see human life as especially worthy of esteem. For example, Lawrence Johnson describes experiments in which rhesus monkeys show extreme reluctance to obtain food by means that would subject monkeys in neighboring cages to electric shock. He describes the case of Washoe, a chimpanzee who learned sign language.[10] Anyone who has tried to learn a foreign language ought to be able to appreciate how astonishing an intellectual feat it is that an essentially nonlinguistic creature could learn a language—a language that is not merely foreign but the language of another species.[11]

However, although he believes Washoe has moral standing, Johnson does not believe that the moral standing of chimpanzees, and indeed of all living creatures, implies we must resolve never to kill. Thus, Johnson (an Australian) supports killing introduced animal species (feral dogs, rabbits, and so forth) to protect Australia's native species, including native plant species.[12]

Is Johnson advocating a speciesist version of the Holocaust? Has he shown himself to be no better than a racist? I think not. Johnson is right to want to take drastic measures to protect Australia's natural flora, and the idea of respecting trees is intelligible. Certainly one thing I feel in the presence of redwoods (or Australia's incredible eucalyptus forests) is something like a feeling of respect. But I doubt that what underlies Johnson's willingness to kill feral dogs is mere respect for Australia's native plants. I suspect his approval of such killings turns to some extent on needs and aesthetic sensibilities of human beings, not just interests of plants. For example, if the endangered native species happened to be a malaria-carrying mosquito, I doubt Johnson would advocate wiping out an exotic species of amphibian simply to protect the mosquitoes.

Aldo Leopold urged us to see ourselves as plain citizens of, rather than conquerors of, the biotic community.[13] But there are some species with whom we can never be fellow citizens. The rabbits that once ate flowers in my backyard in Ohio (or the cardinals currently eating my cherry tomatoes in Arizona) are neighbors, and I cherish their company, minor frictions notwithstanding. I feel no sense of community with mosquitoes, though, and not merely because they are not warm and fuzzy. Some mosquito species are so adapted to making human beings miserable that mortal combat is not accidental; rather, combat is a natural state. It is how such creatures live. I think it is fair to say human beings are not able to respond to malaria-carrying mosquitoes in a caring manner. At very least, most of us would think less of a person who did respond to them in a caring manner. We would regard the person's caring as a parody of respect for nature.[14]

The conclusion that *all* living things have moral standing is unmotivated. For human beings, viewing apes as having moral standing is a form of self-respect. Viewing viruses as having moral standing is not. It is good to have a sense of how amazing living things are, but being able to marvel at living things is not the same as

---

10. Johnson (1991) 64n.

11. This is what I wrote in the original version of this essay. I since have heard that families of lowland gorillas have their own fairly complicated language of hand signals, which leads me to suspect I may have been mistaken in describing chimpanzees as essentially nonlinguistic.

12. Johnson (1991) 174.

13. Leopold (1966) 240.

14. Martha Ramsey has asked me, what about Buddhists who consider it a sign of great spiritual advancement when a monk refrains from killing mosquitoes? What if the mosquitoes were known to be transmitters of malaria parasites? In that case, would letting them live be a way of respecting life, or disrespecting it?

thinking all living things have moral standing. Life as such commands respect only in the limited but important sense that for self-aware and reflective creatures who want to act in ways that make sense, deliberately killing something is an act that does not make sense unless we have good reason to do it. Destroying something for no good reason is (at best) the moral equivalent of vandalism.

7. The History of the Debate

There is an odd project in the history of philosophy that equates what seem to be three distinct projects: (1) determining our essence; (2) specifying how we are different from all other species; and (3) specifying what makes us morally important. Equating these three projects has important ramifications. Suppose, for the sake of argument, that what makes us morally important is that we can suffer. If what makes us morally important is necessarily the same property that constitutes our essence, then our essence is that we can suffer. And if our essence necessarily is what makes us different from all other species, then we can straightforwardly deduce that dogs cannot suffer. (I wish this were merely a tasteless joke.)

Likewise with rationality. If rationality is our essence, then rationality is what makes us morally important and also what makes us unique. Therefore, we can deduce that chimpanzees are not rational. Alternatively, if some other animal becomes rational, does that mean our essence will change? Is that why some people find Washoe, the talking chimpanzee, threatening?

The three projects, needless to say, should not be conflated in the way philosophy seems historically to have conflated them, but we can reject species equality without conflation. If we like, we can select a property with respect to which all living things are the same, then say that that property confers moral standing, then say that all living things have equal moral standing on the basis of that shared property. To infer that all living things have equal standing, though, would be to ignore the possibility that there are other morally important properties with respect to which not all living things are equal.

There is room to wonder whether species egalitarianism is even compatible with respect for nature. Is the moral standing of dolphins truly no higher than that of tuna? Is the moral standing of chimpanzees truly no higher than that of mice? I think any such claims would be not only untrue, but disrespectful. Dolphins and chimpanzees command more respect than species egalitarianism allows.

There is no denying that it demeans us to destroy living things we find beautiful or otherwise beneficial. What about living things in which we find neither beauty nor benefit? It is, upon reflection, obviously in our interest to enrich our lives by discovering in them something beautiful or beneficial, if we can. By and large, we must agree with Leopold that it is too late for conquering the biotic community. Our task now is to find ways of fitting in. Species egalitarianism is one way of trying to understand how we fit in. In the end, it is not an acceptable way. Having respect for nature and being a species egalitarian are different things.

This essay revises David Schmidtz, "Are All Species Equal?" *Journal of Applied Philosophy* 15 (1998): 57–67. Reprinted by permission of Blackwell Publishers.

WORKS CITED

Ackerknecht, Erwin H. *Malaria in the Upper Mississippi Valley, 1760–1900*. Baltimore: Johns Hopkins University Press, 1945.
Ackrill, J. L. "Aristotle on Eudaimonia." *Essays on Aristotle's Ethics*, ed. Amelie O. Rorty, 15–33. Berkeley: University of California Press 1980.
Anderson, James C. "Species Equality and the Foundations of Moral Theory." *Environmental Values* 2 (1993): 347–65.
Aristotle. *Nicomachean Ethics*. Trans. T. Irwin. Indianapolis: Hackett, 1999.
———. *Politics*. Trans. T. A. Sinclair. London: Penguin, 1962.
Arrow, Kenneth J. "A Utilitarian Approach to the Concept of Equality in Public Expenditures." *Quarterly Journal of Economics* 85 (1971): 409–15.
Badhwar, Neera Kapur. "Altruism versus Self-Interest: Sometimes a False Dichotomy." *Social Philosophy and Policy* 10 (1993): 90–117.
Baier, Kurt. *The Moral Point of View*. Ithaca, N.Y.: Cornell University Press, 1958.
Bailey, Martin J. "Approximate Optimality of Aboriginal Property Rights." *Journal of Law and Economics* 35 (1992): 183–98.
Baker, Edwin. "Utility and Rights: Two Justifications for State Action Increasing Equality." *Yale Law Journal* 84 (1974): 39–59.
Barry, Brian. *Why Social Justice Matters*. Cambridge: Polity, 2005.
Becker, Gary S. "Unemployment in Europe and the United States." *Journal des Economistes et des Etudes Humaines* 7 (1996): 99–101.
Beito, David T. "The 'Lodge Practice Evil' Reconsidered: Medical Care through Fraternal Societies, 1900–1930." *Journal of Urban History* 23 (1997): 569–600.
———. "Black Fraternal Hospitals in the Mississippi Delta, 1942–1967." *Journal of Southern History* 65 (1999): 109–40.
Beitz, Charles. *Political Theory and International Relations*. Princeton, N.J.: Princeton University Press, 1979.
Bogart, J. H. "Lockean Provisos and State of Nature Theories." *Ethics* 95 (1985): 828–36.
Bonner, Raymond. *At the Hand of Man: Peril and Hope for Africa's Wildlife*. New York: Knopf, 1993.
Bookchin, Murray. "Social Ecology versus Deep Ecology." *Socialist Review* 88 (1988): 11–29.
Bricker, Phillip. "Prudence." *Journal of Philosophy* 77 (1980): 381–401.
Broadie, Sarah. *Ethics with Aristotle*. New York: Oxford University Press, 1991.

Brock, Gillian. "Just Deserts and Needs." *Southern Journal of Philosophy* 37 (1999): 165–88.
Broome, John. *Weighing Goods: Equality, Uncertainty, and Time.* Oxford: Blackwell, 1991.
Butler, Joseph. *Fifteen Sermons.* Oxford: Clarendon Press, 1874 (first published 1726).
Butler, Victoria. "Elephants: Trimming the Herd." *Bioscience* 48 (1998): 76–81.
Chesher, R. "Practical Problems in Coral Reef Utilization and Management: A Tongan Case Study." *Proceedings of the Fifth International Coral Reef Congress* 4 (1985): 213–24.
Child, Brian. "The Elephant as a Natural Resource." *Wildlife Conservation* 96 (1993): 60–61.
Churchill, Winston S. *My African Journey*, London: Hodder and Stoughton, 1908.
Coleman, Jules L. "Rules and Social Facts." *Harvard Journal of Law and Public Policy*, 14 (1991): 703–25.
Craig, Robin K. "Coral Reefs, Fishing, and Tourism: Tensions in U.S. Ocean Law and Policy Reform." *Stanford Environmental Law Journal* 27 (2008) in press.
Danziger, Sheldon, R. Haveman, and R. Plotnick. "How Income Transfer Programs Affect Work, Savings and Income Distribution." *Journal of Economic Literature* 19 (1981): 975–1028.
Davis, Frederick R. *The Man Who Saved Sea Turtles: Archie Carr and the Origins of Conservation Biology.* New York: Oxford University Press, 2007.
Davis, Lawrence. "Prisoners, Paradox, and Rationality." *American Philosophical Quarterly* 14 (1977): 319–27.
Demsetz, Harold. "Toward a Theory of Property Rights." *American Economic Review* (Papers and Proceedings) 57 (1967): 347–59.
Dukeminier, Jesse, and James E. Krier. *Property.* 3rd ed. Boston: Little, Brown, 1993.
Ellickson, Robert C. "Property in Land." *Yale Law Journal* 102 (1993): 1315–1400.
Elman, Richard M. *The Poorhouse State.* New York: Pantheon Books, 1966.
Elster, Jon. *Ulysses and the Sirens: Studies in Rationality and Irrationality.* Rev. ed. Cambridge: Cambridge University Press, 1984.
Fayrer-Hosken, R. A., D. Grobler, J. J. Van Altena, H. J. Bertschinger, and J. F. Kirkpatrick. "Immunocontraception of African Elephants: A Humane Method to Control Elephant Populations without Behavioural Side Effects." *Nature* 407 (2000): 149.
Feinberg, Joel. *Doing and Deserving.* Princeton, N.J.: Princeton University Press, 1970.
———. "Psychological Egoism." In *Reason and Responsibility*, ed. J. Feinberg, 498–508. Belmont, Calif.: Wadsworth, 1981.
Feldman, Fred. "Desert: Reconsideration of Some Received Wisdom." *Mind* 104 (1995): 63–77.
Fisher, Roger, and William Ury. *Getting to Yes.* 2nd ed. New York: Penguin Books, 1991.
Foot, Philippa. "The Problem of Abortion and the Doctrine of Double Effect." *Oxford Review* 5 (1967): 5–15.
Fosdick, Peggy, and Sam Fosdick. *Last Chance Lost?* York, Pa.: Irvin S. Naylor, 1994.
Frank, Robert. *Passions within Reason.* New York: W. W. Norton Publishing Co. 1988.
Frankfurt, Harry. "Equality as a Moral Ideal." *Ethics* 98 (1987): 21–43.
———. "On the Usefulness of Final Ends." *Iyyun* 41 (1992): 3–19.
French, William C. "Against Biospherical Egalitarianism." *Environmental Ethics* 17 (1995): 39–57.
Fried, Barbara. "Wilt Chamberlain Revisited: Nozick's Justice in Transfer and the Problem of Market-Based Distribution." *Philosophy and Public Affairs* 24 (1995): 226–45.
Fukuyama, Francis. *Trust: The Social Virtues and the Creation of Prosperity.* New York: Free Press, 1995.
Galston, William A. "Cosmopolitan Altruism." *Social Philosophy and Policy* 10 (1993): 118–34.
Gauthier, David. *Morals by Agreement.* Oxford: Oxford University Press, 1986.

Gibbard, Allan. *Wise Choices, Apt Feelings*. Cambridge, Mass.: Harvard University Press, 1990.
Gomez, E., A. Alcala, and A. San Diego. "Status of Philippine Coral Reefs—1981." *Proceedings of the Fourth International Coral Reef Symposium* 1 (1981): 275–85.
Goodin, Robert E. *Protecting the Vulnerable: Toward a Reanalysis of Our Social Responsibilities*. Chicago: University of Chicago Press, 1985.
———. *Reasons for Welfare*. Princeton: Princeton University Press, 1988.
———. *Motivating Political Morality*. Cambridge: Blackwell, 1992.
Gordon, H. Scott. "The Economic Theory of a Common-Property Resource—The Fishery." *Journal of Political Economy* 62 (1954): 124–42.
Green, David G. *Working Class Patients and the Medical Establishment: Self-Help in Britain from the Mid–nineteenth century to 1948*. Aldershot, England: Gower, 1985.
———. *Reinventing Civil Society: The Rediscovery of Welfare without Politics*. London: IEA Health and Welfare Unit, 1993.
Green, David G., and Lawrence G. Cromwell. *Mutual Aid or Welfare State: Australia's Friendly Societies*. Sydney: Allen and Unwin, 1984.
Griswold, Charles L. "Platonic Liberalism: Self-Perfection as a Foundation of Political Theory." *Contré Platon*, ed. Monique Dixsaut. Paris: Vrin (1994): 155–95.
Guha, Ramachandra. "Radical American Environmentalism and Wilderness Preservation: A Third-World Critique." *Environmental Ethics* 11 (1989): 71–83.
Haile, Edward W., ed. *Jamestown Narratives: Eye Witness Accounts of the Virginia Colony, The First Decade, 1607–1617*. Champlain, Va:. Roundhouse, 1998.
Hampton, Jean. "Selflessness and the Loss of Self." *Social Philosophy and Policy* 10 (1993): 135–65.
Hardin, Garrett. "The Tragedy of the Commons." *Science* 162 (1968): 1243–48.
Hare, R. M. "Ethical Theory and Utilitarianism." In *Utilitarianism and Beyond*, ed. A. Sen and B. Williams, 23–38. Cambridge: Cambridge University Press, 1982.
Hargrove, Eugene C. "The Historical Foundations of American Environmental Attitudes." *Environmental Ethics* 1 (1979): 209–40.
———. *Foundations of Environmental Ethics*. Englewood Cliffs, N.J.: Prentice-Hall, 1989.
Hart, H. L. A. *The Concept of Law*. Oxford: Clarendon Press, 1961.
Hayek, F. A. *The Constitution of Liberty*. Chicago: University of Chicago Press, 1960.
Hechter, Michael. "A Theory of Group Solidarity." In *Microfoundations of Macrosociology*, ed. Michael Hechter, 16–57. Philadelphia: Temple University Press, 1983.
Held, Virginia. *Property, Profits, and Economic Justice*. Belmont, Calif.: Wadsworth, 1980.
Hiscocks, K. "The Impact of an Increasing Elephant Population on the Woody Vegetation in Southern Sabi Sand Wildtuin, South Africa." *Koedoe* 42 (1999): 47–55.
Himmelfarb, Gertrude. *The De-moralization of Society*. New York: Knopf, 1994.
Hoffman, Paul. "The Man Who Loves Only Numbers." *Atlantic Monthly*, November 1987, 60.
Holmgren, Margaret. "Justifying Desert Claims: Desert and Opportunity." *Journal of Value Inquiry* 20 (1986): 265–78.
Hugo, Victor. *Les Misérables*. Paris: Hetzel, 1888.
Hume, David. *A Treatise of Human Nature*. Oxford: Clarendon Press, 1978. (Originally published 1739)
———. *An Enquiry Concerning the Principles of Morals*. Indianapolis: Hackett, 1983. (Originally published 1751)
Hume, Ivor N. *The Virginia Adventure*. Charlottesville: University of Virginia Press, 1994.
Irwin, T. H. review of Broadie (1991). *Journal of Philosophy* 90 (1993): 323–29.
Jackson, Peter. *Elephants and Rhinos in Africa: A Time for Decision*. Gland, Switzerland: International Union for Conservation of Nature and Natural Resources, 1982.

Jeffrey, Richard C. *The Logic of Decision.* New York: McGraw-Hill, 1965.
Johanson, Donald, and Maitland Edey. *Lucy: The Beginnings of Humankind.* New York: Touchstone, 1981.
Johnson, Lawrence. *A Morally Deep World.* New York: Cambridge University Press, 1991.
Joubert, S. C. J. "Master Plan for the Management of Kruger National Park." Unpublished, 1996.
Kagan, Shelly. *The Limits of Morality.* New York: Oxford University Press, 1989.
Kant, Immanuel. *Grounding for the Metaphysics of Morals.* Trans. James W. Ellington. Indianapolis: Hackett, 1981. (Originally published 1785)
Kavka, Gregory S. "The Reconciliation Project." *Morality, Reason and Truth,* ed. David Copp and David Zimmerman. Totowa: Rowman and Allanheld (1984): 297–319.
King, Martin Luther. *I Have a Dream: Writings and Speeches that Changed the World.* New York: HarperCollins, 1986.
Kleinig, John. "The Concept of Desert." *American Philosophical Quarterly* 8 (1971): 71–78.
Krug, W. *Private Supply of Protected Land in Southern Africa.* Norwich, U.K.: Centre for Social and Economic Research on the Global Environment, 2001. www.olis.oecd.org.
Lambrechts, Arend Von W. "Meeting Wildlife and Human Needs by Establishing Collaborative Nature Reserves: A Transvaal System." In *Integrating People and Wildlife for a Sustainable Future,* ed. J. Bissonette and P. Krausman, 37–43. Bethesda, Md.: The Wildlife Society, 1995.
Lear, Jonathan, "Inside and Outside the Republic." *Phronesis* 37 (1992): 184–215.
Leopold, Aldo. *A Sand County Almanac.* New York: Oxford University Press, 1966. (Originally published 1949)
Lerner, Abba. *The Economics of Control.* New York: Augustus M. Kelley, 1970.
Levi, Isaac. "Newcomb's Many Problems." *Theory and Decision* 6 (1975): 161–75.
———. *Hard Choices: Decision Making under Unresolved Conflict.* New York: Cambridge University Press, 1986.
Lewis, David. "Prisoners' Dilemma Is a Newcomb Problem." *Philosophy and Public Affairs* 8 (1979): 235–40.
Locke, John. *Second Treatise of Government,* ed. Peter Laslett. Cambridge: Cambridge University Press, 1960. (Originally published 1690)
Lombardi, Louis G. "Inherent Worth, Respect, and Rights." *Environmental Ethics* 5 (1993): 257–70.
Long, Roderick. "Mill's Higher Pleasures and the Choice of Character." *Utilitas* 4 (1992): 279–97.
Louden, Robert. *Morality and Moral Theory.* New York: Oxford University Press, 1992.
Lundberg, Shelly, and Robert D. Plotnick. "Adolescent Premarital Childbearing: Do Economic Incentives Matter?" *Journal of Labor Economics* 13 (1995): 177–200.
MacDonald, Scott. "Ultimate Ends in Practical Reasoning: Aquinas's Aristotelian Psychology and Anscombe's Fallacy." *Philosophical Review* 100 (1991): 31–65.
Maslow, Abraham. *Motivation and Personality.* New York: Harper and Row, 1970.
Matzke, Gordon E., and Nontokozo Nabane. "Outcomes of a Community Controlled Wildlife Utilization Program in a Zambezi Valley Community." *Human Ecology* 24 (1996): 65–85.
McClennen, Edward F. "Constrained Maximization and Resolute Choice." *Social Philosophy and Policy* 5 (1988): 95–118.
McComb, Karen, C. Moss, S. M. Durant, L. Baker, and S. Sayialel. "Matriarchs as Repositories of Social Knowledge in African Elephants." *Science* 292 (2001): 491–94.
Mead, Lawrence M. *Beyond Entitlement: The Social Obligations of Citizenship.* New York: Free Press, 1986.

Mill, John S. *On Liberty.* Harmondsworth, England: Penguin, 1974. (Originally published 1859)
———. *Utilitarianism.* Indianapolis: Hackett, 1979. (Originally published 1861)
Miller, David. *Social Justice.* Oxford: Oxford University Press, 1976.
———. *Principles of Social Justice.* Cambridge, Mass.: Harvard University Press, 1999a.
———. "Justice and Global Inequality." In *Inequality, Globalization, and World Politics,* ed. Andrew Hurrell and Ngaire Woods, 187–210. Oxford: Oxford University Press, 1999b.
Miller, Fred D. "Sovereignty and Political Rights." In *Aristoteles Politik,* ed. Otfried Höffe, 107–19. Berlin: Akademie Verlag, 2001.
Miller, Richard W. "Justice as Social Freedom." In *On the Track of Reason: Essays in Honor of Kai Nielsen,* ed. Kai Nielsen, Roger Beehler, David Copp, and Bela Szabados, 37–55. Boulder, Colo.: Westview, 1992.
———. "Too Much Inequality." *Social Philosophy and Policy* 19 (2002): 275–313.
Morris, Christopher W. "The Relation between Self-Interest and Justice in Contractarian Ethics." *Social Philosophy and Policy* 5 (1988): 119–53.
———. "Punishment and Loss of Moral Standing." *Canadian Journal of Philosophy* 21 (1991): 53–79.
Mosugelo, David K., S. R. Moe, S. Ringrose, and C. Nellemann. "Vegetation Changes during a Thirty-Six-Year Period in Northern Chobe National Park, Botswana." *African Journal of Ecology* 40 (2002): 232–40.
Myers, Norman. "A Farewell to Africa." *International Wildlife* 11 (1981): 36–47.
Nagel, Thomas. *The Possibility of Altruism.* Oxford: Clarendon Press, 1970.
———. *The View from Nowhere.* New York: Oxford University Press, 1986.
———. *Equality and Partiality.* New York: Oxford University Press, 1991.
Narveson, Jan. Review of Larry S.Temkin. *Inequality.* New York: Oxford University Press (1993) in *Philosophy and Phenomenological Research* 56 (1994): 482–86.
———. "Deserving Profits." In *Profits and Morality,* ed. Robin Cowan and Mario Rizzo, 48–97. Chicago: University of Chicago Press, 1995.
———. "Egalitarianism: Baseless, Partial, and Counterproductive." *Ratio* 10 (1997): 280–95.
Nechyba, Thomas J. *Social Approval, Values, and AFDC.* Working paper. Stanford, Calif.: Stanford University, Economics Department, 1997.
Nelson, Alan, "Explanation and Justification in Political Philosophy." *Ethics* 97 (1986): 154–176.
Netting, Robert. "What Alpine Peasants Have in Common." *Human Ecology* 4 (1976): 135–46.
Norton, Brian. *Toward Unity among Environmentalists.* New York: Oxford University Press, 1991.
Nozick, Robert. "Newcomb's Problem and Two Principles of Choice." In *Essays in Honor of Carl G. Hempel,* ed. Nicholas Rescher, 114–46. Dordrecht: Reidel, 1969.
———. *Anarchy, State, and Utopia.* New York: Basic Books, 1974.
Nozick, Robert. "Reflections on Newcomb's Problem." *Scientific American* 238 (1974): 102–8.
———. *The Nature of Rationality.* Princeton, N.J.: Princeton University Press, 1993.
Olsaretti, Serena. *Liberty, Desert, and the Market.* Cambridge: Cambridge University Press, 2004.
Ostrom, Elinor. *Governing the Commons: The Evolution of Institutions for Collective Action.* Cambridge: Cambridge University Press, 1990.
Parker, Ian. "The Gift." *New Yorker,* August 2, 2004, 54–63.
Pettit, Philip. "Satisficing Consequentialism." *Proceedings of the Aristotelian Society,* 58 supp. (1984): 165–76.
———. "Decision Theory and Folk Psychology." *Foundations of Decision Theory.* ed. Michael Bacharach and Susan Hurley, Cambridge: Basil Blackwell (1991): 147–75.

Plato. *Republic.* Translated by G. M. A. Grube. Indianapolis: Hackett, 1974.
Pollock, John L. "How Do You Maximize Expectation Value?" *Nous* 17 (1984): 409–21.
———. "A Theory of Moral Reasoning." *Ethics* 96 (1986): 506–23.
———. "Causal Probability." *Synthese* 132 (2002): 143–85.
Postema, Gerald. "Hume's Reply to the Sensible Knave." *History of Philosophy Quarterly* 5 (1988): 23–40.
———. "Morality In the First Person Plural." *Law and Philosophy* 14 (1995): 35–64.
———. "Conflict, Conversation, and Convention: Reflections on Hume's Account of the Emergence of Norms of Justice." Unpublished, 2007.
Rachels, James. "What People Deserve." In *Can Ethics Provide Answers?* 175–97. Lanham, Md.: Rowman and Littlefield, 1997.
Rakowski, Eric. *Equal Justice.* Oxford: Oxford University Press, 1991.
Rawls, John. "Two Concepts of Rules." *Philosophical Review* 64 (1955): 3–32.
———. *A Theory of Justice.* Cambridge, Mass.: Belknap Press, 1971.
———. "Kantian Constructivism in Moral Theory." *Journal of Philosophy* 77 (1980): 515–72.
———. *A Theory of Justice.* Revised ed. Cambridge: Harvard Press, 1999.
———. "Two Concepts of Rules." Reprinted in John Rawls, *Collected Papers.* Cambridge: Harvard Press, 1999b.
Resnik, Michael, *Choices.* Minneapolis: University of Minnesota Press, 1987.
Rose, Carol. "Possession as the Origin of Property." *University of Chicago Law Review* 52 (1985): 73–88.
———. "The Comedy of the Commons: Custom, Commerce, and Inherently Public Property." *University of Chicago Law Review* 53 (1986): 711–87.
Russell, Bertrand. *Human Society in Ethics and Politics.* London: Allen and Unwin, 1954.
Sagoff, Mark. *The Economy of the Earth.* Cambridge: Cambridge University Press, 1988.
Samuelson, Paul. *Economics.* 9th ed. New York: McGraw-Hill, 1973.
Sanders, John T. "Justice and the Initial Acquisition of Private Property." *Harvard Journal of Law and Public Policy* 10 (1987): 367–99.
Sartorius, Rolf. "Persons and Property." In *Utility and Rights*, ed. R. Frey, 196–214. Minneapolis: University of Minnesota Press, 1984.
Savage, Leonard J. *The Foundations of Statistics.* New York: Dover, 1954.
Sayre-McCord, Geoffrey. "Deception and Reasons to Be Moral." *American Philosophical Quarterly* 26 (1989): 113–22.
———. "On Why Hume's 'General Point of View' Isn't Ideal—and Shouldn't Be." *Social Philosophy and Policy*, 11 (1994): 202–28.
Scheffler, Samuel. *The Rejection of Consequentialism.* New York: Oxford University Press, 1982.
———. "Responsibility, Reactive Attitudes, and Liberalism in Philosophy and Politics." *Philosophy and Public Affairs* 21 (1992): 299–323.
Schmidtz, David. "Justifying the State." *Ethics* 101 (1990a): 89–102.
———. "Scheffler's Hybrid Theory of the Right." *Nous* 24 (1990b): 622–27.
———. "When Is Original Appropriation *Required*?" *Monist* 73 (1990c): 504–18.
———. *The Limits of Government: An Essay on the Public Goods Argument.* Boulder, Colo.: Westview Press, 1991.
———. "Observing the Unobservable." In *On the Reliability of Economic Models: Essays in the Epistemology of Economics*, ed. D. Little, 147–72. Dordrecht: Kluwer Academic, 1995.
———. "When Preservationism Doesn't Preserve." *Environmental Values* 7 (1997b): 327–39.
———. "Islands in a Sea of Obligation: An Essay on the Duty to Rescue." *Law and Philosophy* 19 (2000): 683–705.

———. "The Language of Ethics." In *Ethical Dilemmas in the Water Industry*, ed. C. Davis, 3–16. Washington, D.C.: American Water Works Association, 2001a.
———. "A Place for Cost-Benefit Analysis." *Philosophical Issues* (*Nous* annual supp.) 11 (2001b): 148–71.
———. *Elements of Justice*. New York: Cambridge University Press, 2006.
———. "When Justice Matters." *Ethics* 117 (2007): 433–59.
Schmidtz, David, and Robert E. Goodin. *Social Welfare and Individual Responsibility*. Cambridge, Mass.: Harvard University Press, 1998.
Schmidtz, David, and Elizabeth Willott. "The Tragedy of the Commons." In *Blackwell Companion to Applied Ethics*, ed. R. G. Frey and Christopher Wellman, 662–73. Oxford: Blackwell, 2003.
Seijas, N., and F. Vorhies. "Private Preservation of Wildlife: A Visit to the South African Lowveld." *Freeman*, August 1989, http://www.fee.org/publications/the-freeman/.
Sen, Amartya. "Rational Fools: A Critique of the Behavioral Foundations of Economic Theory." In *Beyond Self-Interest*, ed. Jane Mansbridge, 25–43. Chicago: University of Chicago Press, 1990.
Seung, T. K. and Daniel Bonevac. "Plural Values and Indeterminate Rankings." *Ethics* 102 (1992): 799–813.
Sher, George. *Desert*. Princeton, N.J.: Princeton University Press, 1987.
Siegel, Fred. "Planned Disaster." *New Democrat* (Nov.–Dec. 1996): 14–18.
Simon, Herbert A. "A Behavioral Model of Rational Choice." *Quarterly Journal of Economics* 69 (1955): 99–118.
———. *Models of Thought*. New Haven, Conn.: Yale University Press, 1979.
Singer, Peter. "Famine, Affluence, and Morality." *Philosophy and Public Affairs* 1 (1972): 229–43.
———. *Animal Liberation*. New York: Random House, 1990.
———. *Writings on an Ethical Life*. New York: HarperCollins, 2000.
Slote, Michael. *Beyond Optimizing: A Study of Rational Choice*. Cambridge, Mass.: Harvard University Press, 1989.
Smart, J. J. C., and Bernard Williams. *Utilitarianism: For and Against*. Cambridge: Cambridge University Press, 1973.
Smith, Holly. "Deciding How to Decide: Is There a Regress Problem?" *Foundations of Decision Theory*, ed. M. Bacharach and S. Hurley. Cambridge: Basil Blackwell (1991): 194–219.
Sobel, J. Howard. "Not Every Prisoner's Dilemma Is a Newcomb Problem." In *Paradoxes of Rationality and Cooperation*. ed. Richmond Campbell and Lanning Sowden. Vancouver: University of British Columbia Press, 1985: 263–74.
Songorwa, Alexander N. "Community-Based Wildlife Management in Tanzania: Are the Communities Interested?" *World Development* 27 (1999): 2061–79.
Spector, Horacio. *Autonomy and Rights*. Oxford: Oxford University Press, 1992.
Spenceley, Anna, and Jennifer Seif. *Strategies, Impacts, and Costs of Pro-poor Tourism Approaches in South Africa*. London, U. K.: Pro-Poor Tourism, 2003. www.propoortourism.org.uk/ppt_pubs_workingpapers.html.
Stocker, Michael. *Plural and Conflicting Values*. New York: Oxford University Press, 1990.
Tanner, Michael. *The End of Welfare*. Washington, D.C.: Cato Institute, 1996.
Tanner, Michael, Stephen Moore, and David Hartman. "The Work vs. Welfare Trade-Off." *Policy Analysis* 240 (1995): 1–53.
Taylor, Paul W. "The Ethics of Respect for Nature." *Environmental Ethics* 3 (1981): 197–218.
———. "In Defense of Biocentrism." *Environmental Ethics* 5 (1983): 237–43.
———. *Respect for Nature*. Princeton, N.J.: Princeton University Press, 1986.

Thomson, Judith J. "Killing, Letting Die, and the Trolley Problem." *Monist* 59 (1976): 204–17.
———. *The Realm of Rights*. Cambridge, Mass.: Harvard University Press, 1990.
Ullmann-Margalit, Edna, and Sidney Morgenbesser. "Picking and Choosing." *Social Research* 44 (1977): 757–85.
Unger, Peter. *Living High and Letting Die: Our Illusion of Innocence*. New York: Oxford University Press, 1996.
U.S. Department of Health and Human Services. *Health, United States, 2006*. Washington, D.C.: Government Printing Office, 2006. www.cdc.gov/nchs/data/hus/hus06.pdf#027.
Varner, Gary. *In Nature's Interests?* New York: Oxford University Press, 1998.
Waldron, Jeremy. Enough and as Good Left for Others. *Philosophical Quarterly* 29 (1976): 319–28.
———. "The Rule of Law in Contemporary Liberal Theory." *Ratio Juris* 2 (1989): 79–96.
———. "The Wisdom of the Multitude: Some Reflections on Book 3, Chapter 11 of Aristotle's *Politics*." *Political Theory* 23 (1995): 563–84.
Walzer, Michael. *Spheres of Justice*. New York: Basic Books, 1983.
Watson, Paul. "Tora! Tora! Tora!" In *Earth Ethics*, ed. James Sterba, 341–46. Englewood Cliffs, N.J.: Prentice-Hall, 1995.
Western, David, R. Michael Wright, and Shirley C. Strum, eds. *Natural Connections: Perspectives in Community-Based Conservation*. Washington, D.C.: Island Press, 1994.
White, Robert, "The Urge Towards Competence." *American Journal of Occupational Therapy* 25 (1971): 271–274.
Whyte, Ian, and Richard Fayrer-Hosken. "Playing Elephant God: Ethics of Managing Wild Elephant Populations." In *Elephants and Ethics: Toward a Morality of Coexistence*, ed. Catherine Christen and Christen Wemmer. Baltimore: Johns Hopkins University Press, 2008, in press.
Whyte, Ian. "Headaches and Heartaches: The Elephant Management Dilemma." In *Environmental Ethics: What Really Matters, What Really Works*, ed. David Schmidtz and Elizabeth Willott, 293–305. New York: Oxford University Press, 2002.
Whyte, Ian, R. van Aarde, and S. Pimm. "Managing the Elephants of Kruger National Park." *Animal Conservation* 1 (1998): 77–83.
Williams, Bernard. *Ethics and the Limits of Philosophy*, Cambridge: Harvard University Press, 1985.
Zaitchik, Alan. "On Deserving to Deserve." *Philosophy and Public Affairs* 6 (1977): 370–88.

INDEX

Ackerknecht, 228
Act-utilitarianism, 8, 149, 151
    and exploitation, 127
    and moral dualism, 7,
    recognition rule of, 117–8
    supporting conditions of, 118
Addiction, 123
Agents, 8, 29, 38, 60, 65, 116, 119, 175, 246
    active, 116,
    and institutions, 152
    reflectively rational, 135, 137, 138
    separate, 116, 154
Altruism, 5, 6, 63–6, 68–77, 186
Anderson, James, 242, 244, 246
Aristotle, 7, 52, 69, 75, 99, 123, 242
Arrow, Kenneth, 170

Badhwar, Neera, 98
Baier, Kurt, 139n
Bailey, Martin, 200, 208, 209n
Baker, Edwin, 165, 174
Becker, Gary, 178
Beito, David, 183, 185, 186n
Beitz, Charles, 114n
Benatar, David, 11
Bloomfield, Paul, 12
Bogart, J. H., 195
Bonner, Raymond, 11, 222n
Bookchin, Murray, 235, 237
Brennan, Jason, 12, 143, 162

Bricker, Phillip, 67
Broadie, Sarah, 43, 69n
Brock, Gillian, 95, 110
Broome, John, 166
Buchanan, James, 186
Budget constraint, 18, 62
Butler, Joseph, 30
Butler, Victoria, 223, 225

Cafeteria, 17
Careers, 18, 24, 28, 30, 42–6, 53
Carrying capacity, 200–1, 209, 218–9, 224, 226
    as an aesthetic concept, 216n
Character, 44, 69–73, 77, 93–6, 102n, 103–6, 109–14, 119, 123, 128–9, 134–7, 140–3
Chess, 44, 54, 230
Child, Brian, 231
Childhood,
    as foundation for adulthood, 44
    as something we outgrow, 44
Children, 7, 43n, 63n, 71n, 108, 129, 134, 179–85, 188, 197, 199, 228, 230, 232, 243
    ranking their friends, 246
Churchill, Winston, 237n
Coleman, Jules, 19n, 139n
Communes, 193–4, 201–21
Conflict,
    in priorities, 230
    of rules, 118, 138

Conflict (*continued*)
  in use, 229
  in values, 27–33, 229
Craig, Robin, 197n

Danziger, Sheldon, 177, 181
Davis, Frederick, 198
Davis, Lawrence, 87, 88
Della Rocca, Michael, 43
Demsetz, Harold, 200, 202, 216, 217
Desert
  Desert bases, 106
  Deserving "more than you," 115
  Dignity, 110
  Earning, 105–7
  Earning payment in advance, 105
  Entitlement, 111n, 116
  Excellence, 113
  Hard work, 96
  Jean Valjean (punishment), 104
  Least advantaged, 107
  Luck, 106
  Mere luck, 95
  Need, 110
  As noncomparative, 114–5
  As preinstitutional moral fact, 112
  Puzzles about prediction, 103
  Rawls's Difference Principle, 107
  Respect, 109–10
  As response to active agents, 116
  As response to separate agents, 116
Dietsch, Peter, 114
Dotson, Paul, 114

Ellickson, Robert, 10, 200–8, 211, 213, 217, 227
Elman, Richard, 180
Elster, Jon, 18
Emergencies, 73–4, 138–42, 156, 185, 199, 243. *See also* Trolley
Ends, 5, 15, 23, 58
  biologically given
  Chosen, 52
  Constitutive, 38
  Final, 33, 40, 45
  Global, 18–35
  Instrumental, 38, 41
  Local, 18–35
  Loose, 50
  Maieutic, 39

Prospective, 45, 53, 57, 60
  See also Persons, as ends in themselves
Examples, realistic, 101
Exploitation, 124–30, 140, 184, 200, 243
Externalities, 193, 229

Farrell, Martin, 103
Feinberg, Joel, 61, 94, 96–8, 109, 111
Feldman, Fred, 99n, 105n
Foot, Philippa, 150
Frank, Robert, 59
Frankfurt, Harry, 44, 50n, 54n, 55, 59, 167, 169
Freiman, Chris, 162
French, Peter, 6
French, William, 240
Fried, Barbara, 195
Friends, as equals, 246
Fukuyama, Francis, 182, 184, 185

Galston, William, 75n
Game, 196–200
  negative sum, 187
  in parametric vs. strategic world, 148
  positive sum, 193
  small, 208
  zero sum, 114, 128n, 178
Glannon, Walter, 54
Gauthier, David, 19n, 37n, 93, 130n
Gibbard, Allan, 28n, 70n
Goodin, Robert, 9, 181–2, 186, 188–9, 210
Green, David, 183–5
Griswold, Charles, 77n

Habit, 51, 54–5, 69–70
Hampton, Jean, 5n, 65n, 154n
Hardin, Garrett, 201
Hare, R. M., 165, 169
Hargrove, Eugene, 228n, 234
Hart, H.L.A, 117
Hayek, F. A., 93n
Hechter, Michael, 210
Held, Virginia, 195
Himmelfarb, Gertrude, 184
Holmgren, Margaret, 107–8
Homo economicus, 59–61, 65
Hugo, Victor, 104

Hulet, Gavin, 214
Hume, David, 5, 62

Incompleteness
  of decision theory, 89
  of moral theory, 104, 144, 162
Integrity, 71–4, 117, 123
Ismael, Jenann, 159n

Jamestown, 10, 196, 204–6, 209–10
Jeffrey, Richard, 80–1, 89
Johnson, Cathleen, 10, 12, 172
Johnson, Lawrence, 243, 246–7
Justice
  answerable to requirements of sound practice, 234
  procedural versus substantive, 234

Kagan, Shelley, 152n
Kant, Immanuel, 62, 71n, 110, 119
Kelley, David, 57
King, Martin Luther, 111
Kleinig, John, 96
Kruger, Kobus, 224n

Leopold, Aldo, 235, 248
Levi, Isaac, 28, 81
Lewis, David, 82
Lincoln, Abraham, Gettysburg address, 106n
Locke, John, 194–6, 200–1
Lockean Proviso, 194
  when it permits appropriation, 199
  when it requires appropriation, 200
Lombardi, Louis, 242
Long, Roderick, 69
Louden, Robert, 134

MacDonald, Scott, 38, 40
Marcus, Ruth, 43
Martin, Robert, 11
Maslow, Abraham, 166
Matzke, Gordon E., 236
McClennen, Edward, 73
McComb, Karen, 225
Mead, Lawrence M., 181
Mill, John S., 30, 63, 119, 148, 151
Miller, David, 97, 100, 102, 103, 114, 158
Miller, Fred D., 99, 100
Miller, Richard, 107
Millgram, Elijah, 155n

Moderation, 15–56
Moral principles, conflict in normal vs. abnormal cases, 141
Moral theory, as a game, 157
Morality, as a test, 142
Morris, Christopher, 94, 122
Morris, Elissa, 11
Mosugelo, David, 224
Mutual advantage, 140, 150, 152, 186, 193, 196

Nagel, Thomas, 65, 66, 130, 165, 166, 169, 171
Narveson, Jan, 94, 95, 165, 173
Nechyba, Thomas J., 179, 180
Netting, Robert, 219
Nine, Cara, 12
Norton, Brian, 230, 235
Nozick, Robert, 6, 9, 78–83, 87–90, 93, 108, 154

Olsaretti, Serena, 115
Original appropriation, 195
  and latecomers, 196
Ostrom, Elinor, 11, 211, 217–9

Parker, Ian, 156
Paternalism, 76
Persons, as ends in themselves, 28, 134
Pettit, Philip, 23, 53, 131
Picking, 23, 29, 32, 34, 38, 56, 60, 142
Pincione, Guido, 103, 131
Plato, 71, 131
Pollock, John L., 25, 86
Postema, Gerald, 72, 130
Prudence, 5, 67n, 71–5, 122, 131

Rachels, James, 97, 100, 109
Rainbolt, George, 104n
Rakowski, Eric, 93
Ramsey, Martha, 247
Rationality, reflective, 37, 128, 136
  defined exogenously, 141
  underdetermined rational choice, 29, 33, 56, 142
Ravizza, Mark, 25
Rawls, John, 93–95, 97, 107–9, 111–2, 151, 154
Regan, Tom, 246
Resnik, Michael, 37n

Respect, 239, 244
  for self, 246
Responsibility, 54, 235n, 246
  collective, 175, 183
  for exercising judgment, 163
  externalized, 149, 189
  internalized, 175–9
  static versus dynamic perspectives, 176–88
Rose, Carol, 199, 208–209
Rosenberg, Jay, 20n
Ross, Lainie, 42, 75
Rovane, Carol, 59
Russell, Bertand, 37
Russell, Dan, 182n

Sagoff, Mark, 233
Samuelson, Paul, 170
Sanders, John T., 194, 196
Sartorius, Rolf, 195n
Savage, Leonard J., 79, 80
Saving Private Ryan, 105–7
Sayre-McCord, Geoffrey, 69, 132n, 141n
Satisficing, 15–35, 151–2
Scheffler, Samuel, 93–94, 152
Scherer, Don, 10, 12, 228
Schmidtz, David, 119n, 148n, 149n, 166n, 201n, 210n, 222n
Seijas, N., 215
Self-regard, fragility of, 64, 75
Sen, Amartya, 68
Seung, T. K., 28
Sher, George, 94–95
Siegel, Fred, 180
Simon, Herbert A., 16
Singer, Peter, 8–9, 145–9, 153–8, 163–4, 242–4, 246

Skocpol, Theda, 186
Slote, Michael, 19, 21, 22n, 23–24
Smart, J. J. C., 30
Smith, Adam, 5
Smith, Holly, 31n
Smith, Michael, 8, 9, 102n
Sobel, J. Howard, 82
Spector, Horacio, 131, 150
Spenceley, Anna, 222
Stocker, Michael, 16n, 30n, 119n, 139n
Sturgeon, Nicholas, 30

Tanner, Michael, 179n, 181n
Taylor, Paul, 12, 239–43
Theories
  gaps in, 121
  as maps, 119n, 120, 135, 159–62, 164
  as underdetermined, 142
Thomson, Judith J., 150n, 195
Trolley, 143, 149–50, 153–4

Unger, Peter, 157–8

Vallier, Kevin, 12, 162
Varner, Gary, 235

Waldron, Jeremy, 99n, 100n, 116n, 195n
Walzer, Michael, 97n
Watson, Paul, 155–6, 163
Western, David, R., 229n
Whyte, Ian, 211n, 214, 224–6
Williams, Bernard, 30n, 47, 50
Willott, Elizabeth, 8, 11, 201n, 203n, 222n
Worley, Sara, 49

Zaitchik, Alan, 95n
Zwolinski, Matt, 12